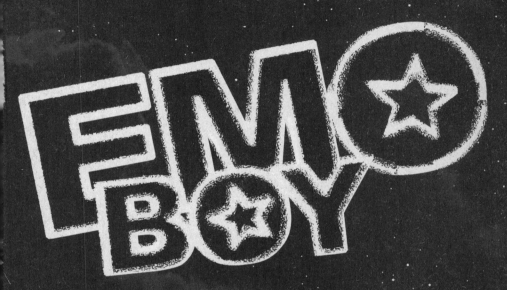

EMO★ BOY

by steve emond

Published by SLG Publishing
Dan Vado - President and Publisher
Jennifer de Guzman - Editor-in-Chief
Art Director - Scott Saavedra
Eleanor Lawson - Production Artist

P.O. Box 26427
San Jose, CA 95159

Emo Boy Volume One: Nobody Cares About Anything Anyway, So Why Don't We All Die? collects issues 1-6 of the SLG Publishing series *Emo Boy*.

www.slgpublishing.com

First Printing: October 2006
Second Printing: March 2008
ISBN 13: 978-1-59362-053-0

Printed in Canada.

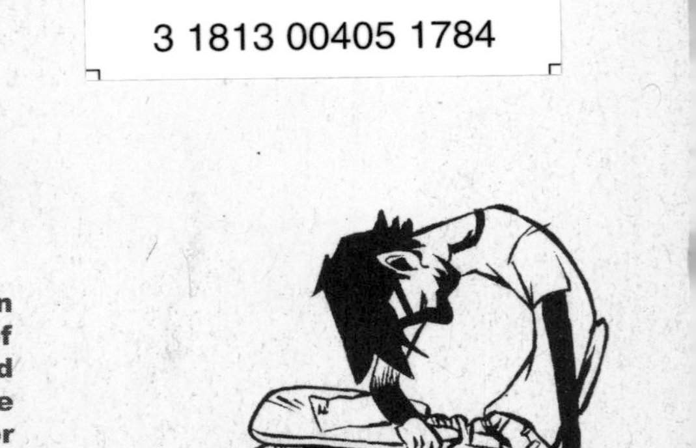

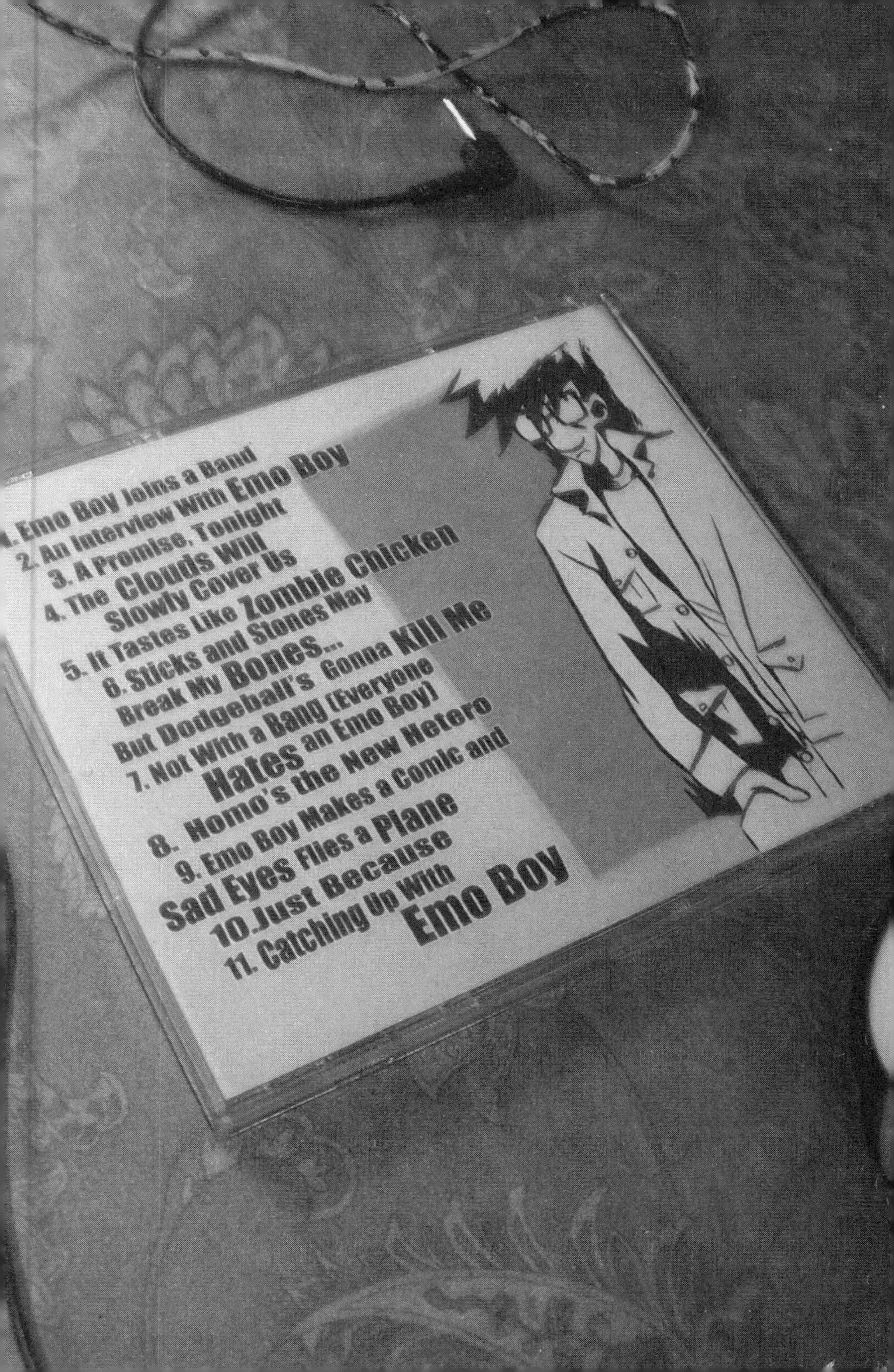
1. Emo Boy Joins a Band
2. An Interview With Emo Boy
3. A Promise, Tonight
4. The Clouds Will
Slowly Cover Us
5. It Tastes Like Zombie Chicken
6. Sticks and Stones May
Break My Bones...
But Dodgeball's Gonna Kill Me
7. Not With a Bang (Everyone
Hates an Emo Boy)
8. Homo's the New Hetero
9. Emo Boy Makes a Comic and
Sad Eyes Flies a Plane
10.Just Because
11. Catching Up With
Emo Boy

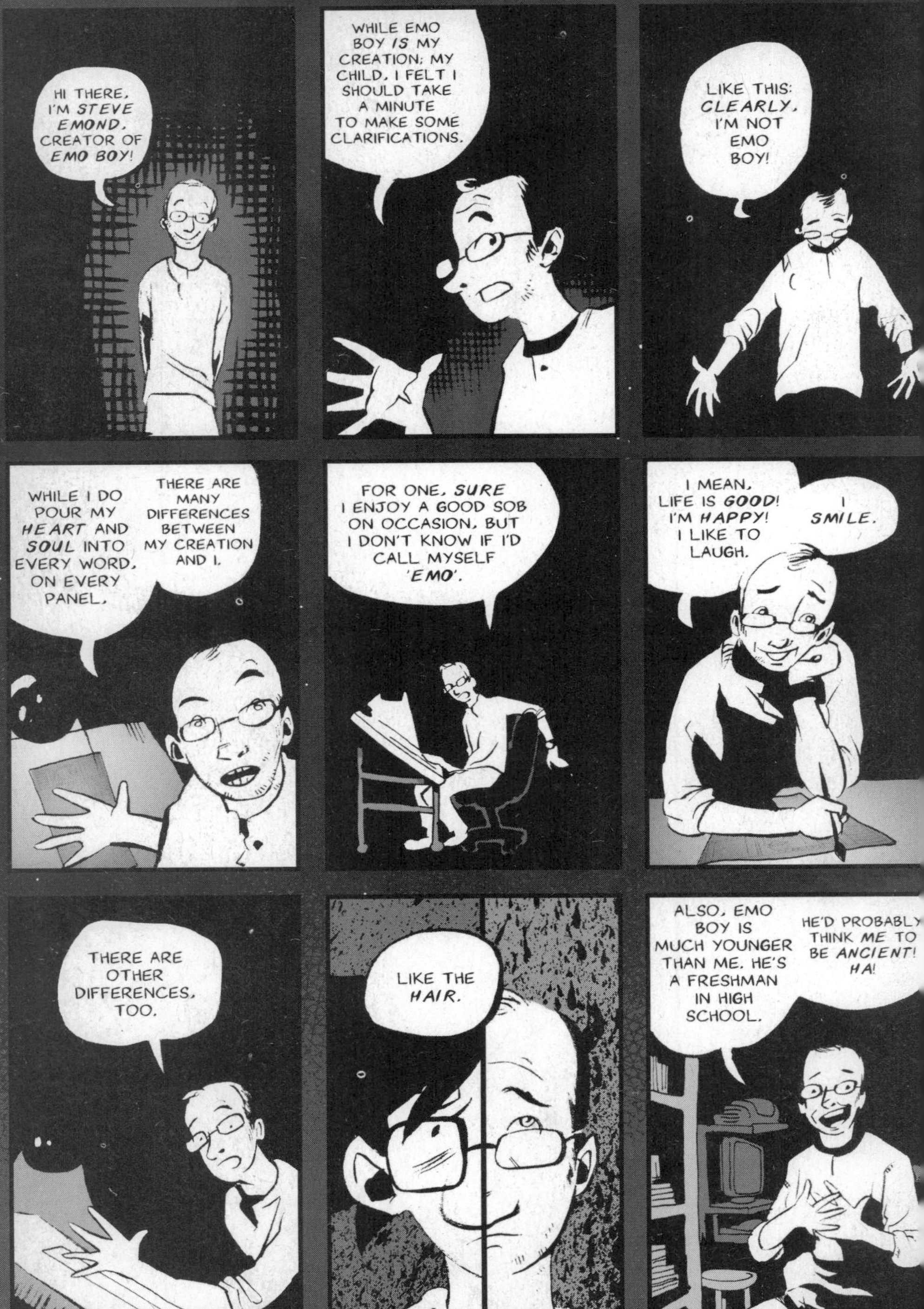
HI THERE, I'M STEVE EMOND, CREATOR OF EMO BOY!
WHILE EMO BOY IS MY CREATION; MY CHILD, I FELT I SHOULD TAKE A MINUTE TO MAKE SOME CLARIFICATIONS.
LIKE THIS: CLEARLY, I'M NOT EMO BOY!
WHILE I DO POUR MY HEART AND SOUL INTO EVERY WORD, ON EVERY PANEL,
THERE ARE MANY DIFFERENCES BETWEEN MY CREATION AND I.
FOR ONE, SURE I ENJOY A GOOD SOB ON OCCASION, BUT I DON'T KNOW IF I'D CALL MYSELF 'EMO'.
I MEAN, LIFE IS GOOD! I'M HAPPY! I LIKE TO LAUGH.
I SMILE.
THERE ARE OTHER DIFFERENCES, TOO.
LIKE THE HAIR.
ALSO, EMO BOY IS MUCH YOUNGER THAN ME. HE'S A FRESHMAN IN HIGH SCHOOL.
HE'D PROBABLY THINK ME TO BE ANCIENT! HA!

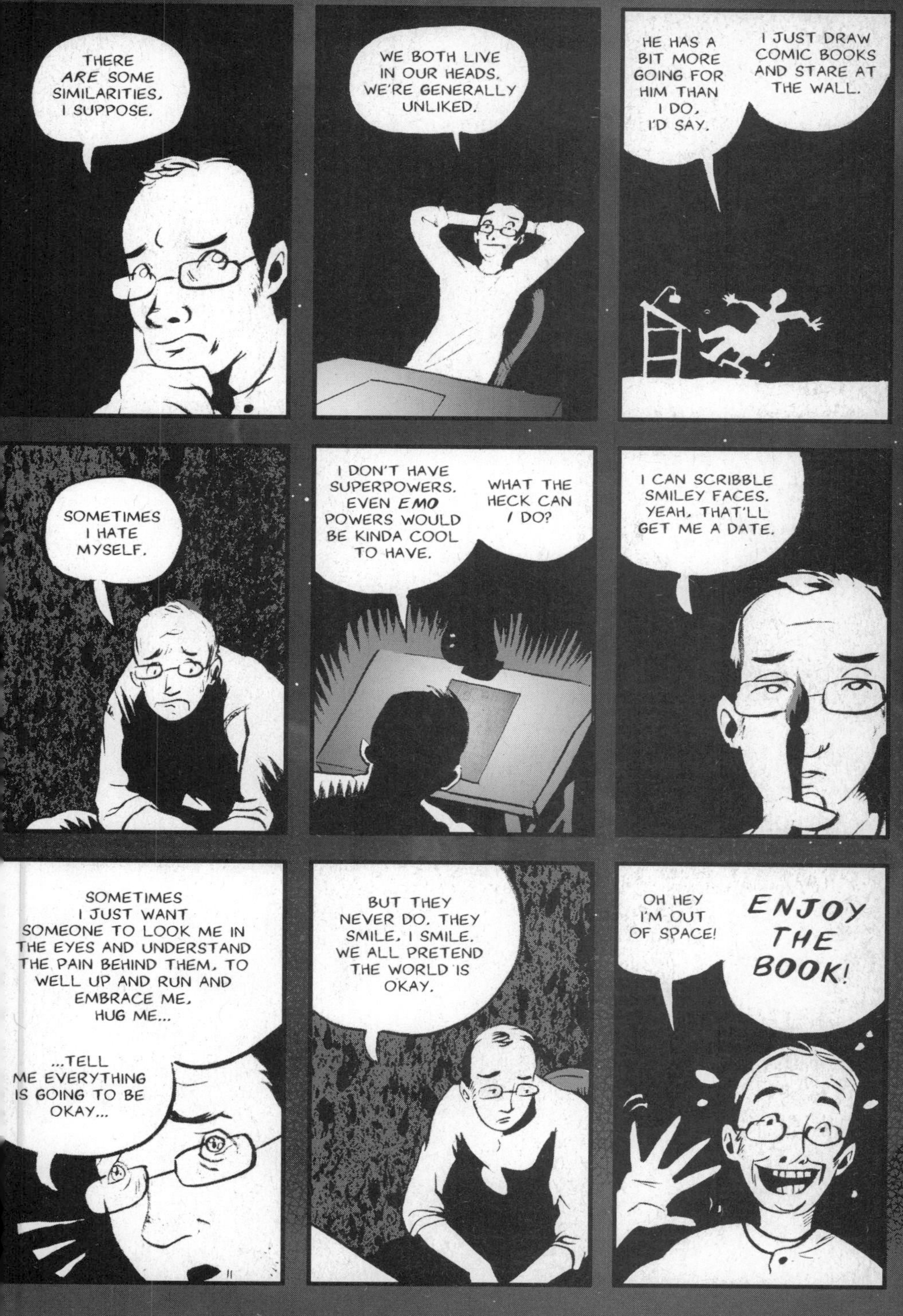
THERE ARE SOME SIMILARITIES, I SUPPOSE.
WE BOTH LIVE IN OUR HEADS. WE'RE GENERALLY UNLIKED.
HE HAS A BIT MORE GOING FOR HIM THAN I DO, I'D SAY.
I JUST DRAW COMIC BOOKS AND STARE AT THE WALL.
SOMETIMES I HATE MYSELF.
I DON'T HAVE SUPERPOWERS. EVEN EMO POWERS WOULD BE KINDA COOL TO HAVE.
WHAT THE HECK CAN I DO?
I CAN SCRIBBLE SMILEY FACES. YEAH, THAT'LL GET ME A DATE.
SOMETIMES I JUST WANT SOMEONE TO LOOK ME IN THE EYES AND UNDERSTAND THE PAIN BEHIND THEM, TO WELL UP AND RUN AND EMBRACE ME, HUG ME...
...TELL ME EVERYTHING IS GOING TO BE OKAY...
BUT THEY NEVER DO. THEY SMILE, I SMILE. WE ALL PRETEND THE WORLD IS OKAY.
OH HEY I'M OUT OF SPACE!
ENJOY THE BOOK!

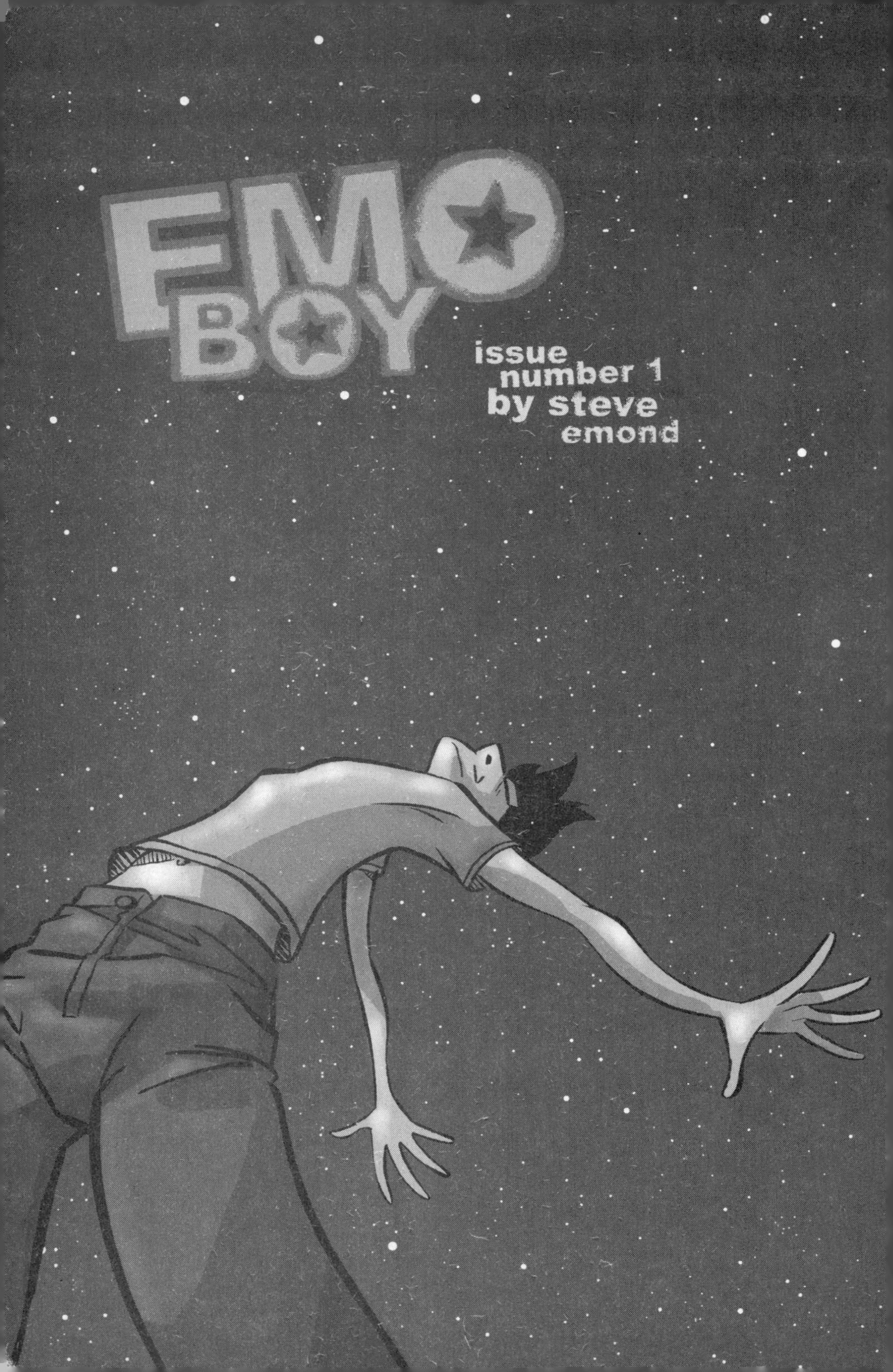
EMO BOY
issue number 1
by steve emond

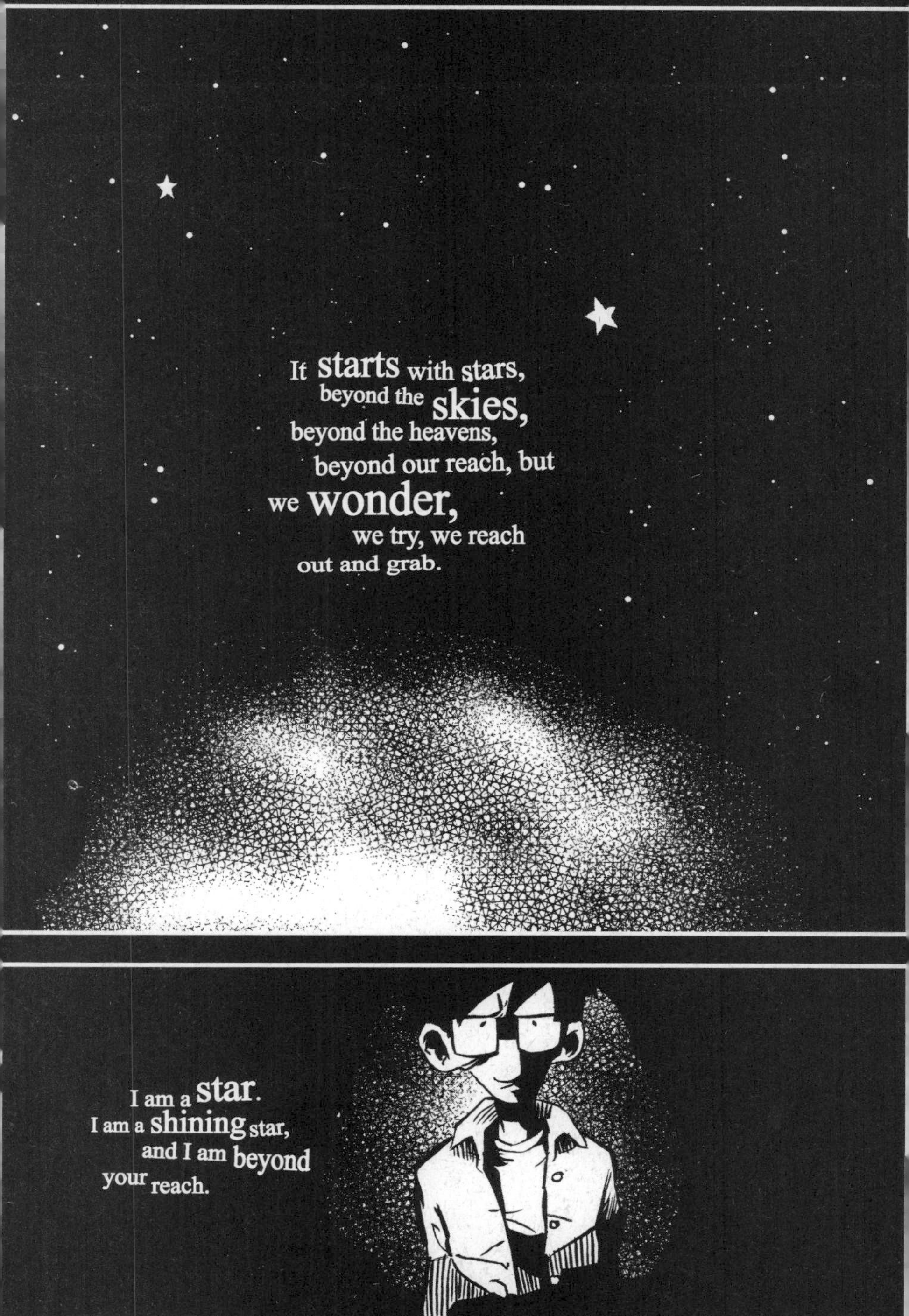
It starts with stars, beyond the skies, beyond the heavens, beyond our reach, but we wonder, we try, we reach out and grab.
I am a star. I am a shining star, and I am beyond your reach.

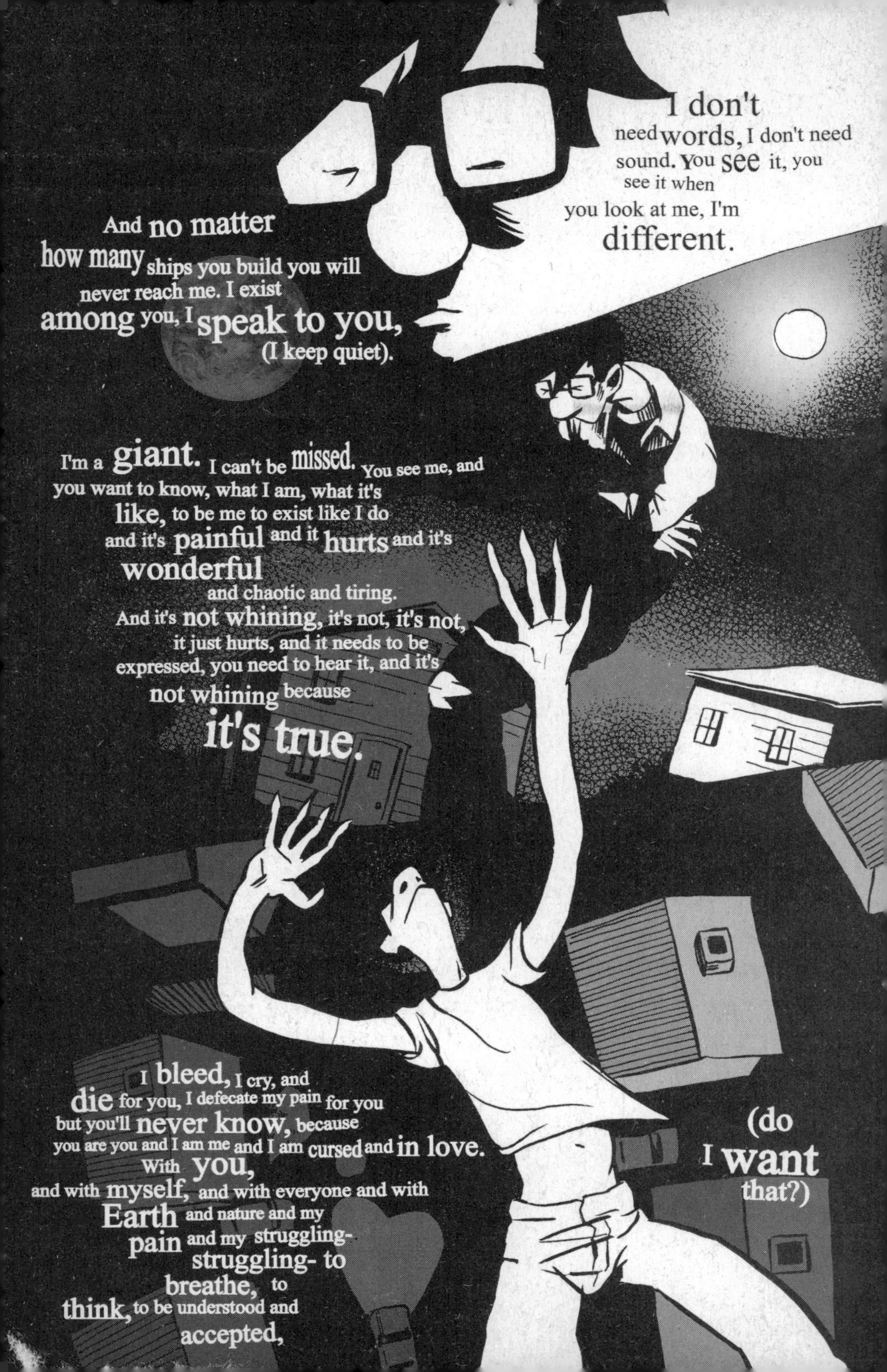
I don't need words, I don't need sound. You see it, you see it when you look at me, I'm different.
And no matter how many ships you build you will never reach me. I exist among you, I speak to you, (I keep quiet).
I'm a giant. I can't be missed. You see me, and you want to know, what I am, what it's like, to be me to exist like I do and it's painful and it hurts and it's wonderful and chaotic and tiring. And it's not whining, it's not, it's not, it just hurts, and it needs to be expressed, you need to hear it, and it's not whining because it's true.
I bleed, I cry, and die for you, I defecate my pain for you but you'll never know, because you are you and I am me and I am cursed and in love. With you, and with myself, and with everyone and with Earth and nature and my pain and my struggling- struggling- to breathe, to think, to be understood and accepted,
(do I want that?)

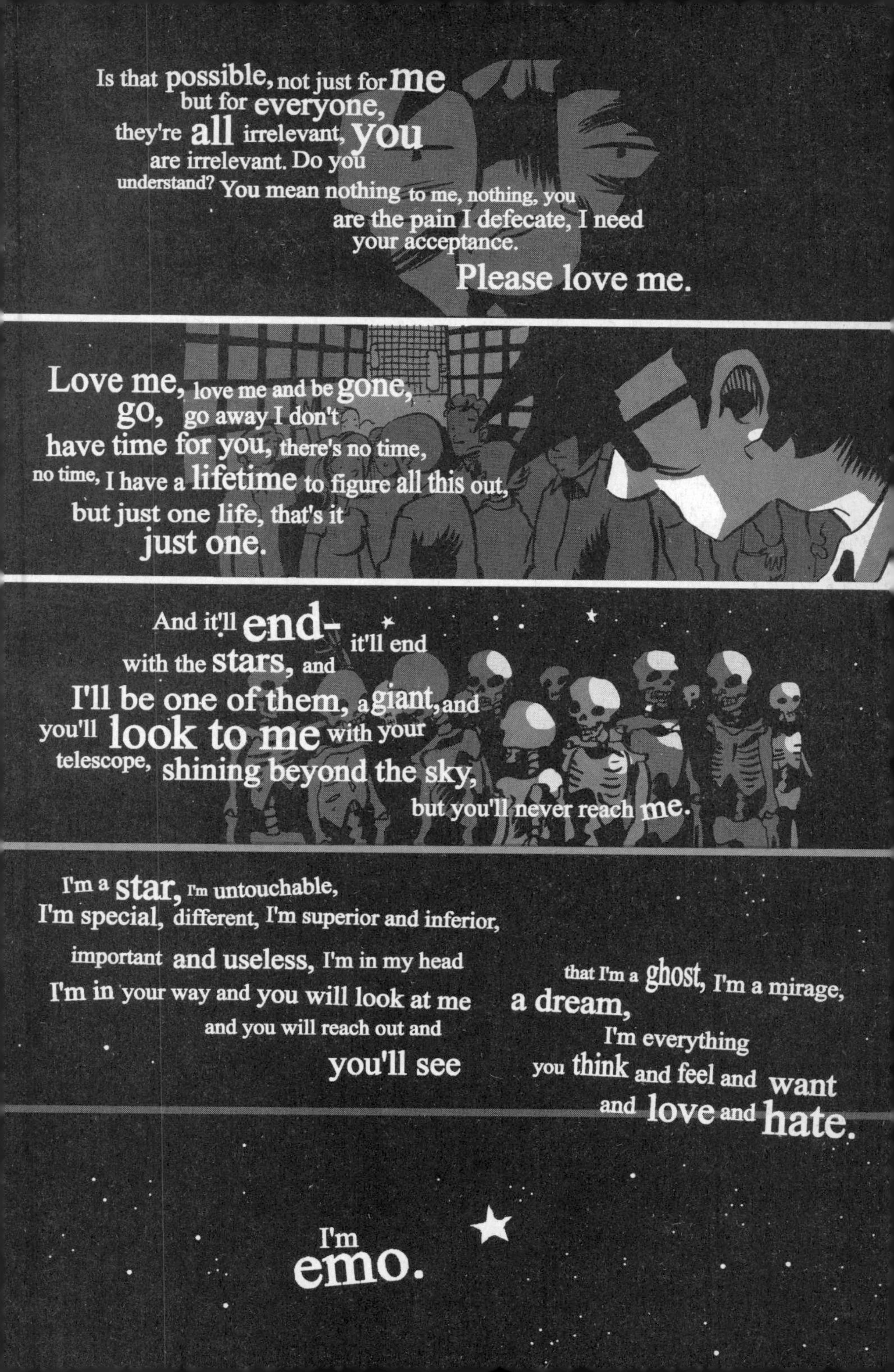
Is that possible, not just for me but for everyone, they're all irrelevant, you are irrelevant. Do you understand? You mean nothing to me, nothing, you are the pain I defecate, I need your acceptance.
Please love me.
Love me, love me and be gone, go, go away I don't have time for you, there's no time, no time, I have a lifetime to figure all this out, but just one life, that's it just one.
And it'll end- it'll end with the stars, and I'll be one of them, a giant, and you'll look to me with your telescope, shining beyond the sky, but you'll never reach me.
I'm a star, I'm untouchable, I'm special, different, I'm superior and inferior, important and useless, I'm in my head I'm in your way and you will look at me and you will reach out and you'll see
that I'm a ghost, I'm a mirage, a dream, I'm everything you think and feel and want and love and hate.
I'm emo.

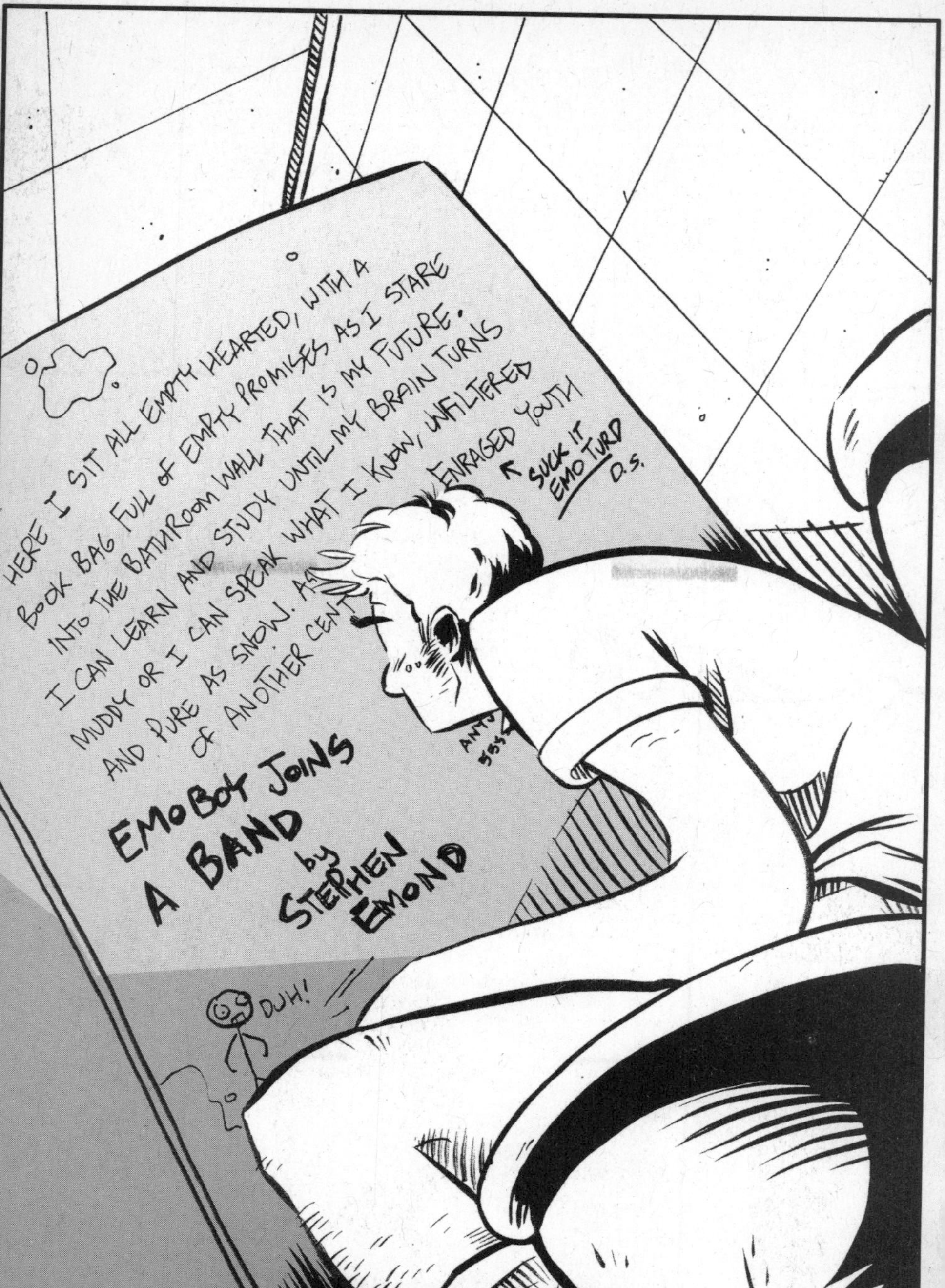
HERE I SIT ALL EMPTY HEARTED, WITH A
BOOK BAG FULL OF EMPTY PROMISES AS I STARE
INTO THE BATHROOM WALL THAT IS MY FUTURE.
I CAN LEARN AND STUDY UNTIL MY BRAIN TURNS
MUDDY OR I CAN SPEAK WHAT I KNOW, UNFILTERED
AND PURE AS SNOW. AS
ENRAGED YOUTH
OF ANOTHER CENT
SUCK IT EMO TURD
D.S.
EMOBOY JOINS A BAND
by STEPHEN EMOND
DUH!

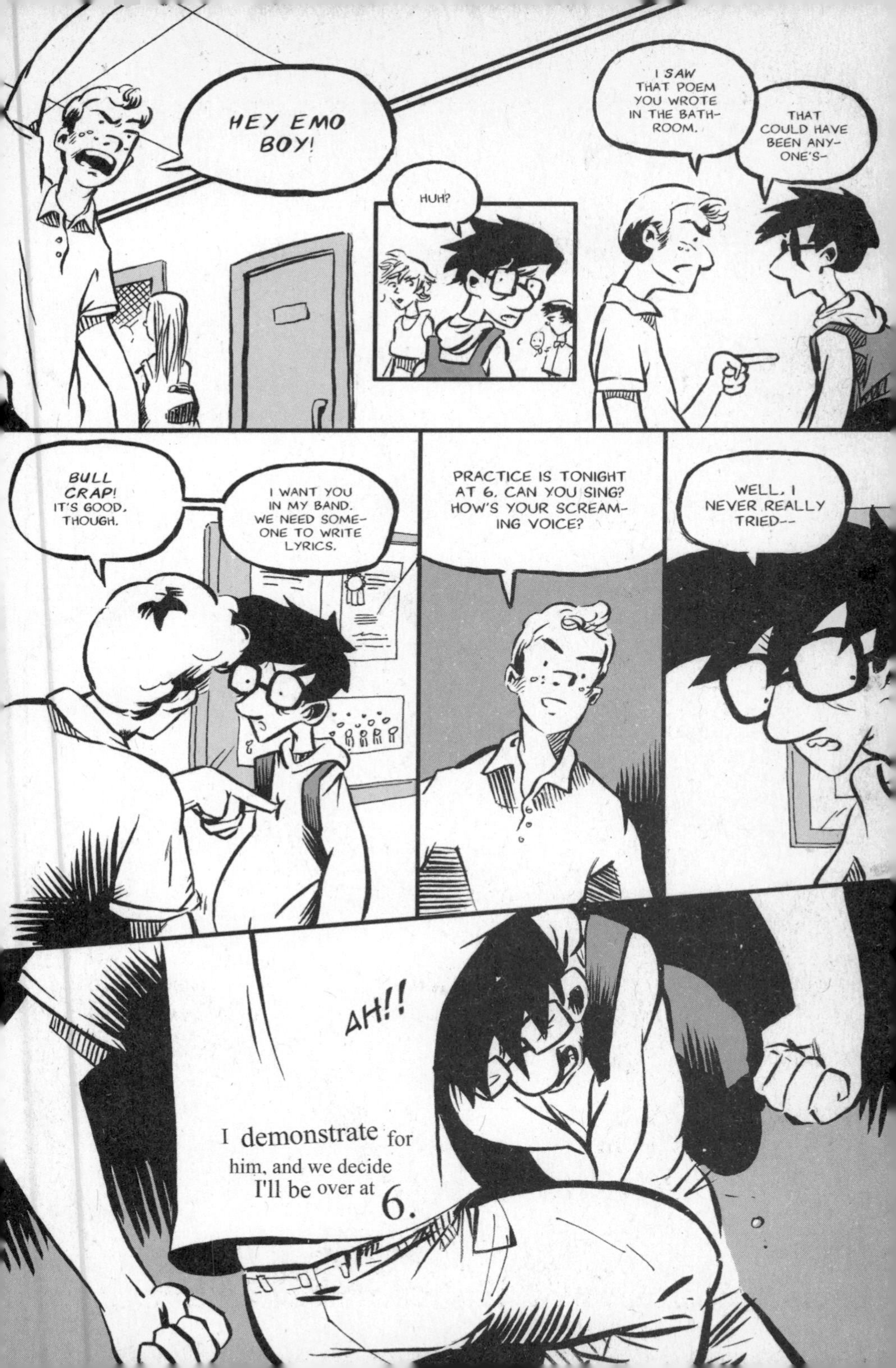
HEY EMO BOY!
HUH?
I SAW THAT POEM YOU WROTE IN THE BATH-ROOM.
THAT COULD HAVE BEEN ANY-ONE'S-
BULL CRAP! IT'S GOOD, THOUGH.
I WANT YOU IN MY BAND. WE NEED SOME-ONE TO WRITE LYRICS.
PRACTICE IS TONIGHT AT 6. CAN YOU SING? HOW'S YOUR SCREAM-ING VOICE?
WELL, I NEVER REALLY TRIED--
AH!!
I demonstrate for him, and we decide I'll be over at 6.

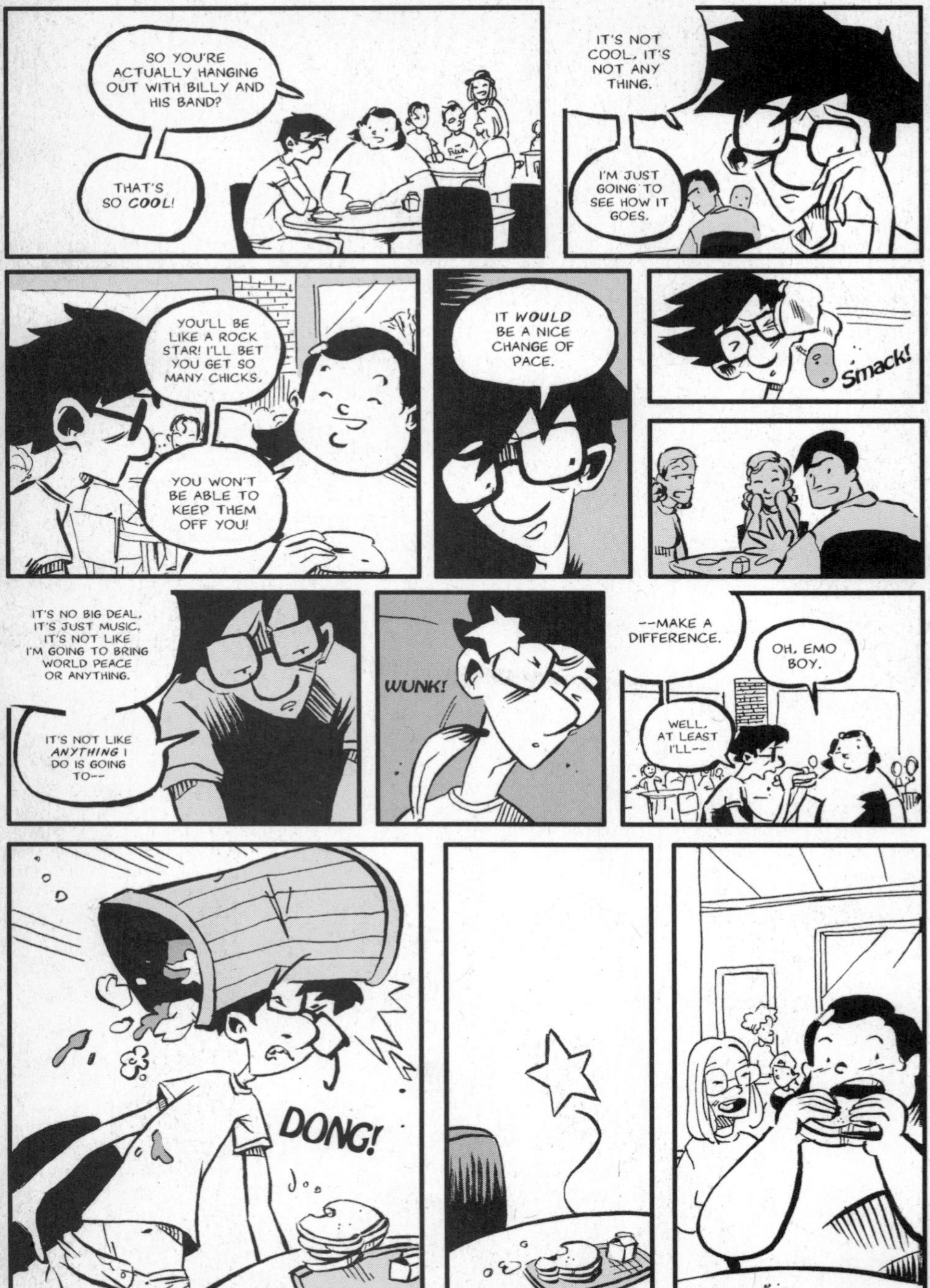
SO YOU'RE ACTUALLY HANGING OUT WITH BILLY AND HIS BAND?
THAT'S SO COOL!
IT'S NOT COOL. IT'S NOT ANY THING.
I'M JUST GOING TO SEE HOW IT GOES.
YOU'LL BE LIKE A ROCK STAR! I'LL BET YOU GET SO MANY CHICKS.
YOU WON'T BE ABLE TO KEEP THEM OFF YOU!
IT WOULD BE A NICE CHANGE OF PACE.
SMACK!
IT'S NO BIG DEAL. IT'S JUST MUSIC. IT'S NOT LIKE I'M GOING TO BRING WORLD PEACE OR ANYTHING.
IT'S NOT LIKE ANYTHING I DO IS GOING TO--
WUNK!
--MAKE A DIFFERENCE.
OH, EMO BOY.
WELL, AT LEAST I'LL--
DONG!

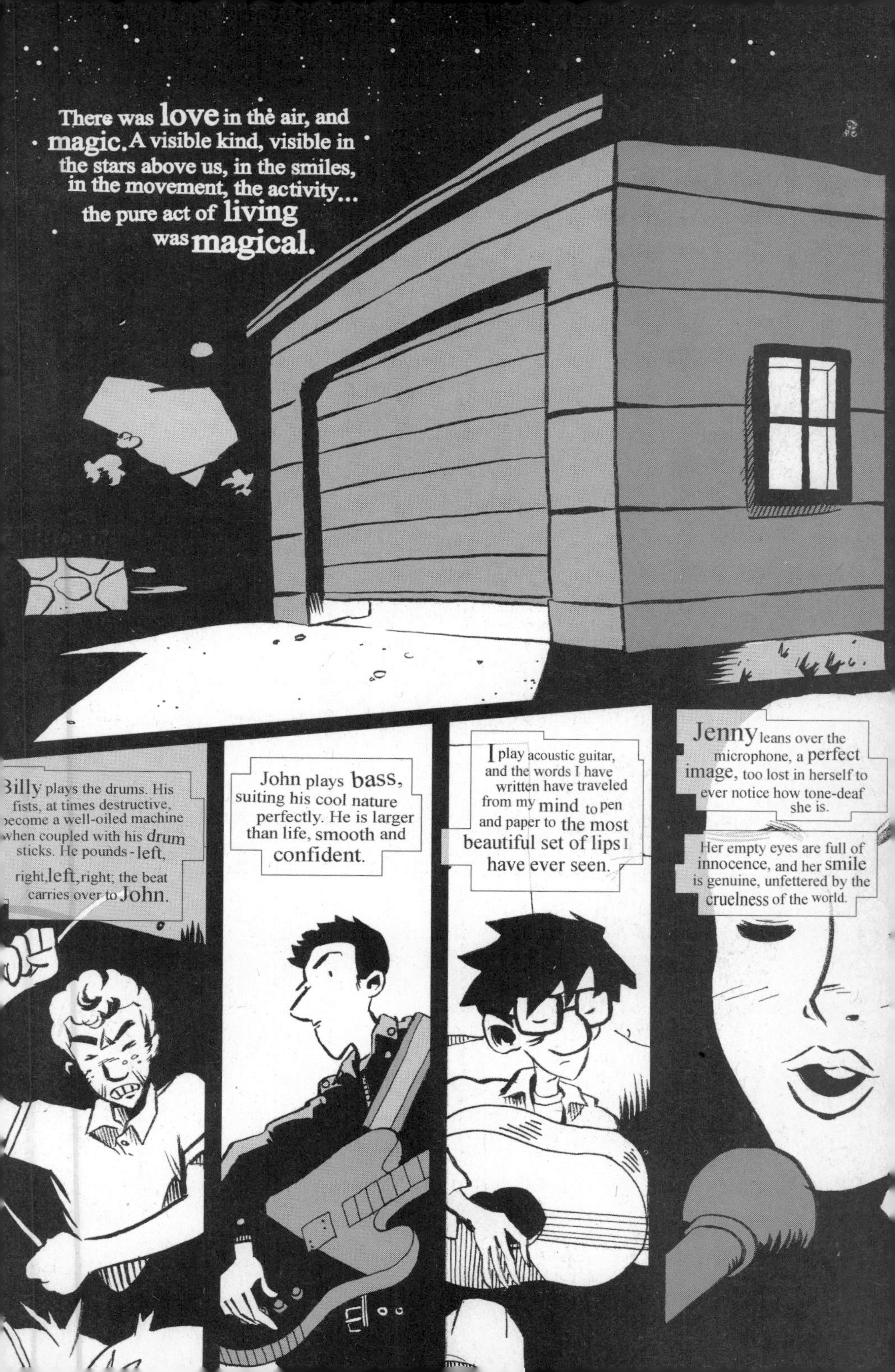
There was love in the air, and magic. A visible kind, visible in the stars above us, in the smiles, in the movement, the activity... the pure act of living was magical.
Billy plays the drums. His fists, at times destructive, become a well-oiled machine when coupled with his drum sticks. He pounds - left, right, left, right; the beat carries over to John.
John plays bass, suiting his cool nature perfectly. He is larger than life, smooth and confident.
I play acoustic guitar, and the words I have written have traveled from my mind to pen and paper to the most beautiful set of lips I have ever seen.
Jenny leans over the microphone, a perfect image, too lost in herself to ever notice how tone-deaf she is.
Her empty eyes are full of innocence, and her smile is genuine, unfettered by the cruelness of the world.

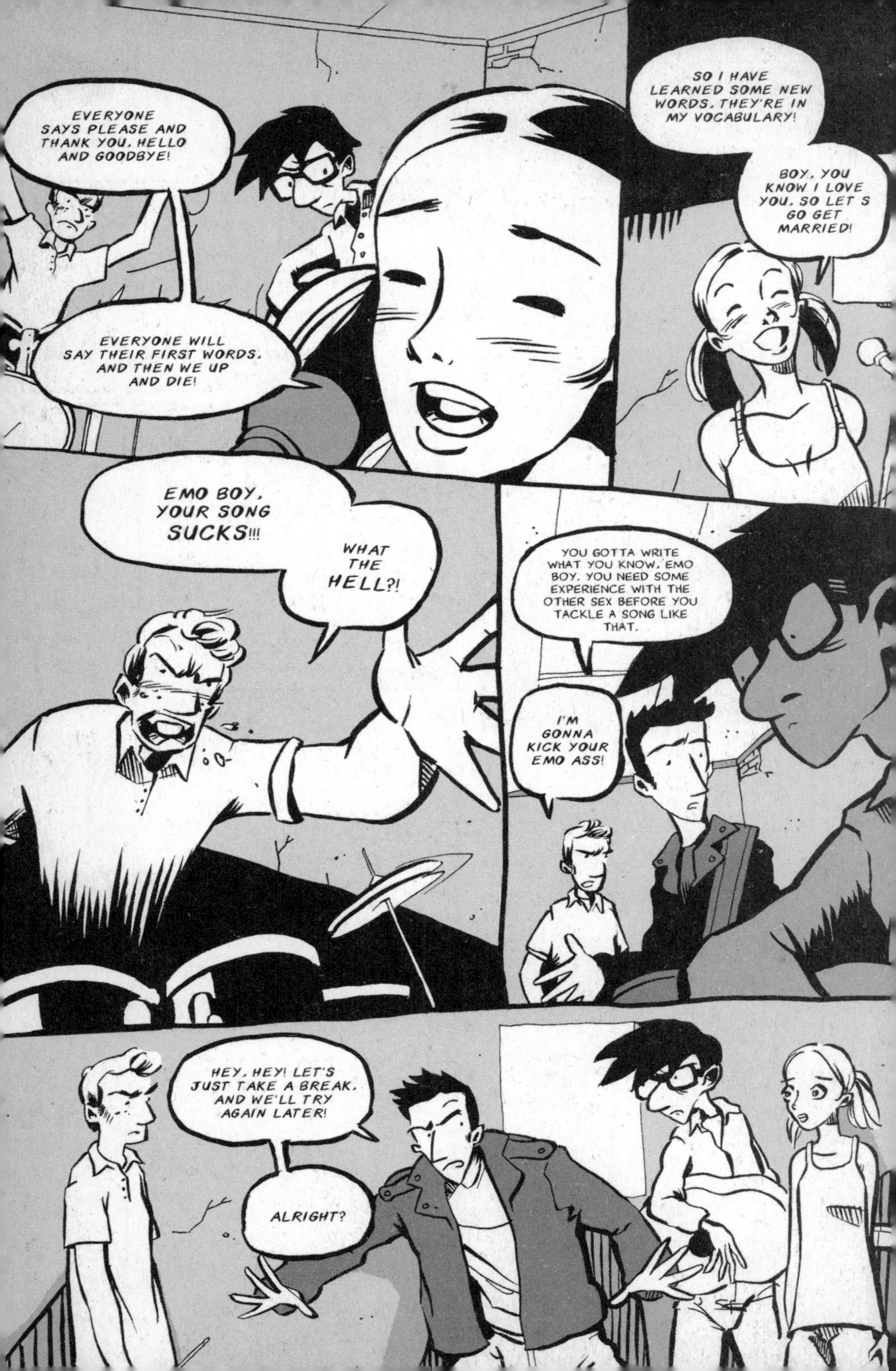
EVERYONE SAYS PLEASE AND THANK YOU, HELLO AND GOODBYE!
EVERYONE WILL SAY THEIR FIRST WORDS, AND THEN WE UP AND DIE!
SO I HAVE LEARNED SOME NEW WORDS, THEY'RE IN MY VOCABULARY!
BOY, YOU KNOW I LOVE YOU, SO LET S GO GET MARRIED!
EMO BOY, YOUR SONG SUCKS!!!
WHAT THE HELL?!
YOU GOTTA WRITE WHAT YOU KNOW, EMO BOY. YOU NEED SOME EXPERIENCE WITH THE OTHER SEX BEFORE YOU TACKLE A SONG LIKE THAT.
I'M GONNA KICK YOUR EMO ASS!
HEY, HEY! LET'S JUST TAKE A BREAK, AND WE'LL TRY AGAIN LATER!
ALRIGHT?

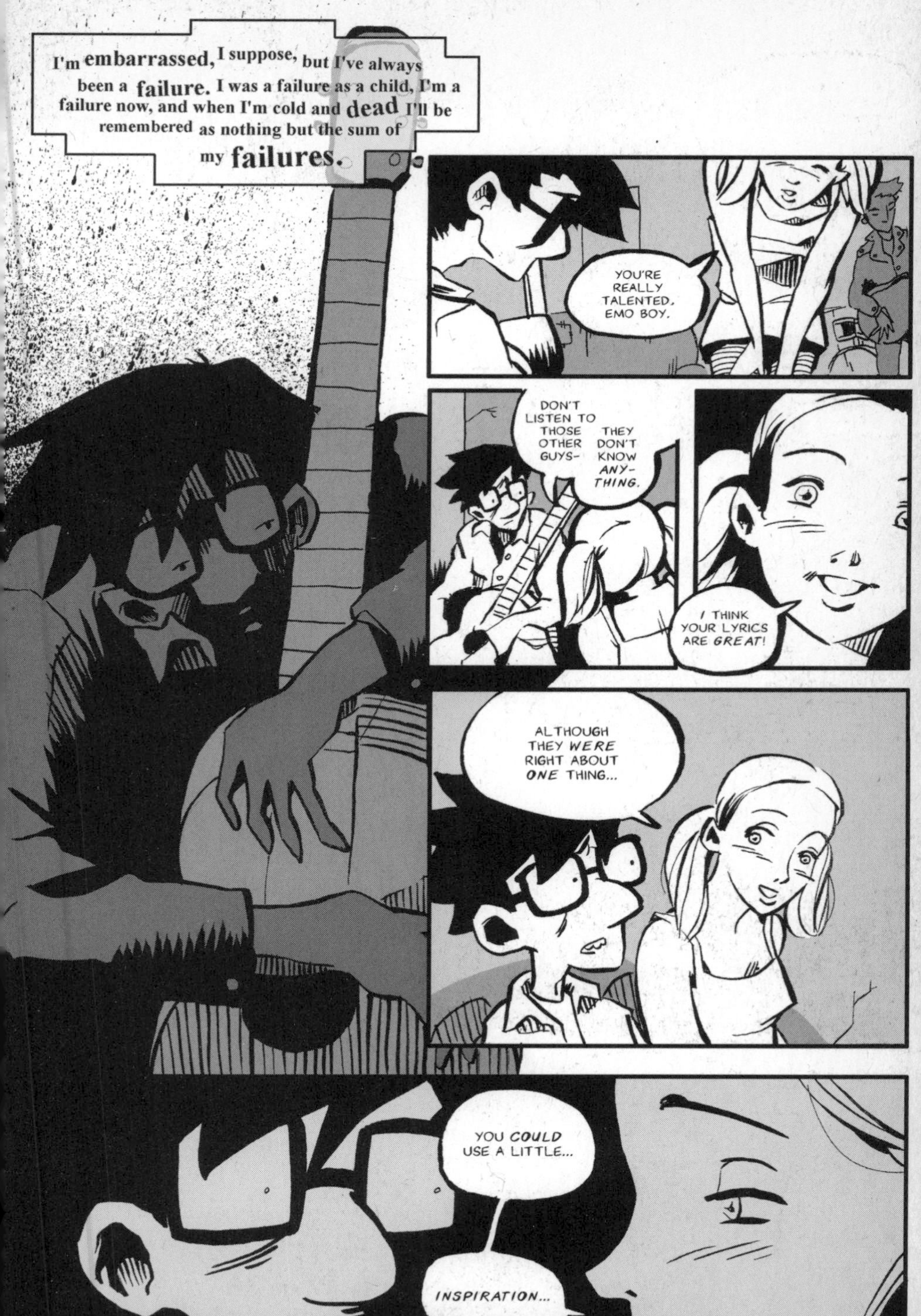

I'm embarrassed, I suppose, but I've always been a failure. I was a failure as a child, I'm a failure now, and when I'm cold and dead I'll be remembered as nothing but the sum of my failures.
YOU'RE REALLY TALENTED, EMO BOY.
DON'T LISTEN TO THOSE OTHER GUYS-
THEY DON'T KNOW ANYTHING.
I THINK YOUR LYRICS ARE GREAT!
ALTHOUGH THEY WERE RIGHT ABOUT ONE THING...
YOU COULD USE A LITTLE...
INSPIRATION...

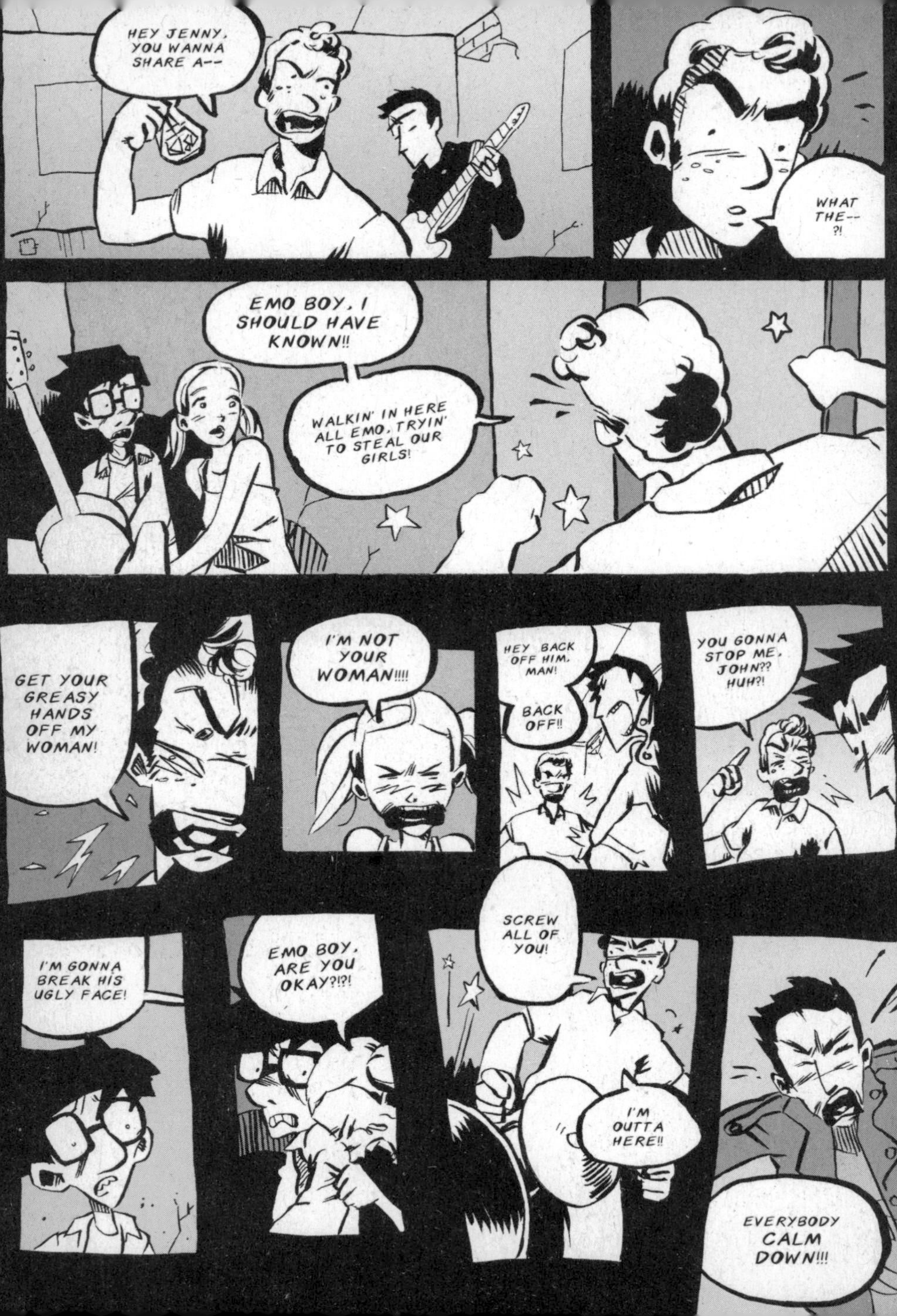
HEY JENNY, YOU WANNA SHARE A--
WHAT THE-- ?!
EMO BOY, I SHOULD HAVE KNOWN!!
WALKIN' IN HERE ALL EMO, TRYIN' TO STEAL OUR GIRLS!
GET YOUR GREASY HANDS OFF MY WOMAN!
I'M NOT YOUR WOMAN!!!!
HEY BACK OFF HIM, MAN!
BACK OFF!!
YOU GONNA STOP ME, JOHN?? HUH?!
I'M GONNA BREAK HIS UGLY FACE!
EMO BOY, ARE YOU OKAY?!?!
SCREW ALL OF YOU!
I'M OUTTA HERE!!
EVERYBODY CALM DOWN!!!

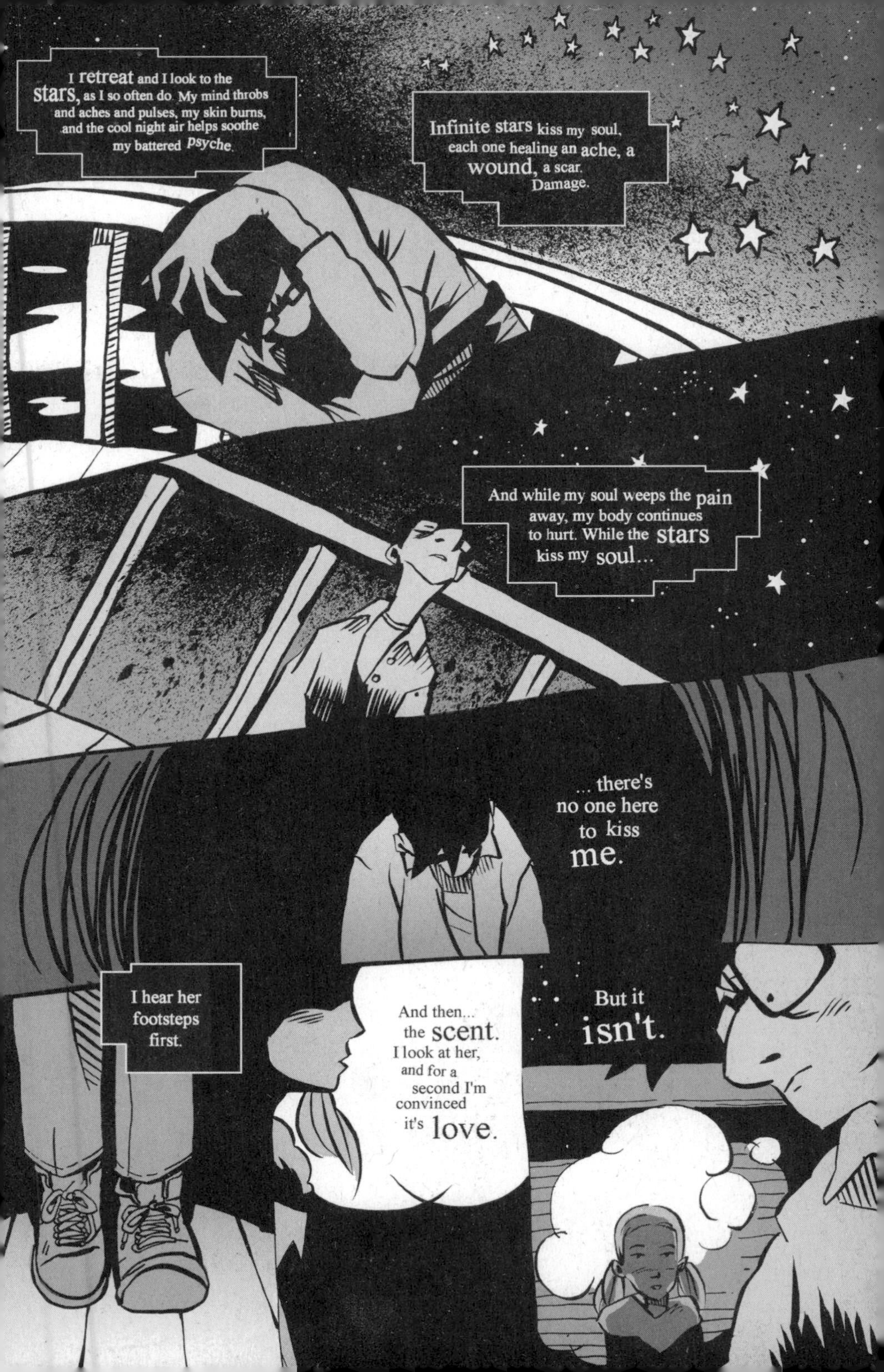
I retreat and I look to the stars, as I so often do. My mind throbs and aches and pulses, my skin burns, and the cool night air helps soothe my battered psyche.
Infinite stars kiss my soul, each one healing an ache, a wound, a scar. Damage.
And while my soul weeps the pain away, my body continues to hurt. While the stars kiss my soul...
... there's no one here to kiss me.
I hear her footsteps first.
And then... the scent. I look at her, and for a second I'm convinced it's love.
But it isn't.

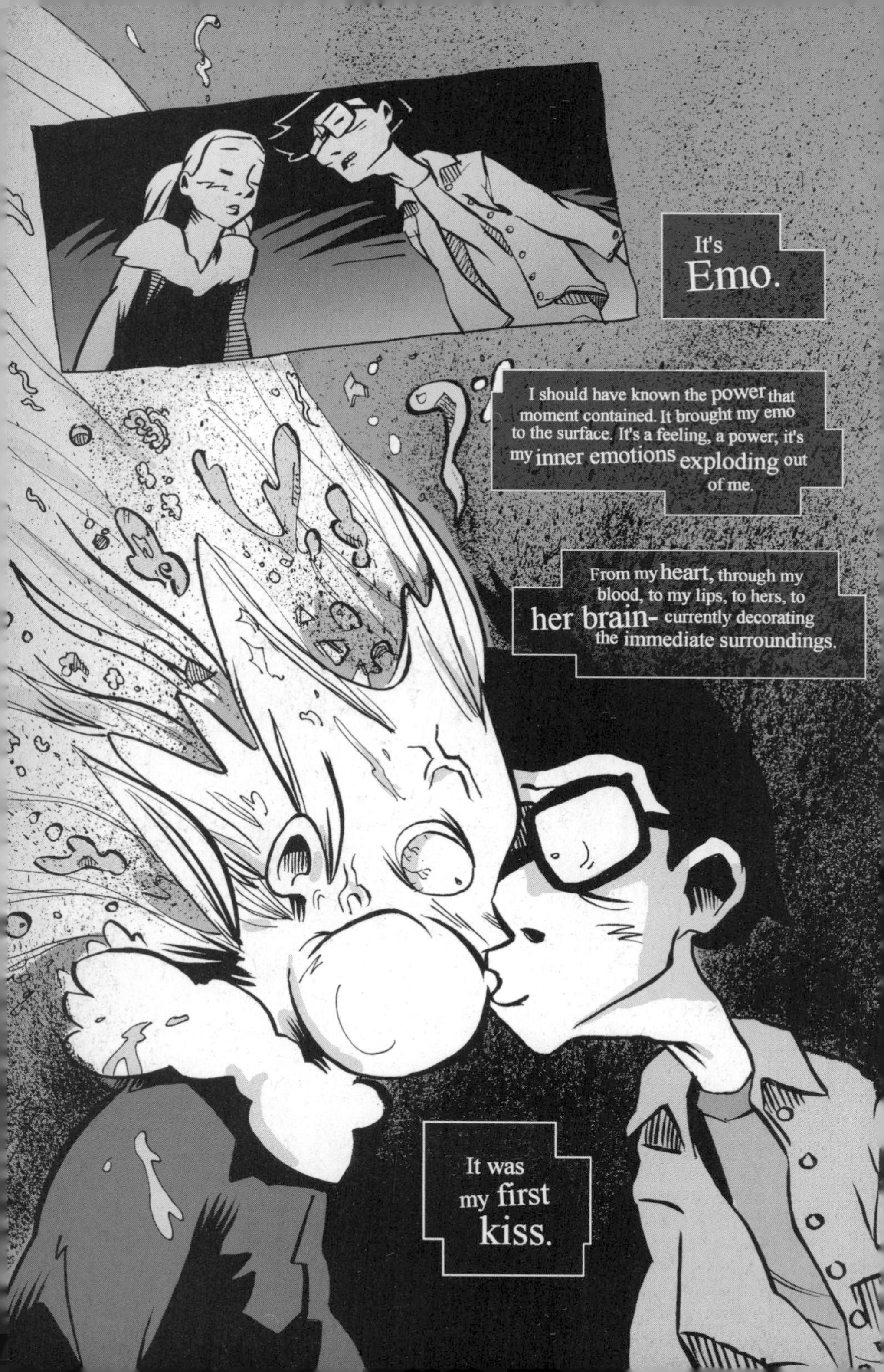
It's Emo.
I should have known the power that moment contained. It brought my emo to the surface. It's a feeling, a power; it's my inner emotions exploding out of me.
From my heart, through my blood, to my lips, to hers, to her brain- currently decorating the immediate surroundings.
It was my first kiss.

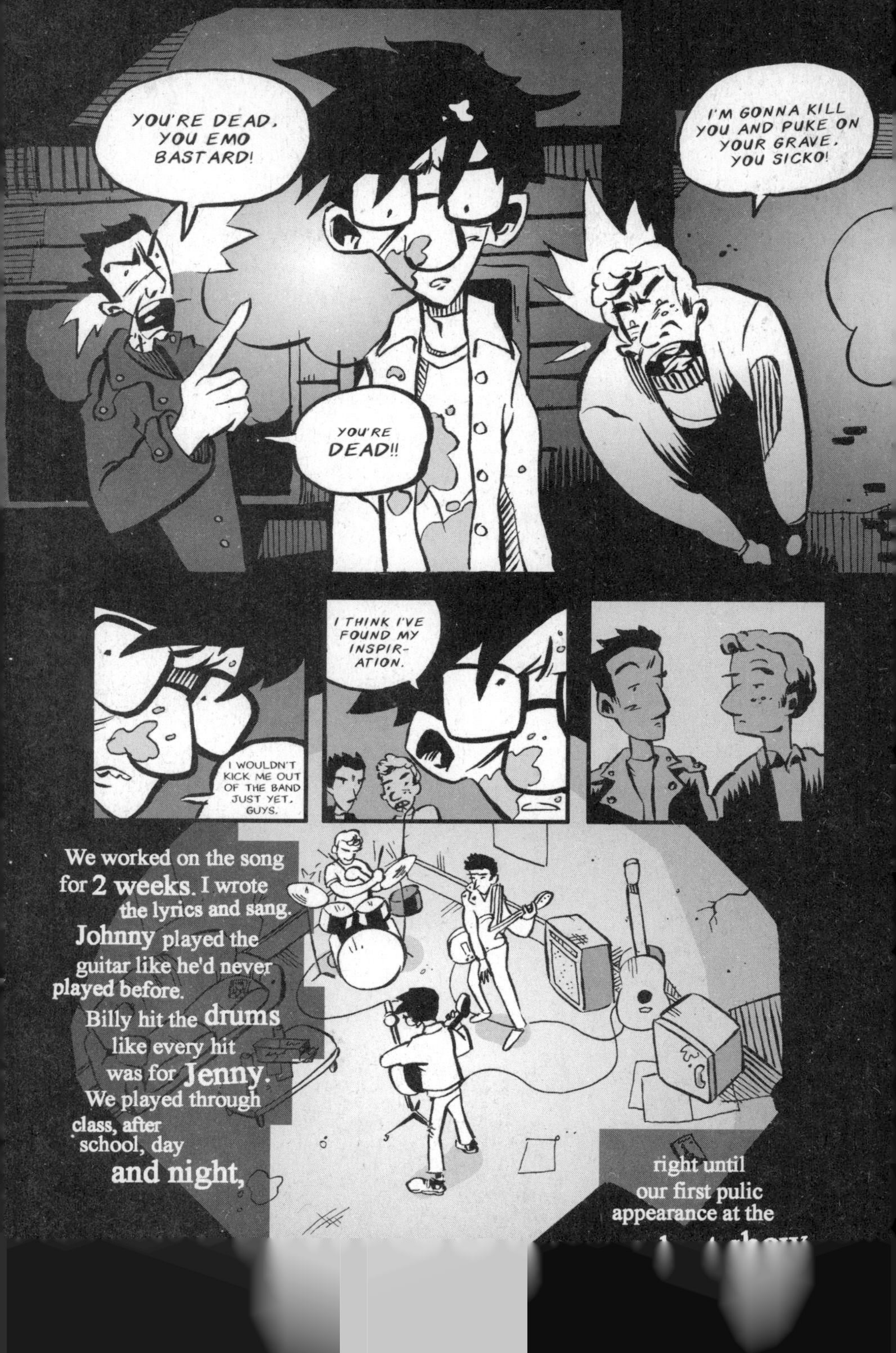
YOU'RE DEAD, YOU EMO BASTARD!
I'M GONNA KILL YOU AND PUKE ON YOUR GRAVE, YOU SICKO!
YOU'RE DEAD!!
I WOULDN'T KICK ME OUT OF THE BAND JUST YET, GUYS.
I THINK I'VE FOUND MY INSPIR-ATION.
We worked on the song for 2 weeks. I wrote the lyrics and sang. Johnny played the guitar like he'd never played before. Billy hit the drums like every hit was for Jenny. We played through class, after school, day and night,
right until our first pulic appearance at the

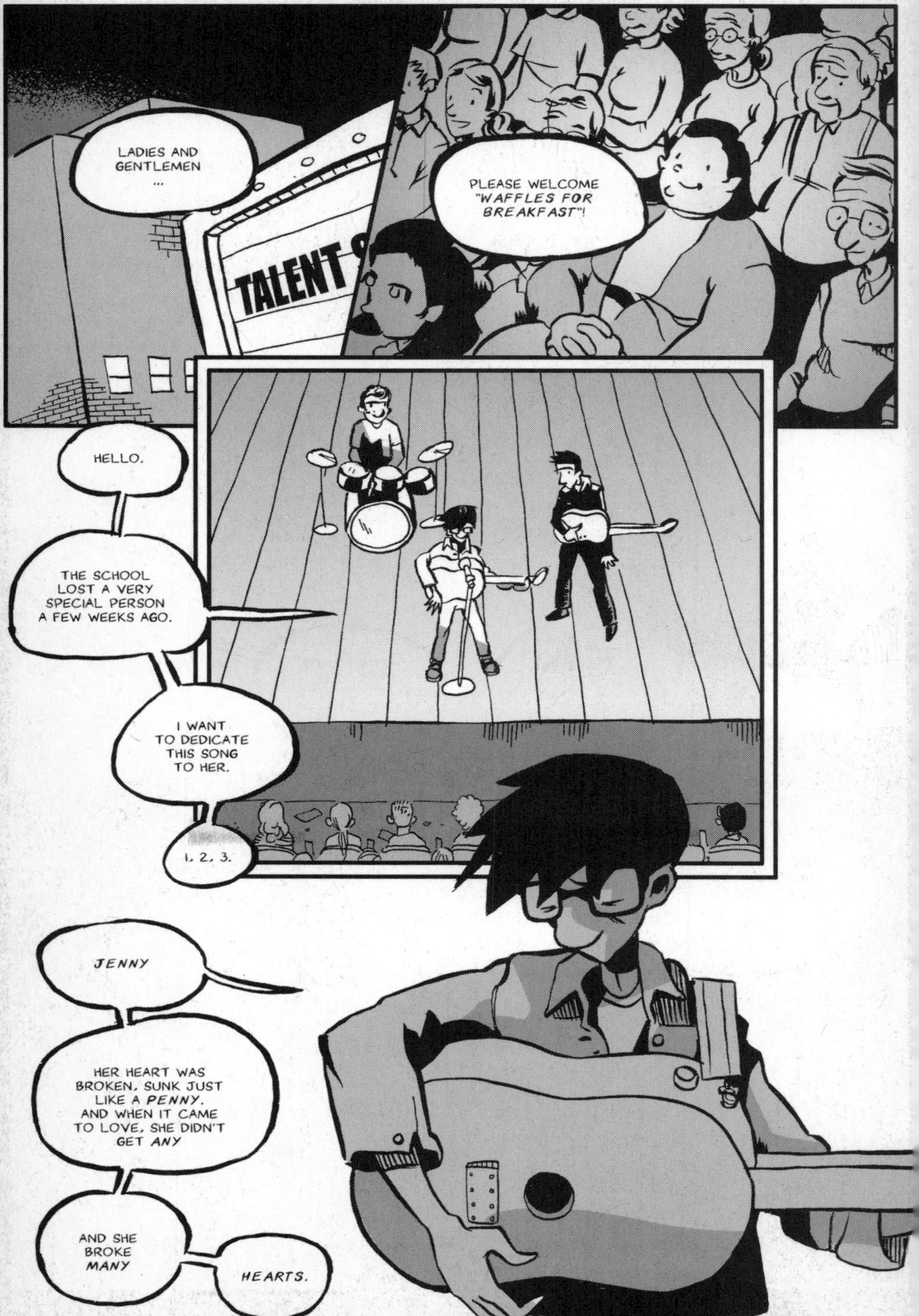
LADIES AND GENTLEMEN ...
PLEASE WELCOME "WAFFLES FOR BREAKFAST"!
TALENT
HELLO.
THE SCHOOL LOST A VERY SPECIAL PERSON A FEW WEEKS AGO.
I WANT TO DEDICATE THIS SONG TO HER.
1, 2, 3.
JENNY
HER HEART WAS BROKEN, SUNK JUST LIKE A PENNY. AND WHEN IT CAME TO LOVE, SHE DIDN'T GET ANY
AND SHE BROKE MANY
HEARTS.

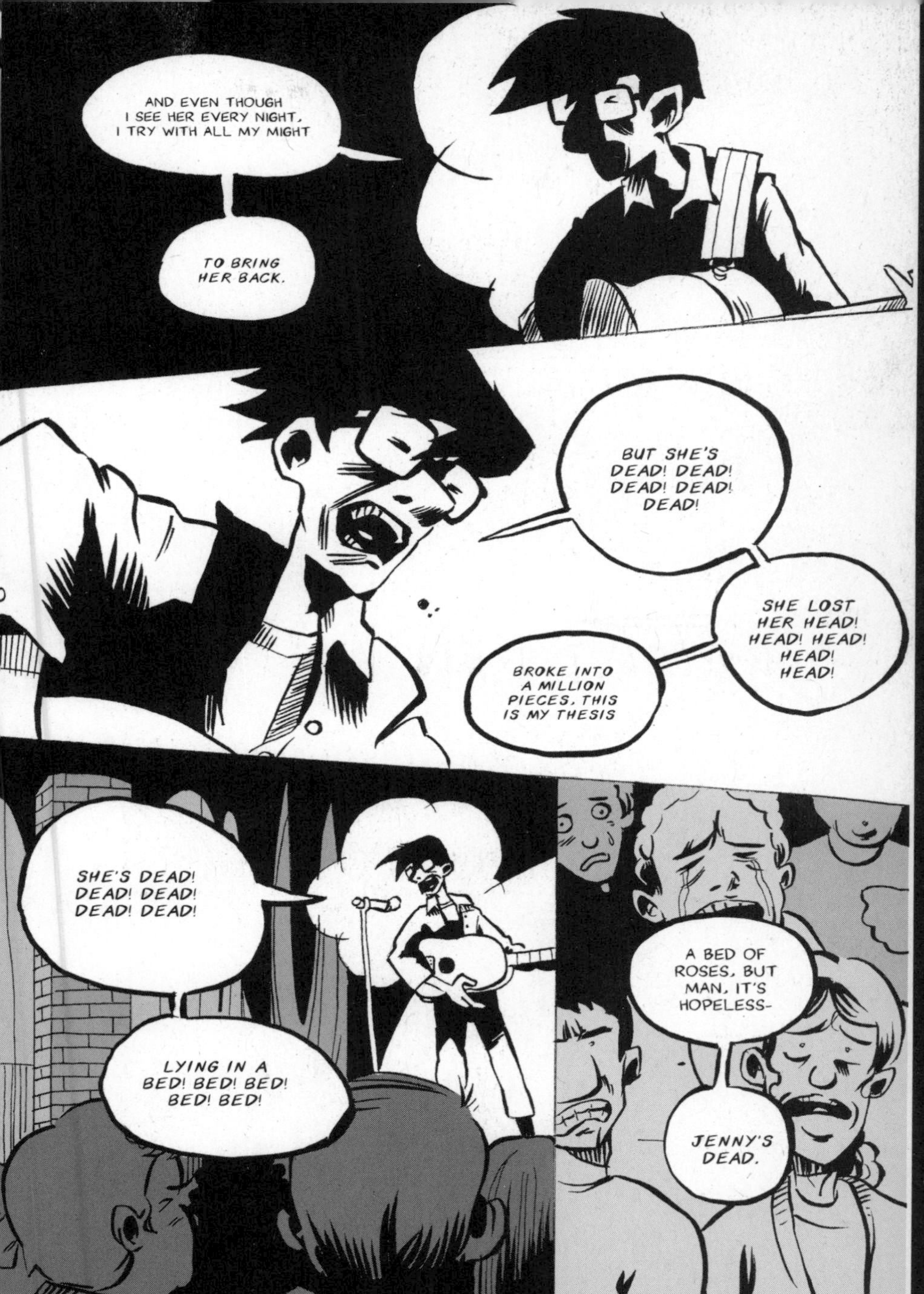
AND EVEN THOUGH I SEE HER EVERY NIGHT, I TRY WITH ALL MY MIGHT
TO BRING HER BACK.
BUT SHE'S DEAD! DEAD! DEAD! DEAD! DEAD!
SHE LOST HER HEAD! HEAD! HEAD! HEAD! HEAD!
BROKE INTO A MILLION PIECES. THIS IS MY THESIS
SHE'S DEAD! DEAD! DEAD! DEAD! DEAD!
LYING IN A BED! BED! BED! BED! BED!
A BED OF ROSES, BUT MAN, IT'S HOPELESS-
JENNY'S DEAD.

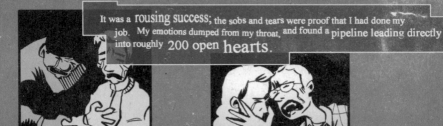

It was a rousing success; the sobs and tears were proof that I had done my job. My emotions dumped from my throat, and found a pipeline leading directly into roughly 200 open hearts.

Tonight was beautiful.

EMO BOY!! GET YOUR EMO ASS OVER HERE!!

YOU RUINED THE SHOW, YOU EMO CLOD! THE WHOLE AUDIENCE IS CRYING! NO ONE IS STAYING TO SEE ANY OF THE OTHER ACTS!! YOU BROUGHT THE WHOLE DAMN SHOW DOWN!

YOU GET OUT OF HERE!!

GO WATCH SOME DAMN CARTOONS OR SOMETHING! BEAT IT, KID!

The life of a rock star

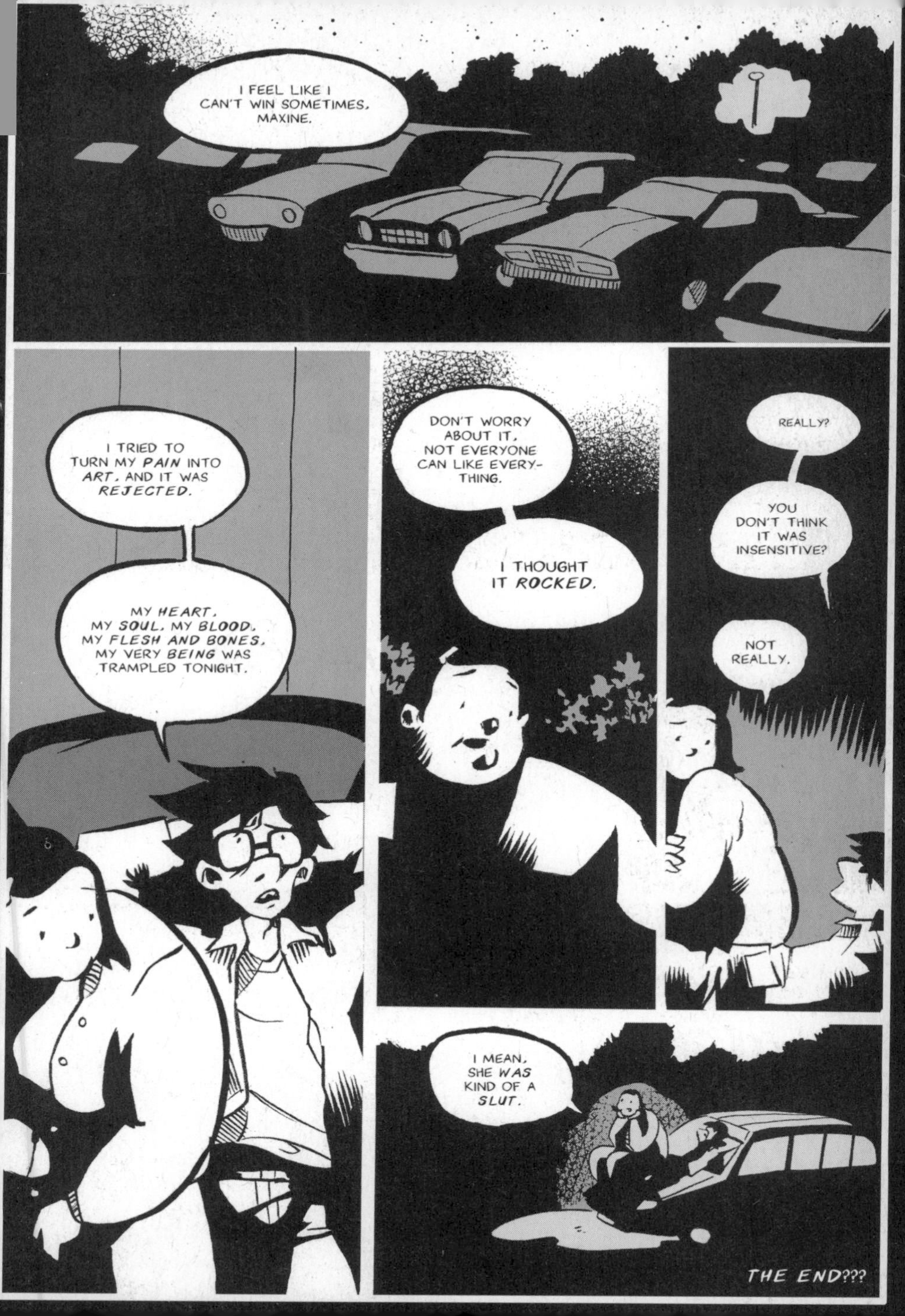
I FEEL LIKE I CAN'T WIN SOMETIMES, MAXINE.
I TRIED TO TURN MY *PAIN* INTO *ART*, AND IT WAS *REJECTED*.
MY *HEART*, MY *SOUL*, MY *BLOOD*, MY *FLESH AND BONES*, MY VERY *BEING* WAS TRAMPLED TONIGHT.
DON'T WORRY ABOUT IT, NOT EVERYONE CAN LIKE EVERY-THING.
I THOUGHT IT *ROCKED*.
REALLY?
YOU DON'T THINK IT WAS INSENSITIVE?
NOT REALLY.
I MEAN, SHE *WAS* KIND OF A *SLUT*.
THE END???

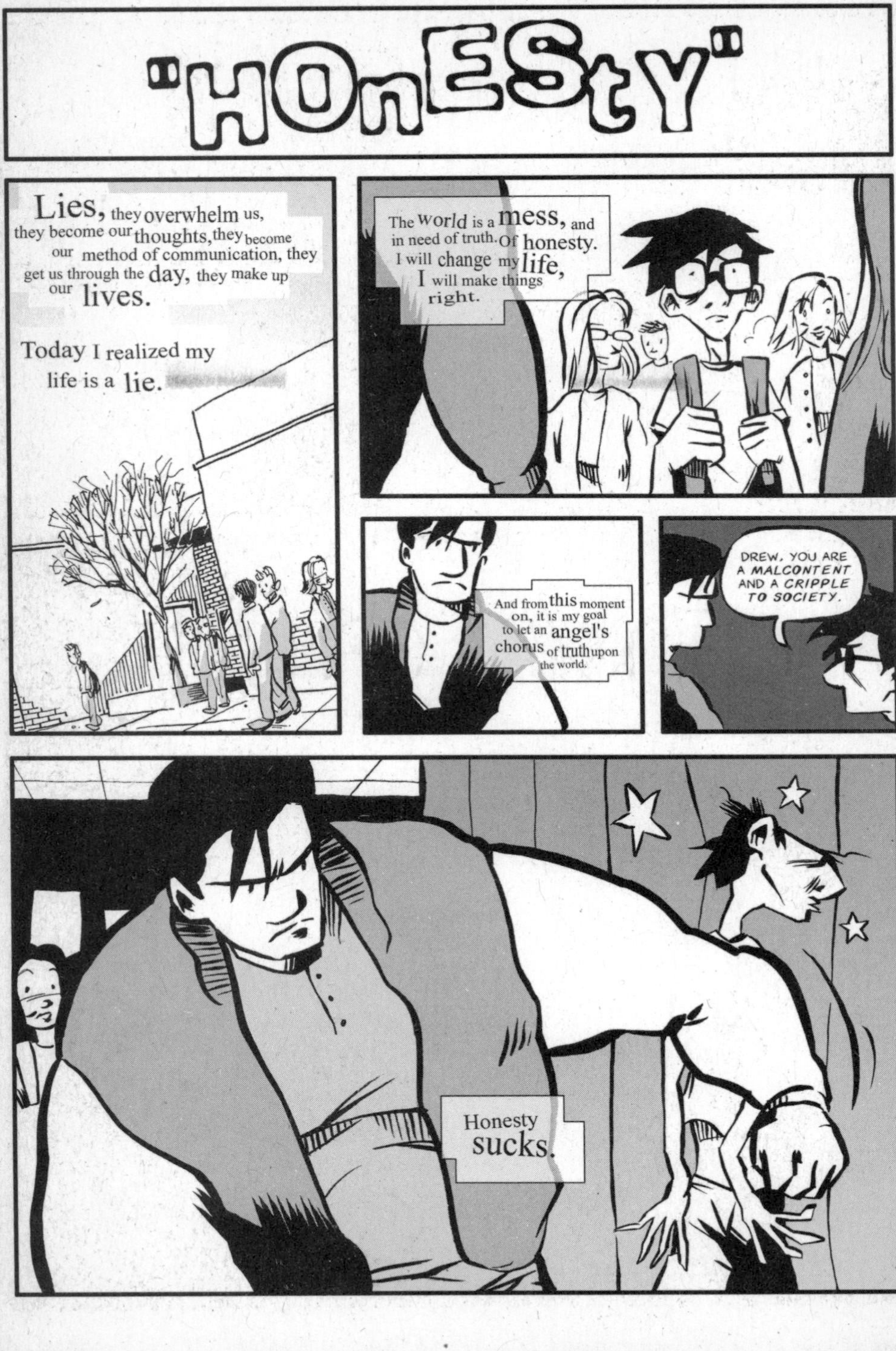
"HOnESty"
Lies, they overwhelm us, they become our thoughts, they become our method of communication, they get us through the day, they make up our lives.
Today I realized my life is a lie.
The world is a mess, and in need of truth. Of honesty. I will change my life, I will make things right.
And from this moment on, it is my goal to let an angel's chorus of truth upon the world.
DREW, YOU ARE A MALCONTENT AND A CRIPPLE TO SOCIETY.
Honesty sucks.

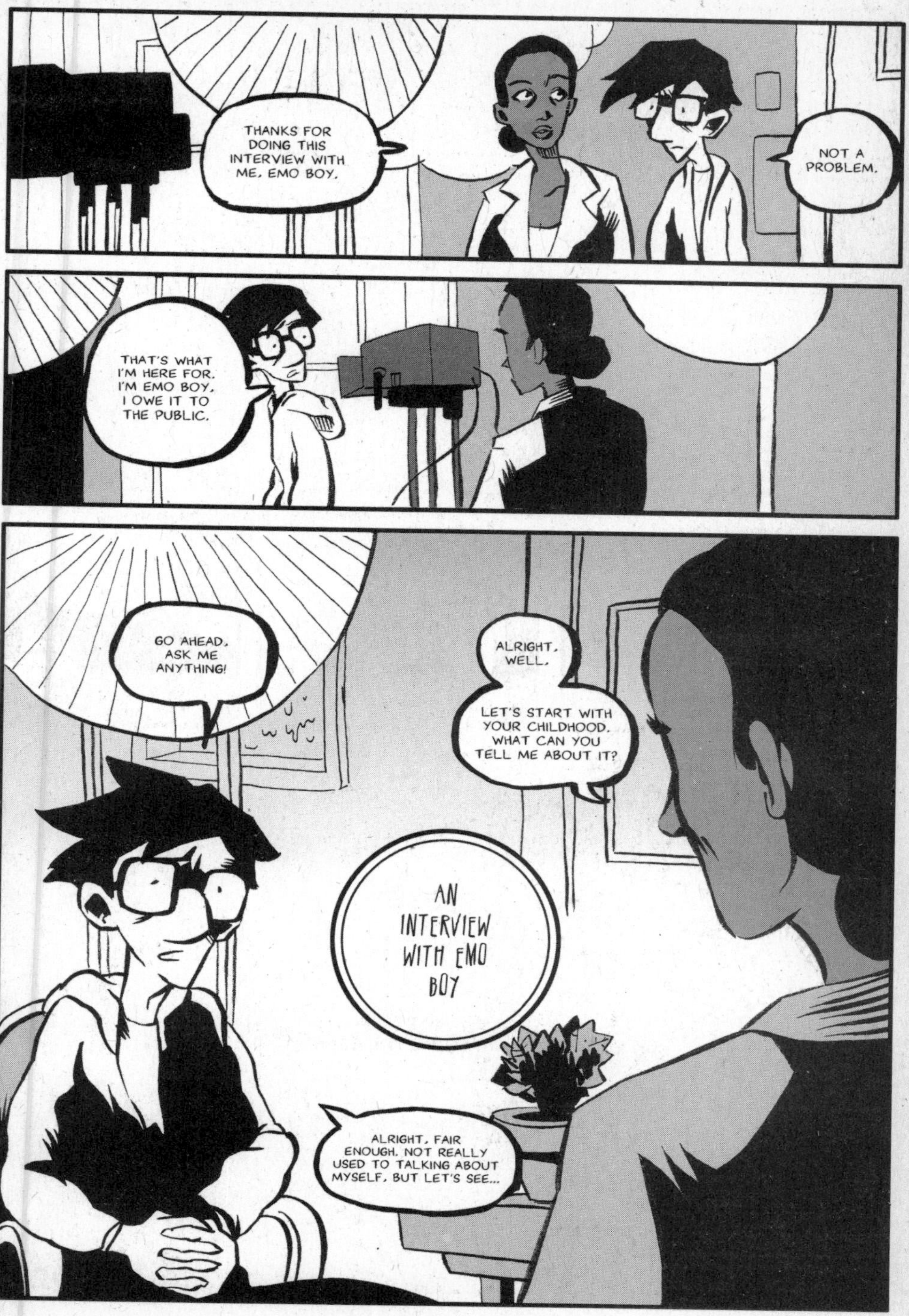
THANKS FOR DOING THIS INTERVIEW WITH ME, EMO BOY.
NOT A PROBLEM.
THAT'S WHAT I'M HERE FOR. I'M EMO BOY, I OWE IT TO THE PUBLIC.
GO AHEAD, ASK ME ANYTHING!
ALRIGHT, WELL.
LET'S START WITH YOUR CHILDHOOD. WHAT CAN YOU TELL ME ABOUT IT?
AN INTERVIEW WITH EMO BOY
ALRIGHT, FAIR ENOUGH. NOT REALLY USED TO TALKING ABOUT MYSELF, BUT LET'S SEE...

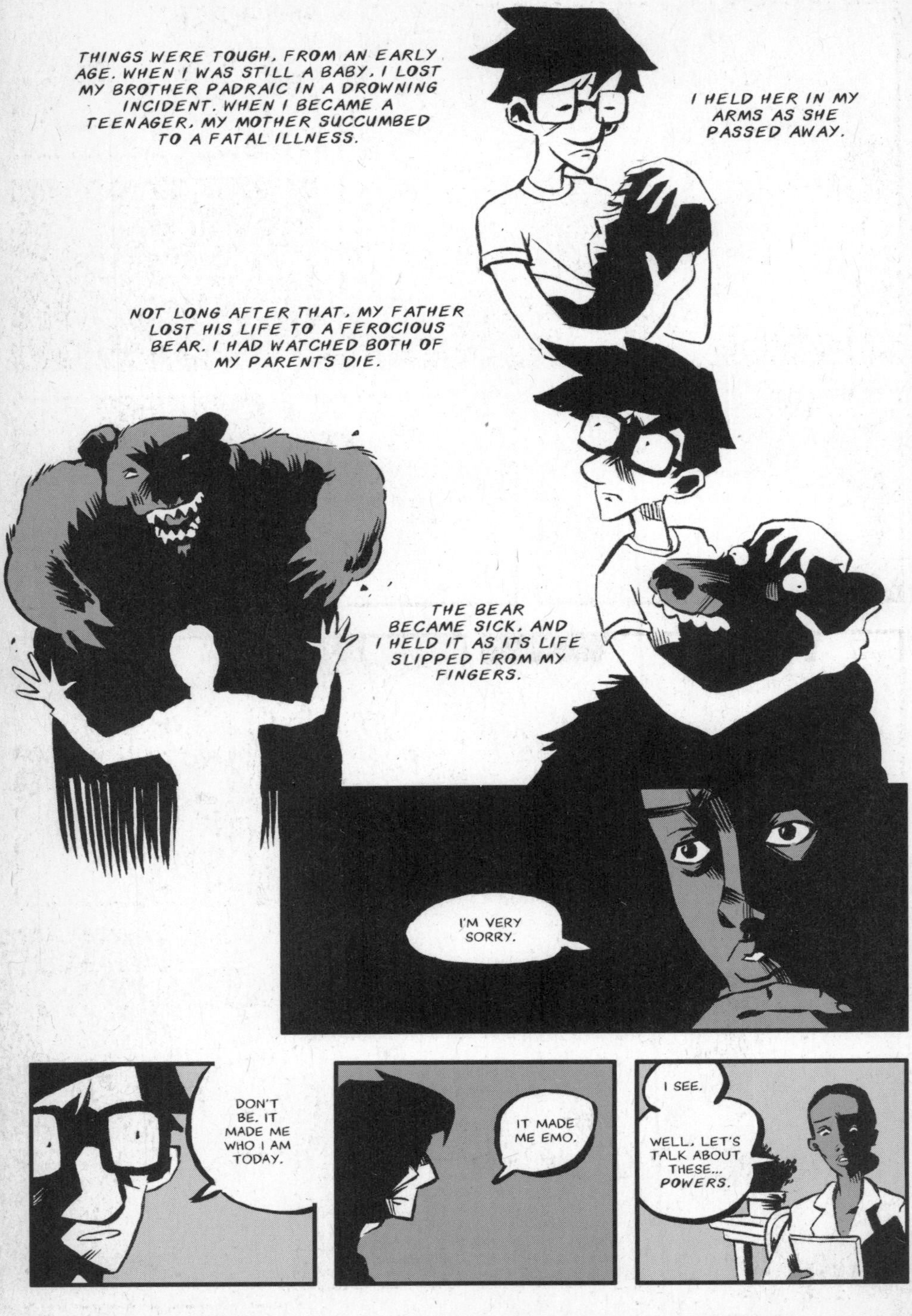
THINGS WERE TOUGH, FROM AN EARLY AGE. WHEN I WAS STILL A BABY, I LOST MY BROTHER PADRAIC IN A DROWNING INCIDENT. WHEN I BECAME A TEENAGER, MY MOTHER SUCCUMBED TO A FATAL ILLNESS.
I HELD HER IN MY ARMS AS SHE PASSED AWAY.
NOT LONG AFTER THAT, MY FATHER LOST HIS LIFE TO A FEROCIOUS BEAR. I HAD WATCHED BOTH OF MY PARENTS DIE.
THE BEAR BECAME SICK, AND I HELD IT AS ITS LIFE SLIPPED FROM MY FINGERS.
I'M VERY SORRY.
DON'T BE. IT MADE ME WHO I AM TODAY.
IT MADE ME EMO.
I SEE.
WELL, LET'S TALK ABOUT THESE... POWERS.

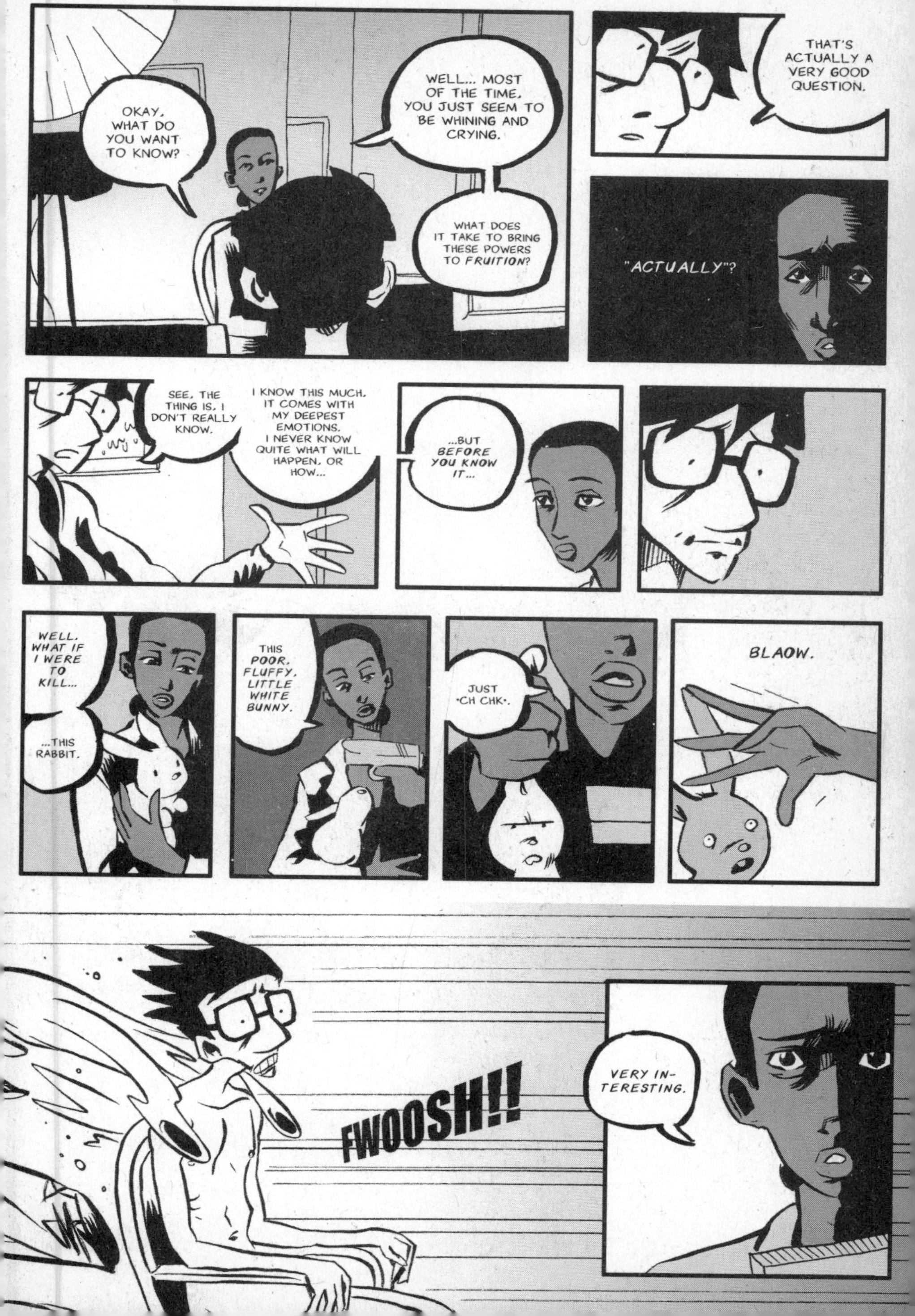
OKAY, WHAT DO YOU WANT TO KNOW?
WELL... MOST OF THE TIME, YOU JUST SEEM TO BE WHINING AND CRYING.
WHAT DOES IT TAKE TO BRING THESE POWERS TO *FRUITION*?
THAT'S ACTUALLY A VERY GOOD QUESTION.
"*ACTUALLY*"?
SEE, THE THING IS, I DON'T REALLY KNOW.
I KNOW THIS MUCH, IT COMES WITH MY DEEPEST EMOTIONS. I NEVER KNOW QUITE WHAT WILL HAPPEN, OR HOW...
...BUT *BEFORE YOU KNOW IT*...
WELL, WHAT IF I WERE TO KILL...
...THIS RABBIT.
THIS *POOR, FLUFFY, LITTLE WHITE BUNNY.*
JUST •CH CHK•.
BLAOW.
FWOOSH!!
VERY IN-TERESTING.

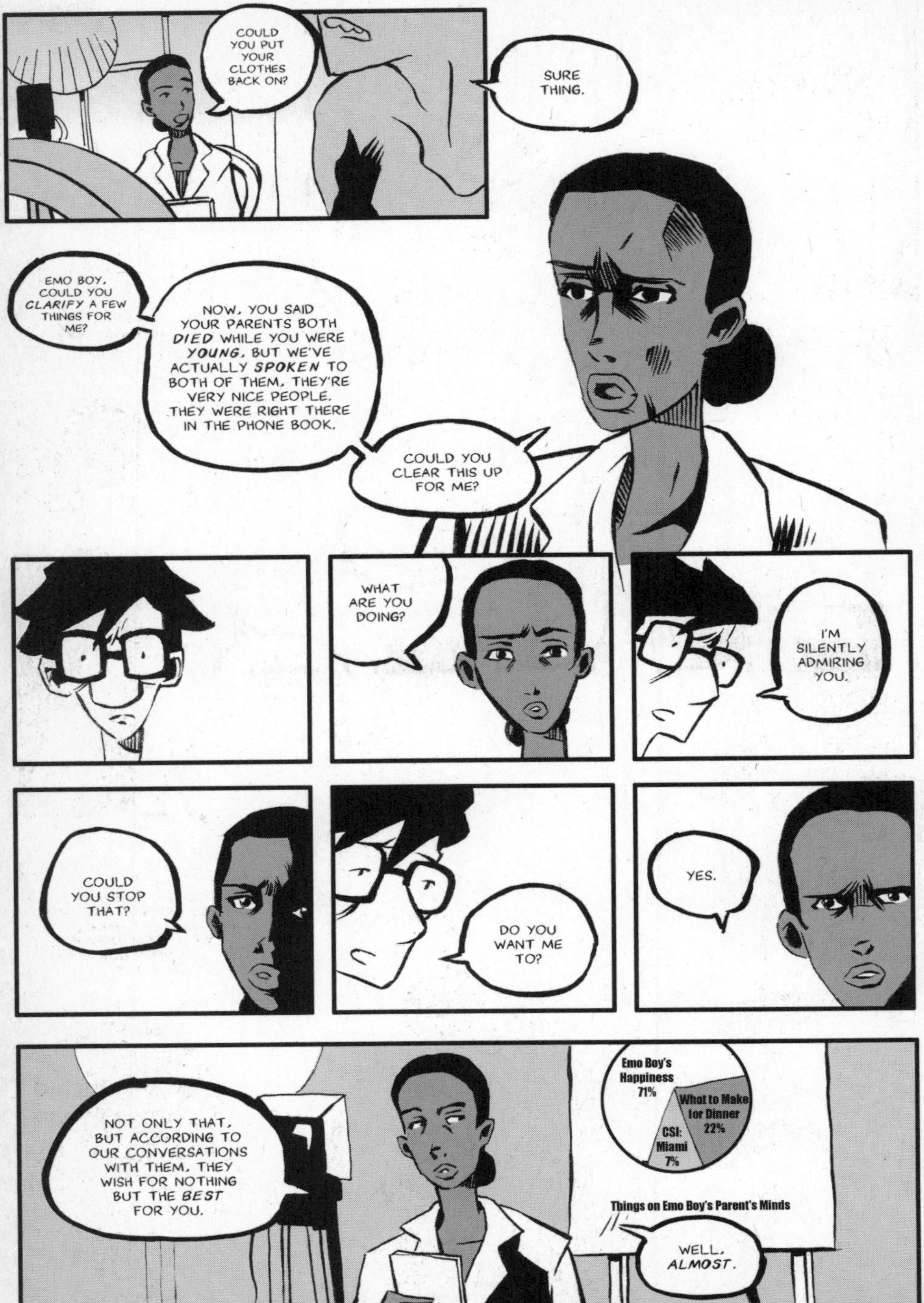

COULD YOU PUT YOUR CLOTHES BACK ON?
SURE THING.
EMO BOY, COULD YOU CLARIFY A FEW THINGS FOR ME?
NOW, YOU SAID YOUR PARENTS BOTH DIED WHILE YOU WERE YOUNG, BUT WE'VE ACTUALLY SPOKEN TO BOTH OF THEM, THEY'RE VERY NICE PEOPLE. THEY WERE RIGHT THERE IN THE PHONE BOOK.
COULD YOU CLEAR THIS UP FOR ME?
WHAT ARE YOU DOING?
I'M SILENTLY ADMIRING YOU.
COULD YOU STOP THAT?
DO YOU WANT ME TO?
YES.
NOT ONLY THAT, BUT ACCORDING TO OUR CONVERSATIONS WITH THEM, THEY WISH FOR NOTHING BUT THE BEST FOR YOU.
Emo Boy's Happiness 71%
What to Make for Dinner 22%
CSI: Miami 7%
Things on Emo Boy's Parent's Minds
WELL, ALMOST.

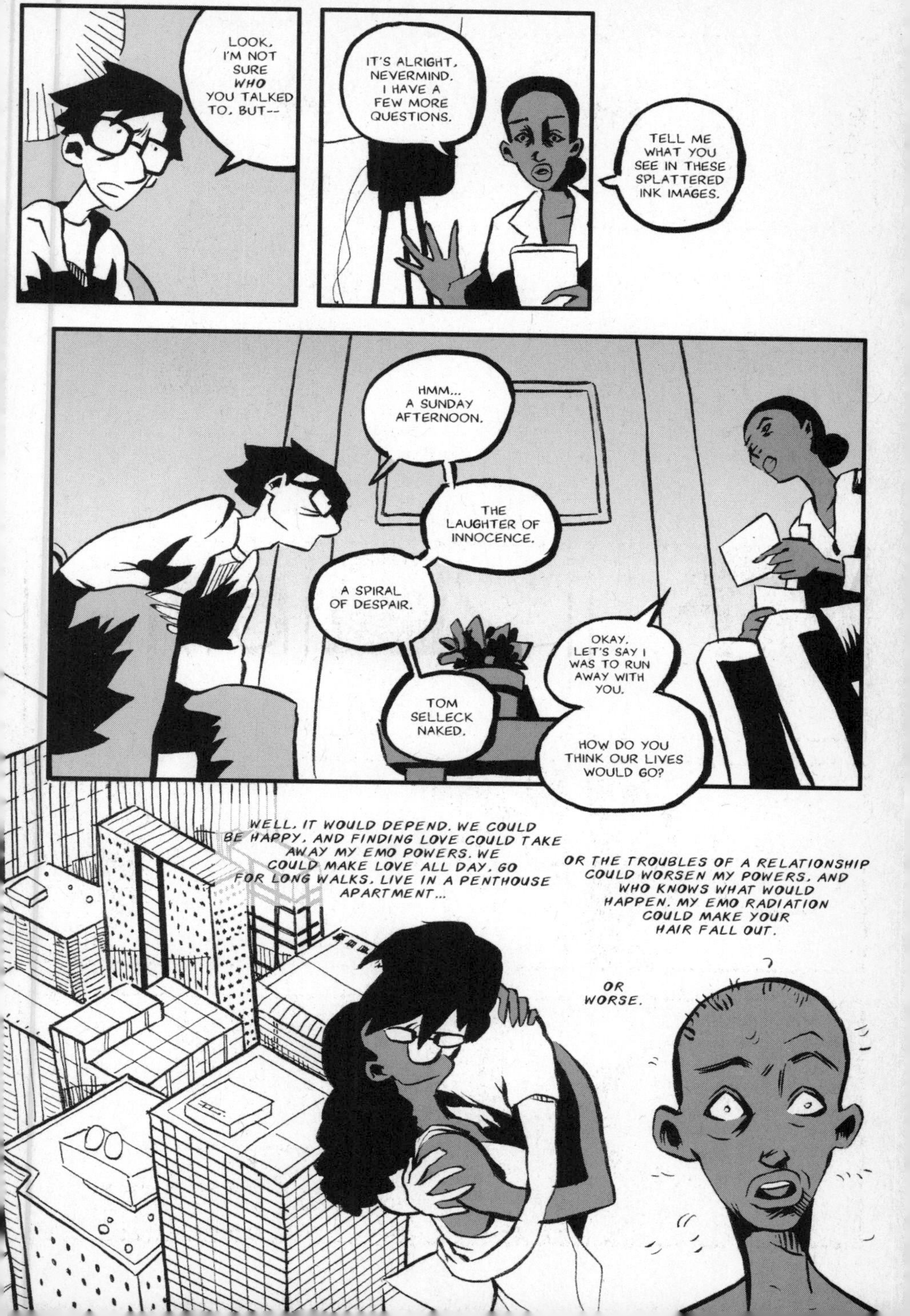
LOOK, I'M NOT SURE WHO YOU TALKED TO, BUT--
IT'S ALRIGHT, NEVERMIND. I HAVE A FEW MORE QUESTIONS.
TELL ME WHAT YOU SEE IN THESE SPLATTERED INK IMAGES.
HMM... A SUNDAY AFTERNOON.
THE LAUGHTER OF INNOCENCE.
A SPIRAL OF DESPAIR.
TOM SELLECK NAKED.
OKAY. LET'S SAY I WAS TO RUN AWAY WITH YOU.
HOW DO YOU THINK OUR LIVES WOULD GO?
WELL, IT WOULD DEPEND. WE COULD BE HAPPY, AND FINDING LOVE COULD TAKE AWAY MY EMO POWERS. WE COULD MAKE LOVE ALL DAY, GO FOR LONG WALKS, LIVE IN A PENTHOUSE APARTMENT...
OR THE TROUBLES OF A RELATIONSHIP COULD WORSEN MY POWERS, AND WHO KNOWS WHAT WOULD HAPPEN. MY EMO RADIATION COULD MAKE YOUR HAIR FALL OUT.
OR WORSE.

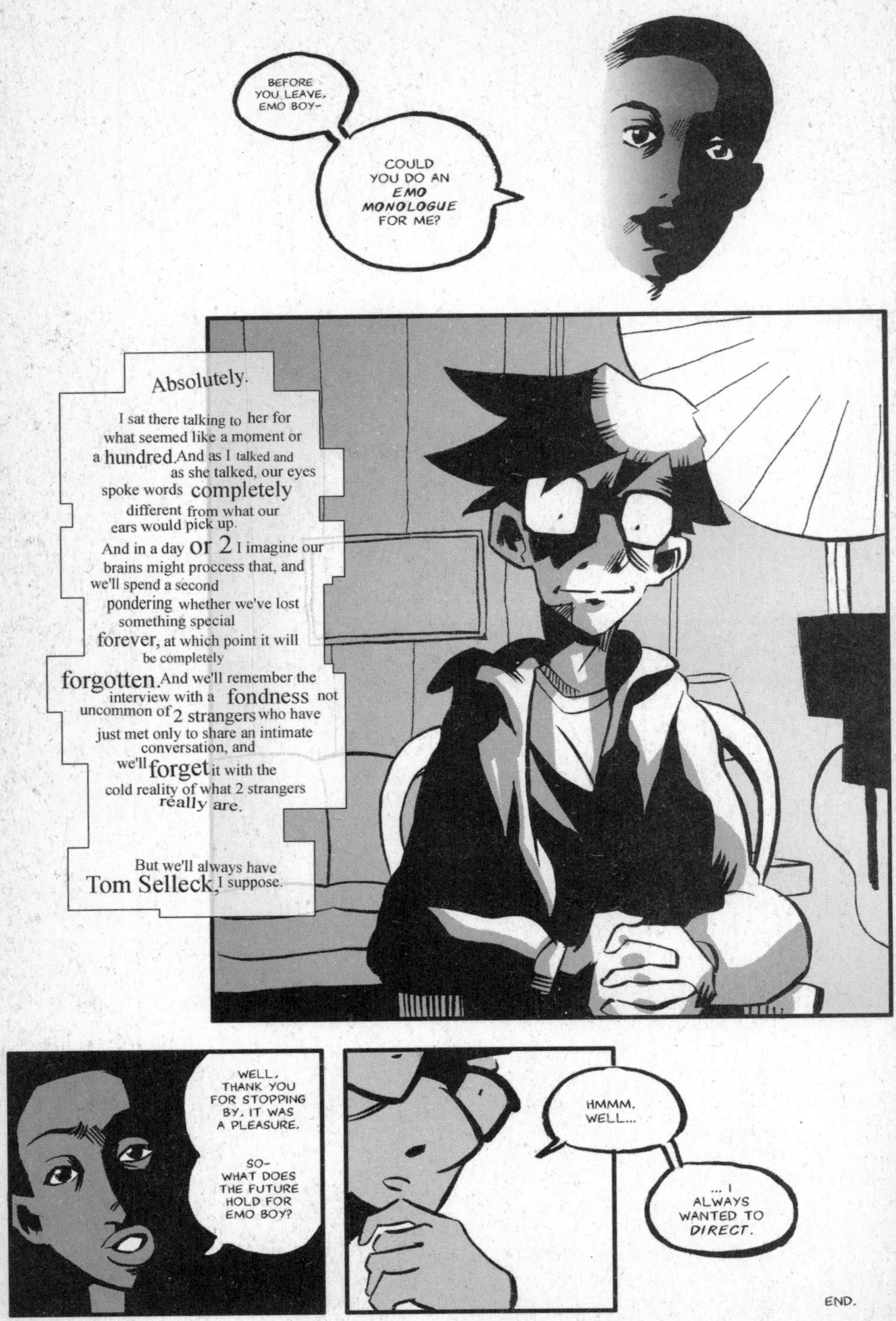
BEFORE YOU LEAVE, EMO BOY-
COULD YOU DO AN *EMO MONOLOGUE* FOR ME?
Absolutely.
I sat there talking to her for what seemed like a moment or a hundred. And as I talked and as she talked, our eyes spoke words completely different from what our ears would pick up.
And in a day or 2 I imagine our brains might proccess that, and we'll spend a second pondering whether we've lost something special forever, at which point it will be completely forgotten. And we'll remember the interview with a fondness not uncommon of 2 strangers who have just met only to share an intimate conversation, and we'll forget it with the cold reality of what 2 strangers really are.
But we'll always have Tom Selleck, I suppose.
WELL, THANK YOU FOR STOPPING BY, IT WAS A PLEASURE.
SO- WHAT DOES THE FUTURE HOLD FOR EMO BOY?
HMMM. WELL...
... I ALWAYS WANTED TO *DIRECT*.
END.

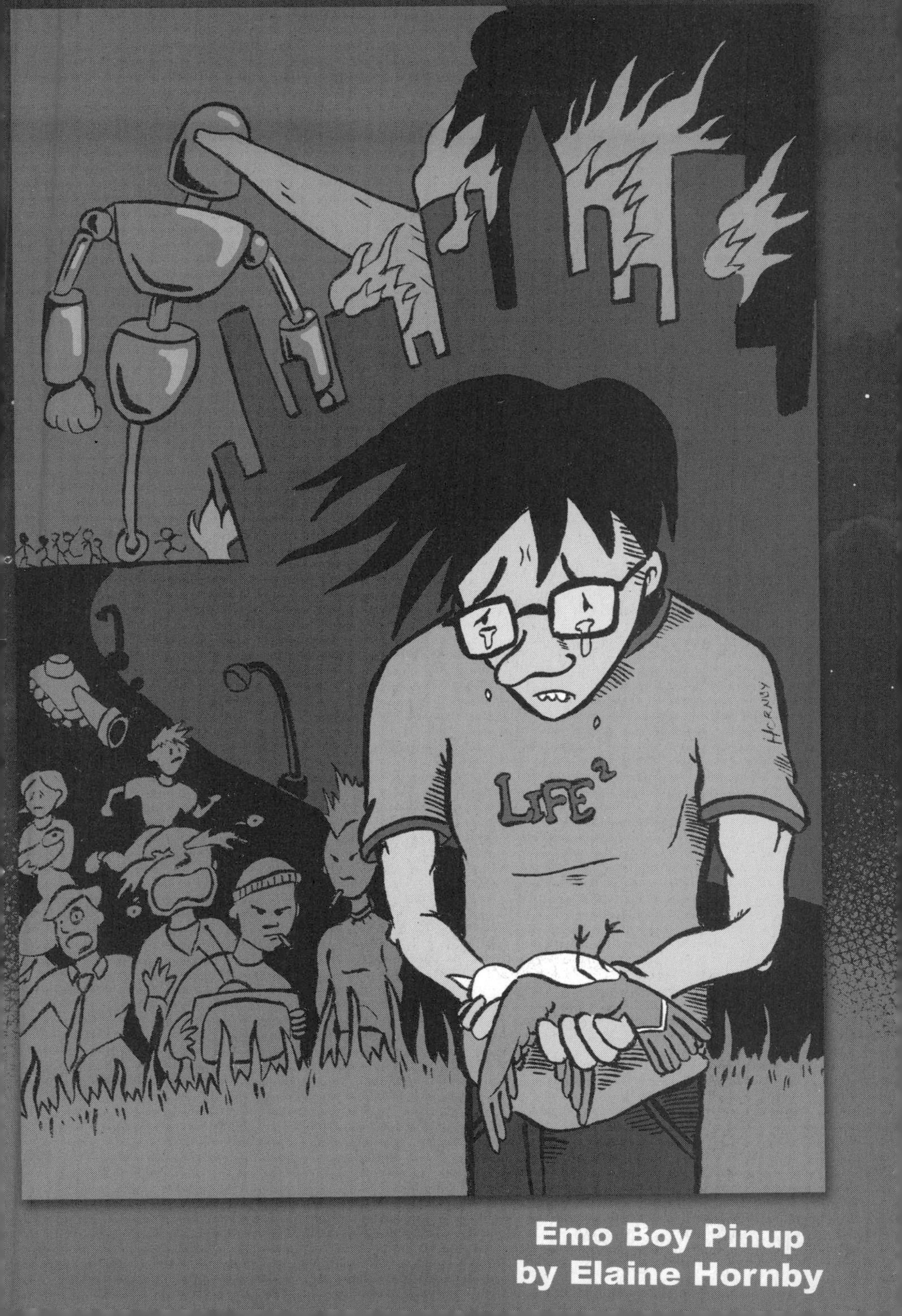
LIFE²
HORNBY

Emo Boy Pinup
by Elaine Hornby

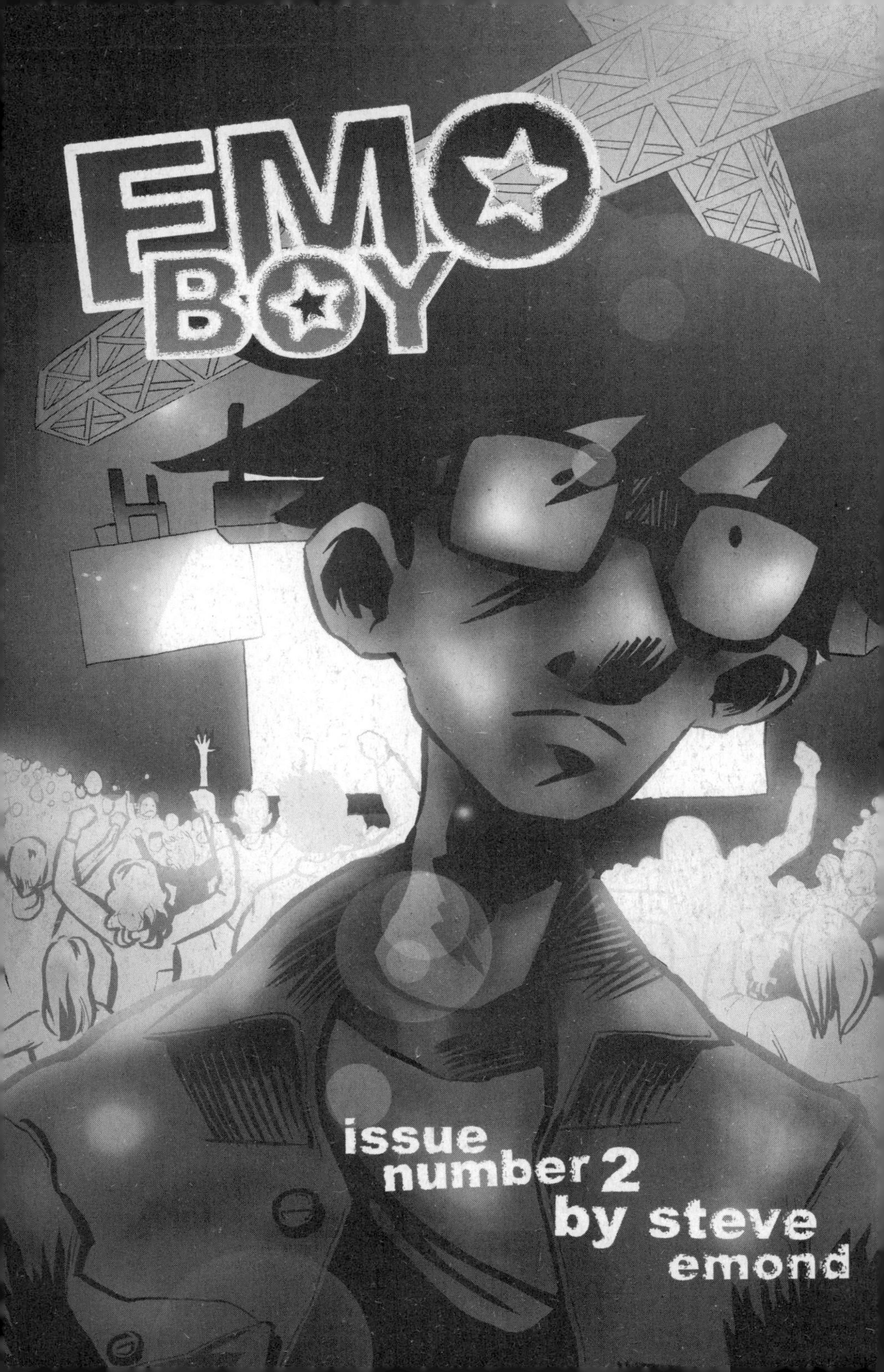
EMO BOY
issue number 2
by steve emond

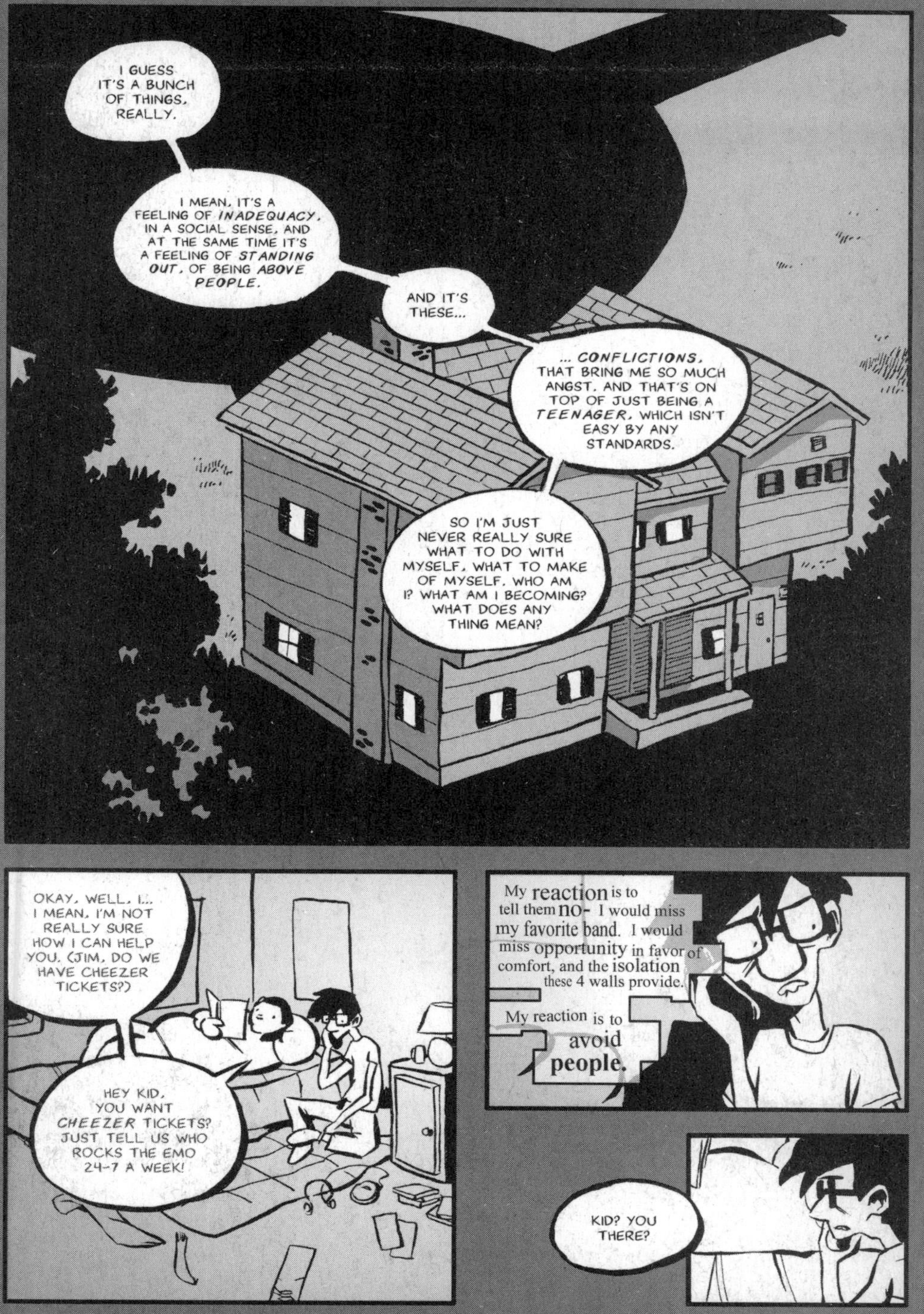
I GUESS IT'S A BUNCH OF THINGS, REALLY.
I MEAN, IT'S A FEELING OF INADEQUACY, IN A SOCIAL SENSE, AND AT THE SAME TIME IT'S A FEELING OF STANDING OUT, OF BEING ABOVE PEOPLE.
AND IT'S THESE...
... CONFLICTIONS, THAT BRING ME SO MUCH ANGST. AND THAT'S ON TOP OF JUST BEING A TEENAGER, WHICH ISN'T EASY BY ANY STANDARDS.
SO I'M JUST NEVER REALLY SURE WHAT TO DO WITH MYSELF, WHAT TO MAKE OF MYSELF. WHO AM I? WHAT AM I BECOMING? WHAT DOES ANY THING MEAN?
OKAY, WELL, I... I MEAN, I'M NOT REALLY SURE HOW I CAN HELP YOU. (JIM, DO WE HAVE CHEEZER TICKETS?)
HEY KID, YOU WANT CHEEZER TICKETS? JUST TELL US WHO ROCKS THE EMO 24-7 A WEEK!
My reaction is to tell them no- I would miss my favorite band. I would miss opportunity in favor of comfort, and the isolation these 4 walls provide.
My reaction is to avoid people.
KID? YOU THERE?

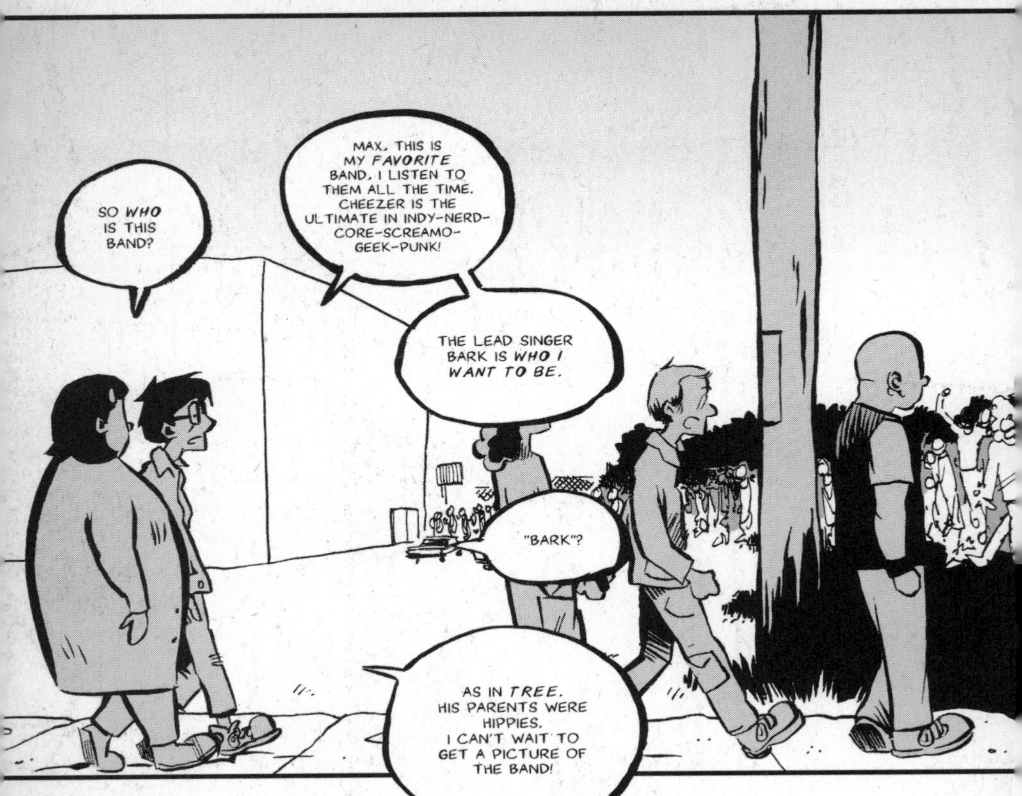
SO WHO IS THIS BAND?
MAX, THIS IS MY FAVORITE BAND. I LISTEN TO THEM ALL THE TIME. CHEEZER IS THE ULTIMATE IN INDY-NERD-CORE-SCREAMO-GEEK-PUNK!
THE LEAD SINGER BARK IS WHO I WANT TO BE.
"BARK"?
AS IN TREE. HIS PARENTS WERE HIPPIES. I CAN'T WAIT TO GET A PICTURE OF THE BAND!

Emo Boy Issue #2: "A Promise, Tonight" by Stephen Emond

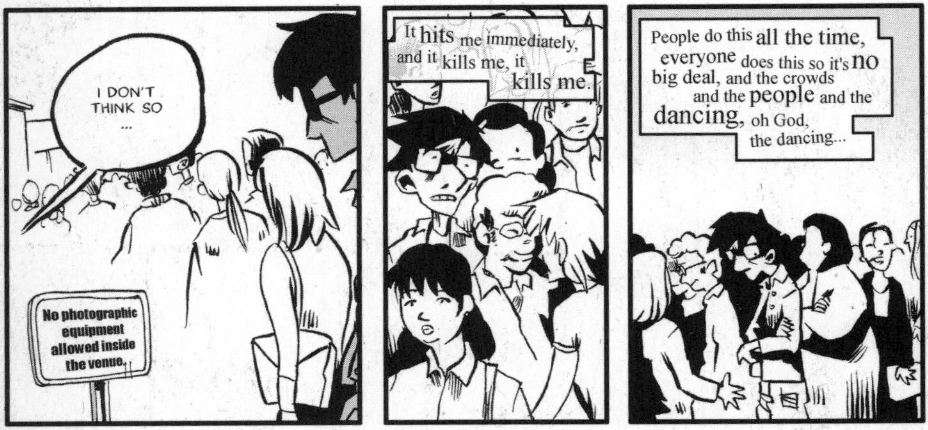
I DON'T THINK SO ...
No photographic equipment allowed inside the venue.
It hits me immediately, and it kills me, it kills me.
People do this all the time, everyone does this so it's no big deal, and the crowds and the people and the dancing, oh God, the dancing...

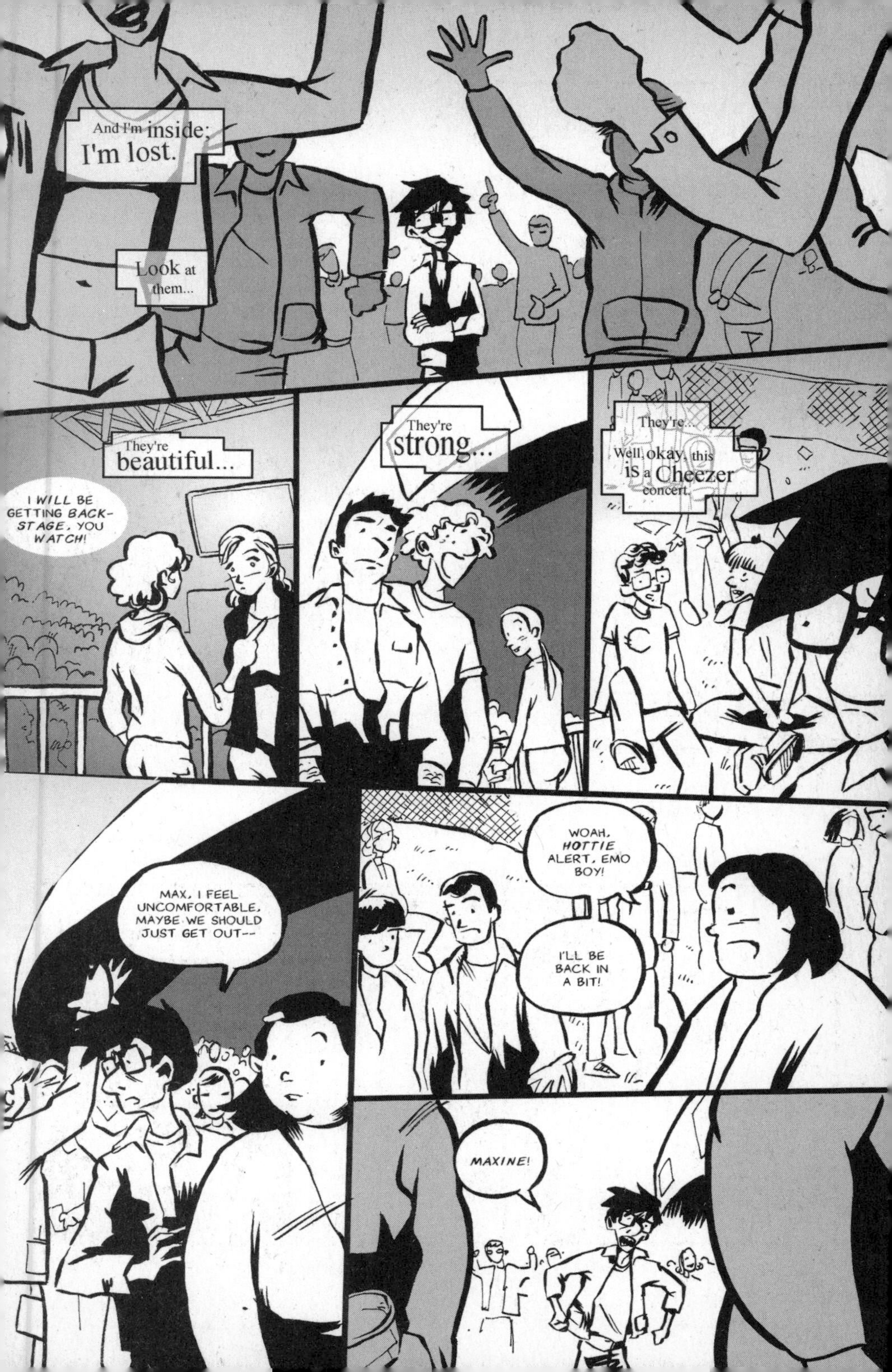

And I'm inside; I'm lost.
Look at them...
They're beautiful...
I WILL BE GETTING BACKSTAGE, YOU WATCH!
They're strong...
They're...
Well, okay, this is a Cheezer concert.
MAX, I FEEL UNCOMFORTABLE, MAYBE WE SHOULD JUST GET OUT--
WOAH, HOTTIE ALERT, EMO BOY!
I'LL BE BACK IN A BIT!
MAXINE!

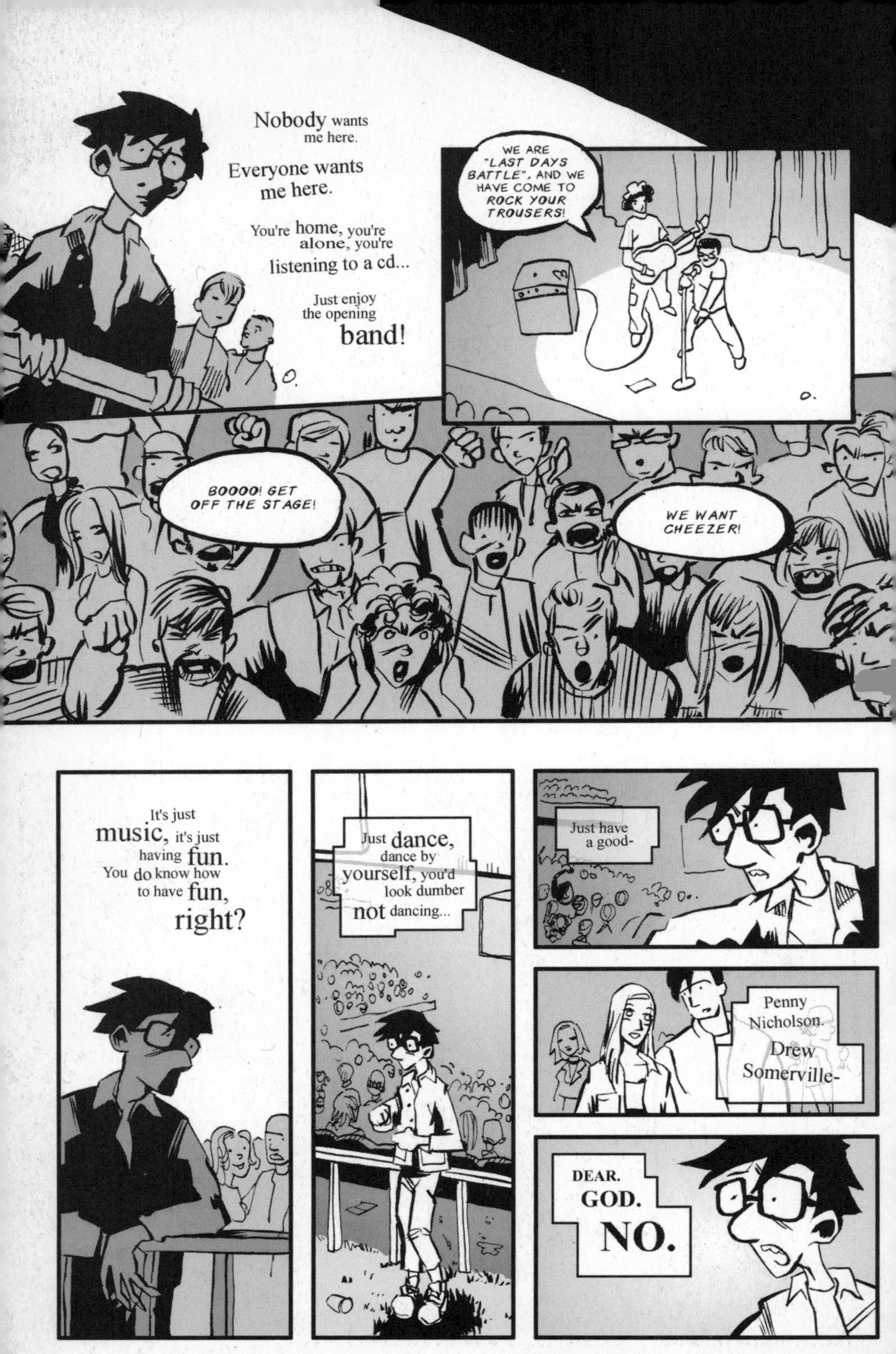
Nobody wants me here.
Everyone wants me here.
You're home, you're alone, you're listening to a cd...
Just enjoy the opening band!
WE ARE "LAST DAYS BATTLE", AND WE HAVE COME TO ROCK YOUR TROUSERS!
BOOOO! GET OFF THE STAGE!
WE WANT CHEEZER!
It's just music, it's just having fun. You do know how to have fun, right?
Just dance, dance by yourself, you'd look dumber not dancing...
Just have a good-
Penny Nicholson. Drew Somerville-
DEAR. GOD. NO.

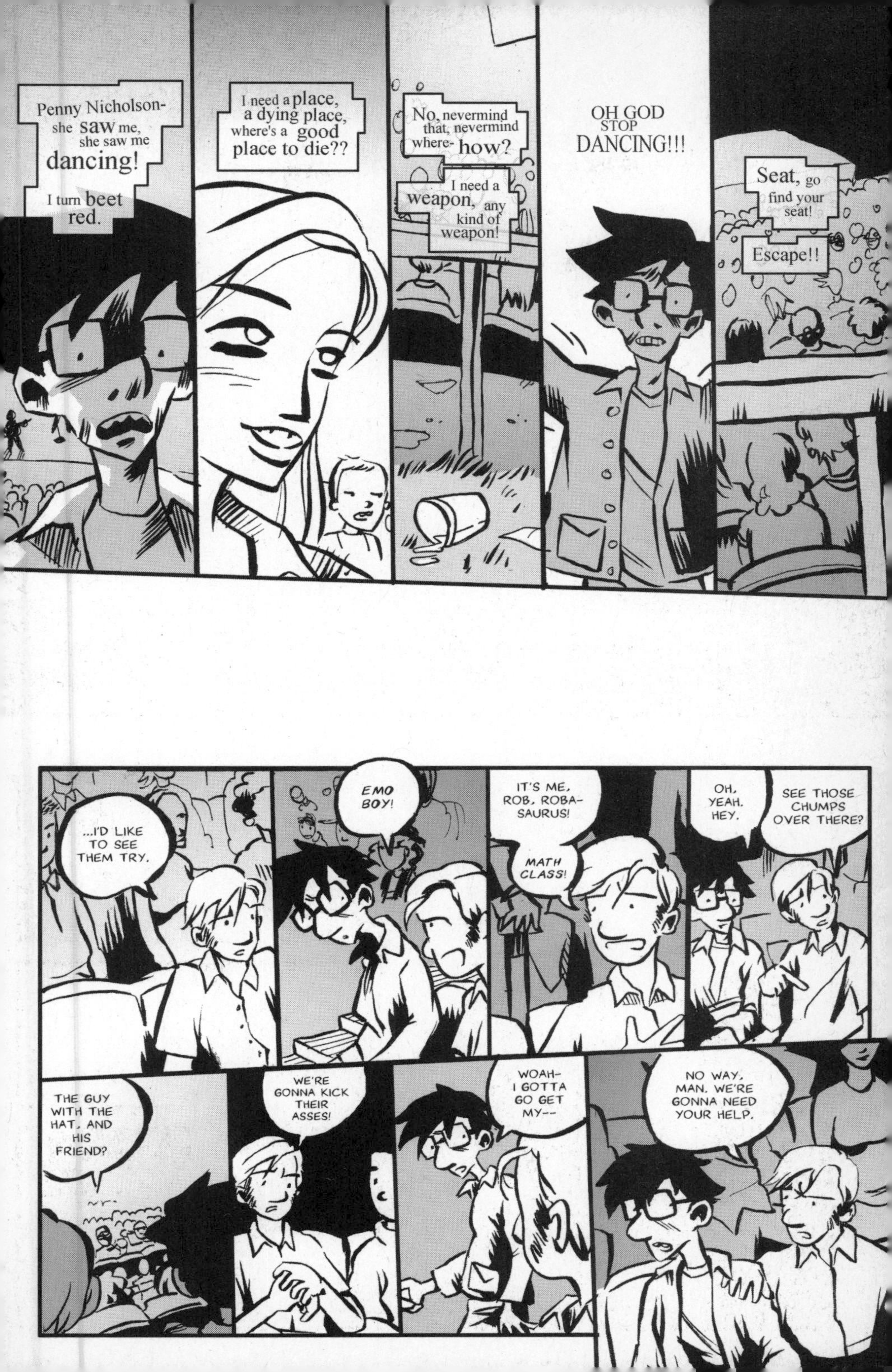
Penny Nicholson- she saw me, she saw me dancing!
I turn beet red.
I need a place, a dying place, where's a good place to die??
No, nevermind that, nevermind where- how?
I need a weapon, any kind of weapon!
OH GOD STOP DANCING!!!
Seat, go find your seat!
Escape!!
...I'D LIKE TO SEE THEM TRY.
EMO BOY!
IT'S ME, ROB, ROBA-SAURUS!
MATH CLASS!
OH, YEAH. HEY.
SEE THOSE CHUMPS OVER THERE?
THE GUY WITH THE HAT, AND HIS FRIEND?
WE'RE GONNA KICK THEIR ASSES!
WOAH- I GOTTA GO GET MY--
NO WAY, MAN. WE'RE GONNA NEED YOUR HELP.

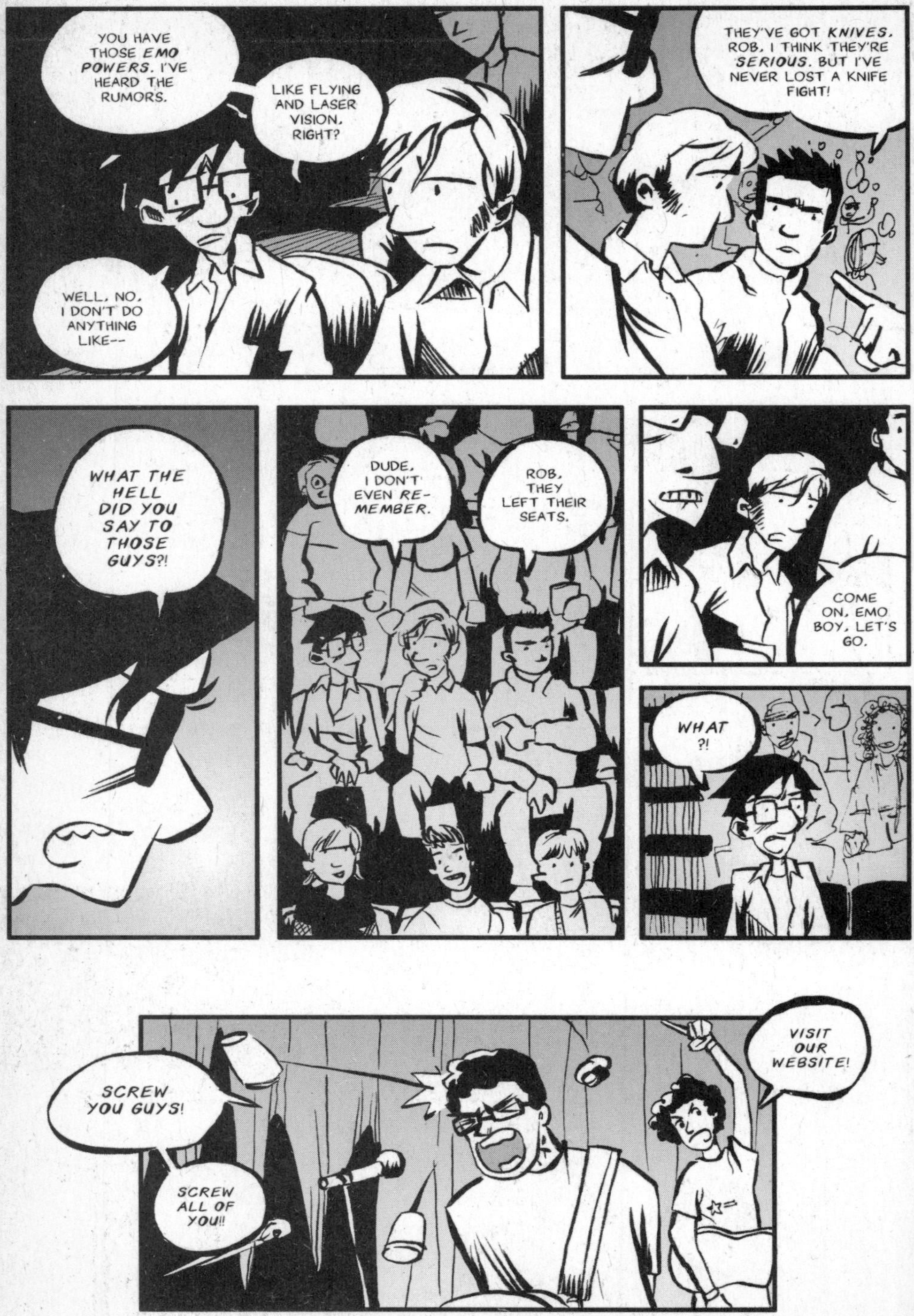
YOU HAVE THOSE *EMO POWERS*. I'VE HEARD THE RUMORS.
LIKE FLYING AND LASER VISION, RIGHT?
WELL, NO, I DON'T DO ANYTHING LIKE--
THEY'VE GOT *KNIVES*, ROB, I THINK THEY'RE *SERIOUS*. BUT I'VE NEVER LOST A KNIFE FIGHT!
WHAT THE HELL DID YOU SAY TO THOSE GUYS?!
DUDE, I DON'T EVEN *RE-MEMBER*.
ROB, THEY LEFT THEIR SEATS.
COME ON, EMO BOY, LET'S GO.
WHAT ?!
SCREW YOU GUYS!
SCREW ALL OF YOU!!
VISIT OUR WEBSITE!

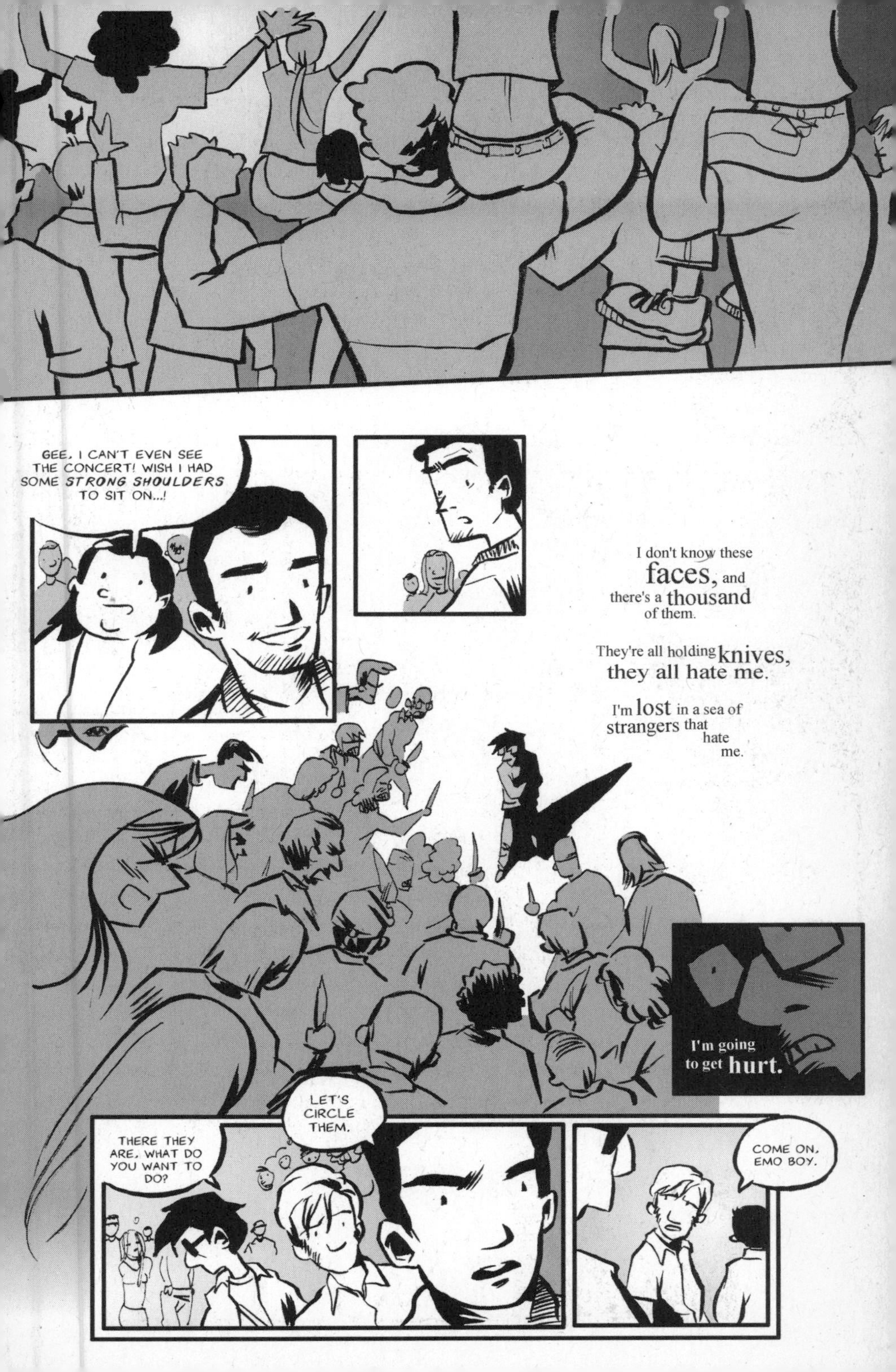
GEE, I CAN'T EVEN SEE THE CONCERT! WISH I HAD SOME *STRONG SHOULDERS* TO SIT ON...!
I don't know these faces, and there's a thousand of them.
They're all holding knives, they all hate me.
I'm lost in a sea of strangers that hate me.
I'm going to get **hurt.**
THERE THEY ARE. WHAT DO YOU WANT TO DO?
LET'S CIRCLE THEM.
COME ON, EMO BOY.

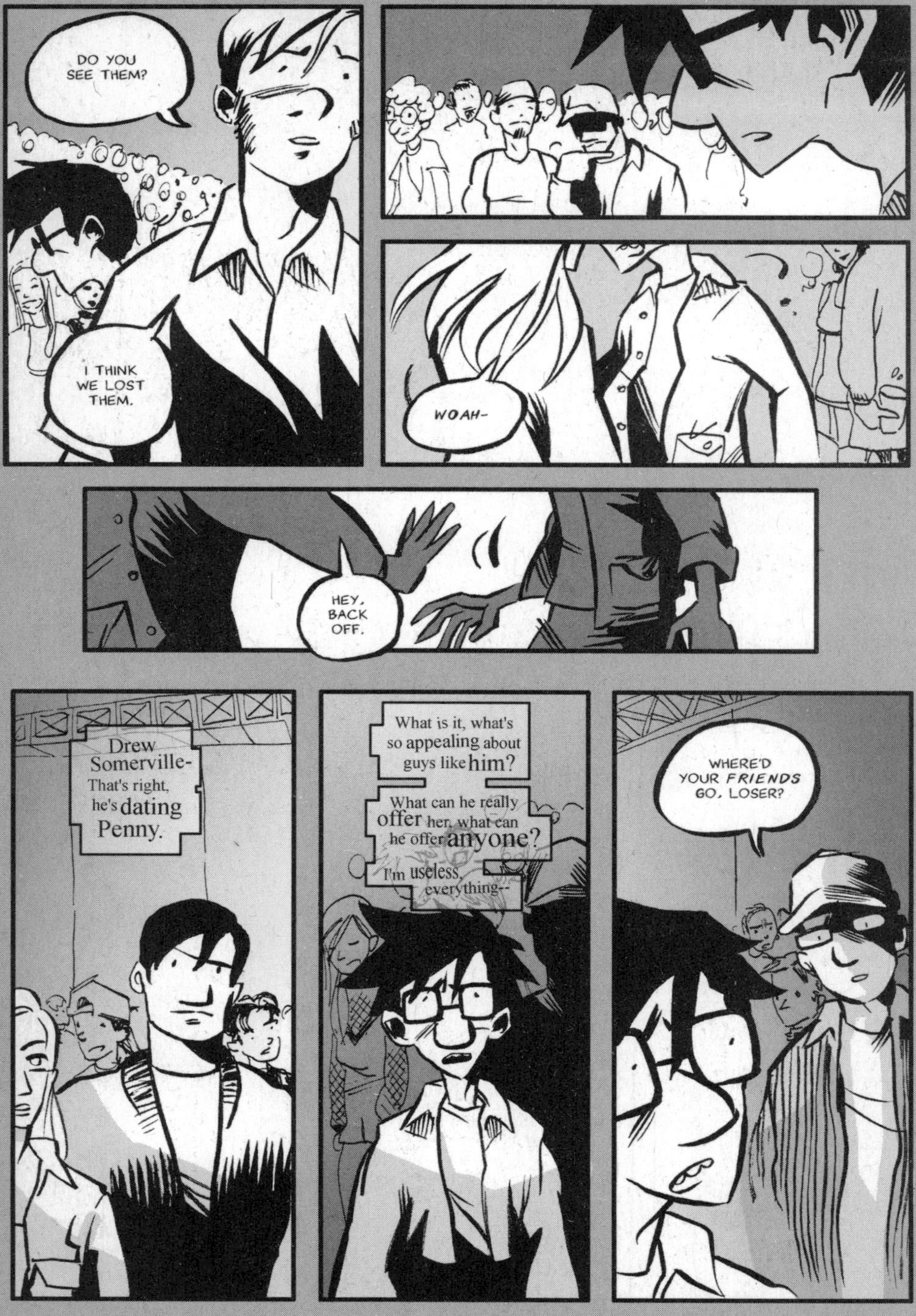
DO YOU SEE THEM?
I THINK WE LOST THEM.
WOAH-
HEY, BACK OFF.
Drew Somerville- That's right, he's dating Penny.
What is it, what's so appealing about guys like him?
What can he really offer her, what can he offer anyone?
I'm useless, everything--
WHERE'D YOUR FRIENDS GO, LOSER?

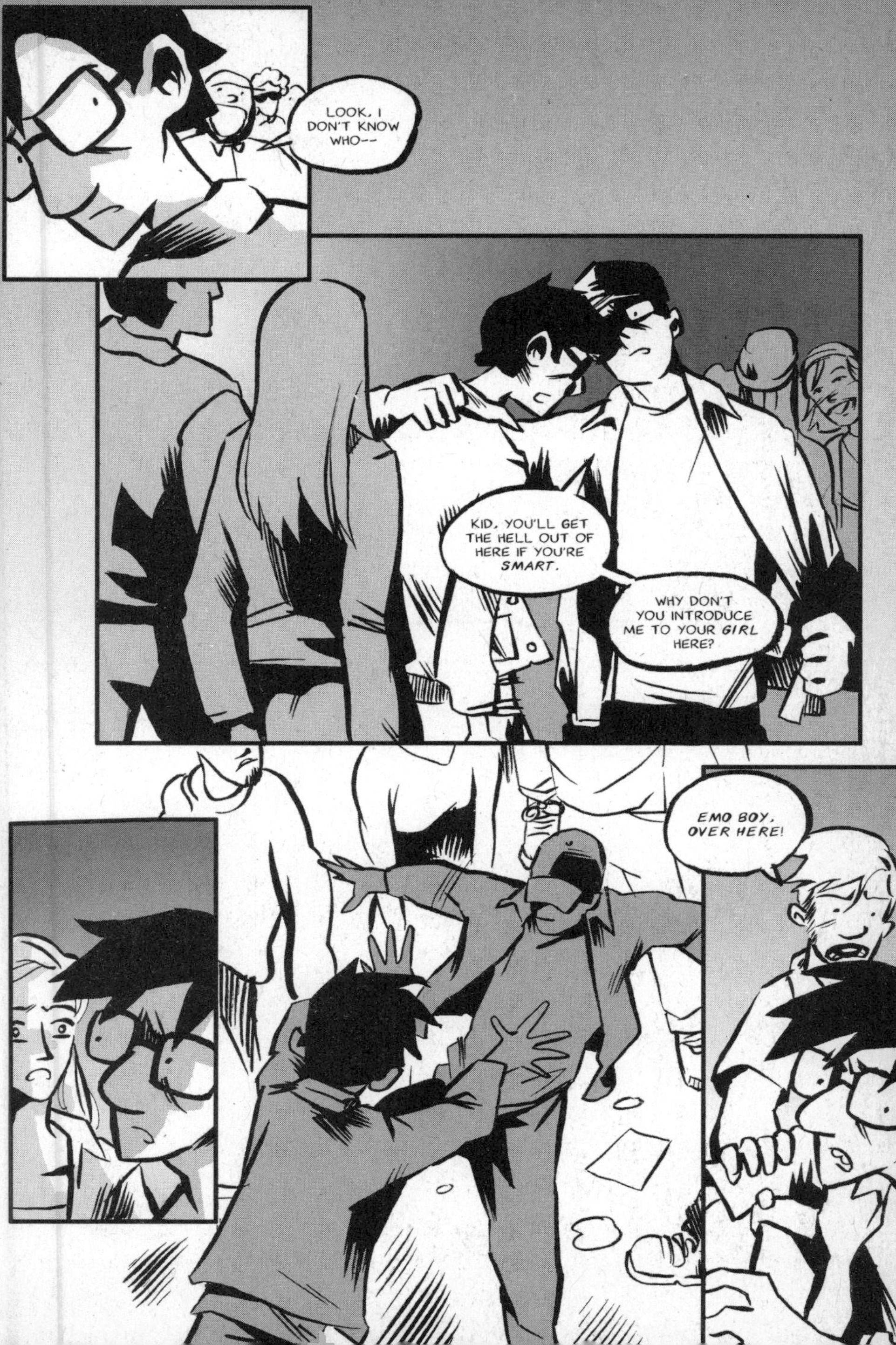
LOOK, I DON'T KNOW WHO--
KID, YOU'LL GET THE HELL OUT OF HERE IF YOU'RE *SMART*.
WHY DON'T YOU INTRODUCE ME TO YOUR *GIRL* HERE?
EMO BOY, OVER HERE!

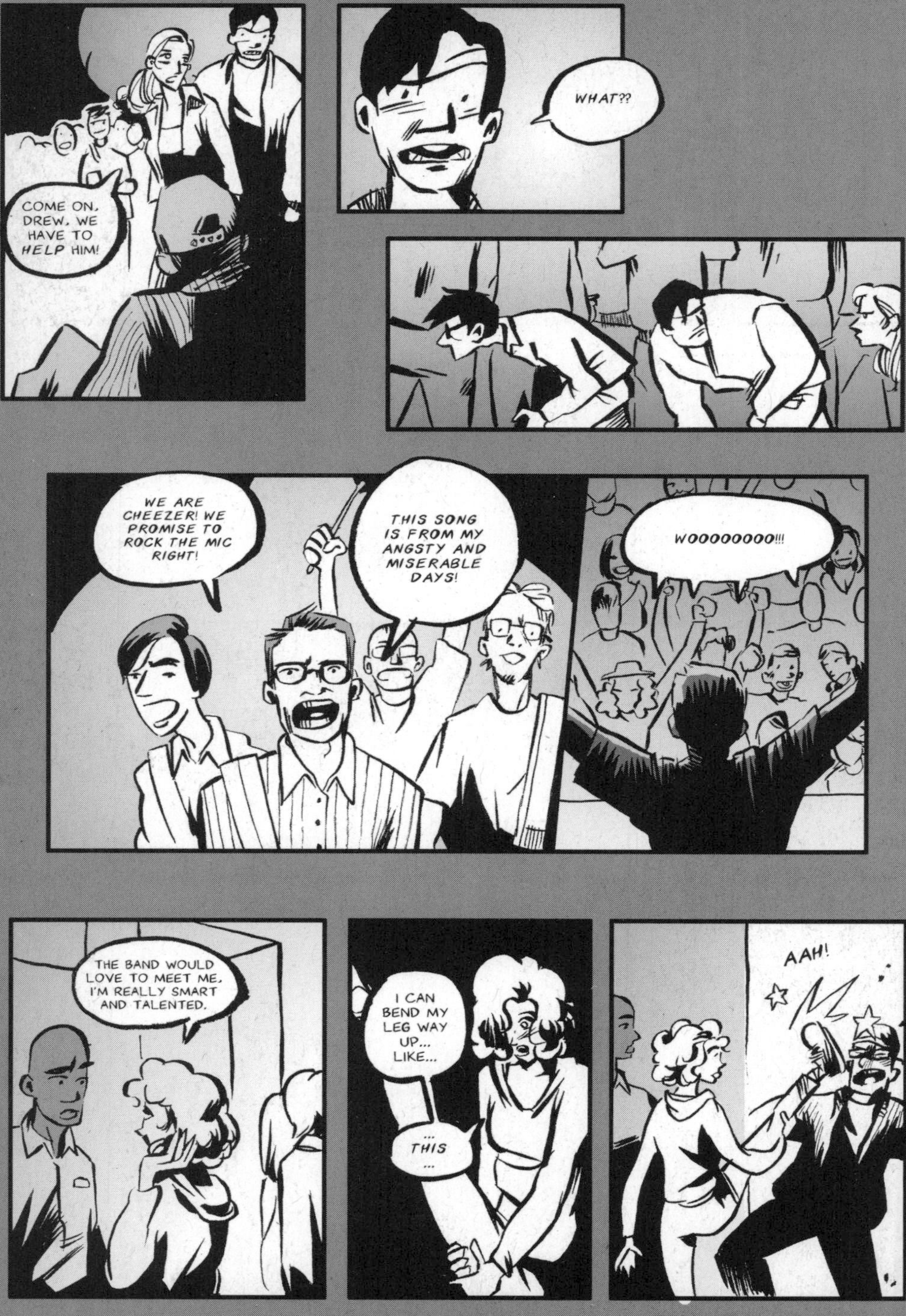
COME ON, DREW, WE HAVE TO HELP HIM!
WHAT??
WE ARE CHEEZER! WE PROMISE TO ROCK THE MIC RIGHT!
THIS SONG IS FROM MY ANGSTY AND MISERABLE DAYS!
WOOOOOOOO!!!
THE BAND WOULD LOVE TO MEET ME. I'M REALLY SMART AND TALENTED.
I CAN BEND MY LEG WAY UP... LIKE...
... THIS ...
AAH!

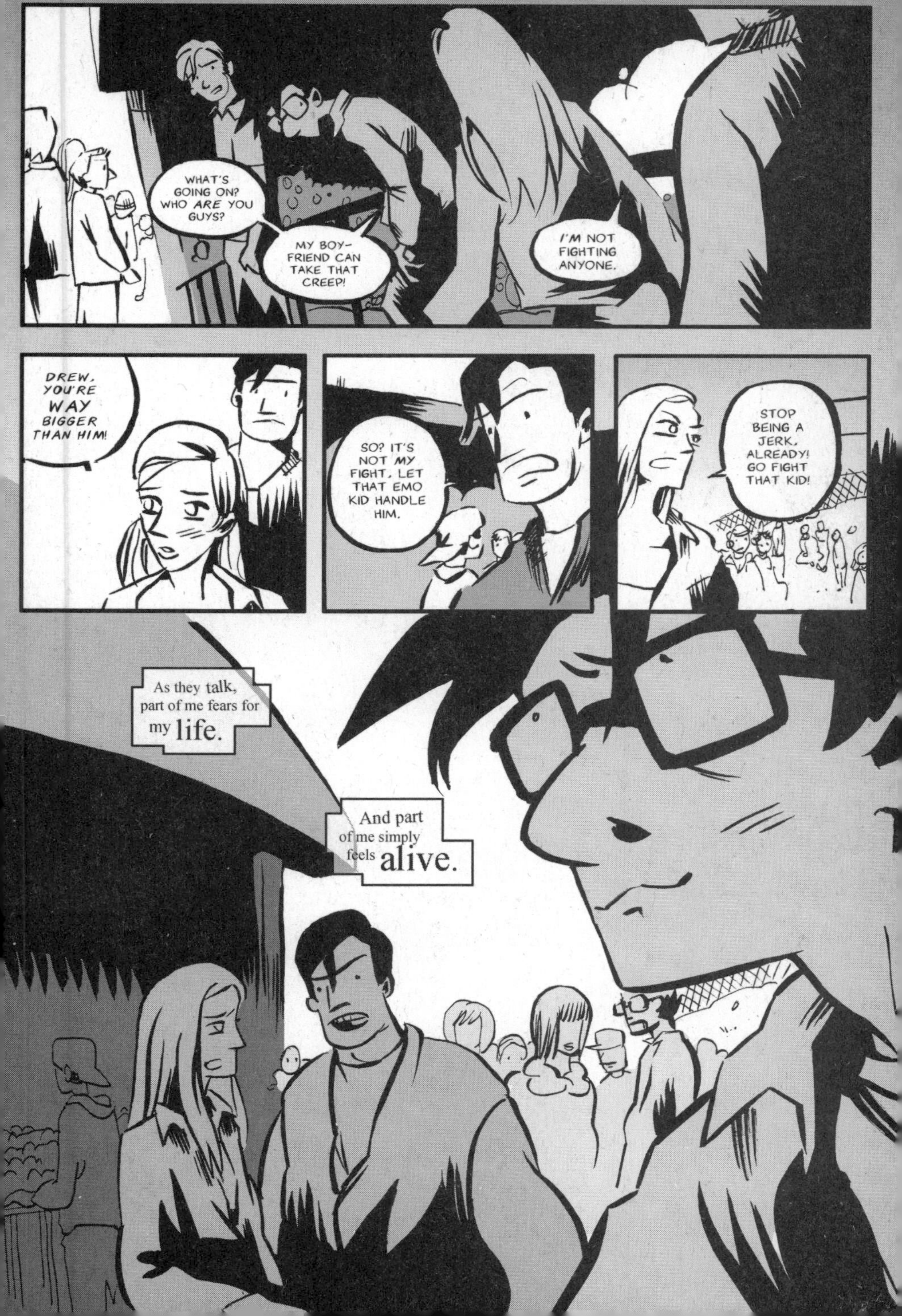
WHAT'S GOING ON? WHO ARE YOU GUYS?
MY BOY-FRIEND CAN TAKE THAT CREEP!
I'M NOT FIGHTING ANYONE.
DREW, YOU'RE WAY BIGGER THAN HIM!
SO? IT'S NOT MY FIGHT. LET THAT EMO KID HANDLE HIM.
STOP BEING A JERK, ALREADY! GO FIGHT THAT KID!
As they talk, part of me fears for my life.
And part of me simply feels alive.

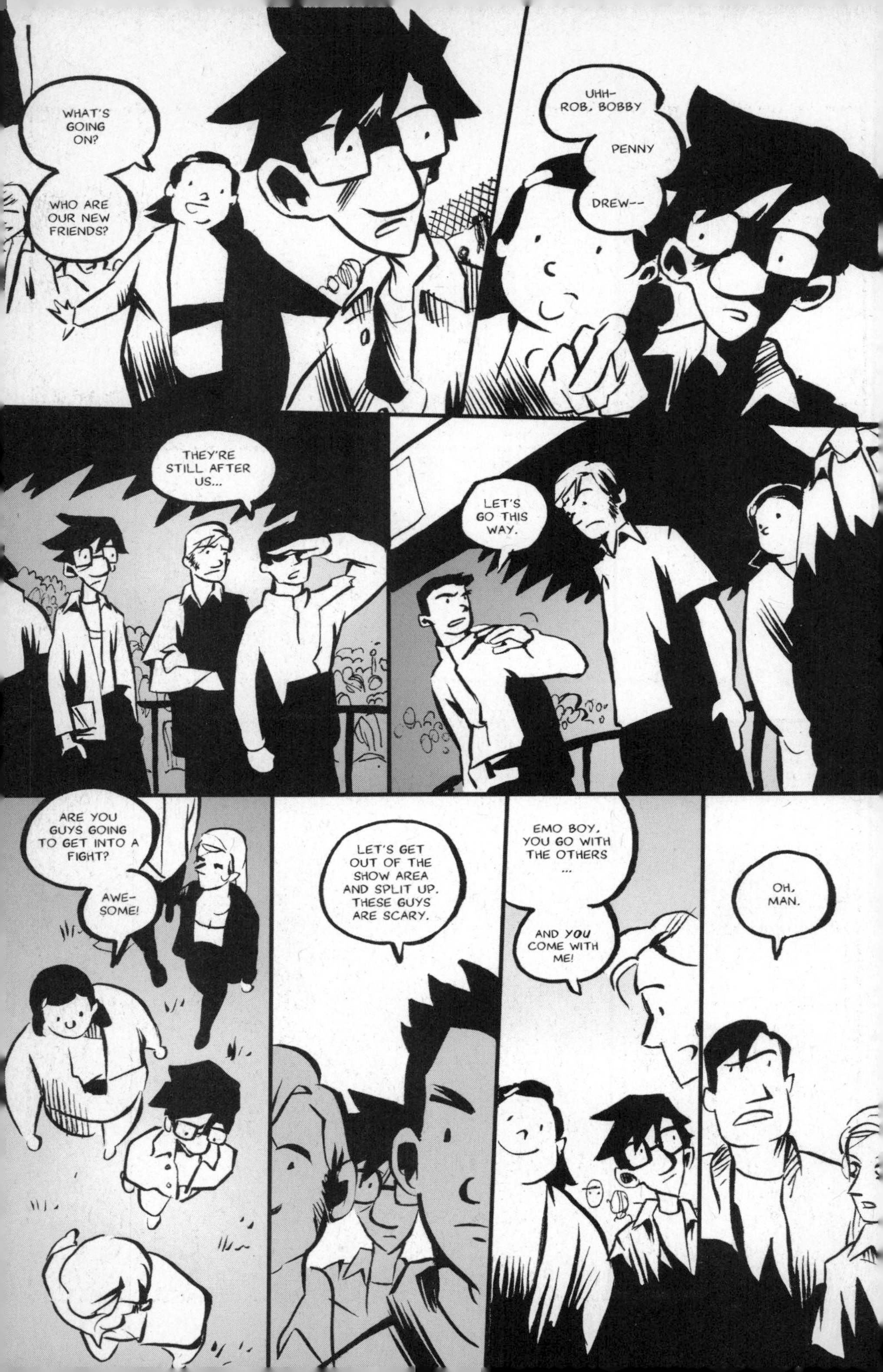
WHAT'S GOING ON?
WHO ARE OUR NEW FRIENDS?
UHH- ROB, BOBBY
PENNY
DREW--
THEY'RE STILL AFTER US...
LET'S GO THIS WAY.
ARE YOU GUYS GOING TO GET INTO A FIGHT?
AWE-SOME!
LET'S GET OUT OF THE SHOW AREA AND SPLIT UP. THESE GUYS ARE SCARY.
EMO BOY, YOU GO WITH THE OTHERS ...
AND YOU COME WITH ME!
OH, MAN.

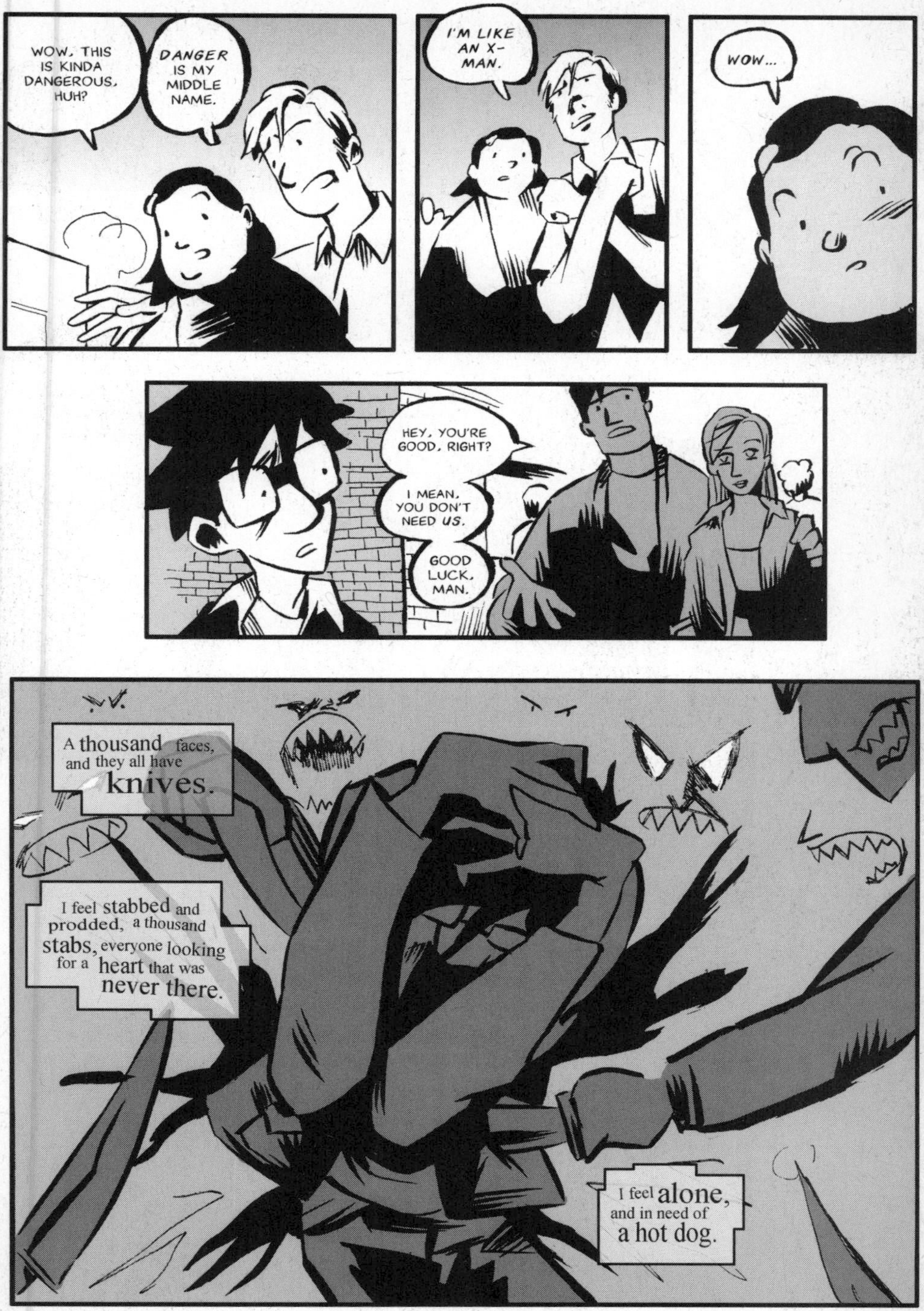

WOW, THIS IS KINDA DANGEROUS, HUH?
DANGER IS MY MIDDLE NAME.
I'M LIKE AN X-MAN.
WOW...
HEY, YOU'RE GOOD, RIGHT?
I MEAN, YOU DON'T NEED US.
GOOD LUCK, MAN.
A thousand faces, and they all have knives.
I feel stabbed and prodded, a thousand stabs, everyone looking for a heart that was never there.
I feel alone, and in need of a hot dog.

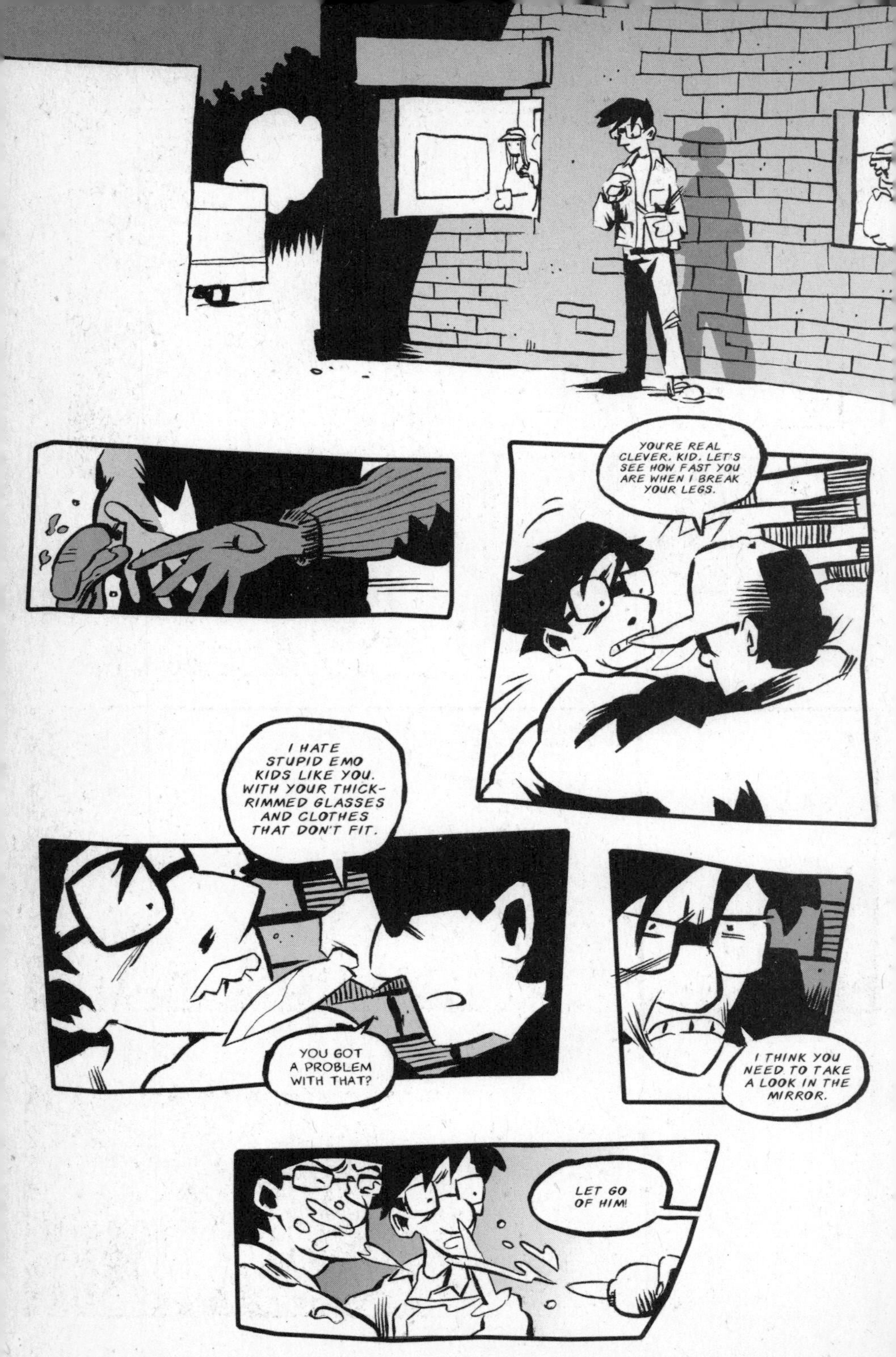
YOU'RE REAL CLEVER, KID. LET'S SEE HOW FAST YOU ARE WHEN I BREAK YOUR LEGS.
I HATE STUPID EMO KIDS LIKE YOU. WITH YOUR THICK-RIMMED GLASSES AND CLOTHES THAT DON'T FIT.
YOU GOT A PROBLEM WITH THAT?
I THINK YOU NEED TO TAKE A LOOK IN THE MIRROR.
LET GO OF HIM!

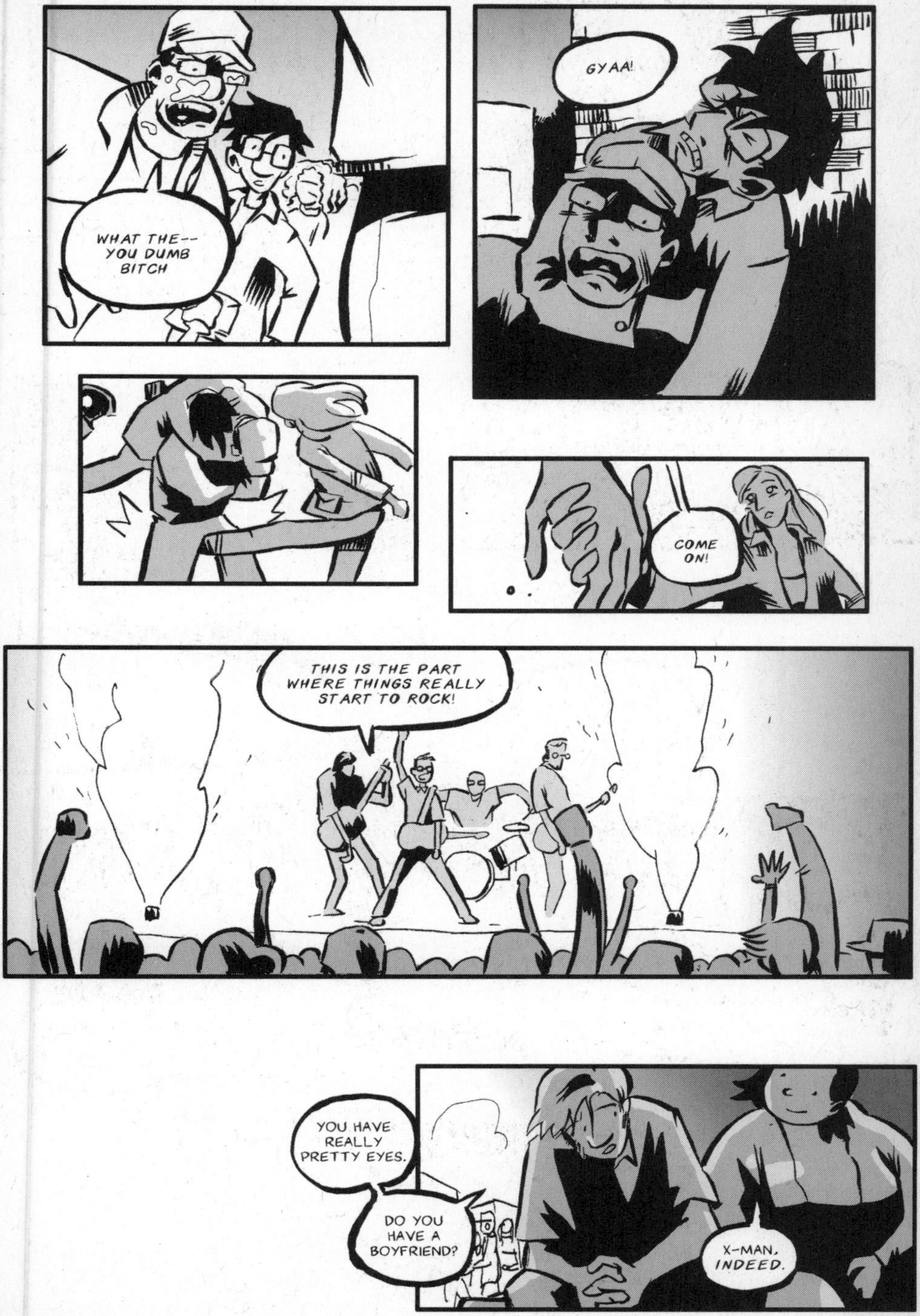
WHAT THE-- YOU DUMB BITCH
GYAA!
COME ON!
THIS IS THE PART WHERE THINGS REALLY START TO ROCK!
YOU HAVE REALLY PRETTY EYES.
DO YOU HAVE A BOYFRIEND?
X-MAN, INDEED.

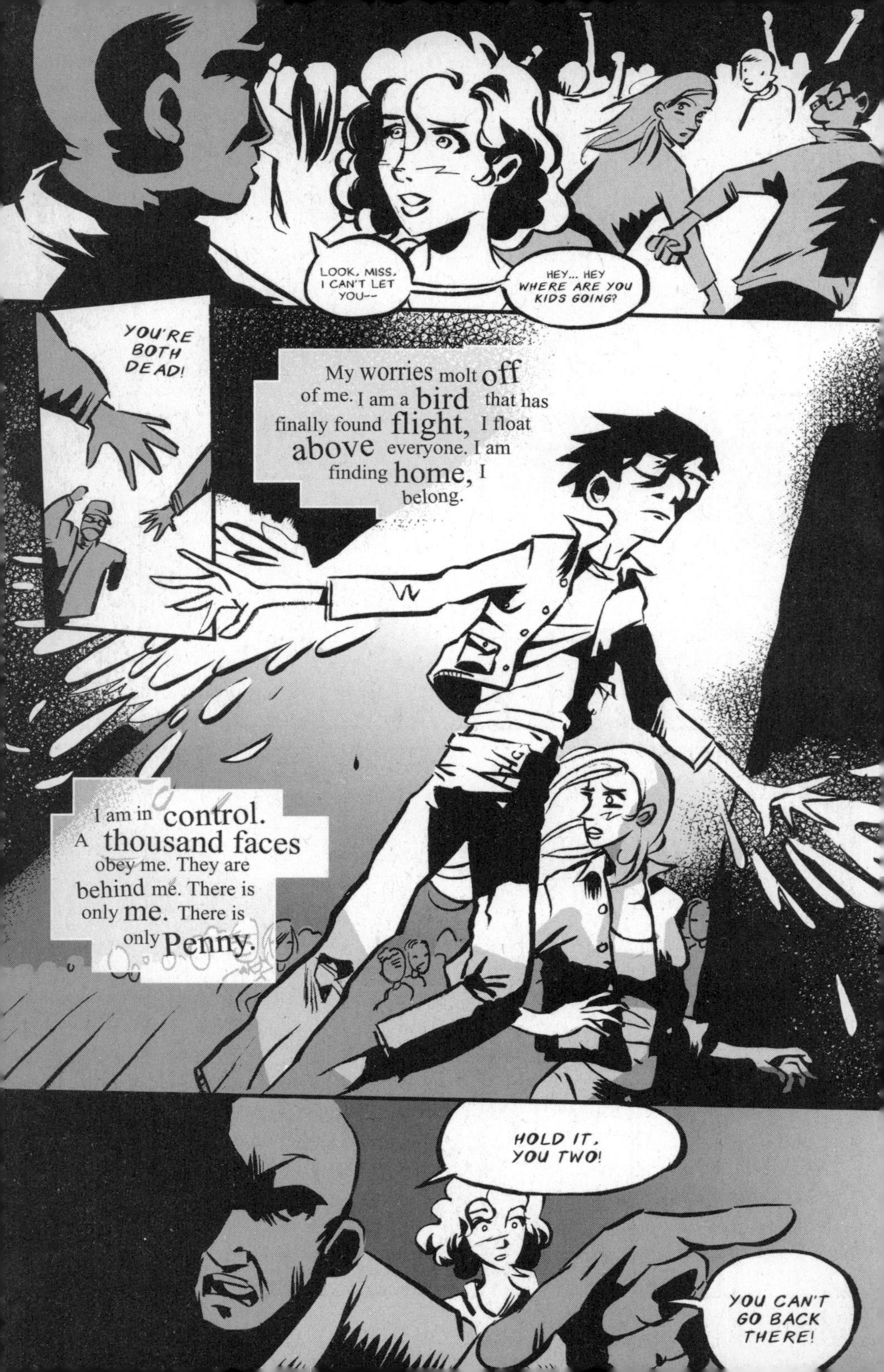

LOOK, MISS, I CAN'T LET YOU--
HEY... HEY WHERE ARE YOU KIDS GOING?
YOU'RE BOTH DEAD!
My worries molt off of me. I am a bird that has finally found flight, I float above everyone. I am finding home, I belong.
I am in control. A thousand faces obey me. They are behind me. There is only me. There is only Penny.
HOLD IT, YOU TWO!
YOU CAN'T GO BACK THERE!

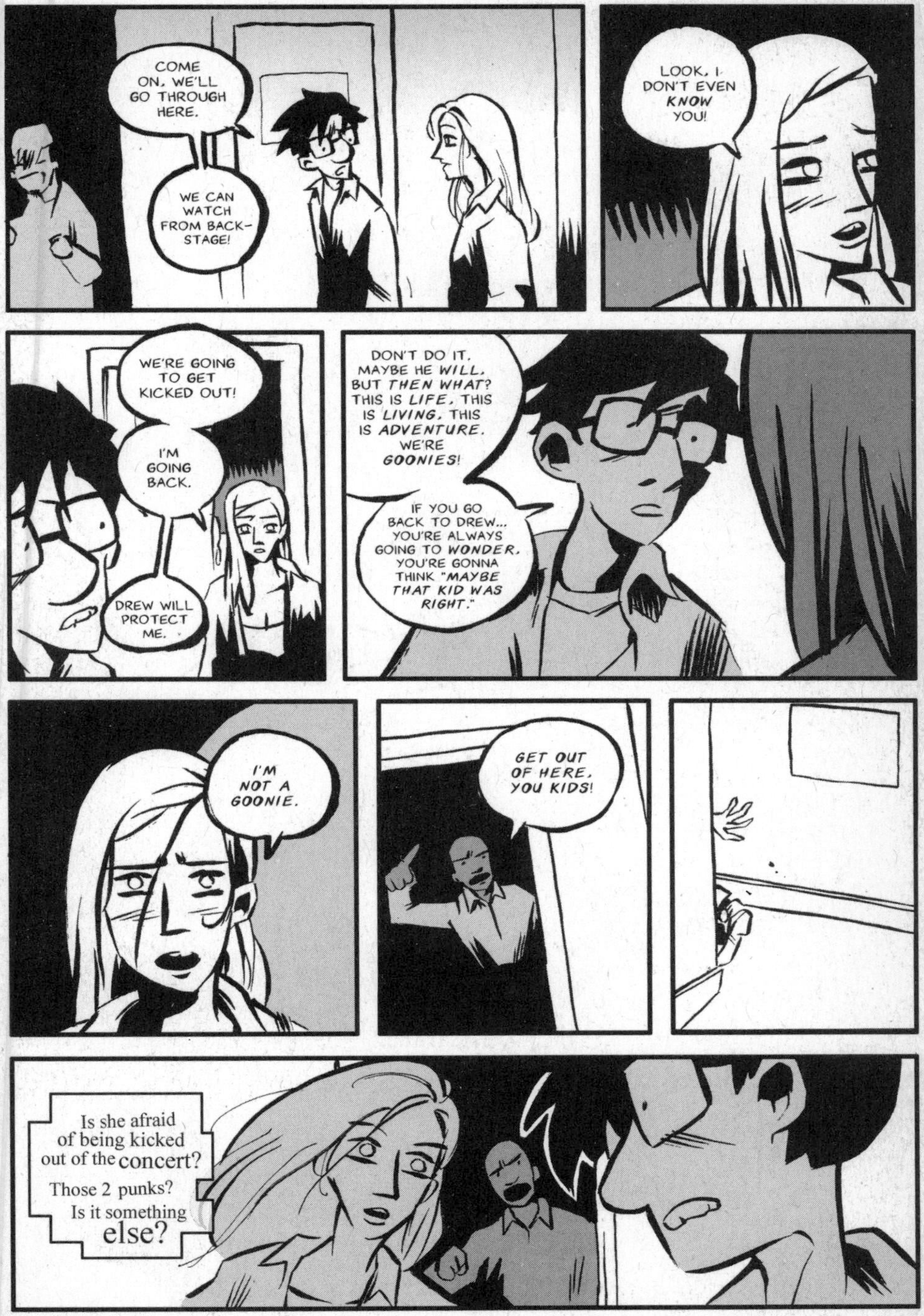
COME ON. WE'LL GO THROUGH HERE.
WE CAN WATCH FROM BACK-STAGE!
LOOK, I DON'T EVEN KNOW YOU!
WE'RE GOING TO GET KICKED OUT!
I'M GOING BACK.
DREW WILL PROTECT ME.
DON'T DO IT. MAYBE HE WILL. BUT THEN WHAT? THIS IS LIFE. THIS IS LIVING. THIS IS ADVENTURE. WE'RE GOONIES!
IF YOU GO BACK TO DREW... YOU'RE ALWAYS GOING TO WONDER. YOU'RE GONNA THINK "MAYBE THAT KID WAS RIGHT."
I'M NOT A GOONIE.
GET OUT OF HERE, YOU KIDS!
Is she afraid of being kicked out of the concert? Those 2 punks? Is it something else?

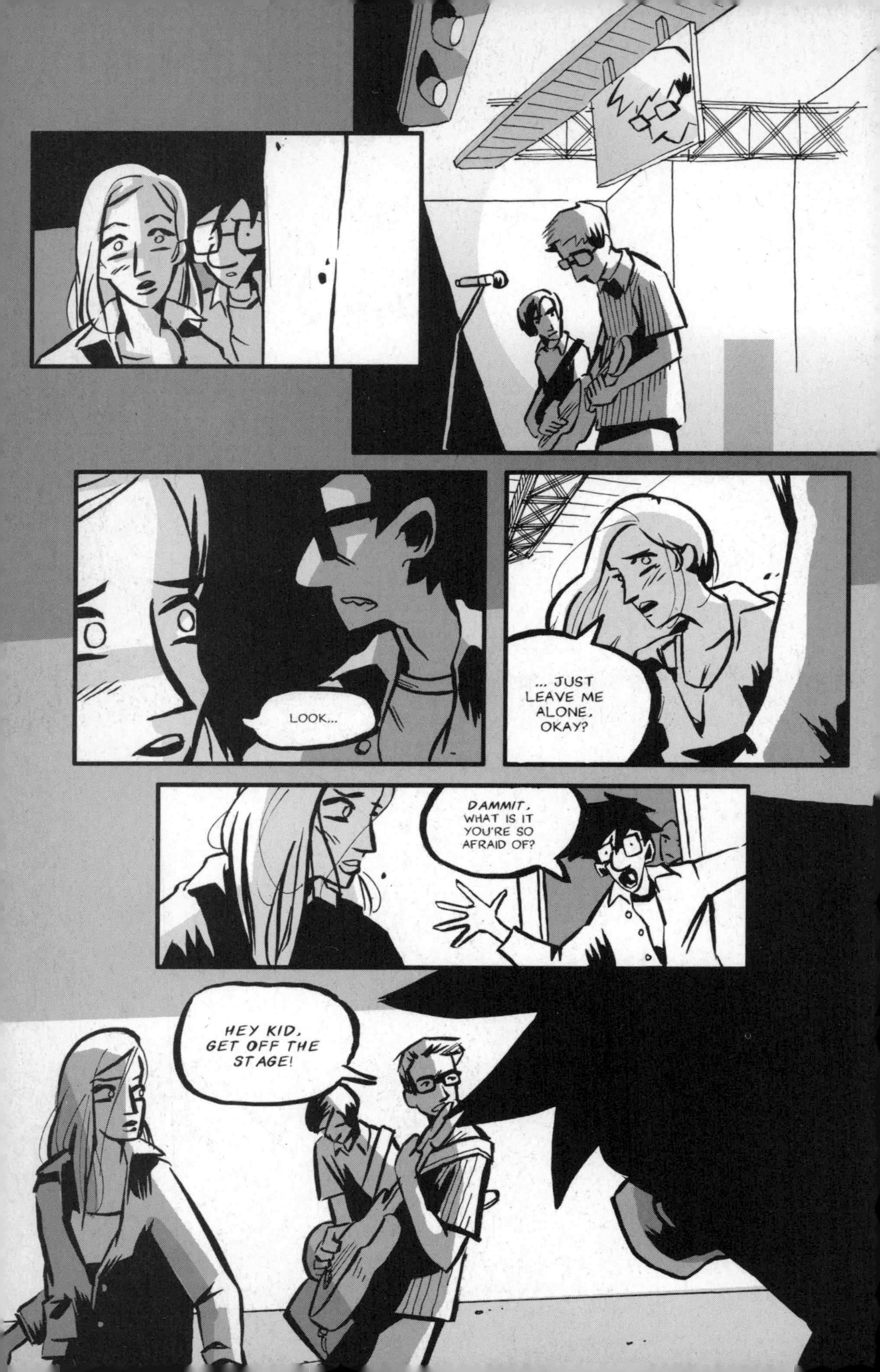
LOOK...
... JUST LEAVE ME ALONE, OKAY?
DAMMIT, WHAT IS IT YOU'RE SO AFRAID OF?
HEY KID, GET OFF THE STAGE!

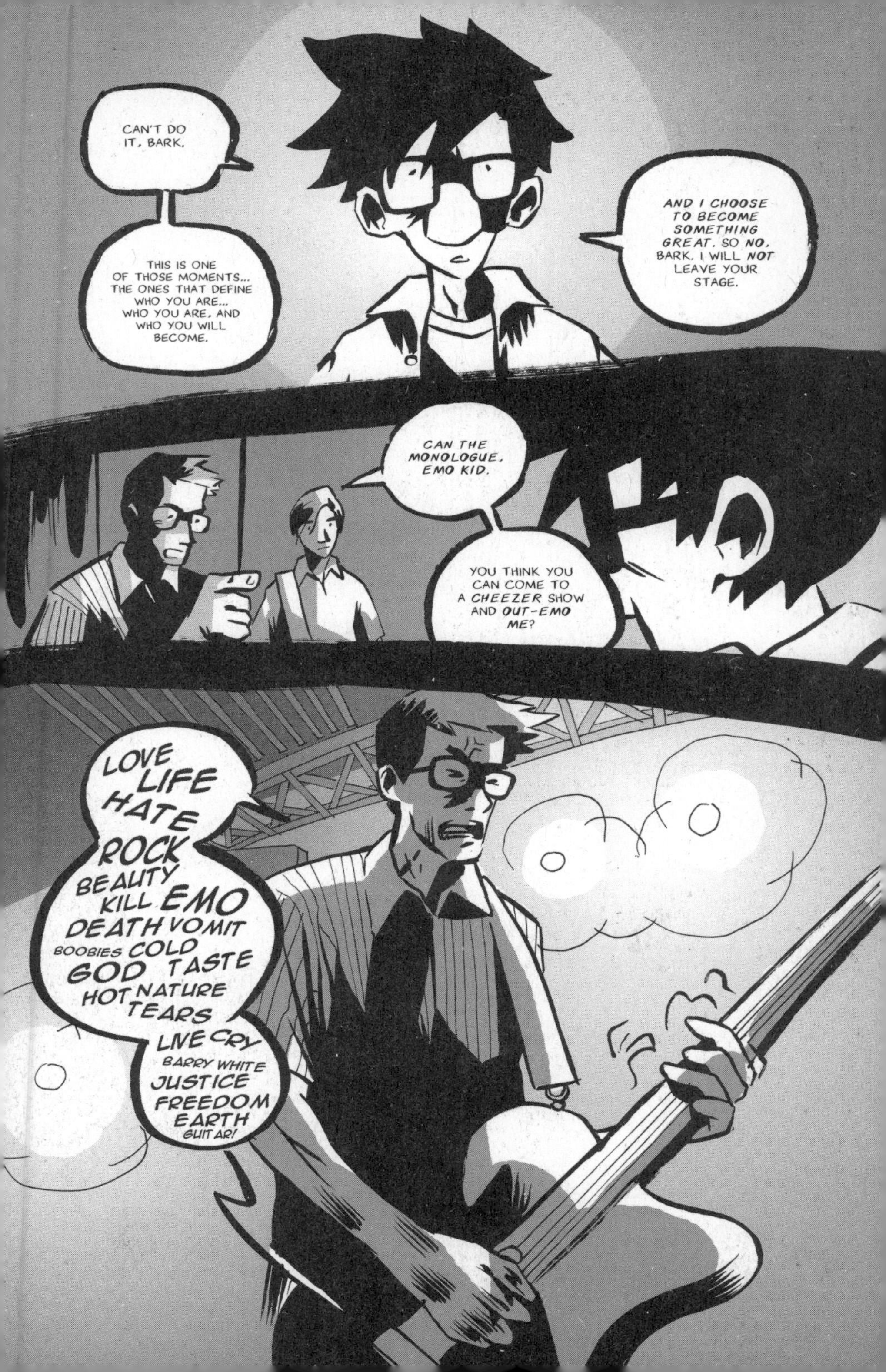
CAN'T DO IT, BARK.
THIS IS ONE OF THOSE MOMENTS... THE ONES THAT DEFINE WHO YOU ARE... WHO YOU ARE, AND WHO YOU WILL BECOME.
AND I CHOOSE TO BECOME SOMETHING GREAT. SO NO, BARK. I WILL NOT LEAVE YOUR STAGE.
CAN THE MONOLOGUE, EMO KID.
YOU THINK YOU CAN COME TO A CHEEZER SHOW AND OUT-EMO ME?
LOVE LIFE HATE ROCK BEAUTY KILL EMO DEATH VOMIT BOOBIES COLD GOD TASTE HOT NATURE TEARS LIVE CRY BARRY WHITE JUSTICE FREEDOM EARTH GUITAR!

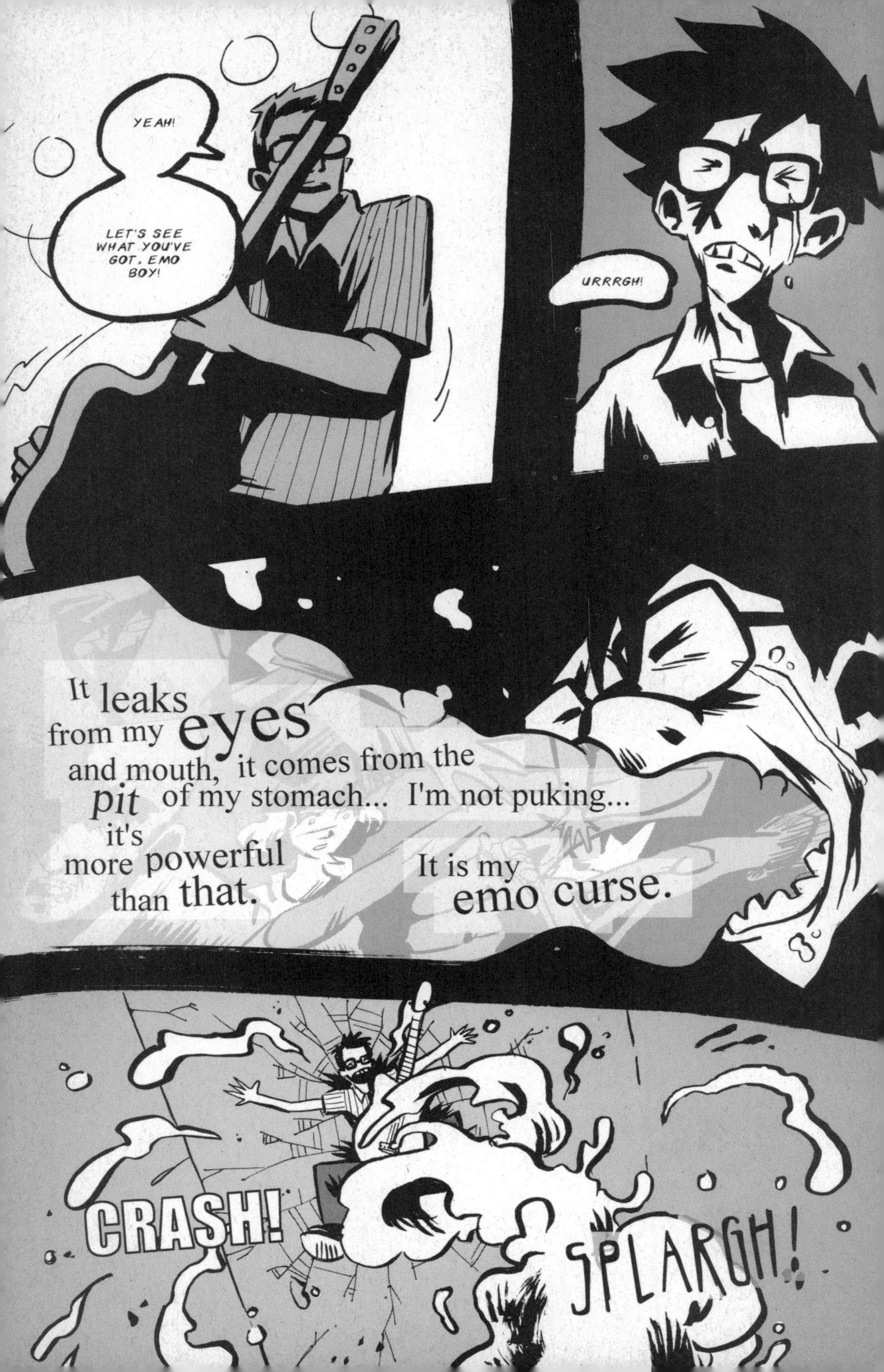
YEAH!
LET'S SEE WHAT YOU'VE GOT, EMO BOY!
URRRGH!
It leaks from my eyes and mouth, it comes from the pit of my stomach... I'm not puking... it's more powerful than that.
It is my emo curse.
CRASH!
SPLARGH!

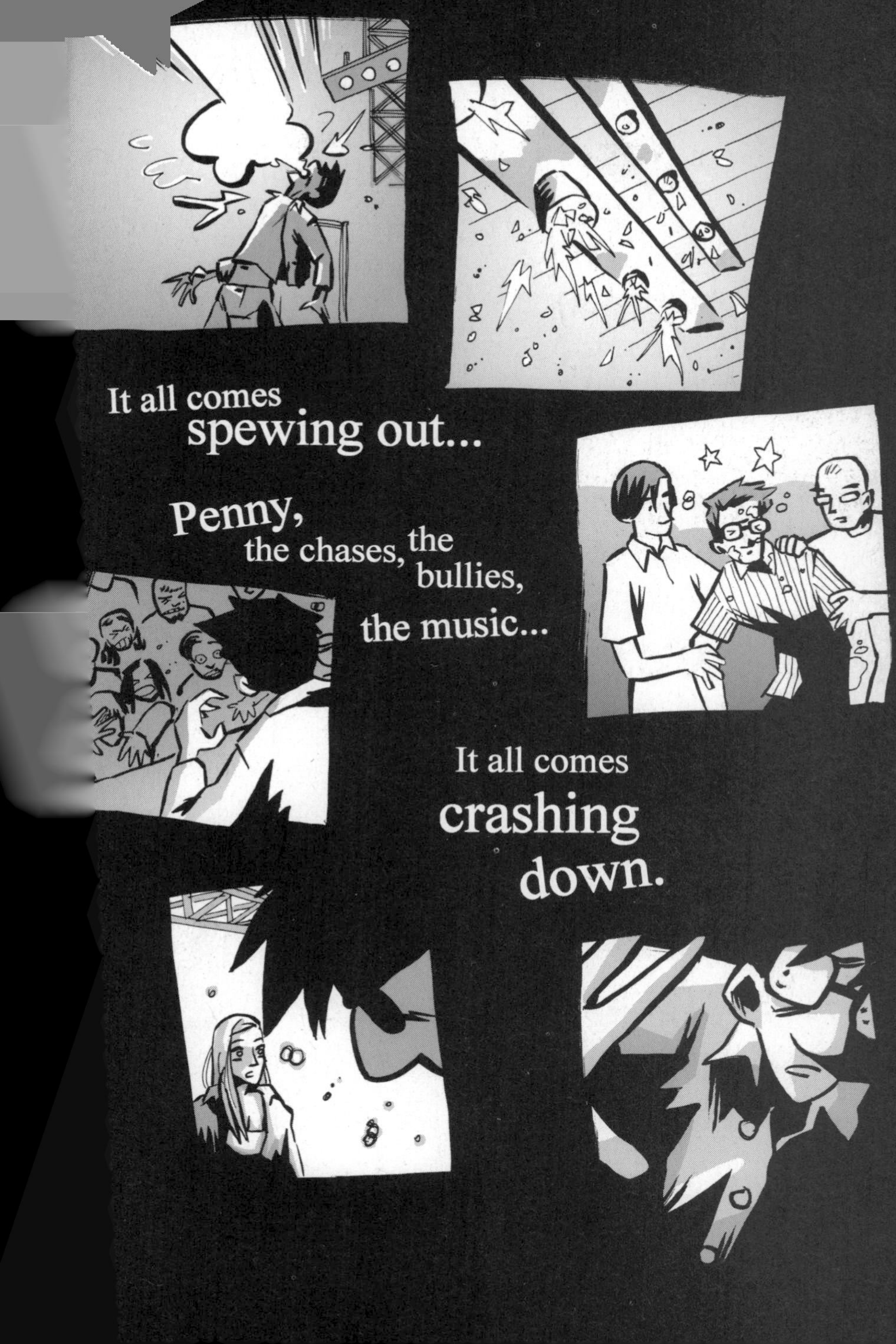

It all comes spewing out...
Penny,
the chases,
the bullies,
the music...
It all comes crashing down.

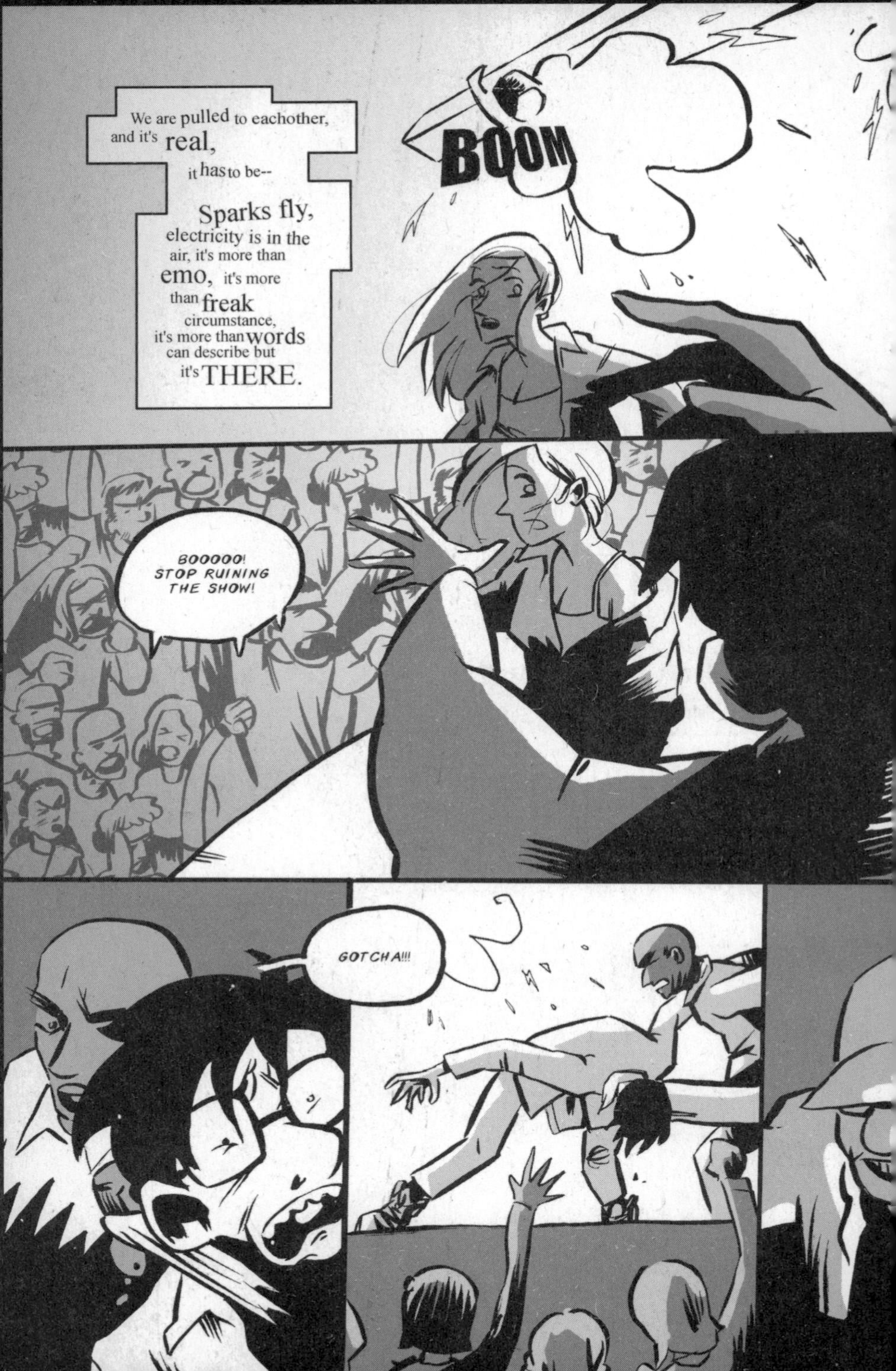
We are pulled to eachother, and it's real, it has to be--
Sparks fly, electricity is in the air, it's more than emo, it's more than freak circumstance, it's more than words can describe but it's THERE.
BOOM
BOOOOO! STOP RUINING THE SHOW!
GOTCHA!!!

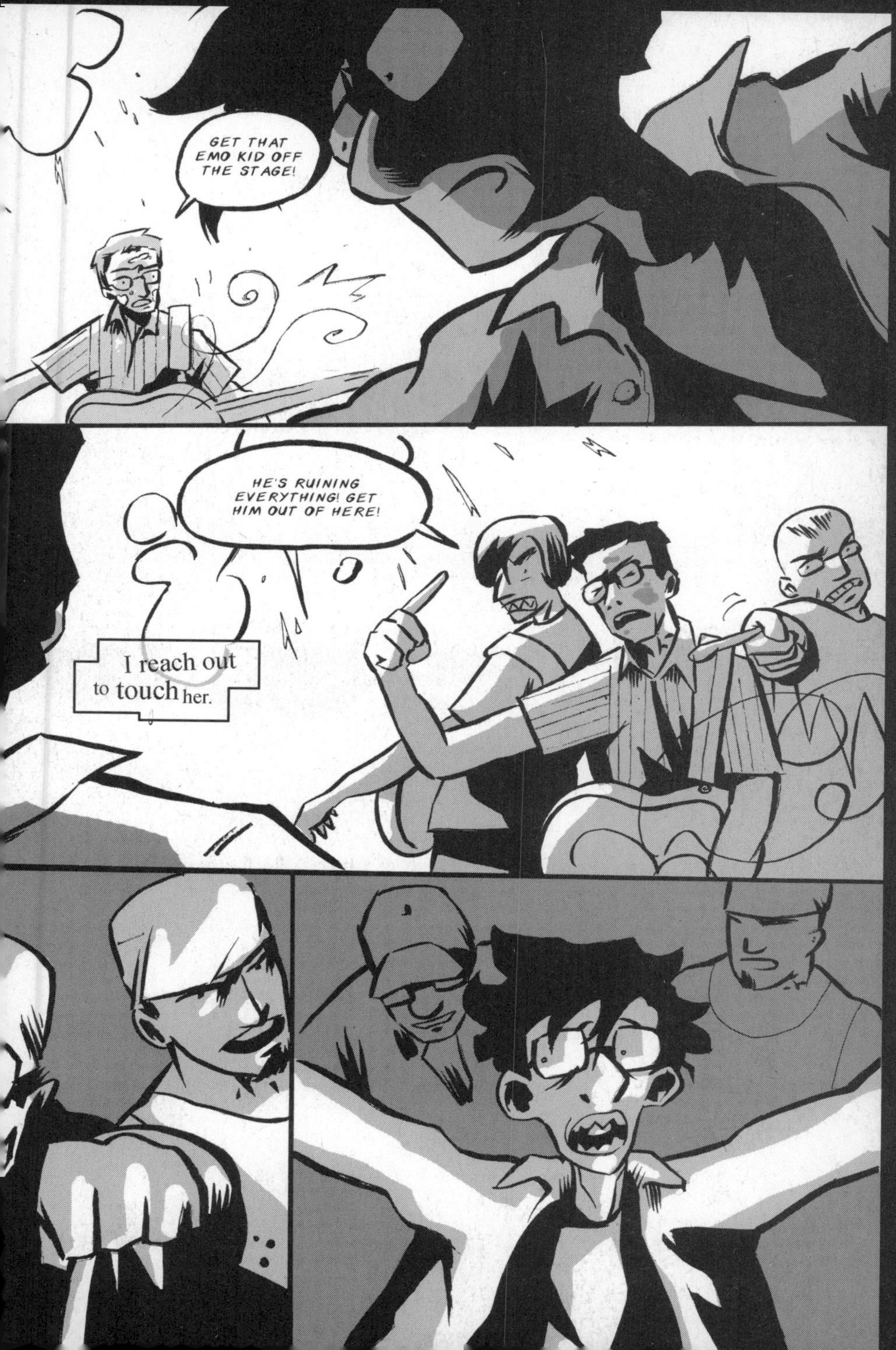
GET THAT EMO KID OFF THE STAGE!
HE'S RUINING EVERYTHING! GET HIM OUT OF HERE!
I reach out to touch her.

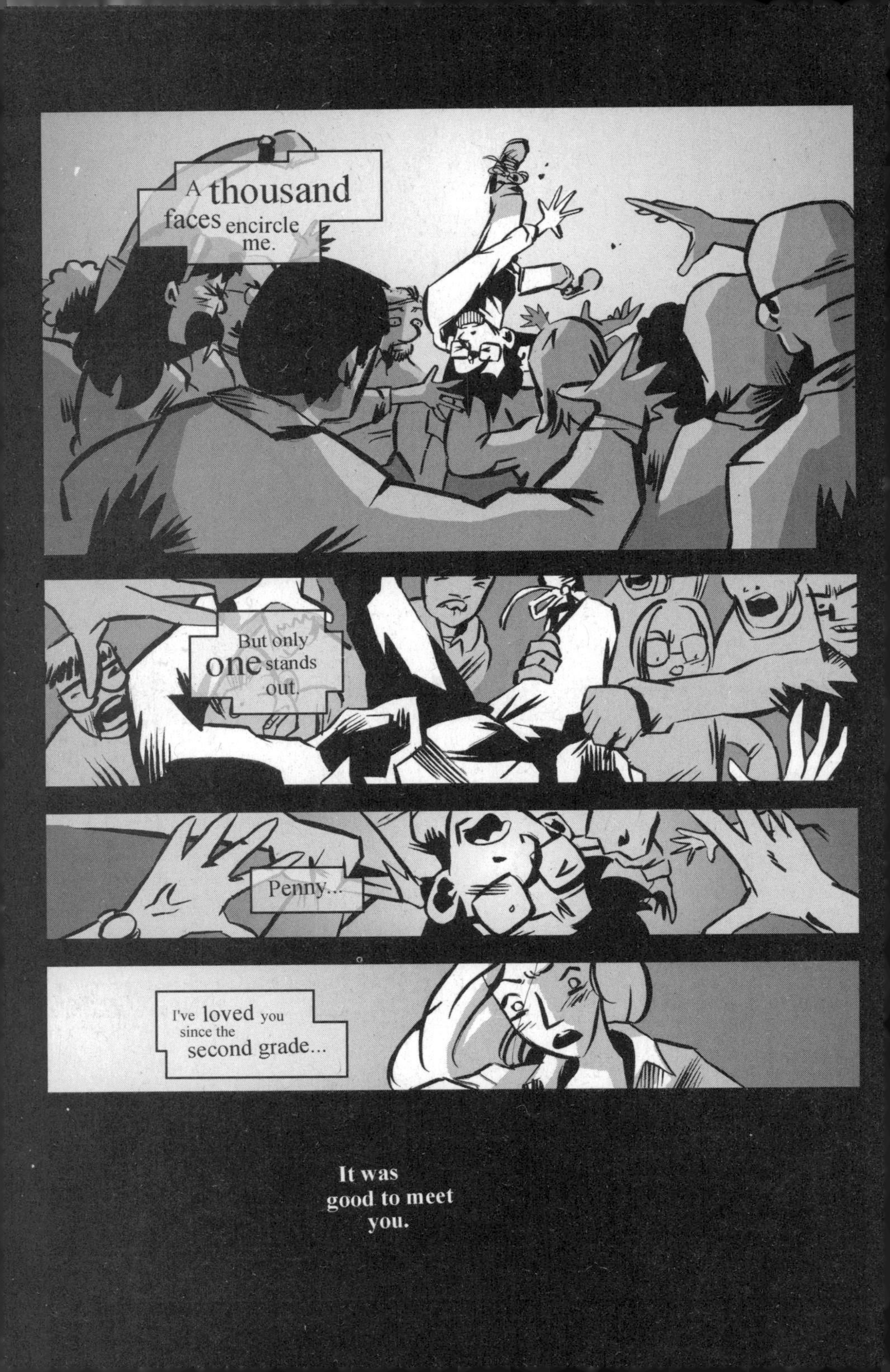
A thousand faces encircle me.
But only one stands out.
Penny...
I've loved you since the second grade...

It was
good to meet
you.

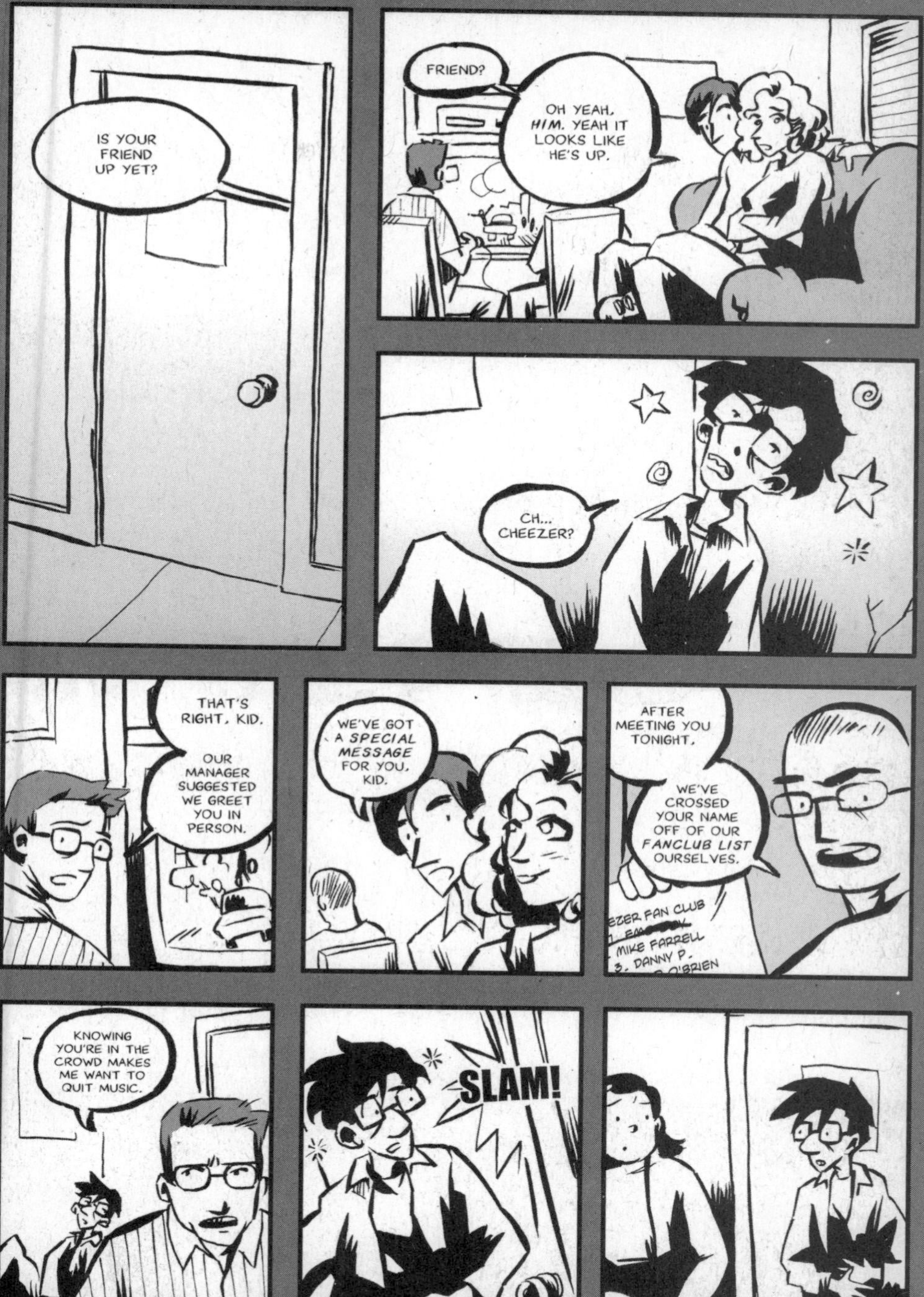

IS YOUR FRIEND UP YET?
FRIEND?
OH YEAH, *HIM*. YEAH IT LOOKS LIKE HE'S UP.
CH... CHEEZER?
THAT'S RIGHT, KID.
OUR MANAGER SUGGESTED WE GREET YOU IN PERSON.
WE'VE GOT A *SPECIAL MESSAGE* FOR YOU, KID.
AFTER MEETING YOU TONIGHT,
WE'VE CROSSED YOUR NAME OFF OF OUR *FANCLUB LIST* OURSELVES.
MIKE FARRELL
DANNY P.
KNOWING YOU'RE IN THE CROWD MAKES ME WANT TO QUIT MUSIC.
SLAM!

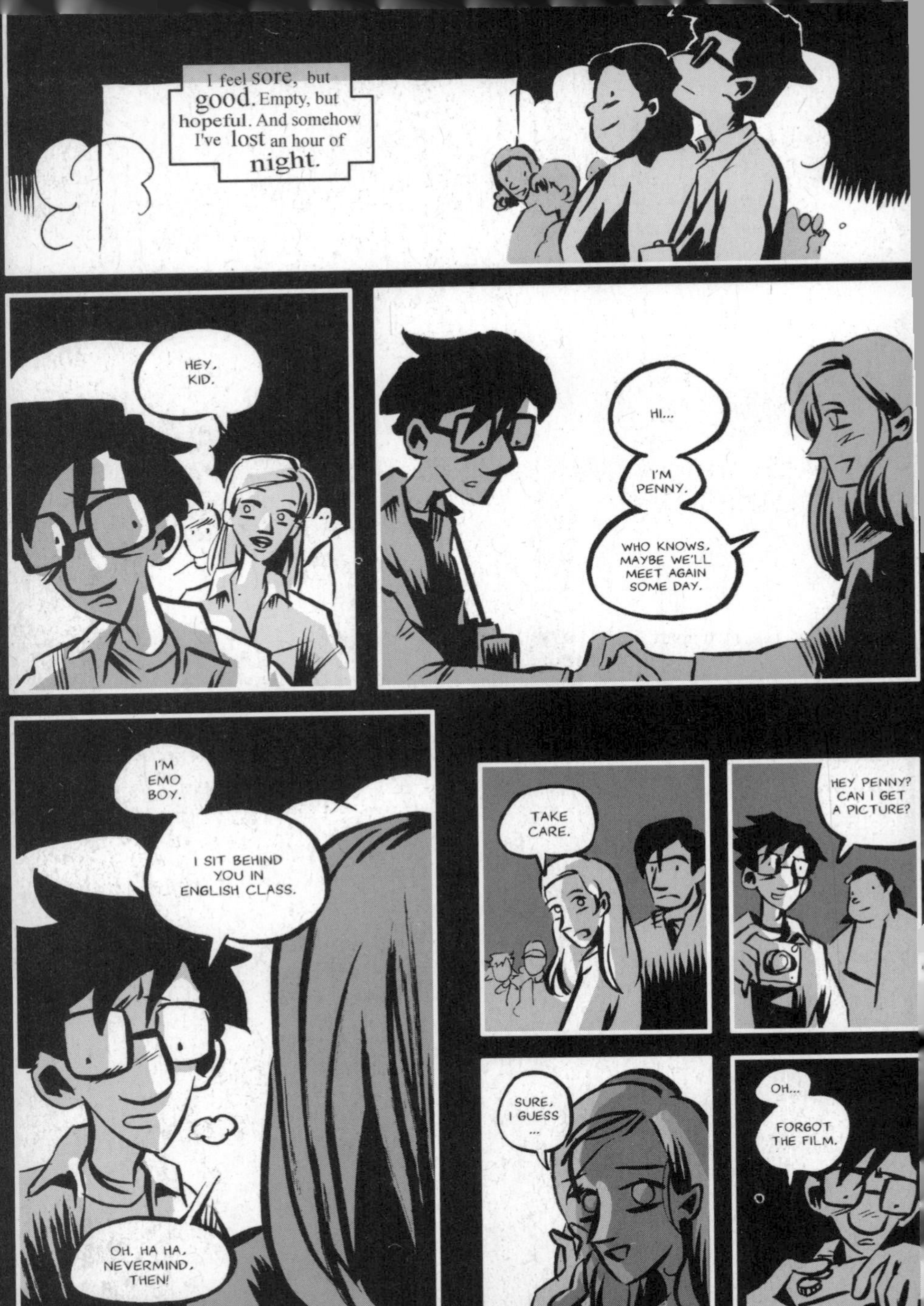
I feel sore, but good. Empty, but hopeful. And somehow I've lost an hour of night.
HEY, KID.
HI...
I'M PENNY.
WHO KNOWS, MAYBE WE'LL MEET AGAIN SOME DAY.
I'M EMO BOY.
I SIT BEHIND YOU IN ENGLISH CLASS.
OH. HA HA, NEVERMIND, THEN!
TAKE CARE.
HEY PENNY? CAN I GET A PICTURE?
SURE, I GUESS ...
OH...
FORGOT THE FILM.

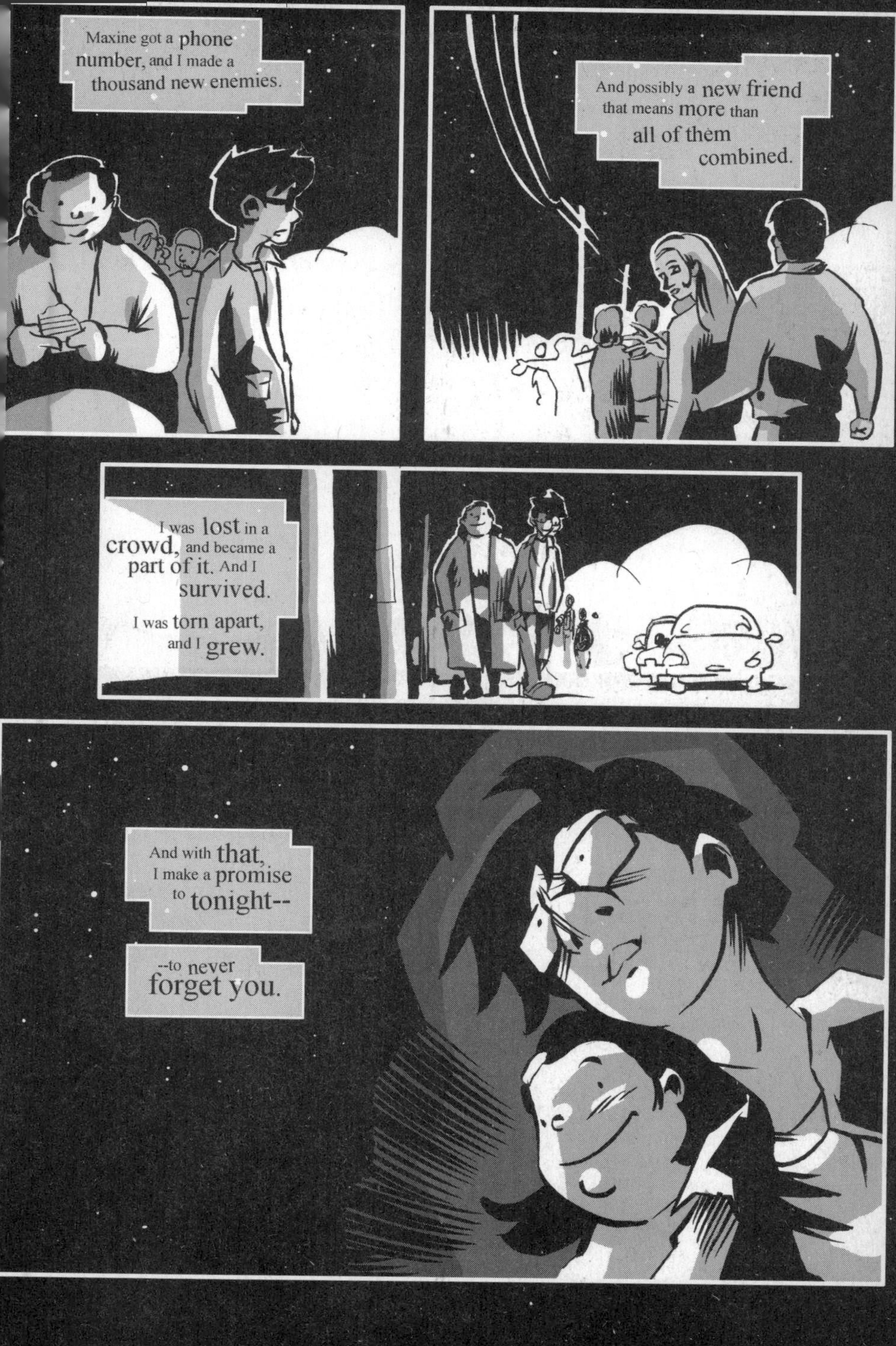
Maxine got a phone number, and I made a thousand new enemies.
And possibly a new friend that means more than all of them combined.
I was lost in a crowd, and became a part of it. And I survived.
I was torn apart, and I grew.
And with that, I make a promise to tonight--
--to never forget you.

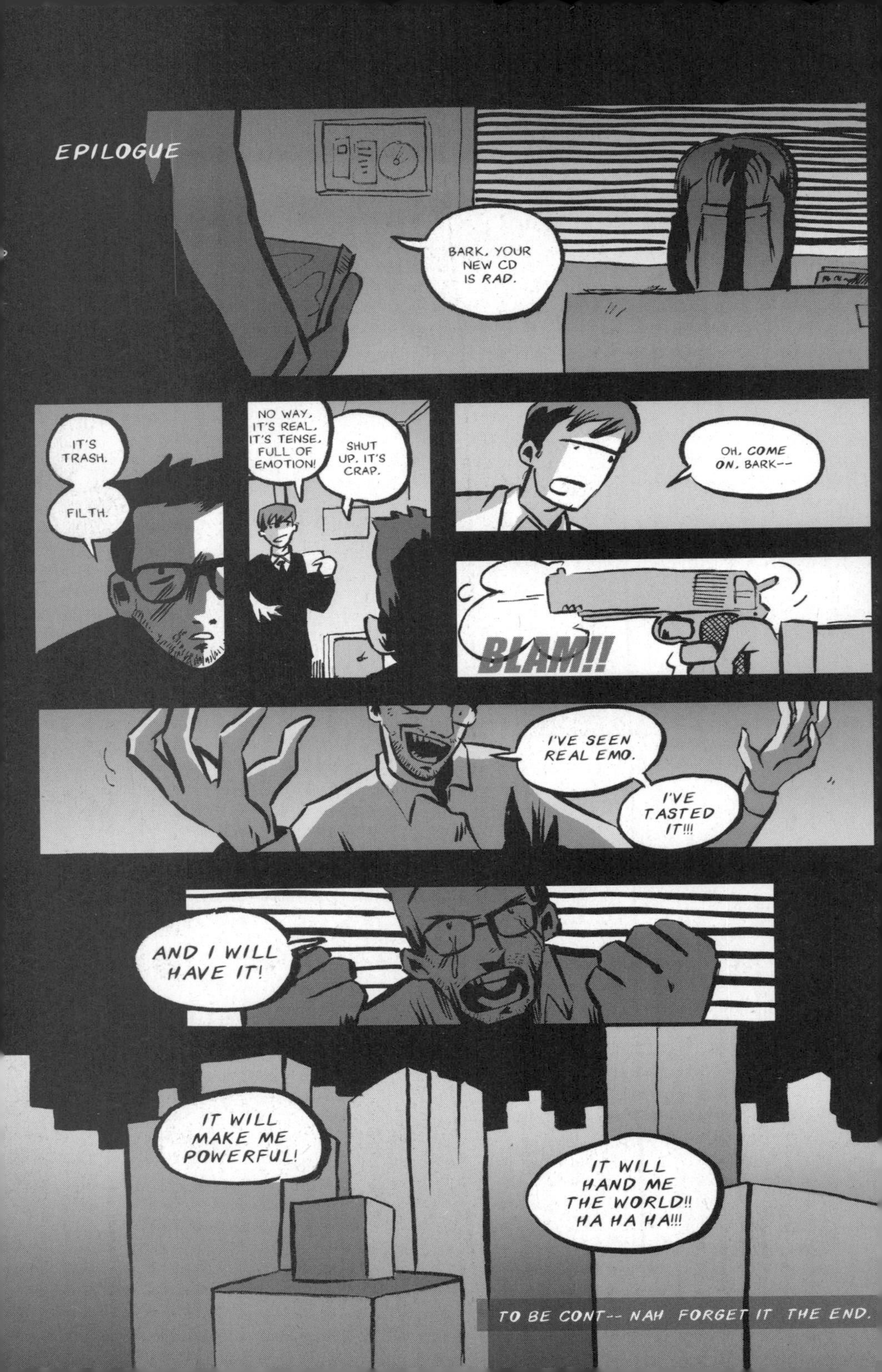
EPILOGUE
BARK, YOUR NEW CD IS RAD.
IT'S TRASH.
FILTH.
NO WAY, IT'S REAL, IT'S TENSE, FULL OF EMOTION!
SHUT UP. IT'S CRAP.
OH, COME ON, BARK--
BLAM!!
I'VE SEEN REAL EMO.
I'VE TASTED IT!!!
AND I WILL HAVE IT!
IT WILL MAKE ME POWERFUL!
IT WILL HAND ME THE WORLD!! HA HA HA!!!
TO BE CONT-- NAH FORGET IT THE END.

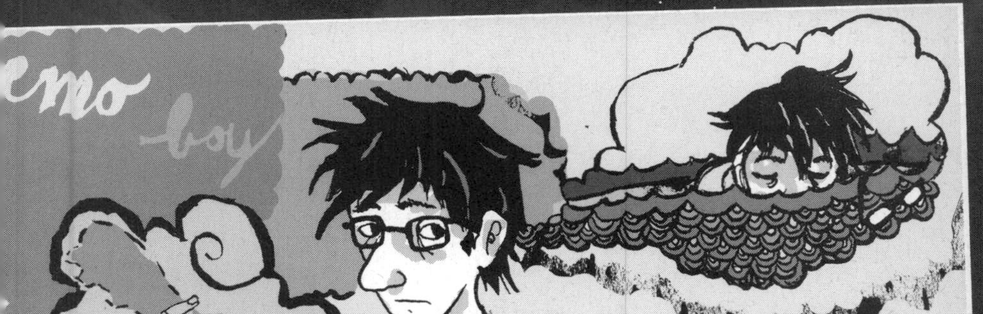
emo
boy

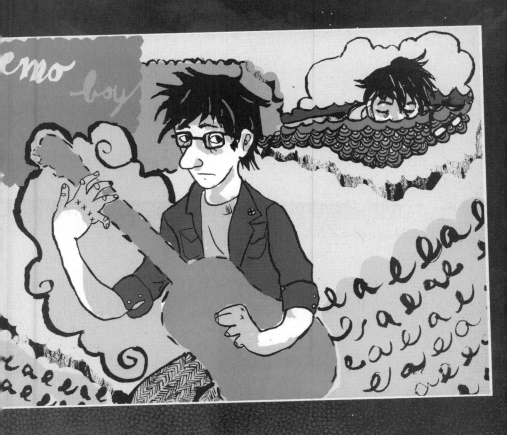

**Emo Boy
Pinup by
Meg Hunt**

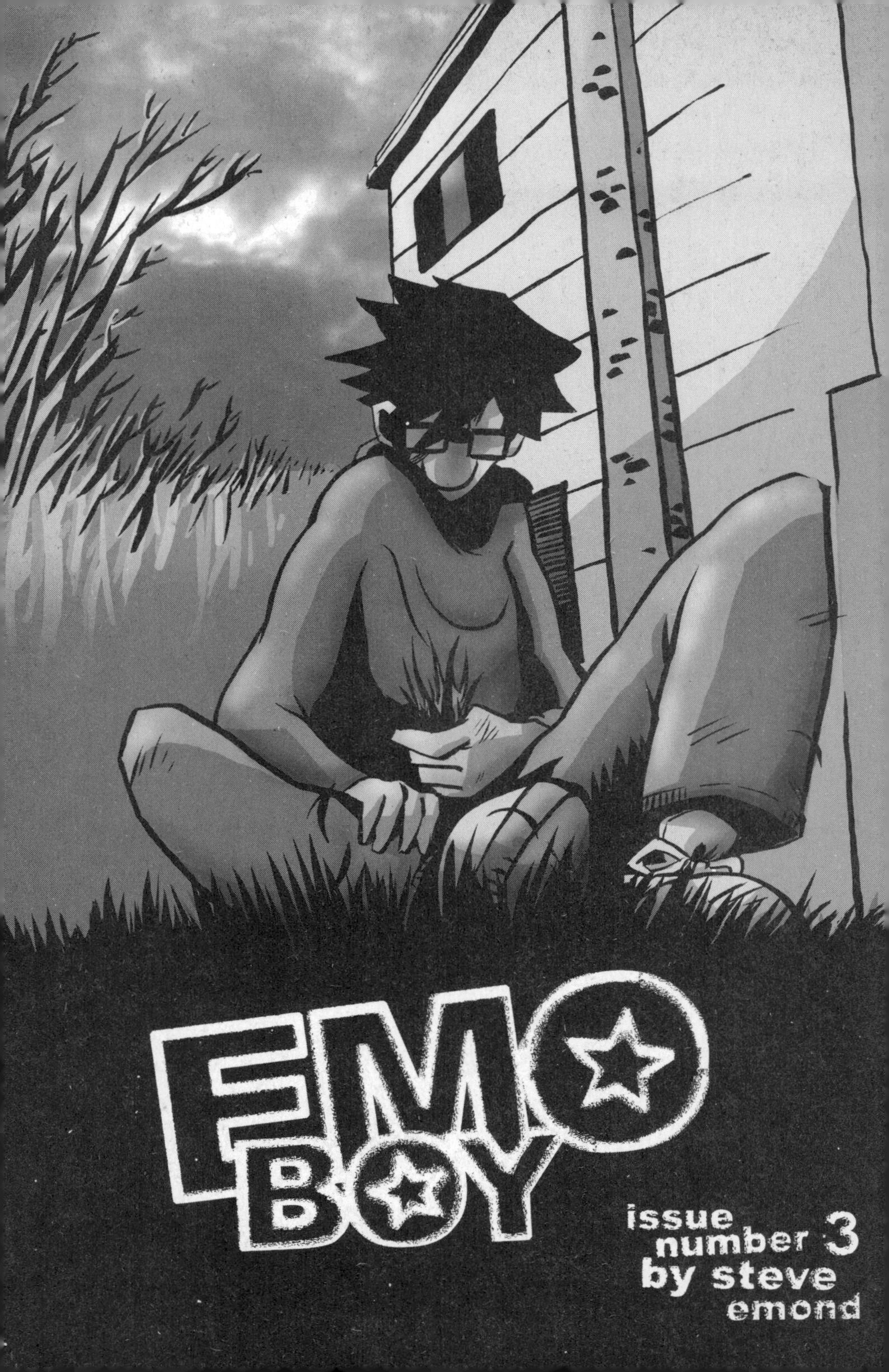
EMO BOY
issue number 3
by steve emond

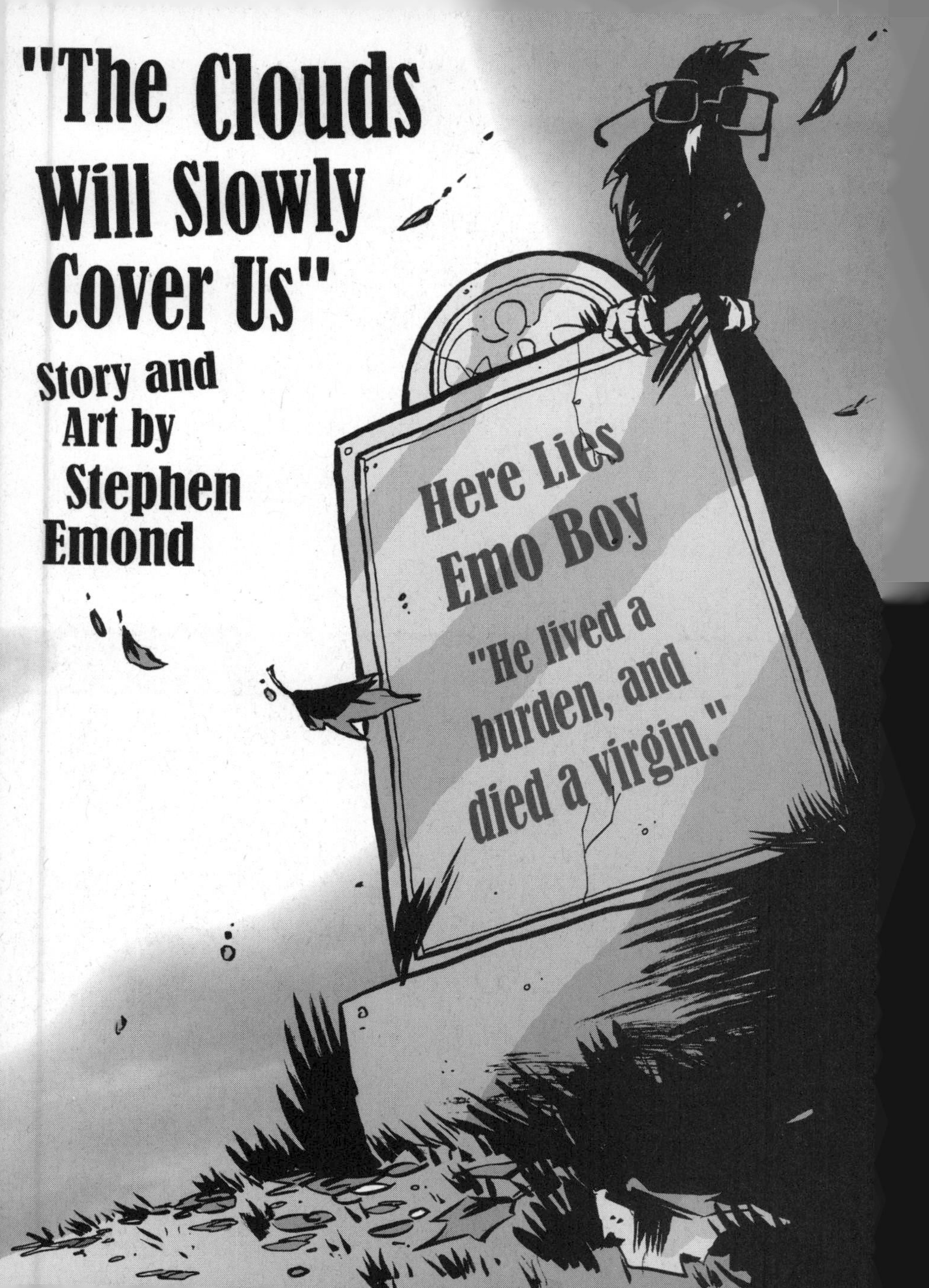
"The Clouds Will Slowly Cover Us"
Story and Art by Stephen Emond
Here Lies Emo Boy
"He lived a burden, and died a virgin."

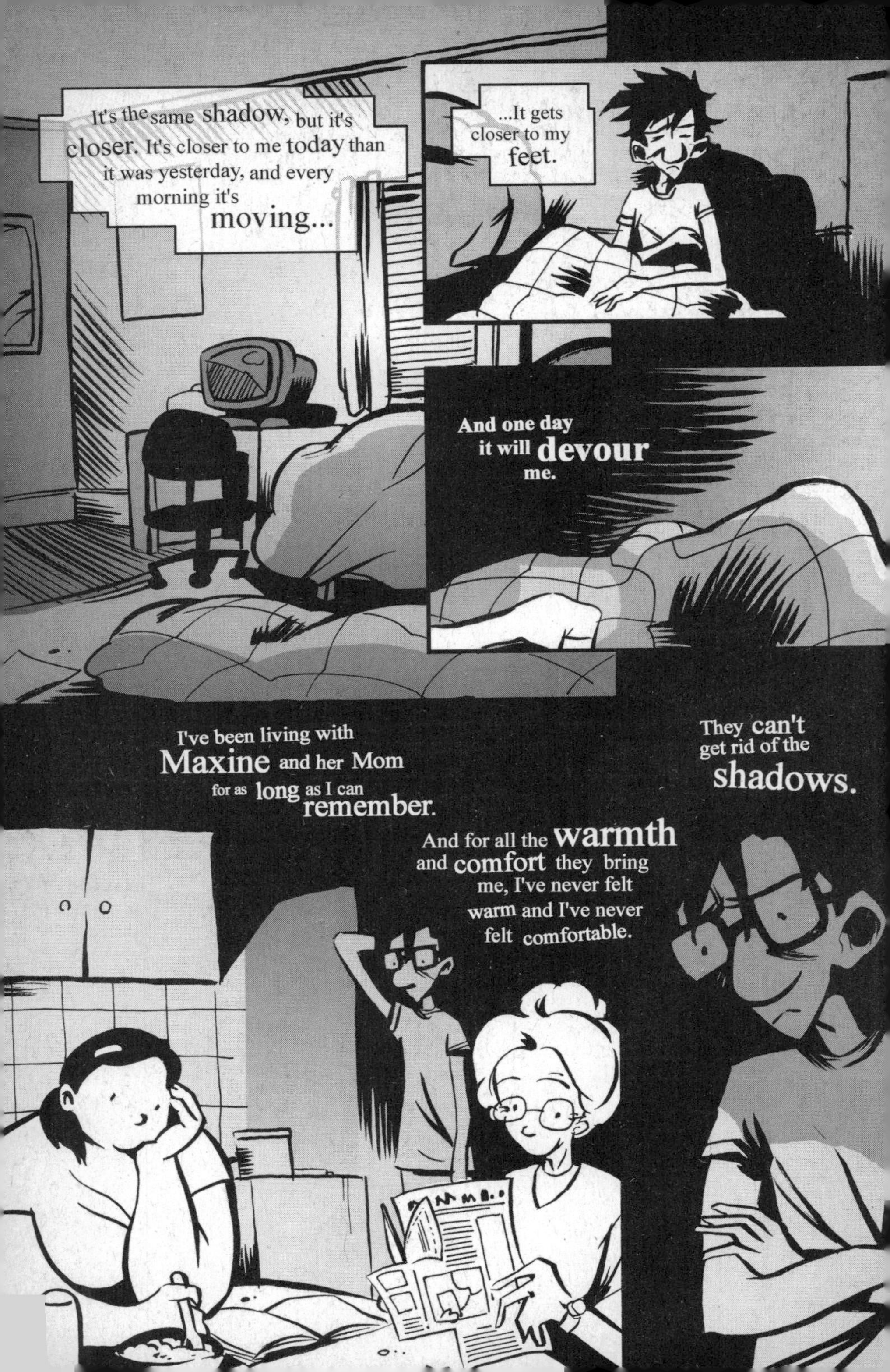

It's the same shadow, but it's closer. It's closer to me today than it was yesterday, and every morning it's moving...
...It gets closer to my feet.
And one day it will devour me.
I've been living with Maxine and her Mom for as long as I can remember.
They can't get rid of the shadows.
And for all the warmth and comfort they bring me, I've never felt warm and I've never felt comfortable.

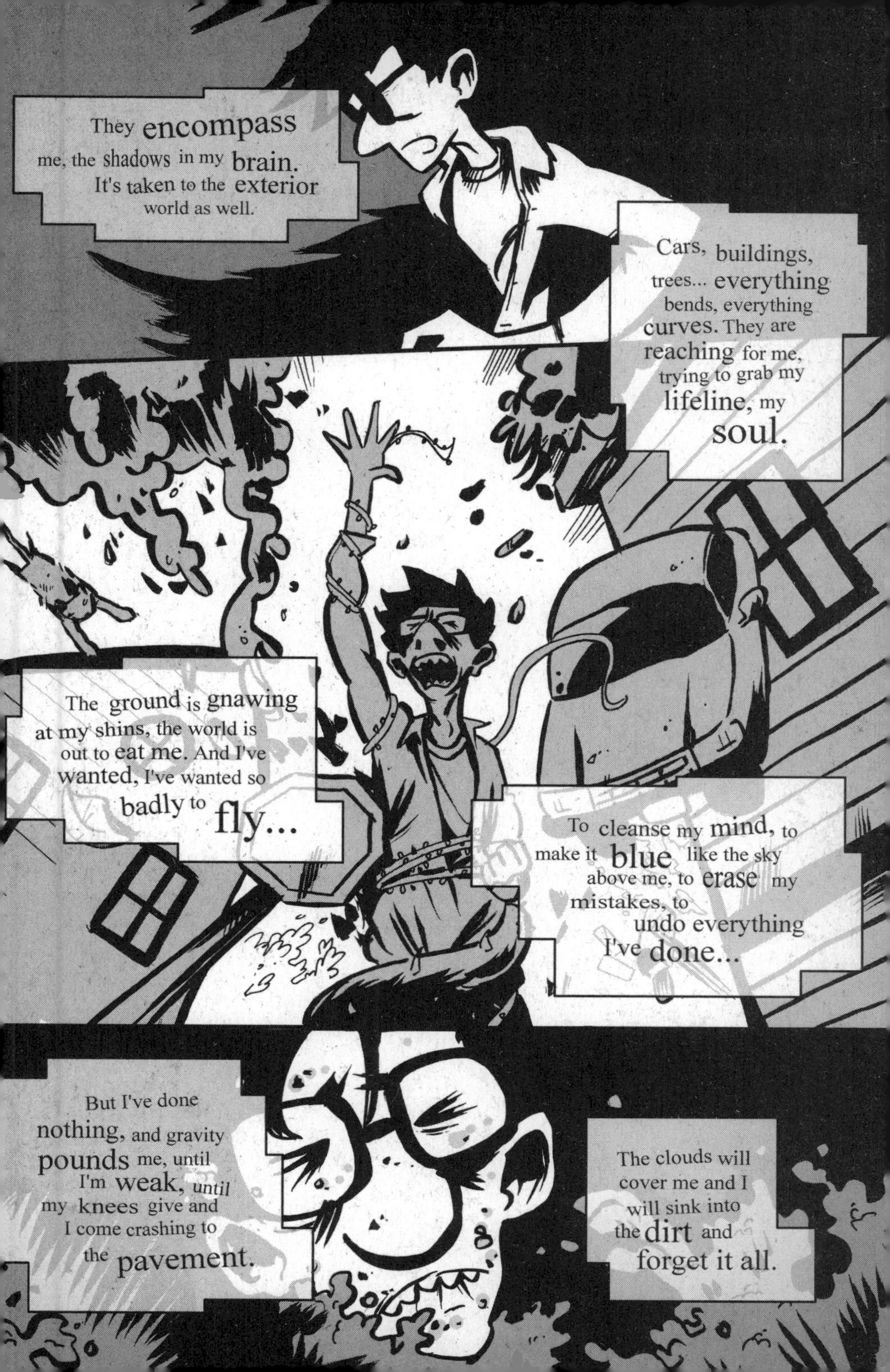
They encompass me, the shadows in my brain. It's taken to the exterior world as well.
Cars, buildings, trees... everything bends, everything curves. They are reaching for me, trying to grab my lifeline, my soul.
The ground is gnawing at my shins, the world is out to eat me. And I've wanted, I've wanted so badly to fly...
To cleanse my mind, to make it blue like the sky above me, to erase my mistakes, to undo everything I've done...
But I've done nothing, and gravity pounds me, until I'm weak, until my knees give and I come crashing to the pavement.
The clouds will cover me and I will sink into the dirt and forget it all.

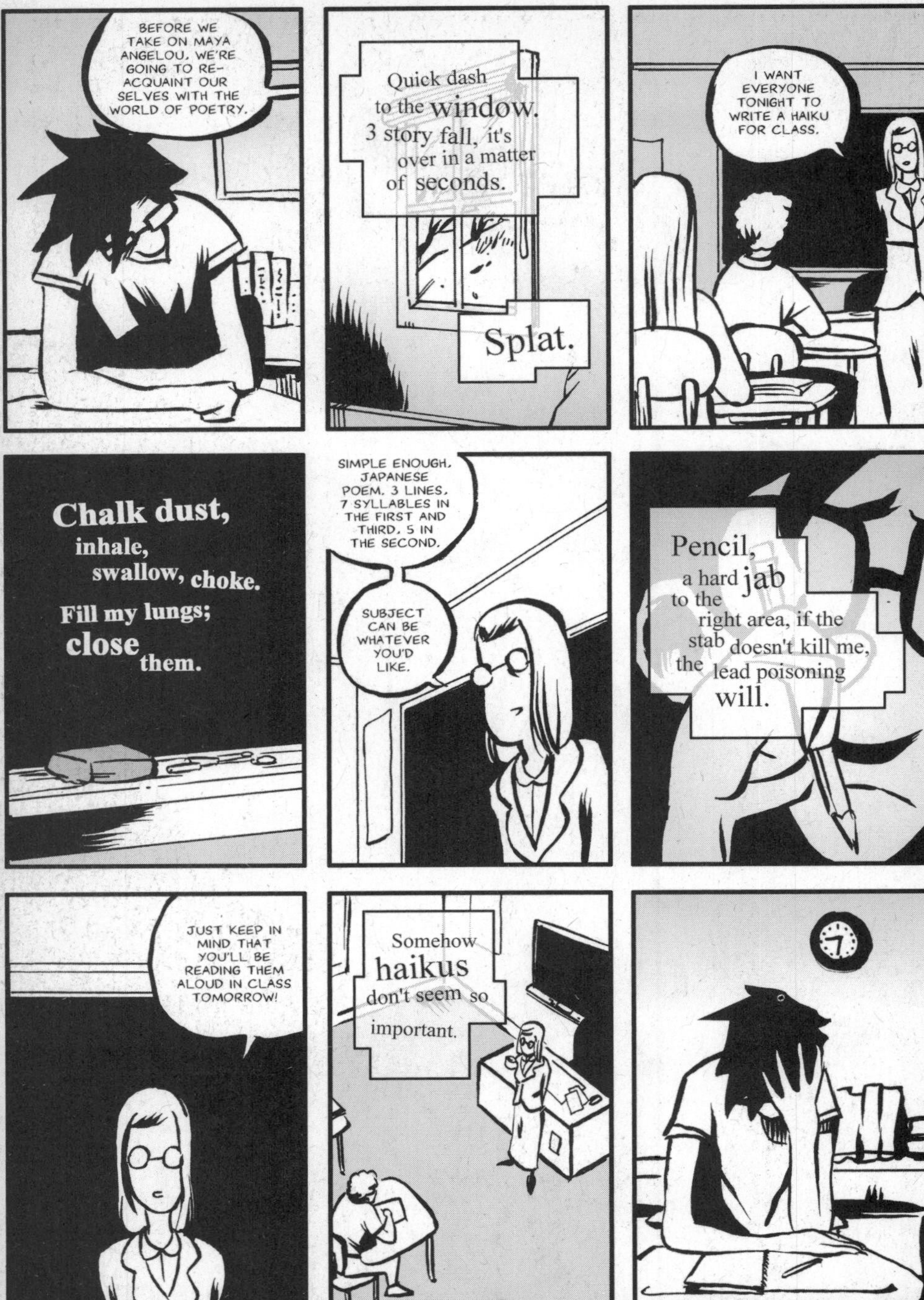
BEFORE WE TAKE ON MAYA ANGELOU, WE'RE GOING TO RE-ACQUAINT OUR SELVES WITH THE WORLD OF POETRY.
Quick dash to the window. 3 story fall, it's over in a matter of seconds.
Splat.
I WANT EVERYONE TONIGHT TO WRITE A HAIKU FOR CLASS.
Chalk dust, inhale, swallow, choke. Fill my lungs; close them.
SIMPLE ENOUGH. JAPANESE POEM. 3 LINES. 7 SYLLABLES IN THE FIRST AND THIRD, 5 IN THE SECOND.
SUBJECT CAN BE WHATEVER YOU'D LIKE.
Pencil, a hard jab to the right area, if the stab doesn't kill me, the lead poisoning will.
JUST KEEP IN MIND THAT YOU'LL BE READING THEM ALOUD IN CLASS TOMORROW!
Somehow haikus don't seem so important.

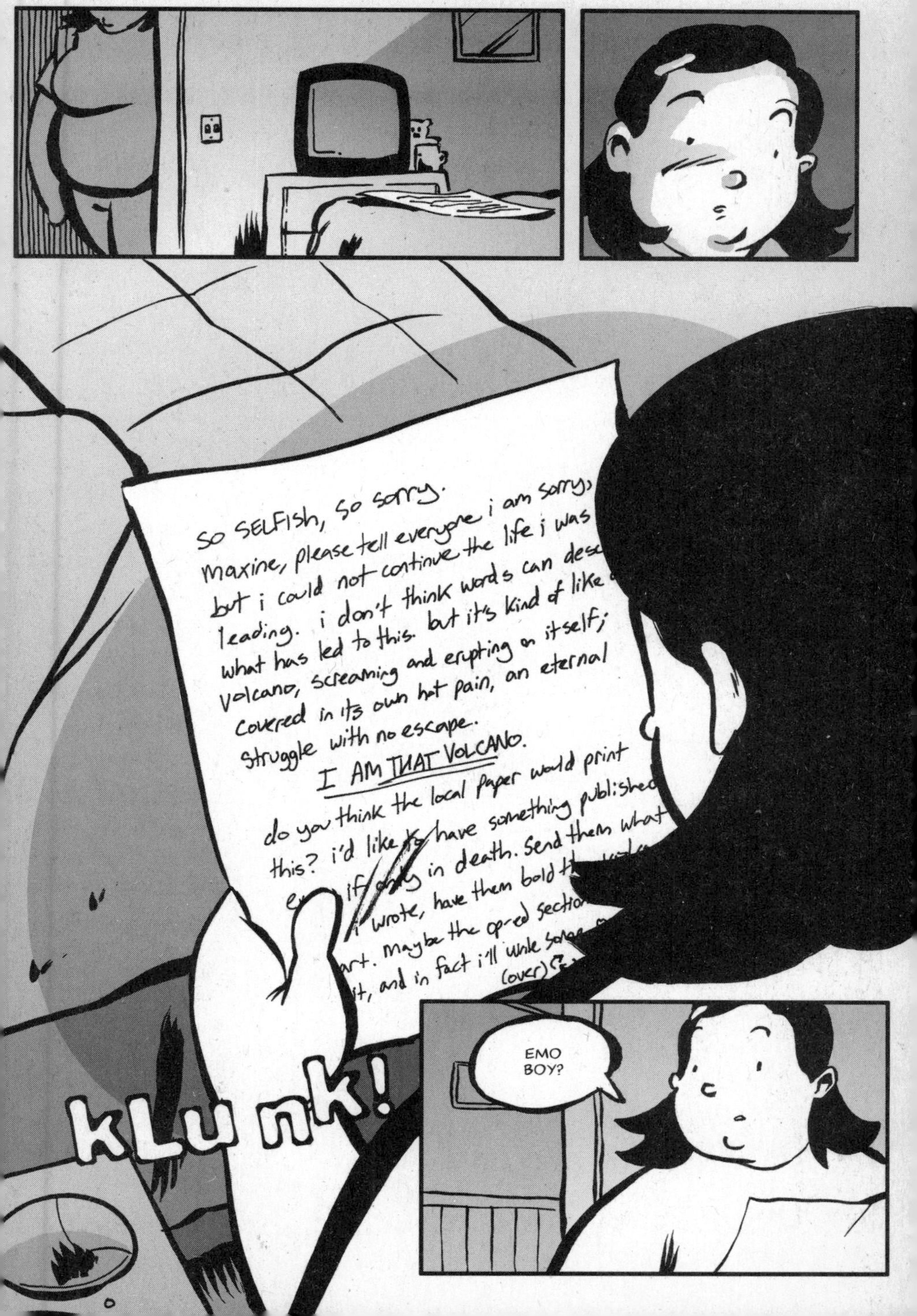

so SELFISH, so sorry.
maxine, please tell everyone i am sorry,
but i could not continue the life i was
leading. i don't think words can
what has led to this. but it's kind of like
volcano, screaming and erupting on itself;
covered in its own hot pain, an eternal
struggle with no escape.
I AM THAT VOLCANO.
do you think the local paper would print
this? i'd like to have something published
if in death. Send them what
i wrote, have them bold the
art. maybe the op-ed section
it, and in fact i'll write
(over)
kLunk!
EMO BOY?

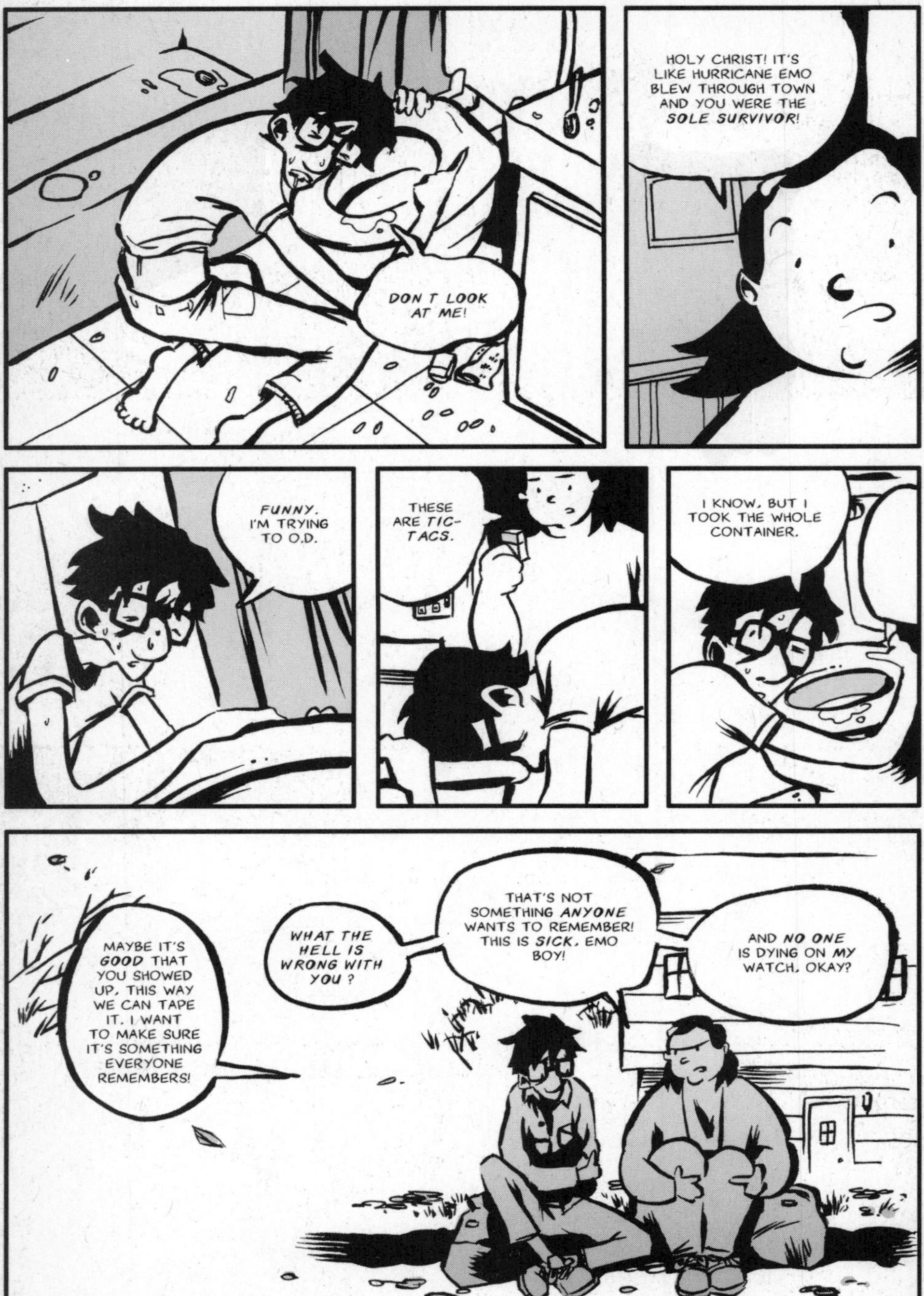
DON T LOOK AT ME!
HOLY CHRIST! IT'S LIKE HURRICANE EMO BLEW THROUGH TOWN AND YOU WERE THE *SOLE SURVIVOR*!
FUNNY. I'M TRYING TO O.D.
THESE ARE *TIC-TACS.*
I KNOW, BUT I TOOK THE WHOLE CONTAINER.
MAYBE IT'S *GOOD* THAT YOU SHOWED UP, THIS WAY WE CAN TAPE IT. I WANT TO MAKE SURE IT'S SOMETHING EVERYONE REMEMBERS!
WHAT THE HELL IS WRONG WITH YOU ?
THAT'S NOT SOMETHING *ANYONE* WANTS TO REMEMBER! THIS IS *SICK*, EMO BOY!
AND *NO ONE* IS DYING ON *MY* WATCH, OKAY?

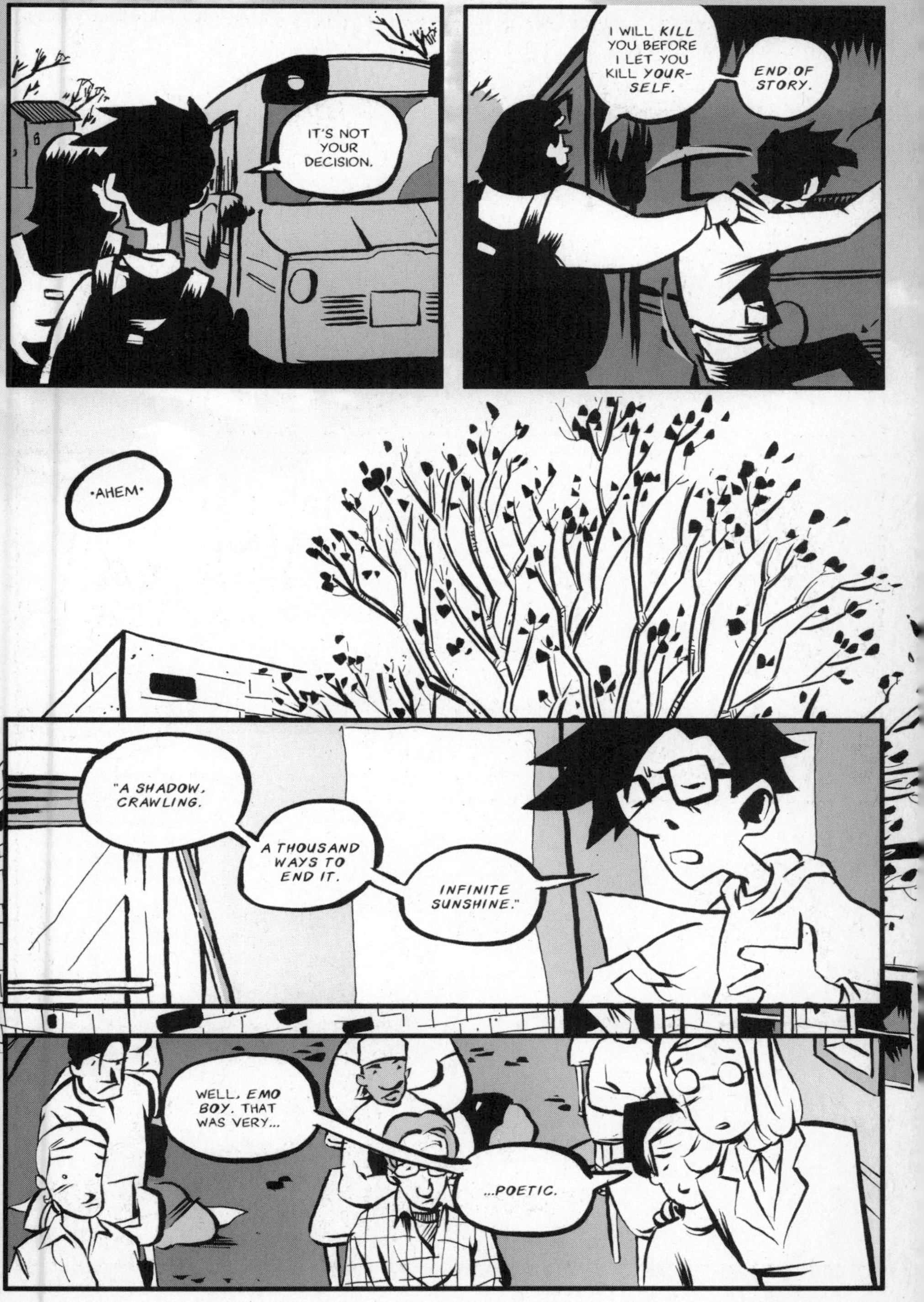
IT'S NOT YOUR DECISION.
I WILL KILL YOU BEFORE I LET YOU KILL YOUR-SELF.
END OF STORY.
•AHEM•
"A SHADOW. CRAWLING.
A THOUSAND WAYS TO END IT.
INFINITE SUNSHINE."
WELL, EMO BOY, THAT WAS VERY...
...POETIC.

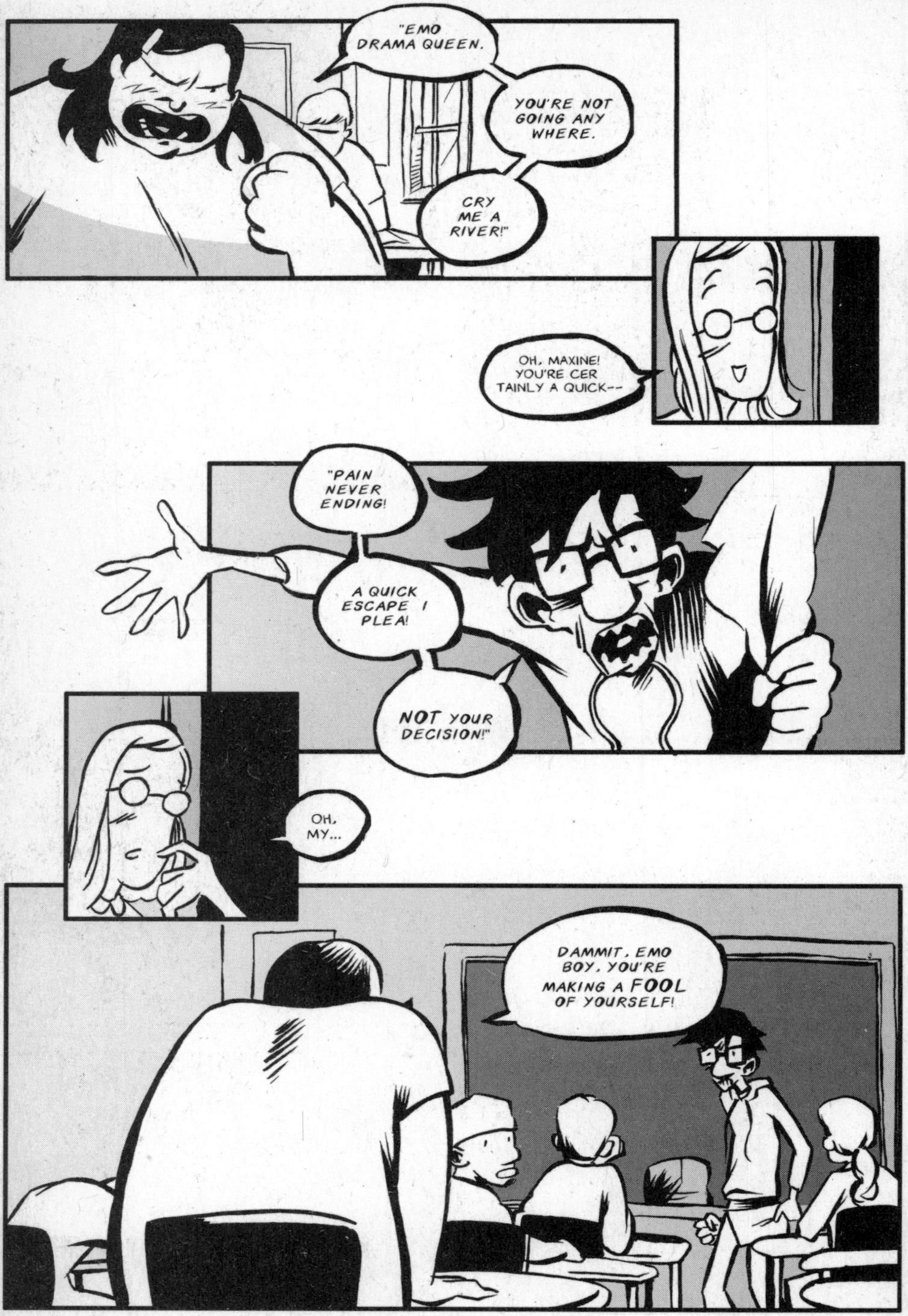
"EMO DRAMA QUEEN.
YOU'RE NOT GOING ANY WHERE.
CRY ME A RIVER!"
OH, MAXINE! YOU'RE CER TAINLY A QUICK--
"PAIN NEVER ENDING!
A QUICK ESCAPE I PLEA!
NOT YOUR DECISION!"
OH, MY...
DAMMIT, EMO BOY, YOU'RE MAKING A FOOL OF YOURSELF!

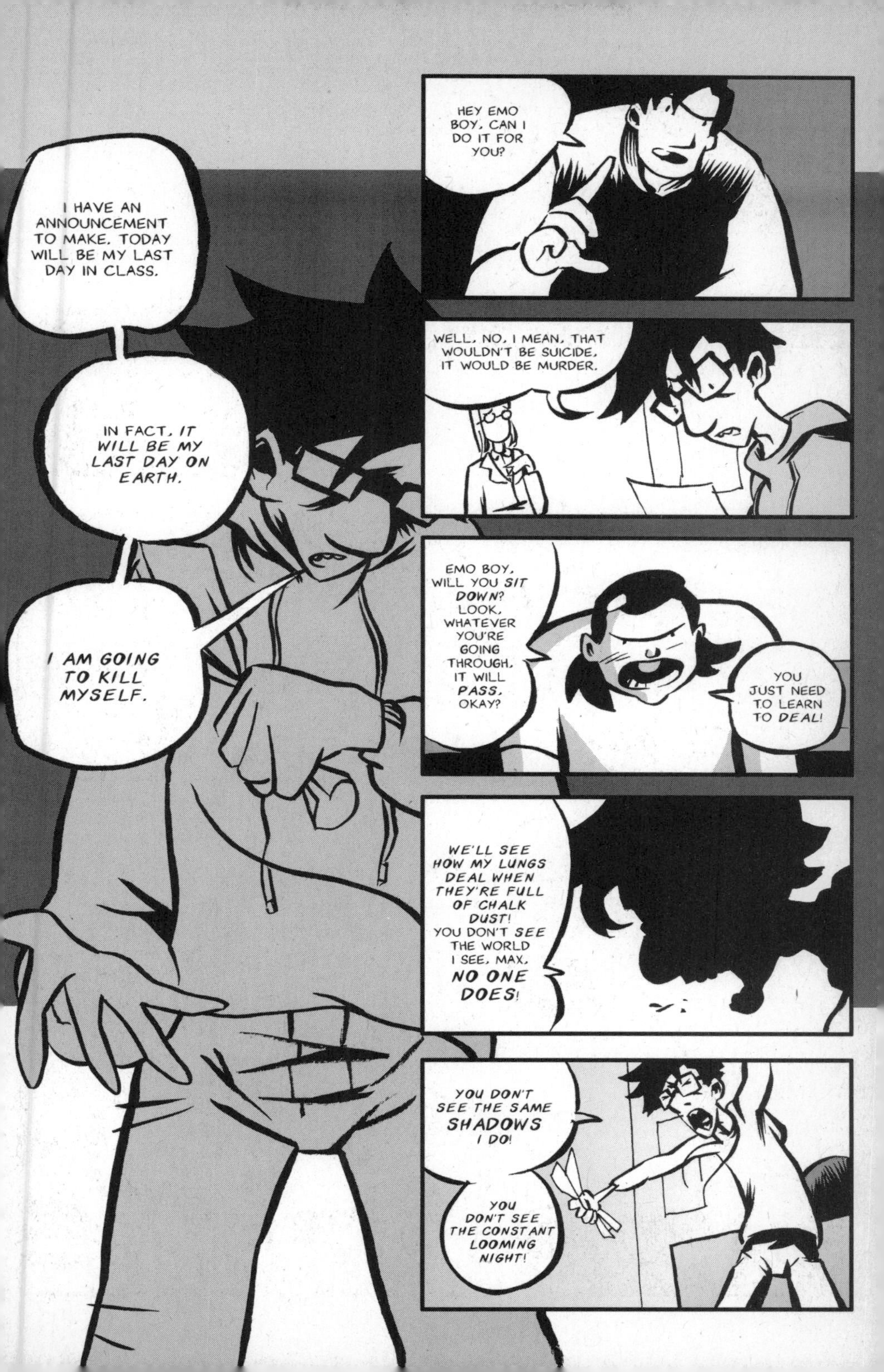
I HAVE AN ANNOUNCEMENT TO MAKE. TODAY WILL BE MY LAST DAY IN CLASS.
IN FACT, IT WILL BE MY LAST DAY ON EARTH.
I AM GOING TO KILL MYSELF.
HEY EMO BOY, CAN I DO IT FOR YOU?
WELL, NO, I MEAN, THAT WOULDN'T BE SUICIDE, IT WOULD BE MURDER.
EMO BOY, WILL YOU SIT DOWN? LOOK, WHATEVER YOU'RE GOING THROUGH, IT WILL PASS, OKAY?
YOU JUST NEED TO LEARN TO DEAL!
WE'LL SEE HOW MY LUNGS DEAL WHEN THEY'RE FULL OF CHALK DUST! YOU DON'T SEE THE WORLD I SEE, MAX, NO ONE DOES!
YOU DON'T SEE THE SAME SHADOWS I DO!
YOU DON'T SEE THE CONSTANT LOOMING NIGHT!

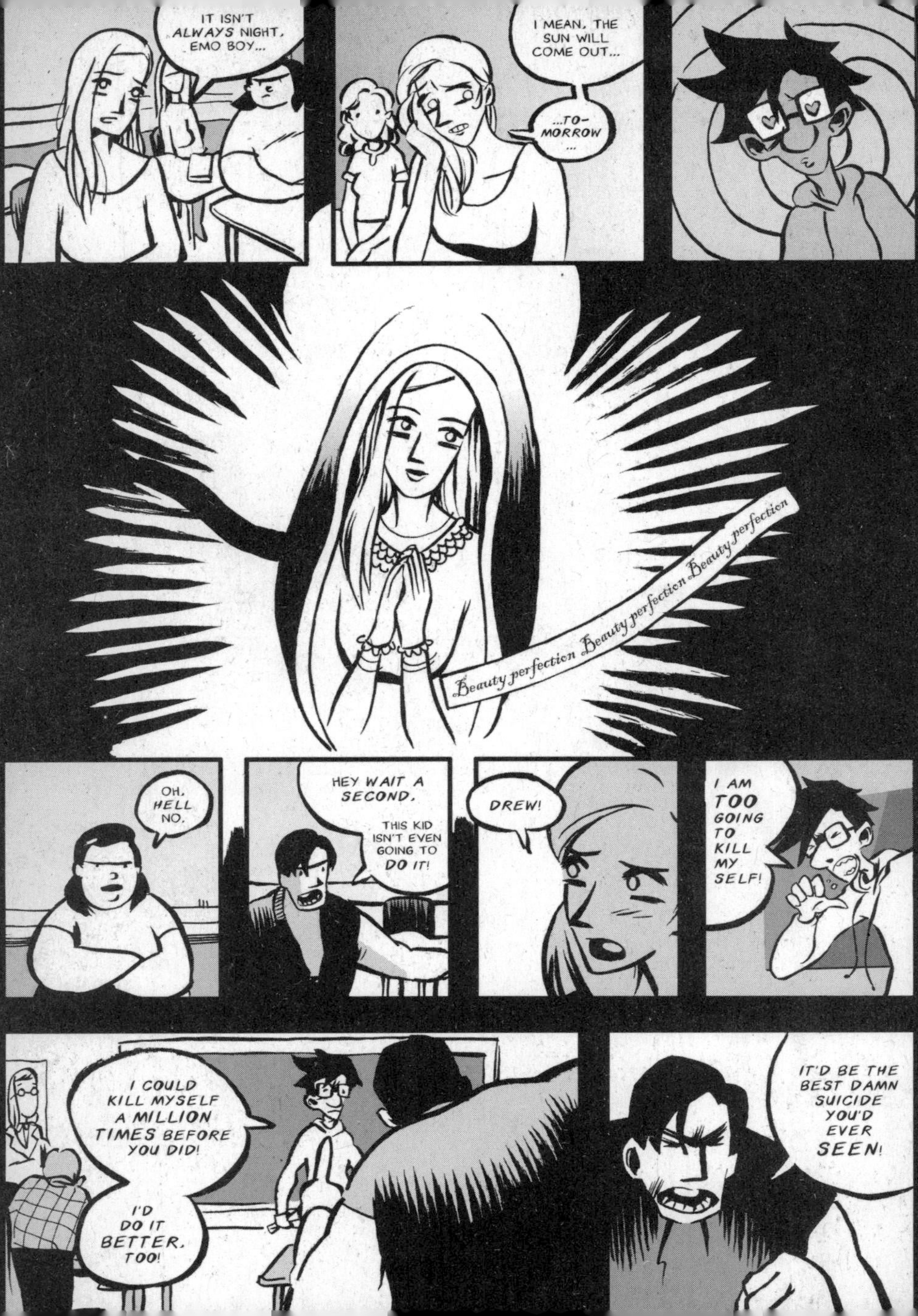
IT ISN'T ALWAYS NIGHT, EMO BOY...
I MEAN, THE SUN WILL COME OUT...
...TO-MORROW...
Beauty perfection Beauty perfection Beauty perfection
OH, HELL NO.
HEY WAIT A SECOND.
THIS KID ISN'T EVEN GOING TO DO IT!
DREW!
I AM TOO GOING TO KILL MY SELF!
I COULD KILL MYSELF A MILLION TIMES BEFORE YOU DID!
I'D DO IT BETTER, TOO!
IT'D BE THE BEST DAMN SUICIDE YOU'D EVER SEEN!

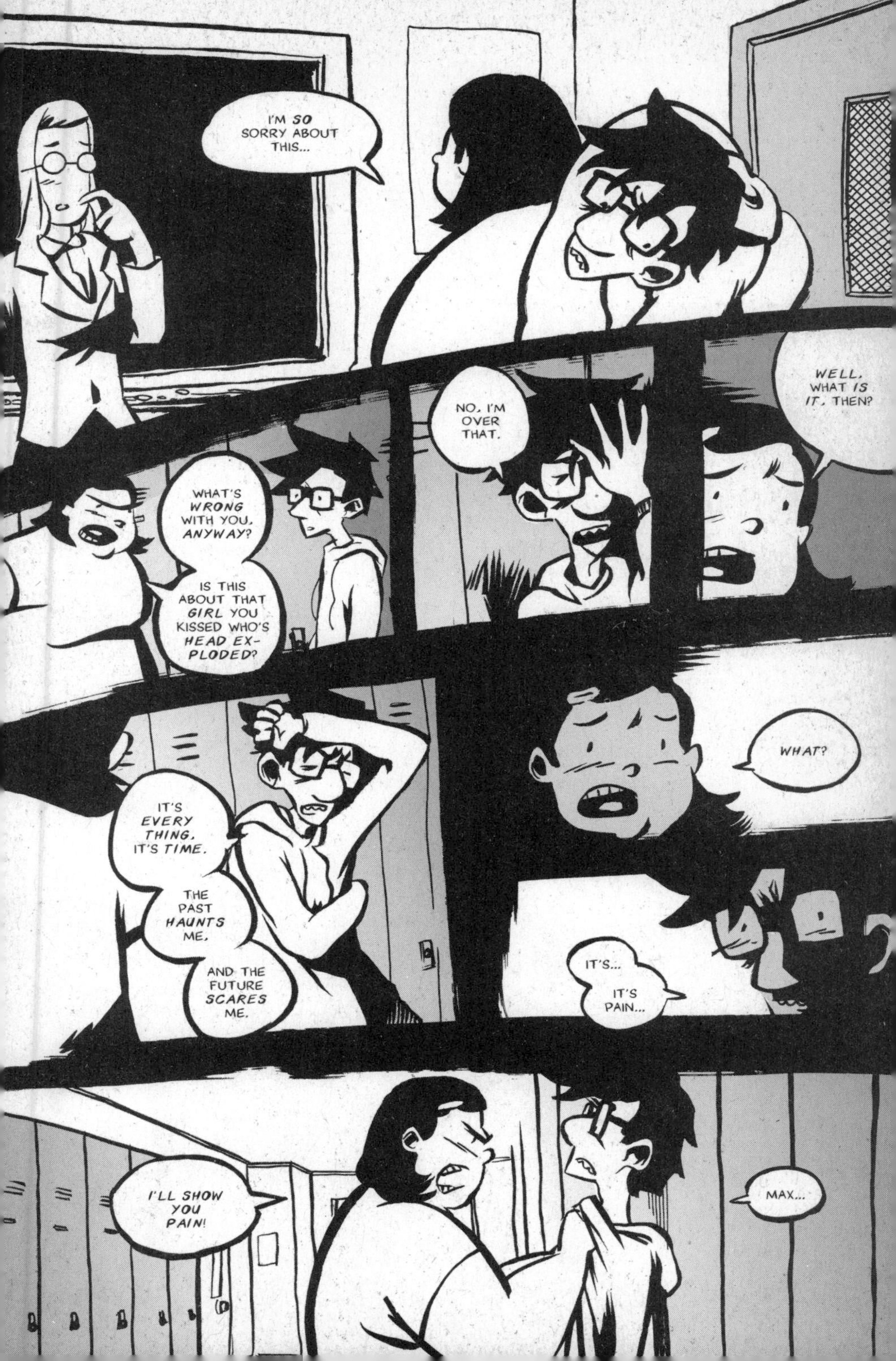
I'M SO SORRY ABOUT THIS...
WHAT'S WRONG WITH YOU, ANYWAY?
IS THIS ABOUT THAT GIRL YOU KISSED WHO'S HEAD EX-PLODED?
NO, I'M OVER THAT.
WELL, WHAT IS IT, THEN?
IT'S EVERY THING, IT'S TIME.
THE PAST HAUNTS ME,
AND THE FUTURE SCARES ME.
WHAT?
IT'S...
IT'S PAIN...
I'LL SHOW YOU PAIN!
MAX...

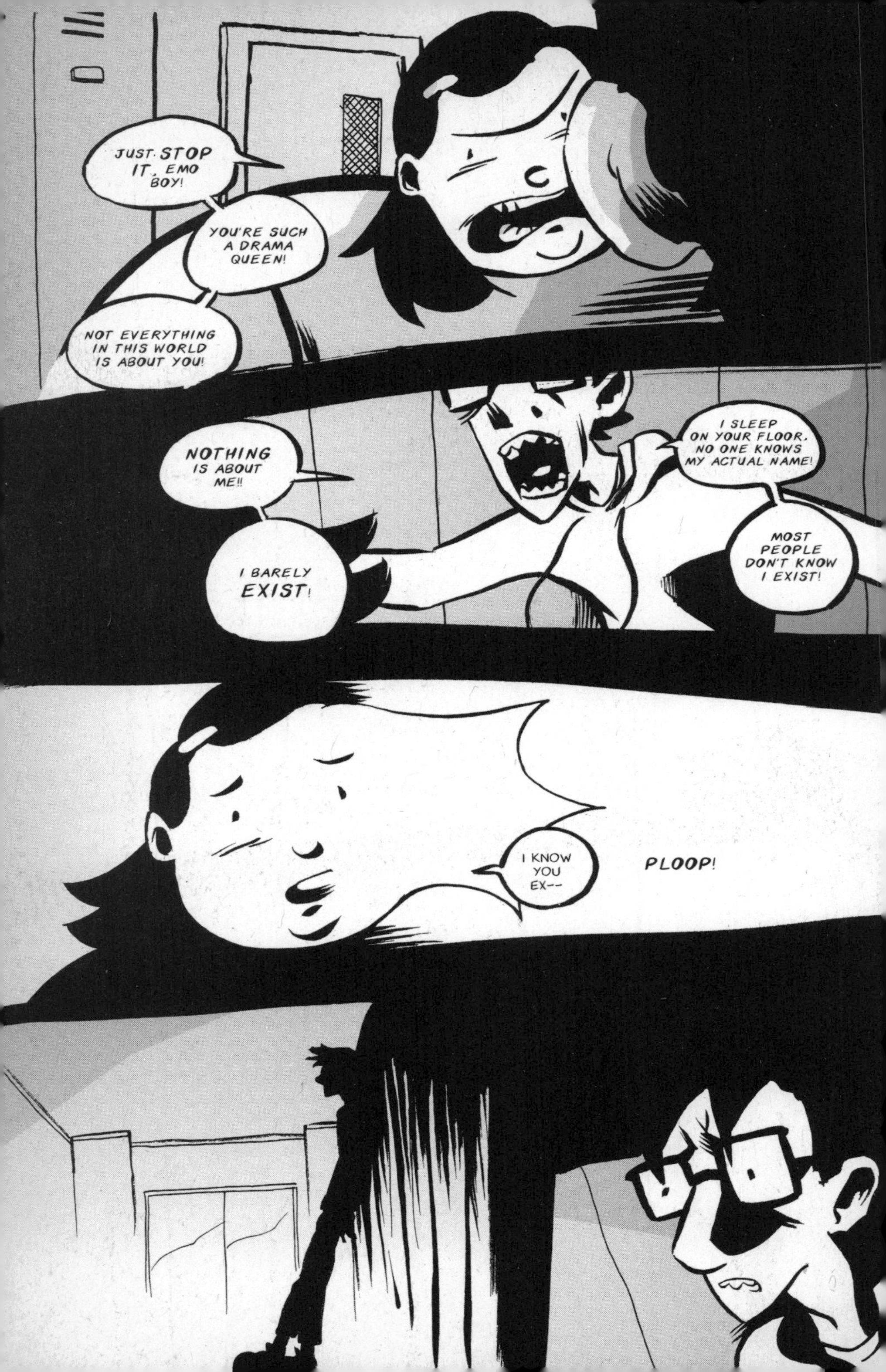
JUST. STOP IT, EMO BOY!
YOU'RE SUCH A DRAMA QUEEN!
NOT EVERYTHING IN THIS WORLD IS ABOUT YOU!
NOTHING IS ABOUT ME!!
I BARELY EXIST!
I SLEEP ON YOUR FLOOR, NO ONE KNOWS MY ACTUAL NAME!
MOST PEOPLE DON'T KNOW I EXIST!
I KNOW YOU EX--
PLOOP!

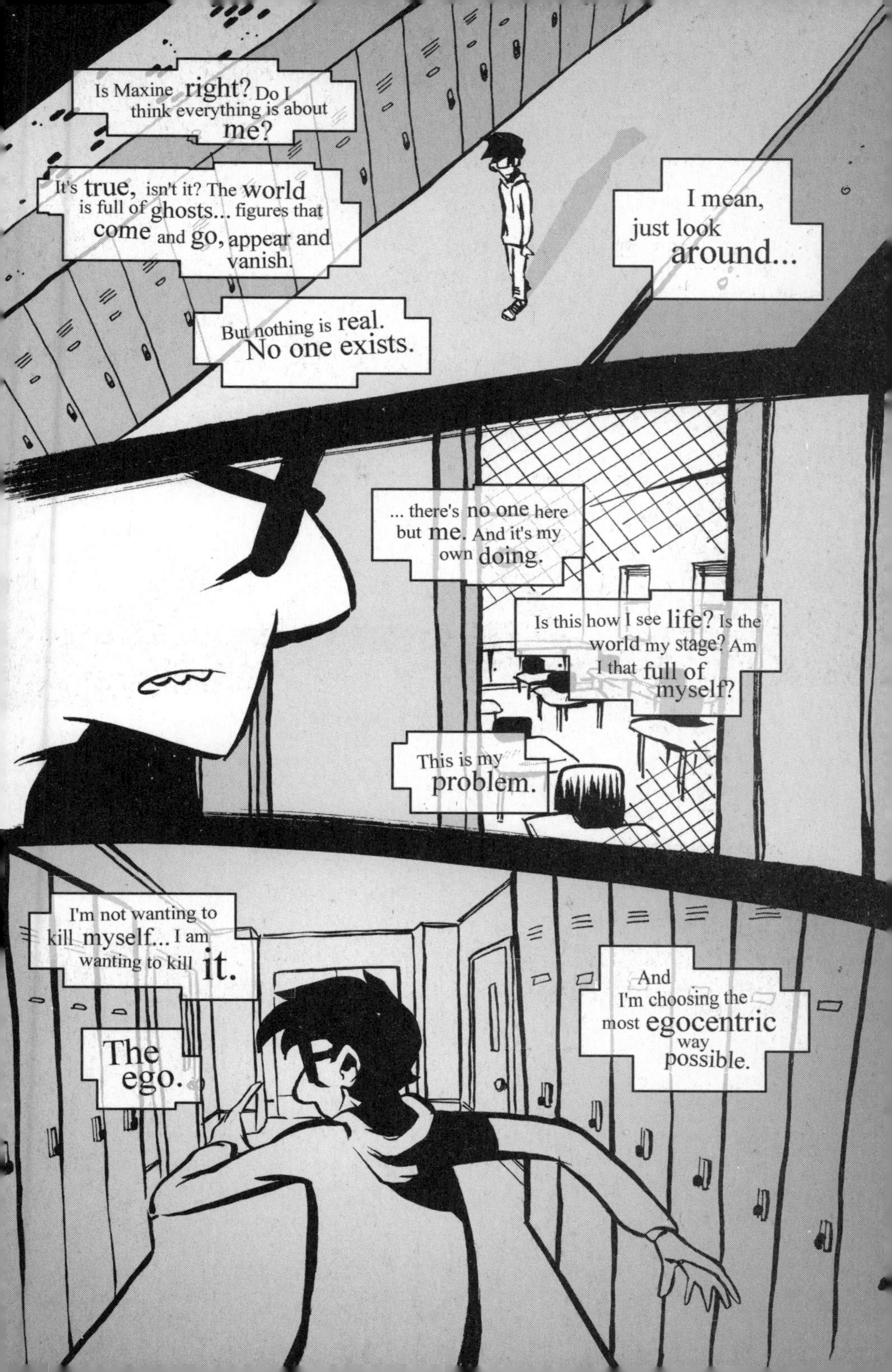
Is Maxine right? Do I think everything is about me?
It's true, isn't it? The world is full of ghosts... figures that come and go, appear and vanish.
But nothing is real. No one exists.
I mean, just look around...
... there's no one here but me. And it's my own doing.
Is this how I see life? Is the world my stage? Am I that full of myself?
This is my problem.
I'm not wanting to kill myself... I am wanting to kill it.
The ego.
And I'm choosing the most egocentric way possible.

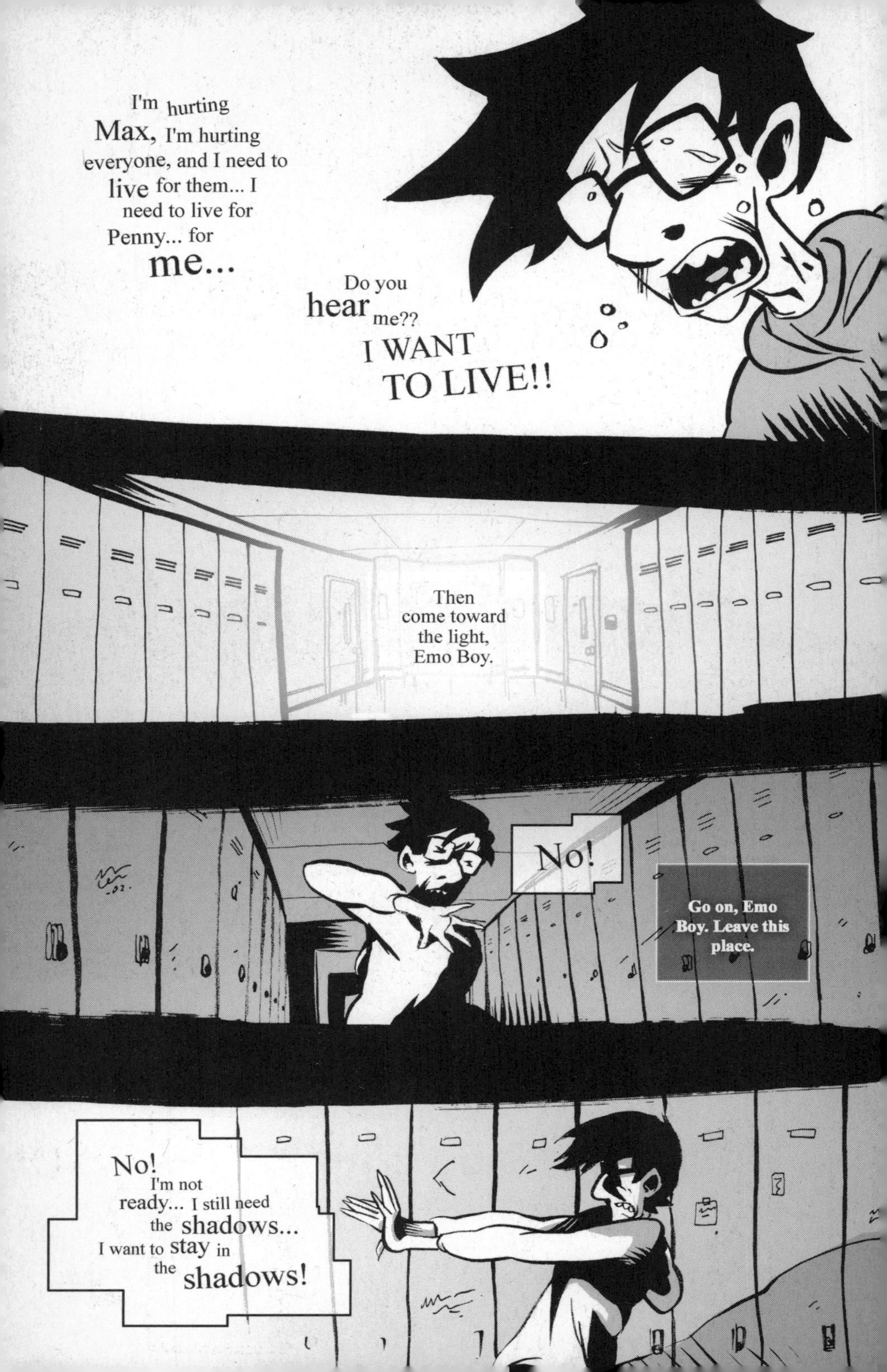
I'm hurting Max, I'm hurting everyone, and I need to live for them... I need to live for Penny... for me...
Do you hear me?? I WANT TO LIVE!!
Then come toward the light, Emo Boy.
No!
Go on, Emo Boy. Leave this place.
No! I'm not ready... I still need the shadows... I want to stay in the shadows!

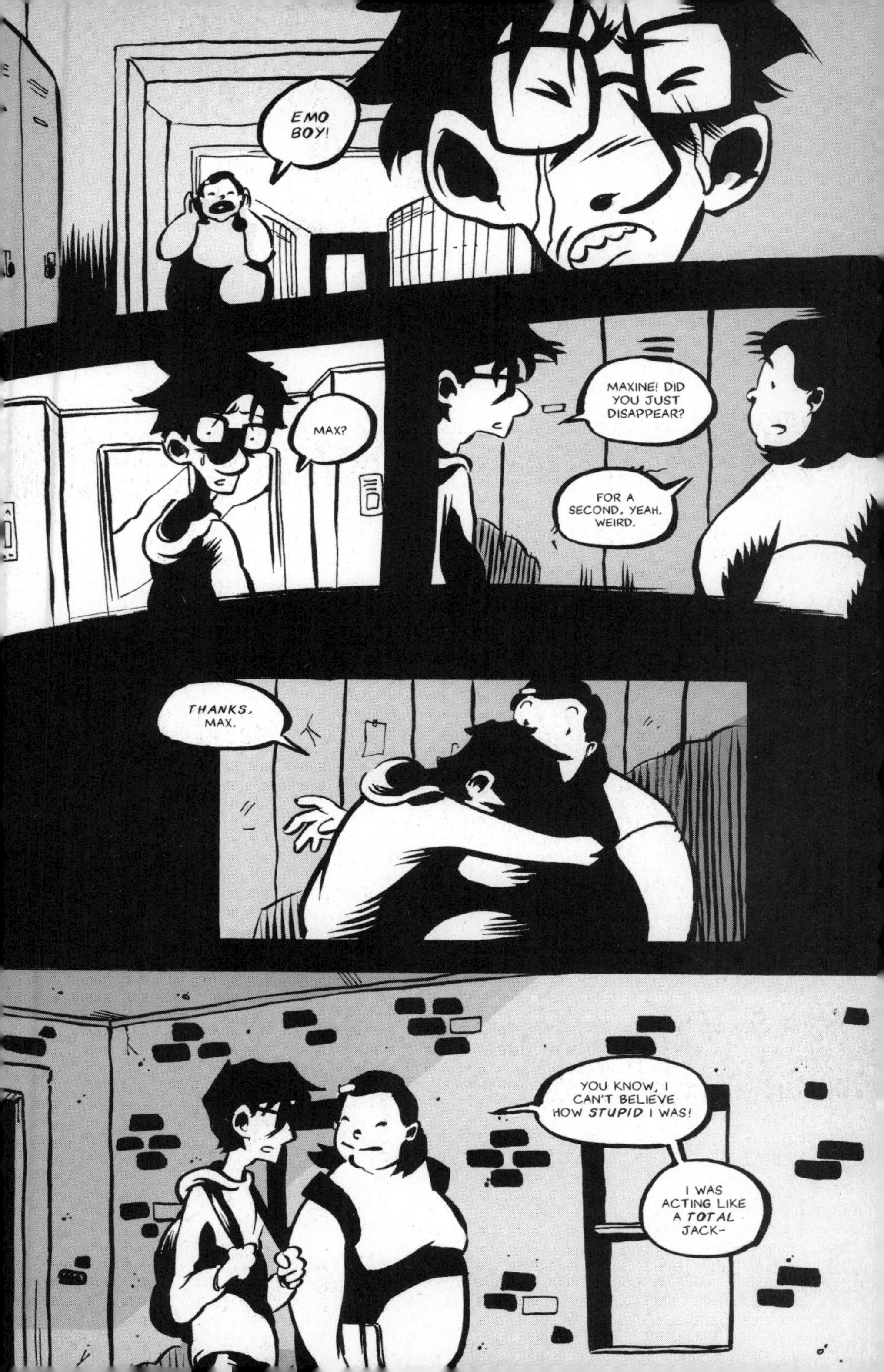
EMO BOY!
MAX?
MAXINE! DID YOU JUST DISAPPEAR?
FOR A SECOND, YEAH. WEIRD.
THANKS, MAX.
YOU KNOW, I CAN'T BELIEVE HOW STUPID I WAS!
I WAS ACTING LIKE A TOTAL JACK-

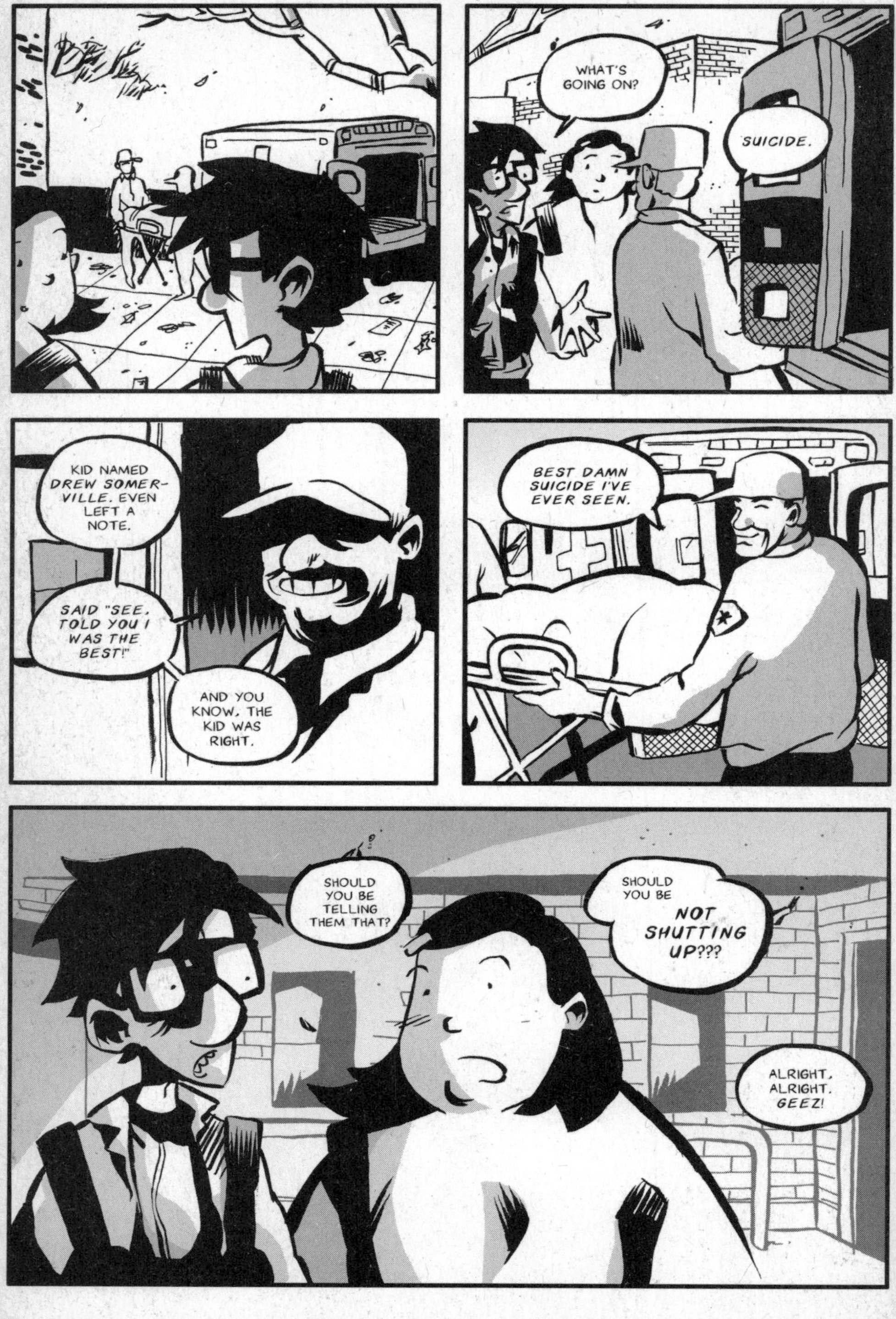
WHAT'S GOING ON?
SUICIDE.
KID NAMED DREW SOMERVILLE. EVEN LEFT A NOTE.
SAID "SEE. TOLD YOU I WAS THE BEST!"
AND YOU KNOW, THE KID WAS RIGHT.
BEST DAMN SUICIDE I'VE EVER SEEN.
SHOULD YOU BE TELLING THEM THAT?
SHOULD YOU BE NOT SHUTTING UP???
ALRIGHT, ALRIGHT. GEEZ!

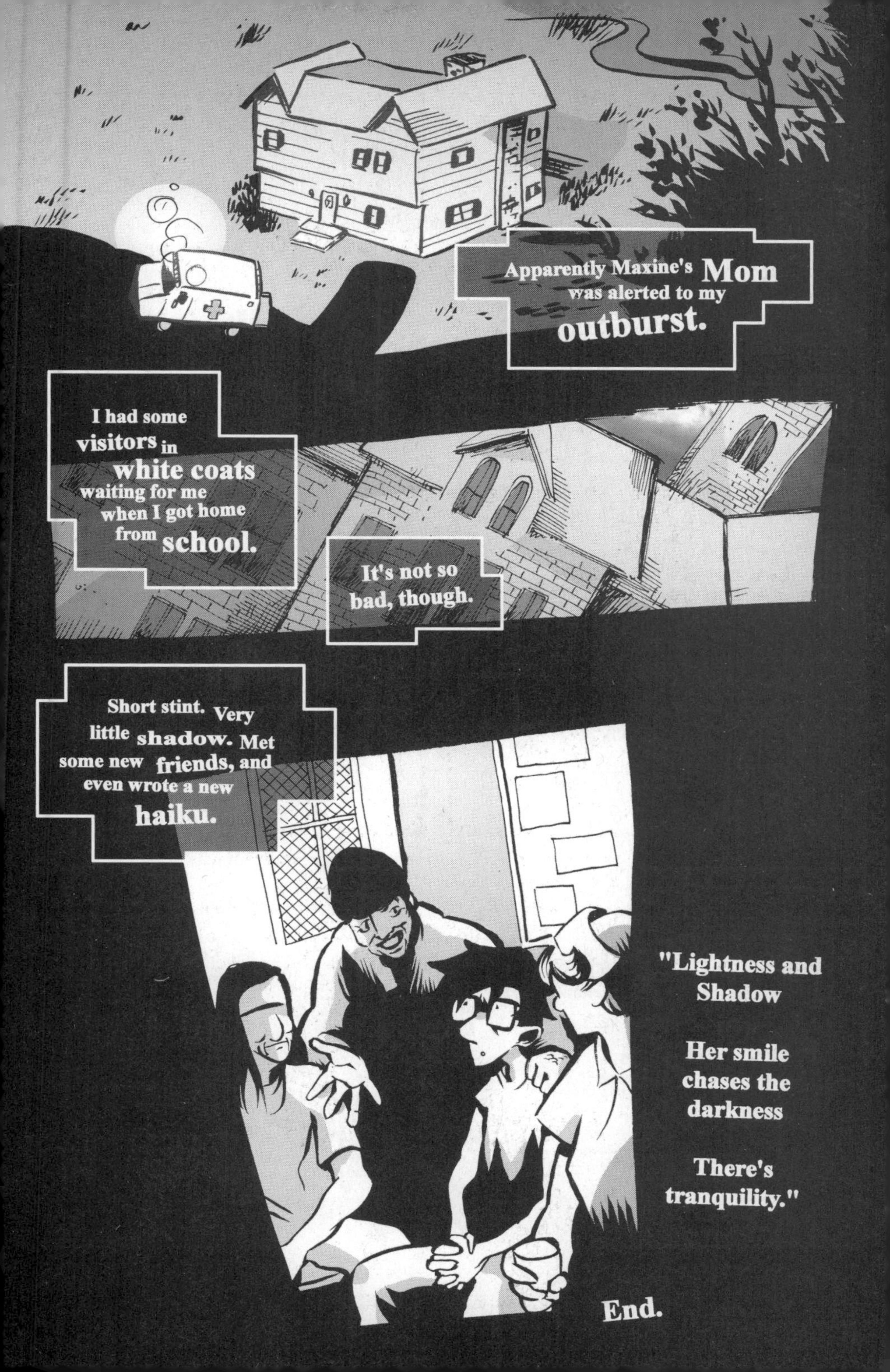

Apparently Maxine's Mom was alerted to my outburst.
I had some visitors in white coats waiting for me when I got home from school.
It's not so bad, though.
Short stint. Very little shadow. Met some new friends, and even wrote a new haiku.
"Lightness and Shadow

Her smile chases the darkness

There's tranquility."
End.

"It tastes like zombie chicken"

story and art
by stephen emond

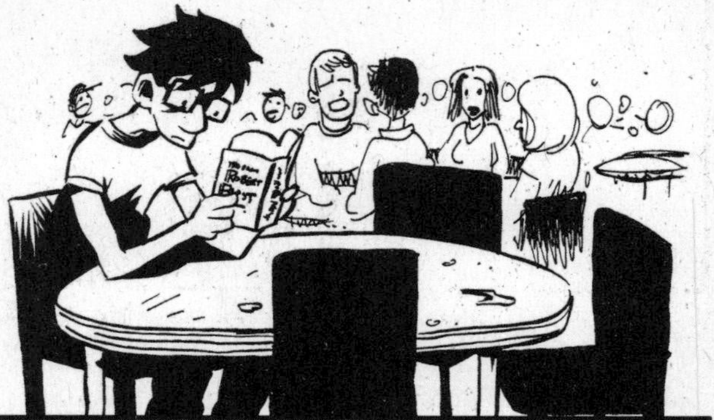

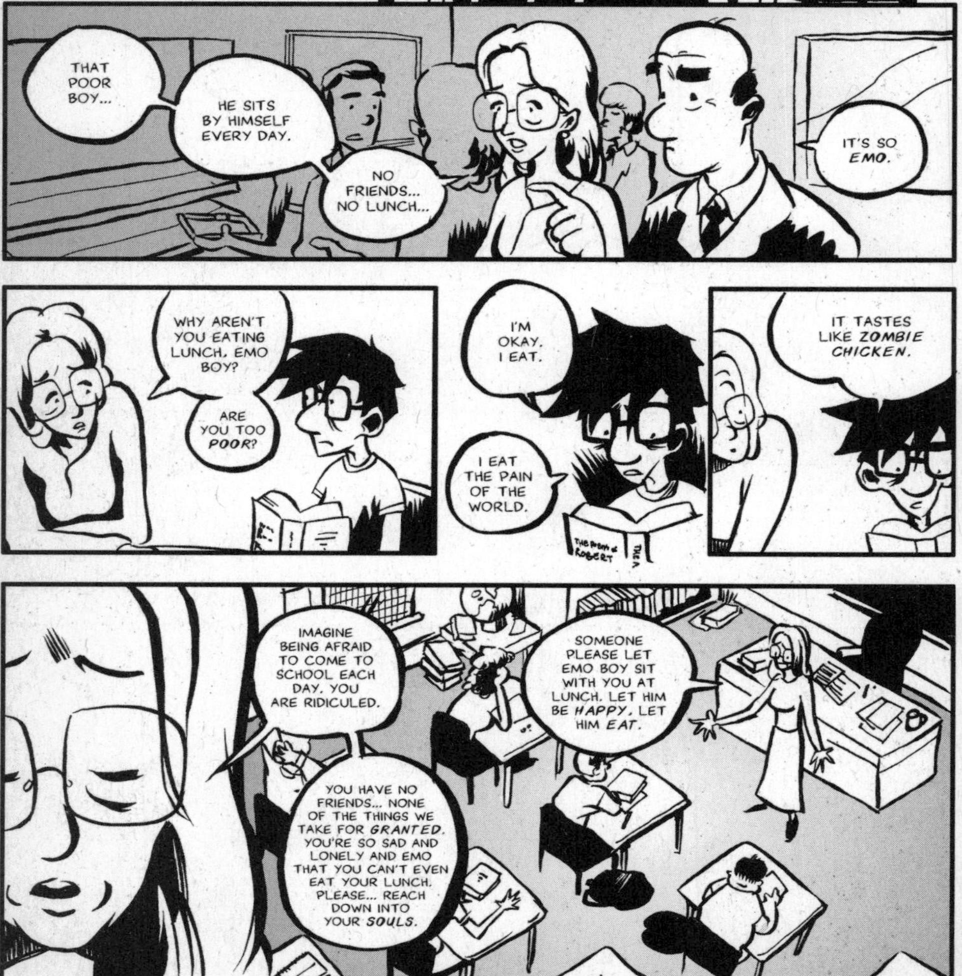

THAT POOR BOY...
HE SITS BY HIMSELF EVERY DAY.
NO FRIENDS... NO LUNCH...
IT'S SO *EMO.*
WHY AREN'T YOU EATING LUNCH, EMO BOY?
ARE YOU TOO *POOR*?
I'M OKAY. I EAT.
I EAT THE PAIN OF THE WORLD.
IT TASTES LIKE *ZOMBIE CHICKEN.*
IMAGINE BEING AFRAID TO COME TO SCHOOL EACH DAY. YOU ARE RIDICULED.
YOU HAVE NO FRIENDS... NONE OF THE THINGS WE TAKE FOR *GRANTED.* YOU'RE SO SAD AND LONELY AND EMO THAT YOU CAN'T EVEN EAT YOUR LUNCH. PLEASE... REACH DOWN INTO YOUR *SOULS.*
SOMEONE PLEASE LET EMO BOY SIT WITH YOU AT LUNCH. LET HIM BE *HAPPY.* LET HIM *EAT.*

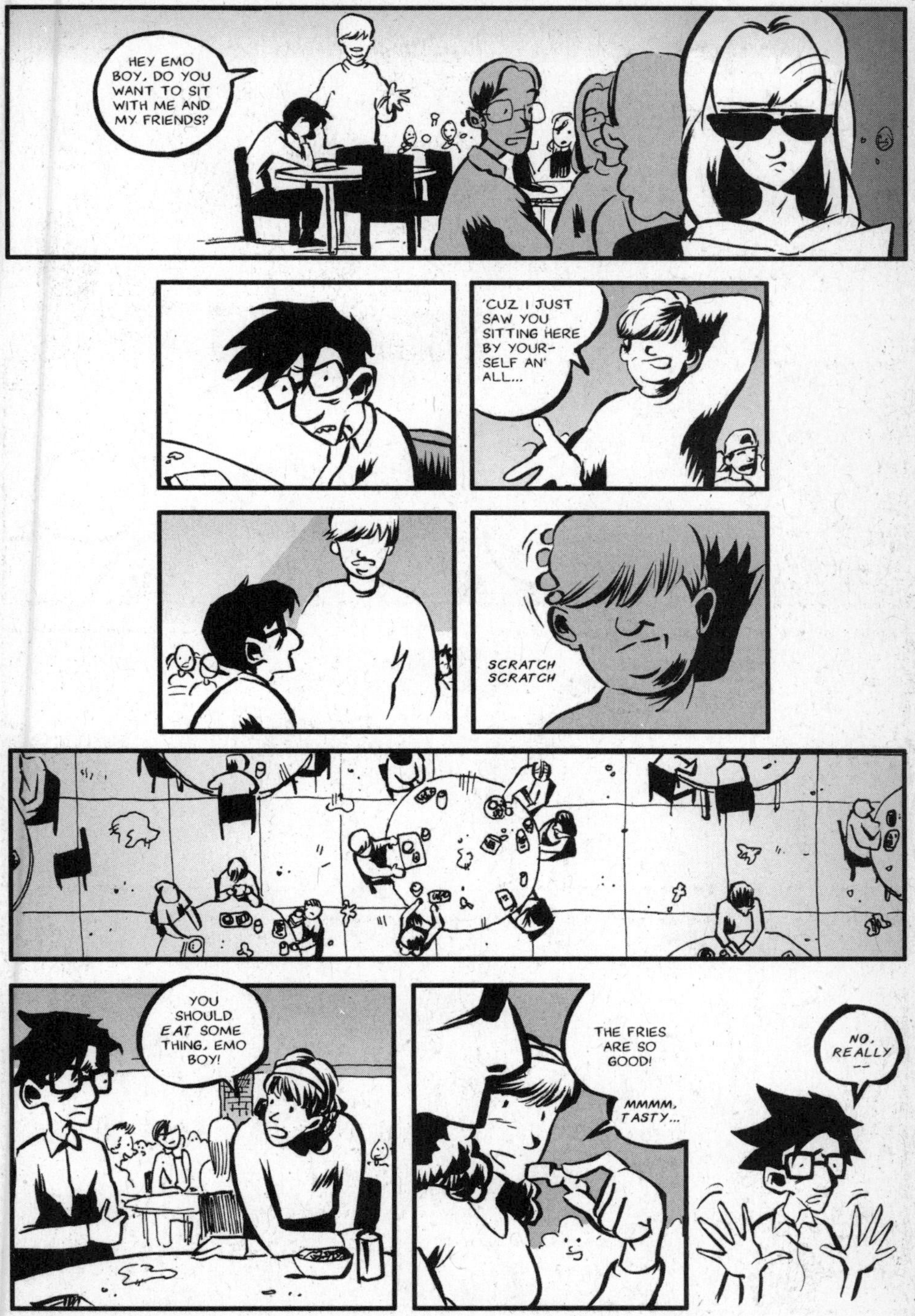
HEY EMO BOY, DO YOU WANT TO SIT WITH ME AND MY FRIENDS?
'CUZ I JUST SAW YOU SITTING HERE BY YOUR-SELF AN' ALL...
SCRATCH SCRATCH
YOU SHOULD EAT SOME THING, EMO BOY!
THE FRIES ARE SO GOOD!
MMMM, TASTY...
NO, REALLY --

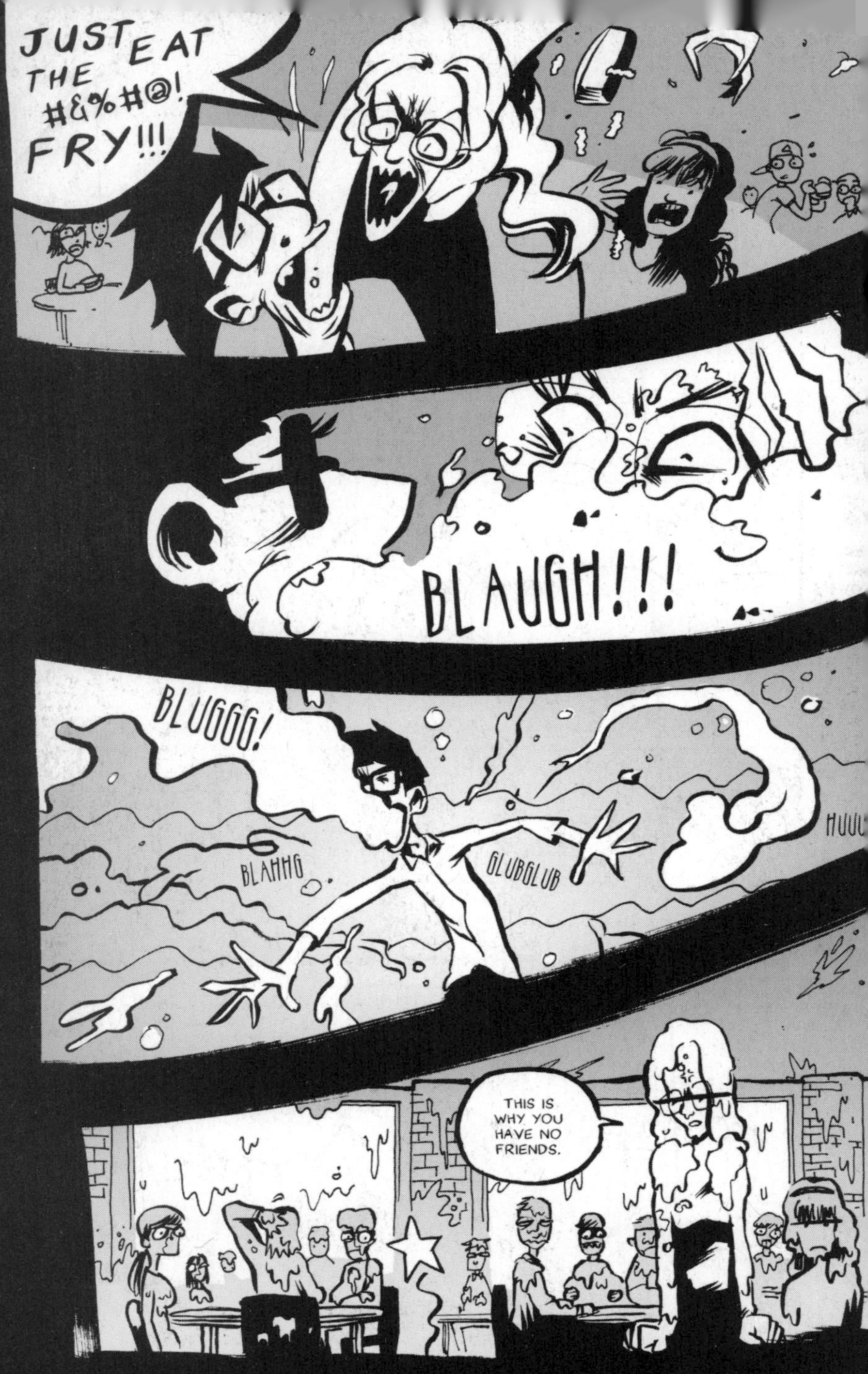
JUST EAT THE #&%#@! FRY!!!
BLAUGH!!!
BLUGGG!
BLAHHG
GLUBGLUB
HUUU
THIS IS WHY YOU HAVE NO FRIENDS.

STICKS AND STONES MAY BREAK MY BONES...

...but Dodgeball's gonna kill me.

story and art by Steve Emond

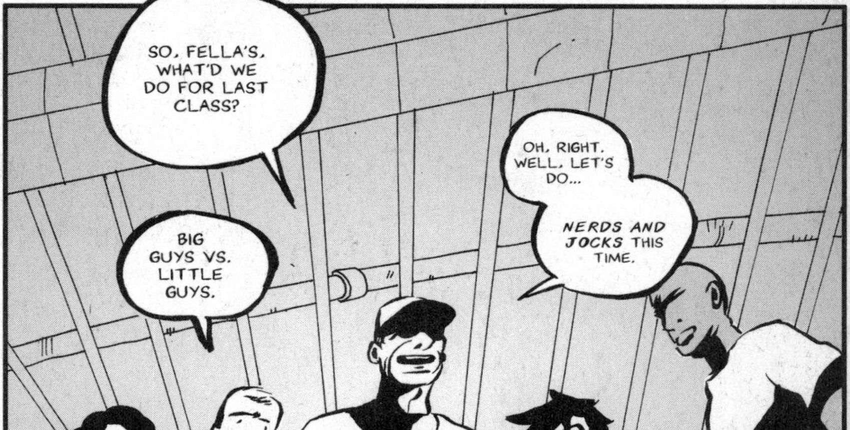
SO, FELLA'S, WHAT'D WE DO FOR LAST CLASS?
BIG GUYS VS. LITTLE GUYS.
OH, RIGHT. WELL, LET'S DO...
NERDS AND JOCKS THIS TIME.

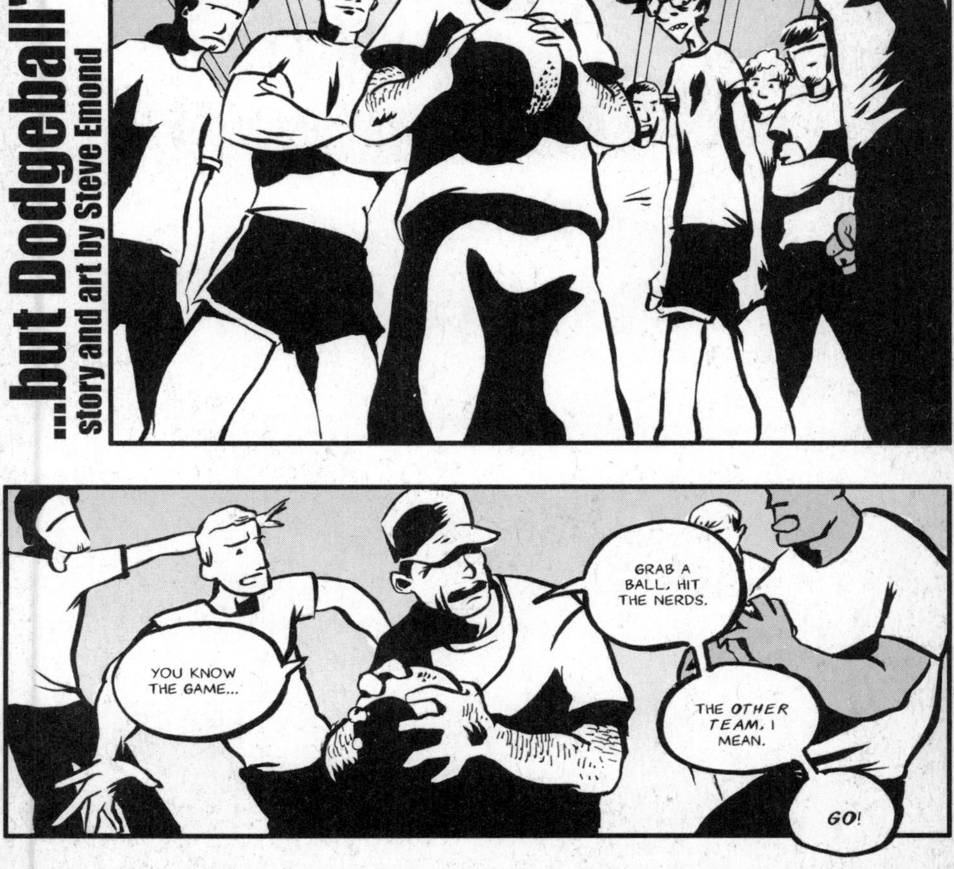
YOU KNOW THE GAME...
GRAB A BALL, HIT THE NERDS.
THE OTHER TEAM, I MEAN.
GO!

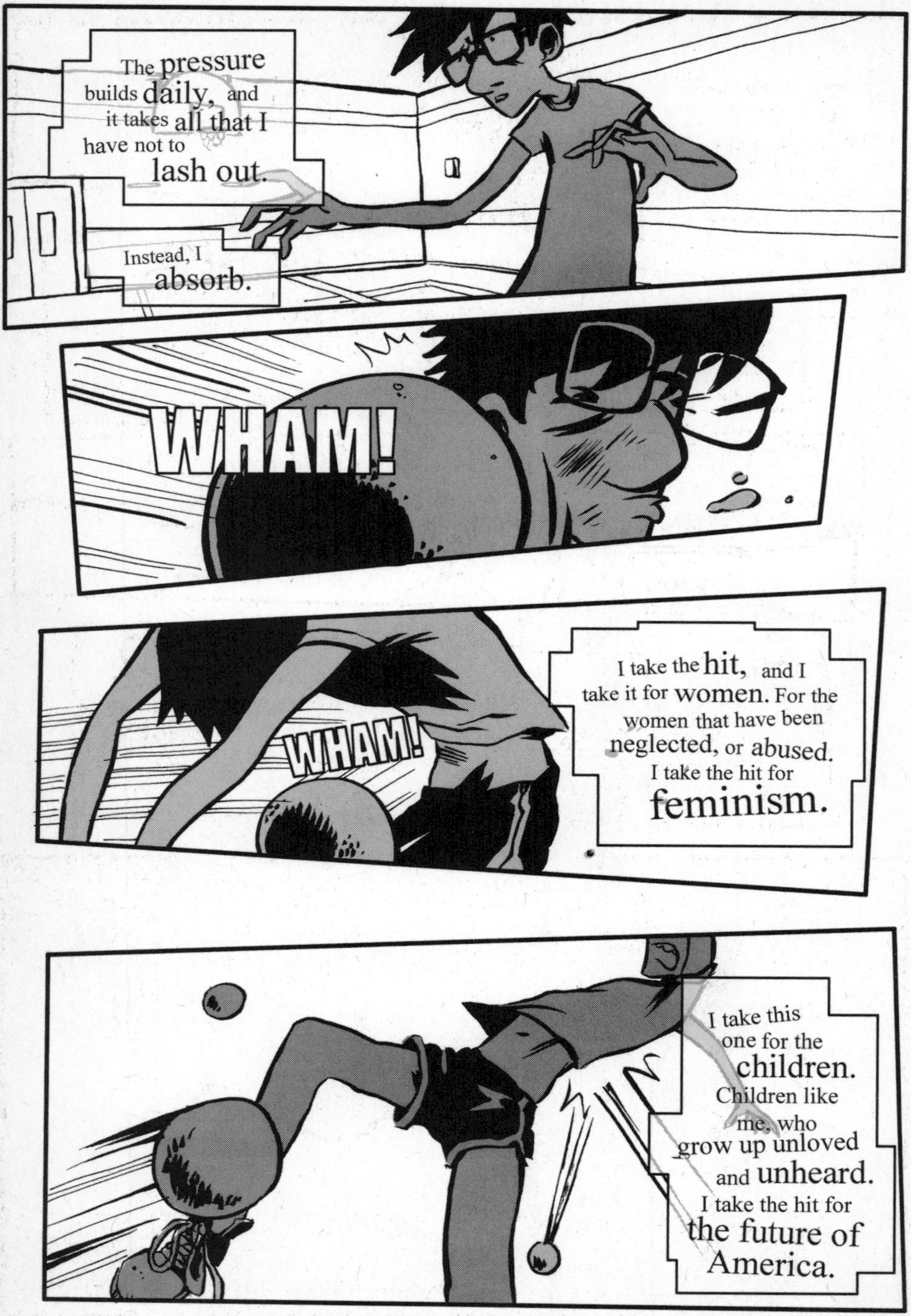
The pressure builds daily, and it takes all that I have not to lash out.
Instead, I absorb.
WHAM!
WHAM!
I take the hit, and I take it for women. For the women that have been neglected, or abused. I take the hit for feminism.
I take this one for the children. Children like me, who grow up unloved and unheard. I take the hit for the future of America.

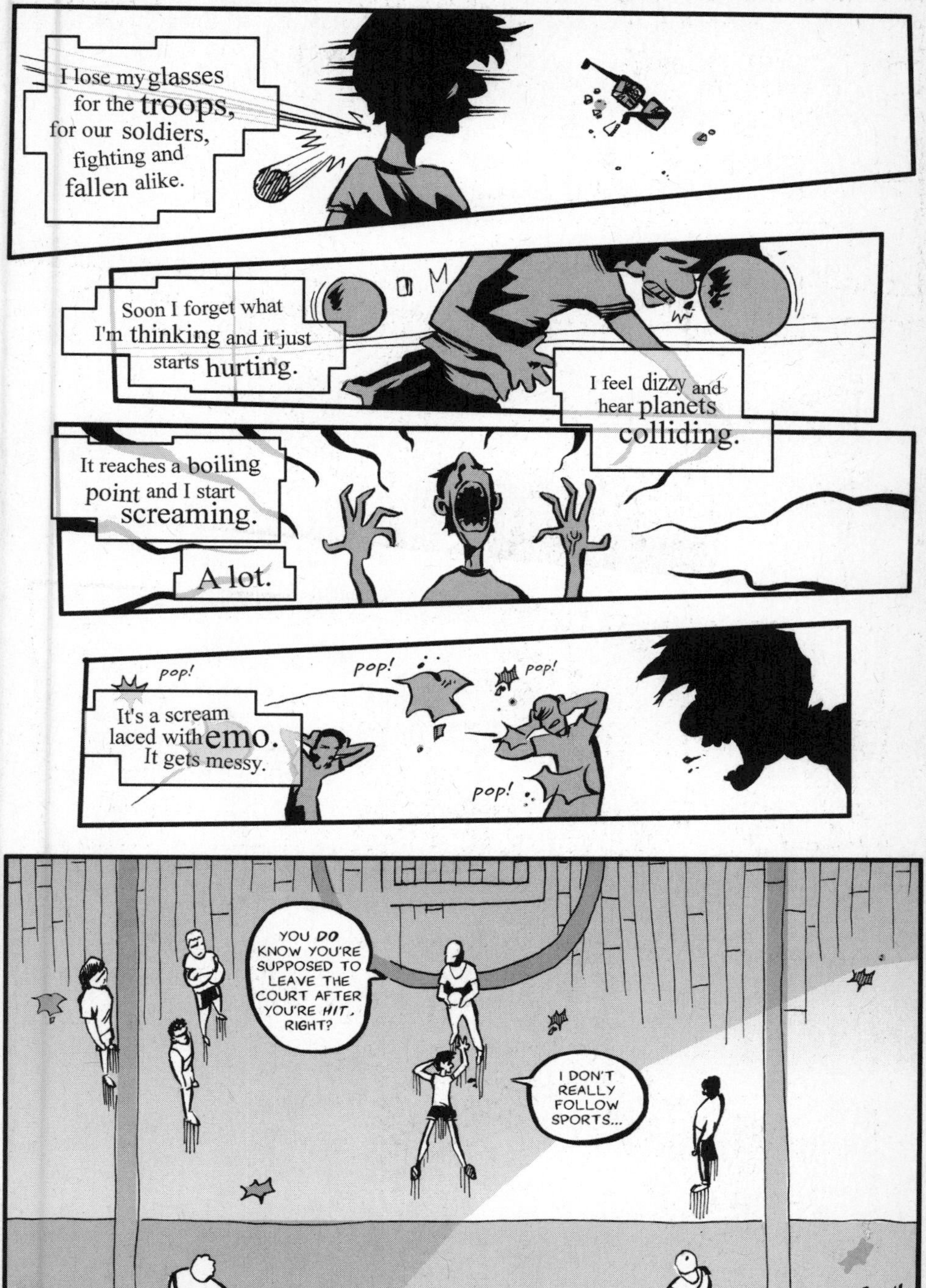
I lose my glasses for the troops, for our soldiers, fighting and fallen alike.
Soon I forget what I'm thinking and it just starts hurting.
I feel dizzy and hear planets colliding.
It reaches a boiling point and I start screaming.
A lot.
pop!
It's a scream laced with emo. It gets messy.
pop!
pop!
pop!
YOU DO KNOW YOU'RE SUPPOSED TO LEAVE THE COURT AFTER YOU'RE HIT, RIGHT?
I DON'T REALLY FOLLOW SPORTS...
The End!

Emo Boy 1990-2005

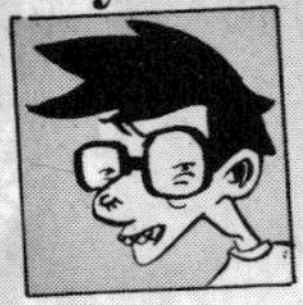

Emo Boy, 15, died this week of causes unknown, but seemingly stemmed from the great amounts of emo he is well-known for. He died early in the morning at home, after a routinely sleepless night.

Born in 1990, Emo Boy had little recollection of his upbringing. He lived with his friend Maxine Butters and her family for the majority of his short and horrendous life.

A student in the 9th grade, Emo Boy suffered severe unpopularity and failing grades. Despite this, he was known to have a rather large ego and very little of anything to back it up. Aside from Maxine, he had no friends. His classmates did acknowledge his passing, however, with a pizza party. Naples from downtown donated several large pizzas free of charge to help celebrate the event.

While Emo Boy accomplished little in class, he was quite famous outside of the school for what can only be called his emo "powers". These powers were often very stupid and did not help the community in any visible way. Such powers as projectile vomiting and cranial-explosions had become somewhat routine to Emo Boy, causing a mass headache for most of the townsfolk. Trouble followed Emo Boy everywhere in life, and we can only assume it will continue in death.

Emo Boy had several hobbies, including listening to depressing music and writing bad poetry. He was often overheard mumbling said poetry to himself when thought to be alone. He also played guitar; his crowning achievement being his dreadful dedication to the lovely and sorely missed Jennie Finch at this years high school talent show, which surely has earned him a place in Hell.

Not that we editorialize around here.

Cool Kids Get Laid More than Nerds

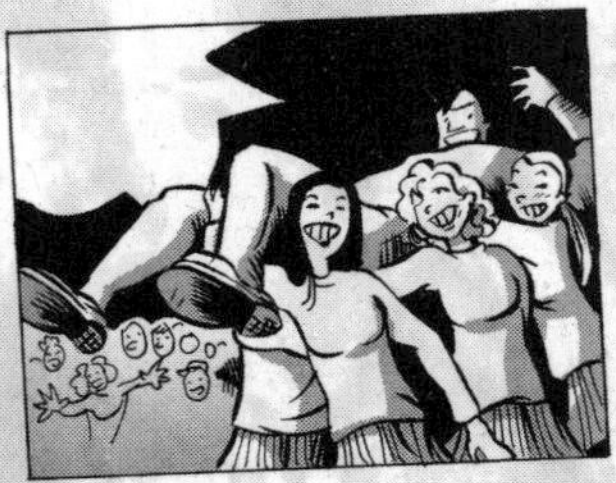

A recent poll shows that the cooler kids in school get more attention from the opposite sex than their nerdier counterparts. High school Freshman Drew Somerville understands it to be a normal part of today's culture. "Hey, if I'm going to spend time working out, and combing my hair, I would expect to get some female attention. Just like if I

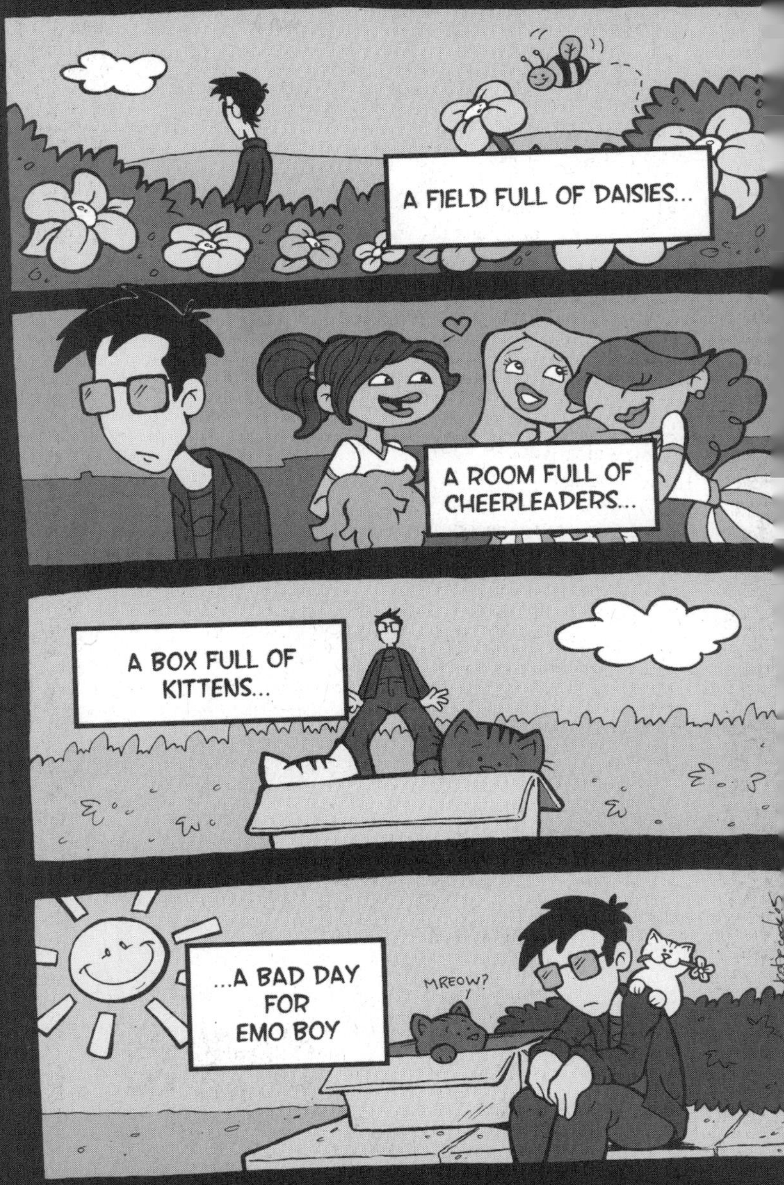
A FIELD FULL OF DAISIES...
A ROOM FULL OF CHEERLEADERS...
A BOX FULL OF KITTENS...
...A BAD DAY FOR EMO BOY
MREOW?

"A BAD DAY FOR EMO BOY"
BY KATIE COOK

Emo Boy Pinup by Katie C

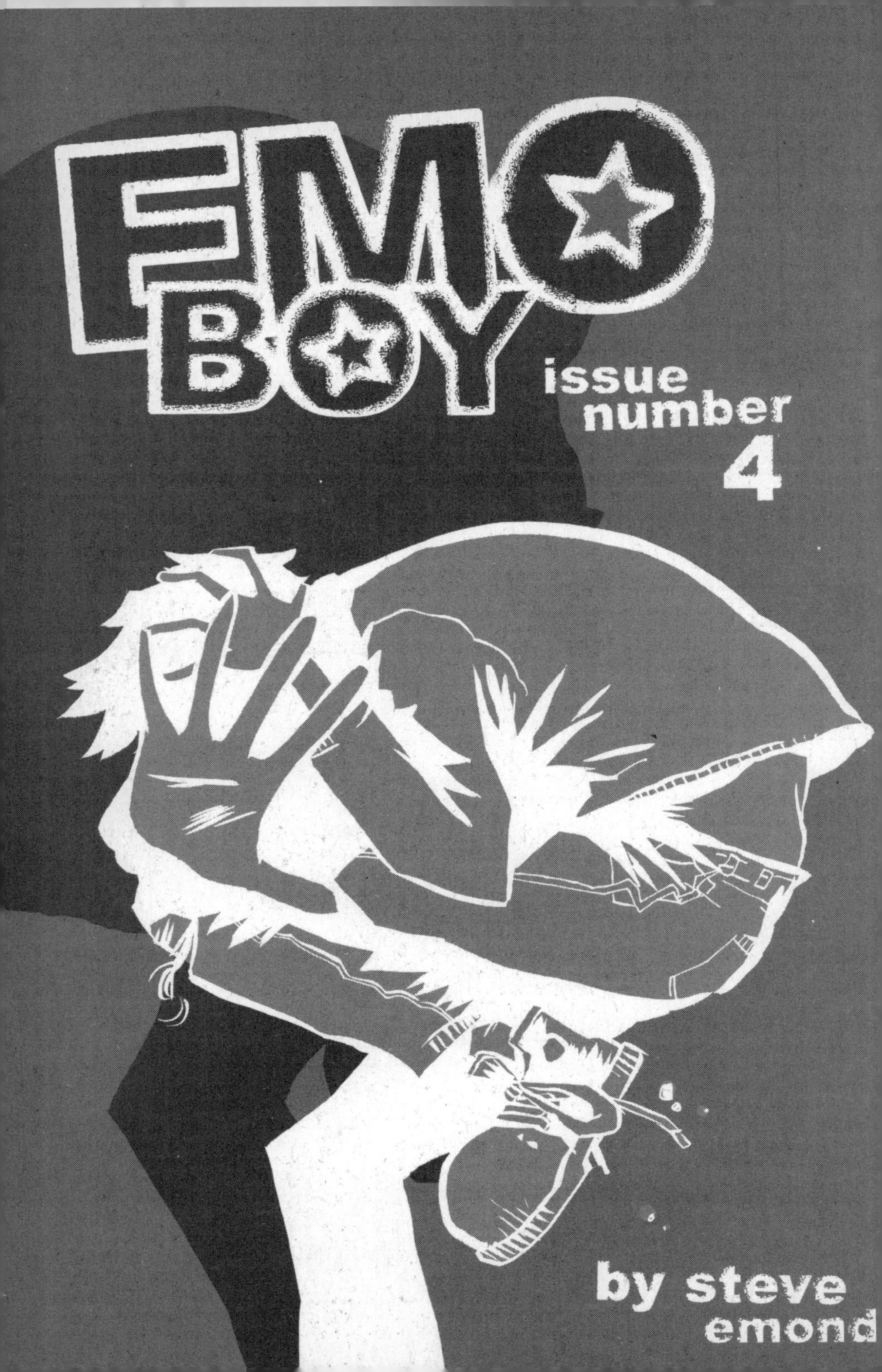
EMO BOY
issue number 4
by steve emond

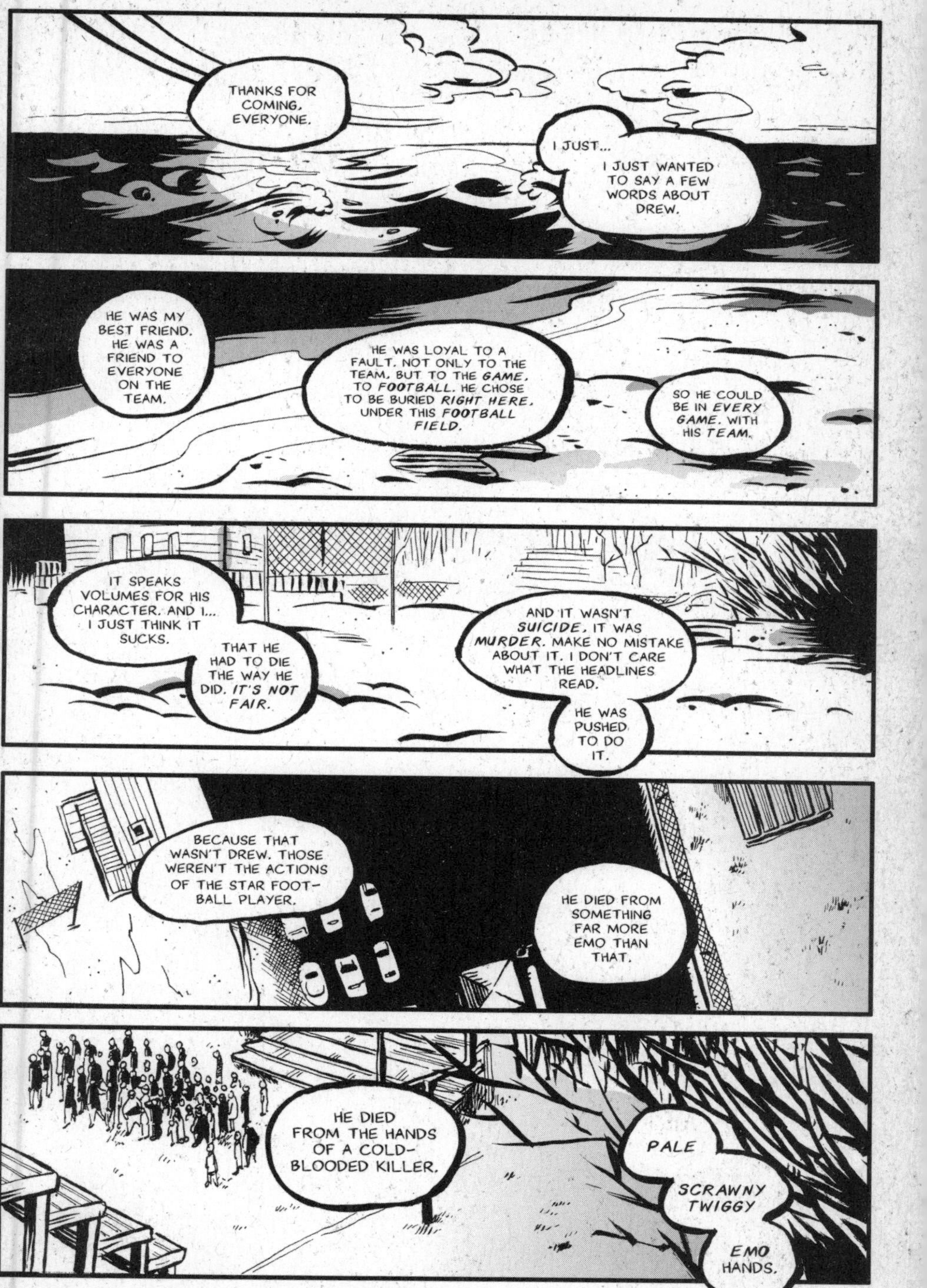
THANKS FOR COMING, EVERYONE.
I JUST...
I JUST WANTED TO SAY A FEW WORDS ABOUT DREW.
HE WAS MY BEST FRIEND. HE WAS A FRIEND TO EVERYONE ON THE TEAM.
HE WAS LOYAL TO A FAULT. NOT ONLY TO THE TEAM, BUT TO THE *GAME*, TO *FOOTBALL*. HE CHOSE TO BE BURIED *RIGHT HERE*, UNDER THIS *FOOTBALL FIELD*.
SO HE COULD BE IN *EVERY GAME*, WITH HIS *TEAM*.
IT SPEAKS VOLUMES FOR HIS CHARACTER, AND I... I JUST THINK IT SUCKS.
THAT HE HAD TO DIE THE WAY HE DID. *IT'S NOT FAIR*.
AND IT WASN'T *SUICIDE*, IT WAS *MURDER*. MAKE NO MISTAKE ABOUT IT. I DON'T CARE WHAT THE HEADLINES READ.
HE WAS PUSHED TO DO IT.
BECAUSE THAT WASN'T DREW. THOSE WEREN'T THE ACTIONS OF THE STAR FOOT-BALL PLAYER.
HE DIED FROM SOMETHING FAR MORE EMO THAN THAT.
HE DIED FROM THE HANDS OF A COLD-BLOODED KILLER.
PALE
SCRAWNY TWIGGY
EMO HANDS.

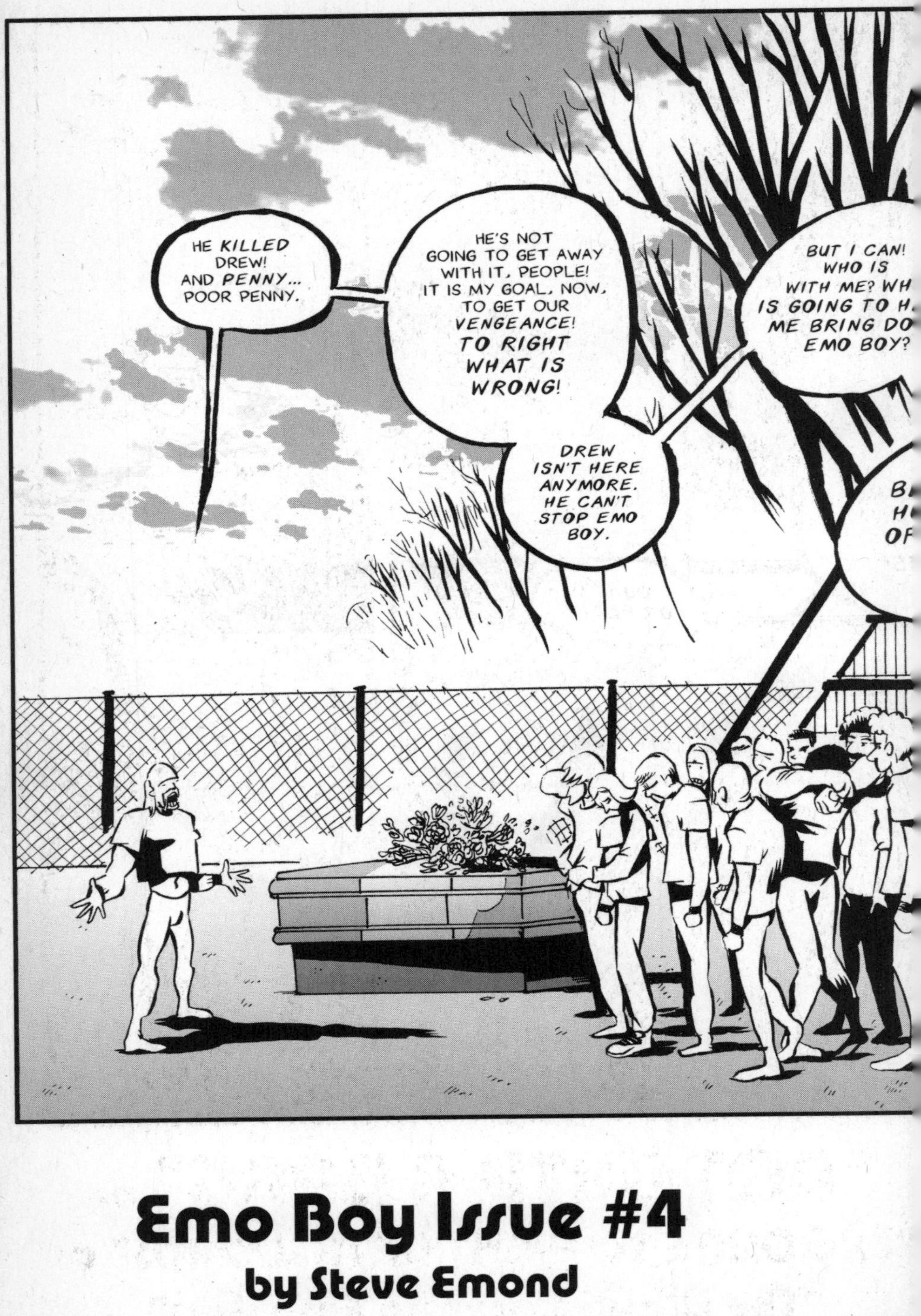
HE KILLED DREW! AND PENNY... POOR PENNY.
HE'S NOT GOING TO GET AWAY WITH IT, PEOPLE! IT IS MY GOAL, NOW, TO GET OUR VENGEANCE! TO RIGHT WHAT IS WRONG!
DREW ISN'T HERE ANYMORE. HE CAN'T STOP EMO BOY.
BUT I CAN! WHO IS WITH ME? WH IS GOING TO H ME BRING DO EMO BOY?

Emo Boy Issue #4

by Steve Emond

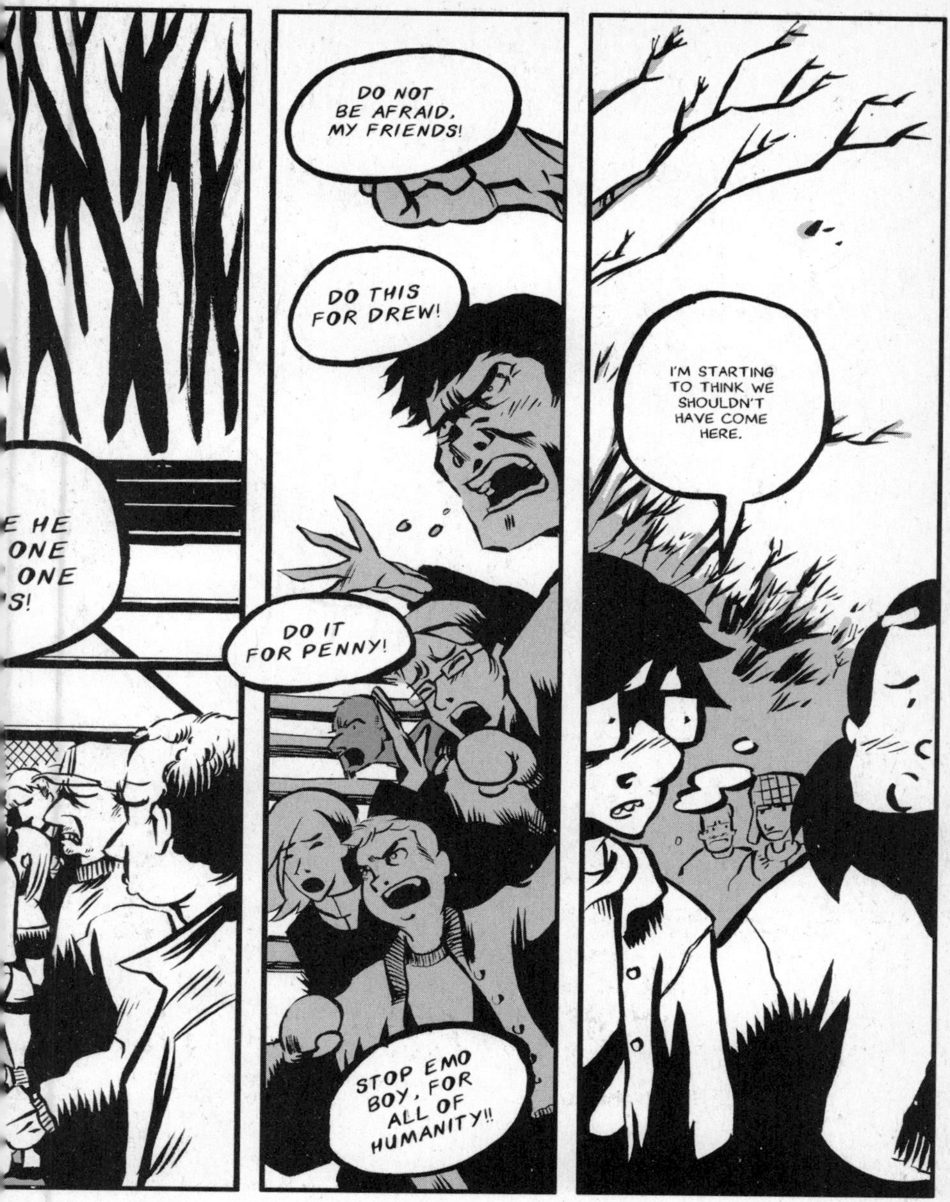
E HE
ONE
ONE
S!
DO NOT BE AFRAID, MY FRIENDS!
DO THIS FOR DREW!
DO IT FOR PENNY!
STOP EMO BOY, FOR ALL OF HUMANITY!!
I'M STARTING TO THINK WE SHOULDN'T HAVE COME HERE.

"NOT WITH A BANG" or
"CHOOSING TO FIGHT WITH WORDS" or
"The World Hates an Emo Boy"

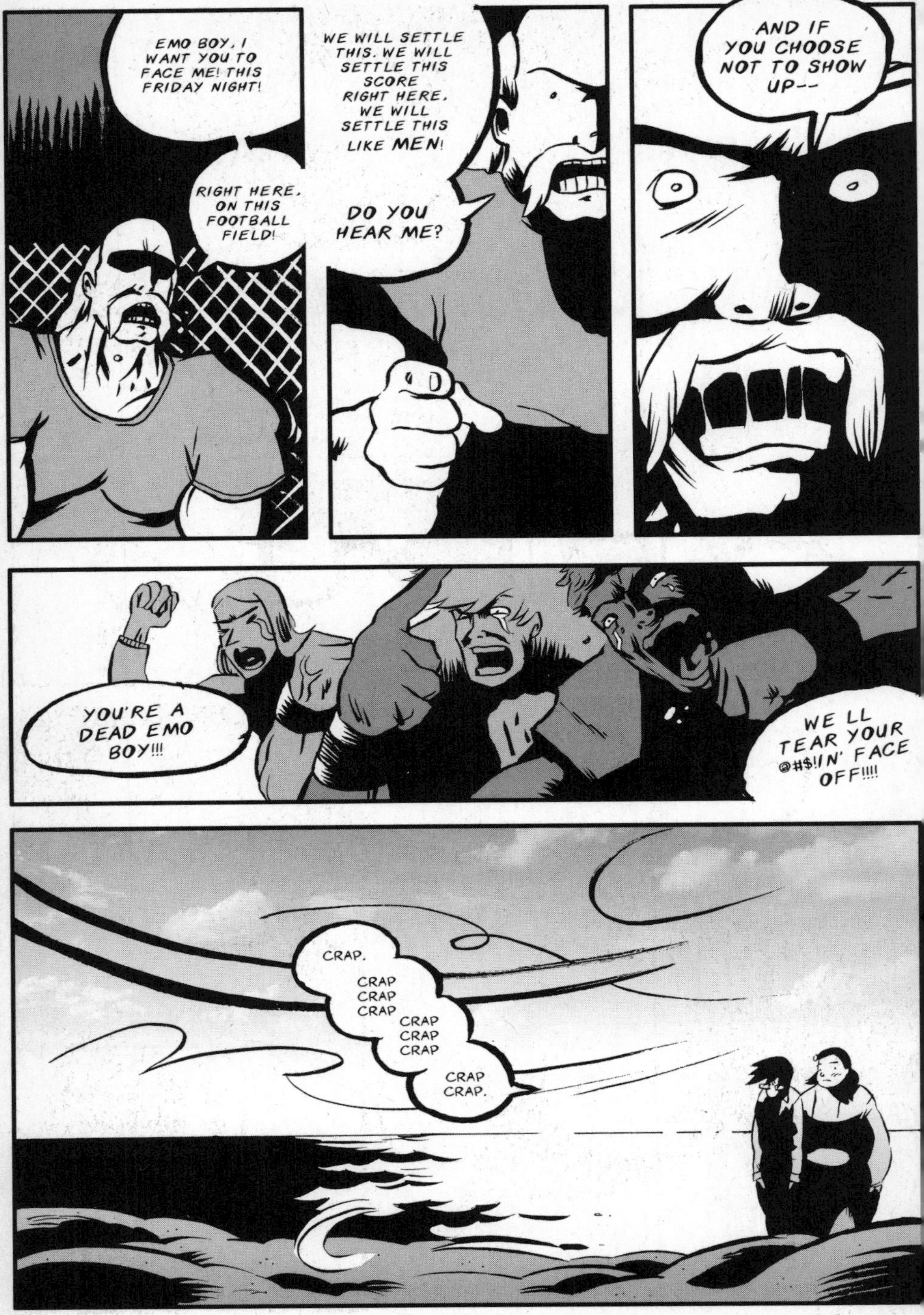
EMO BOY, I WANT YOU TO FACE ME! THIS FRIDAY NIGHT!
RIGHT HERE, ON THIS FOOTBALL FIELD!
WE WILL SETTLE THIS. WE WILL SETTLE THIS SCORE RIGHT HERE. WE WILL SETTLE THIS LIKE MEN!
DO YOU HEAR ME?
AND IF YOU CHOOSE NOT TO SHOW UP--
YOU'RE A DEAD EMO BOY!!!
WE LL TEAR YOUR @#$!IN' FACE OFF!!!!
CRAP.
CRAP CRAP CRAP
CRAP CRAP CRAP
CRAP CRAP.

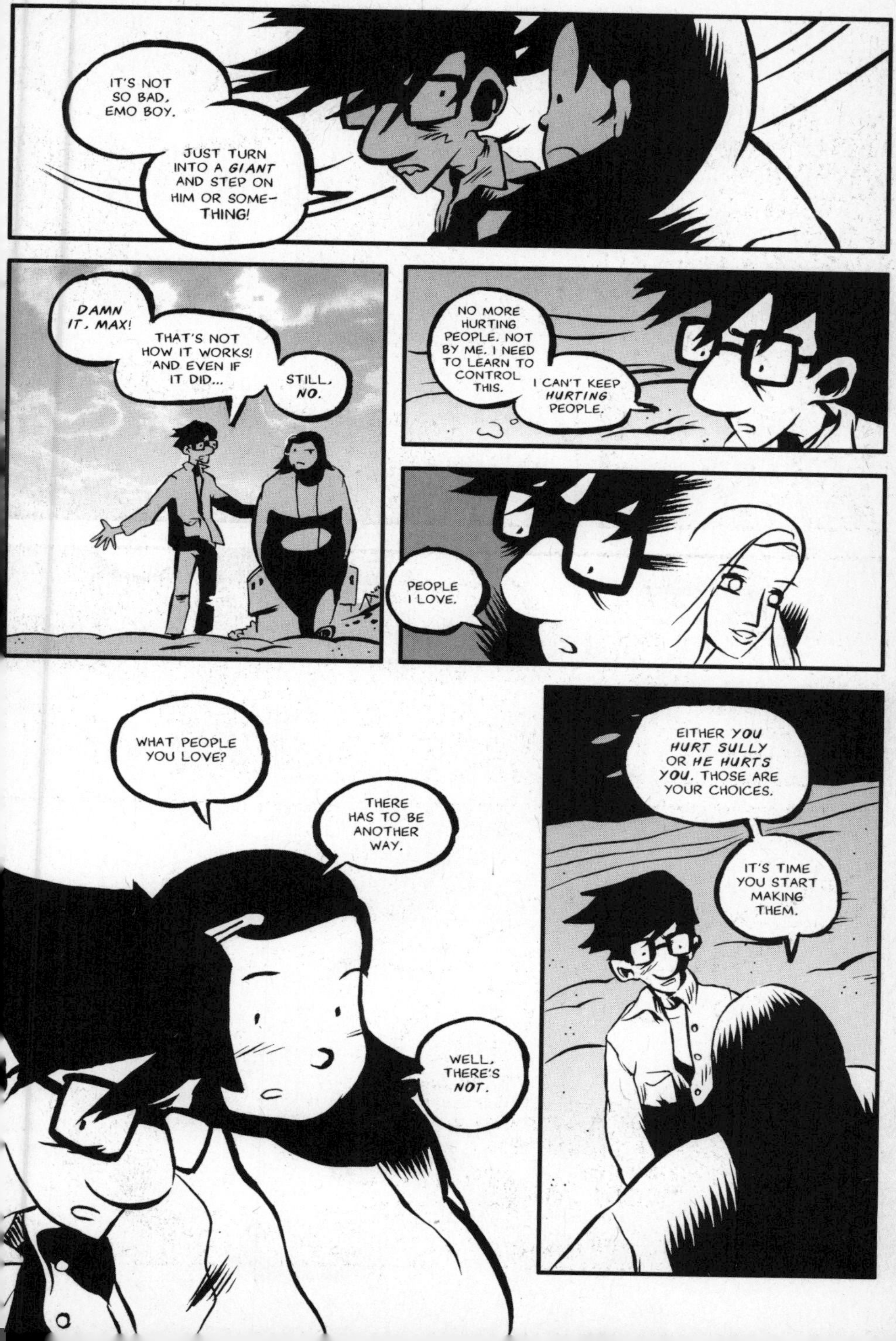
IT'S NOT SO BAD, EMO BOY.
JUST TURN INTO A GIANT AND STEP ON HIM OR SOME-THING!
DAMN IT, MAX!
THAT'S NOT HOW IT WORKS! AND EVEN IF IT DID...
STILL, NO.
NO MORE HURTING PEOPLE. NOT BY ME. I NEED TO LEARN TO CONTROL THIS.
I CAN'T KEEP HURTING PEOPLE.
PEOPLE I LOVE.
WHAT PEOPLE YOU LOVE?
THERE HAS TO BE ANOTHER WAY.
WELL, THERE'S NOT.
EITHER YOU HURT SULLY OR HE HURTS YOU. THOSE ARE YOUR CHOICES.
IT'S TIME YOU START MAKING THEM.

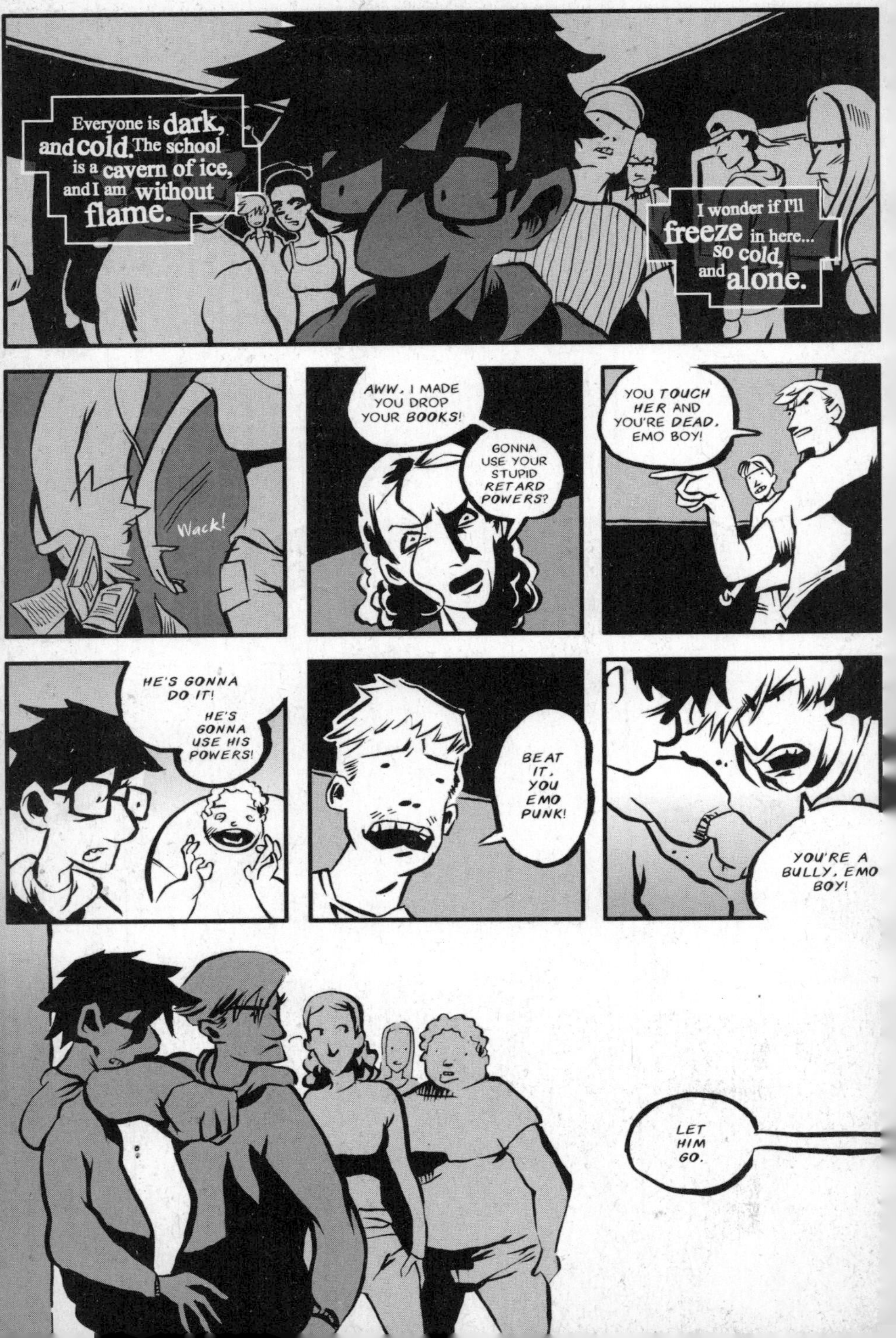
Everyone is dark, and cold. The school is a cavern of ice, and I am without flame.
I wonder if I'll freeze in here... so cold, and alone.
Wack!
AWW, I MADE YOU DROP YOUR BOOKS!
GONNA USE YOUR STUPID RETARD POWERS?
YOU TOUCH HER AND YOU'RE DEAD, EMO BOY!
HE'S GONNA DO IT!
HE'S GONNA USE HIS POWERS!
BEAT IT, YOU EMO PUNK!
YOU'RE A BULLY, EMO BOY!
LET HIM GO.

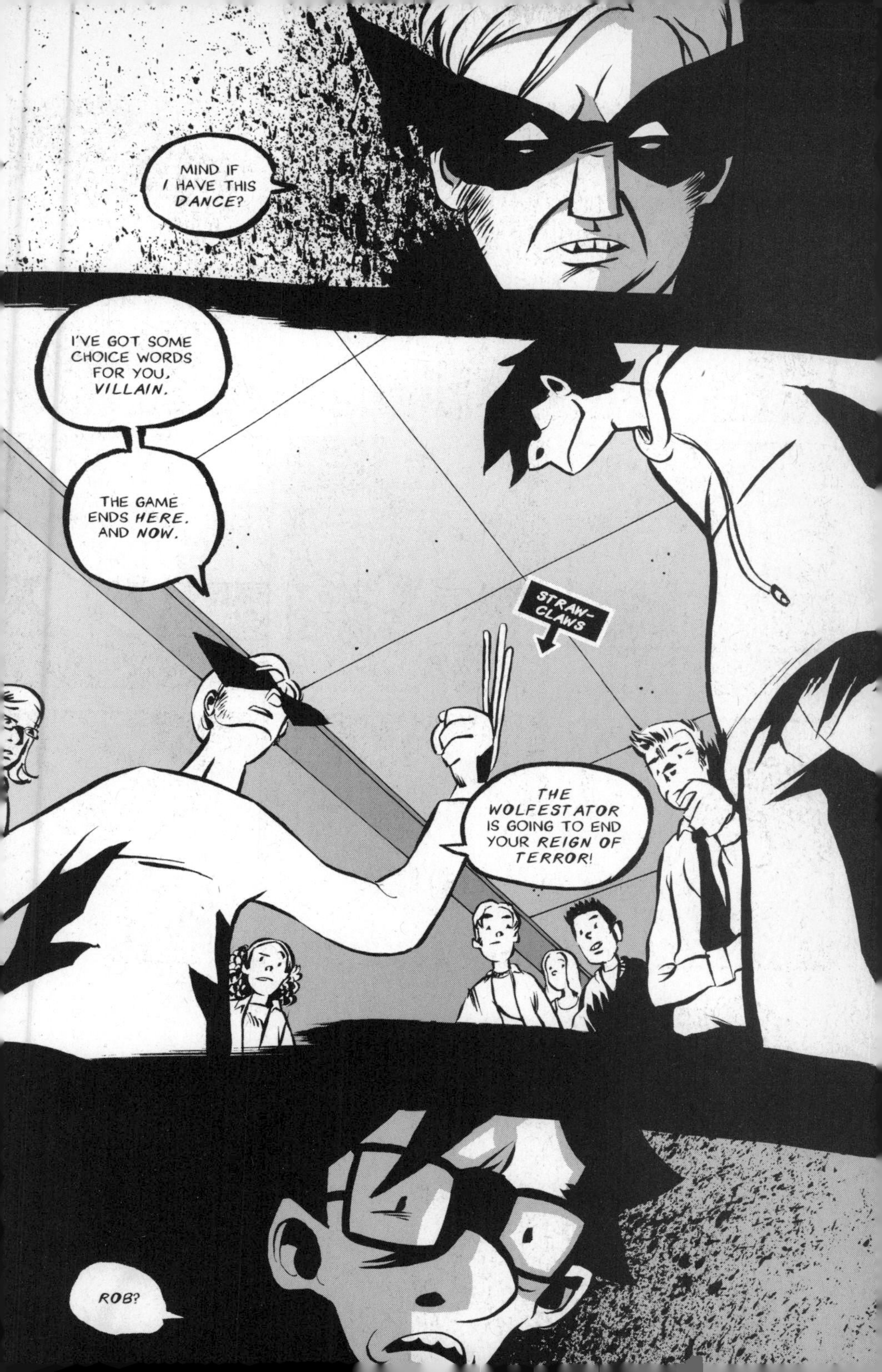
MIND IF I HAVE THIS *DANCE*?
I'VE GOT SOME CHOICE WORDS FOR YOU, *VILLAIN.*
THE GAME ENDS *HERE.* AND *NOW.*
STRAW-CLAWS
THE WOLFESTATOR IS GOING TO END YOUR *REIGN OF TERROR*!
ROB?

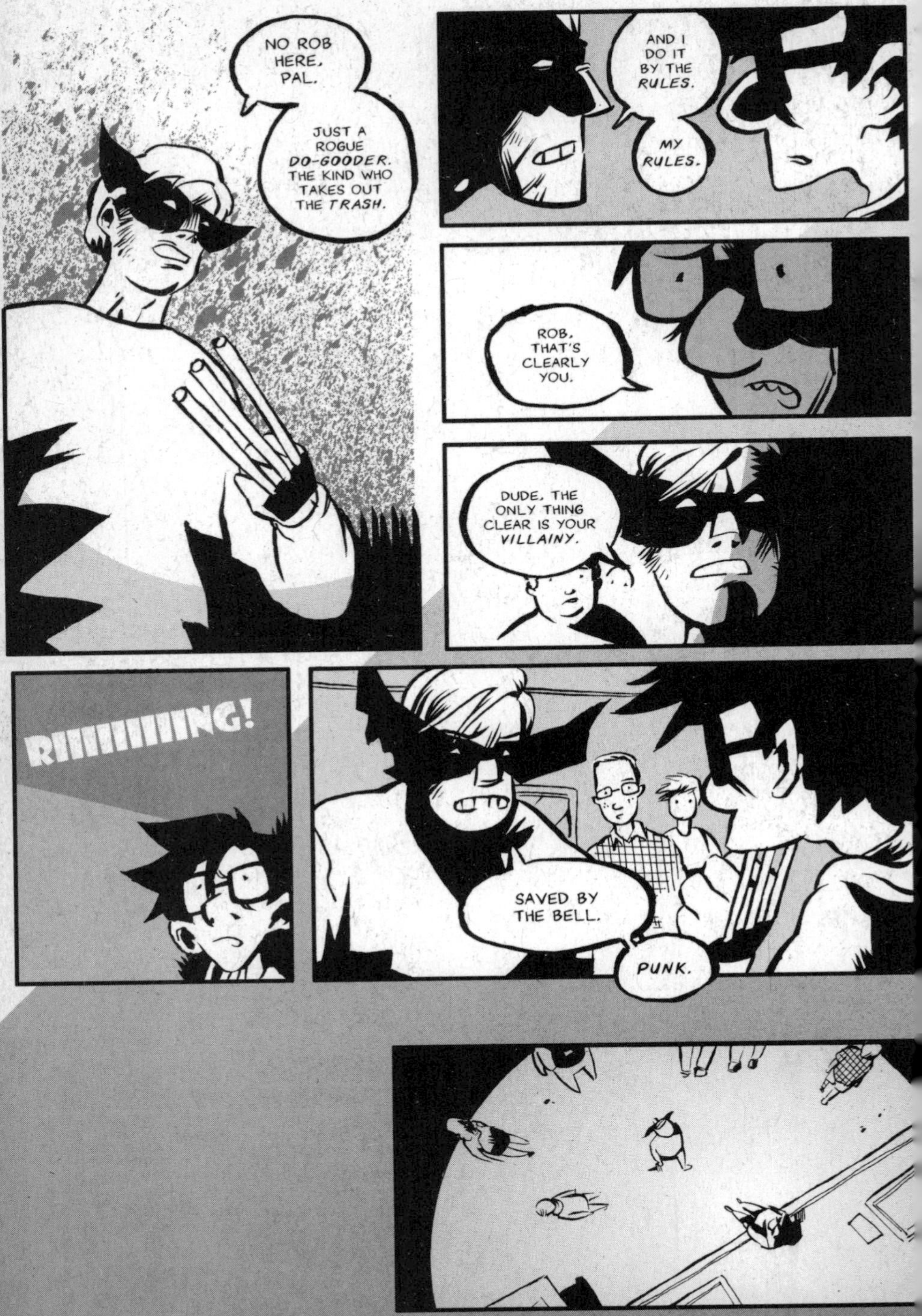
NO ROB HERE, PAL.
JUST A ROGUE *DO-GOODER*. THE KIND WHO TAKES OUT THE *TRASH*.
AND I DO IT BY THE *RULES*.
MY *RULES*.
ROB, THAT'S CLEARLY YOU.
DUDE, THE ONLY THING CLEAR IS YOUR *VILLAINY*.
RIIIIIIIIING!
SAVED BY THE BELL.
PUNK.

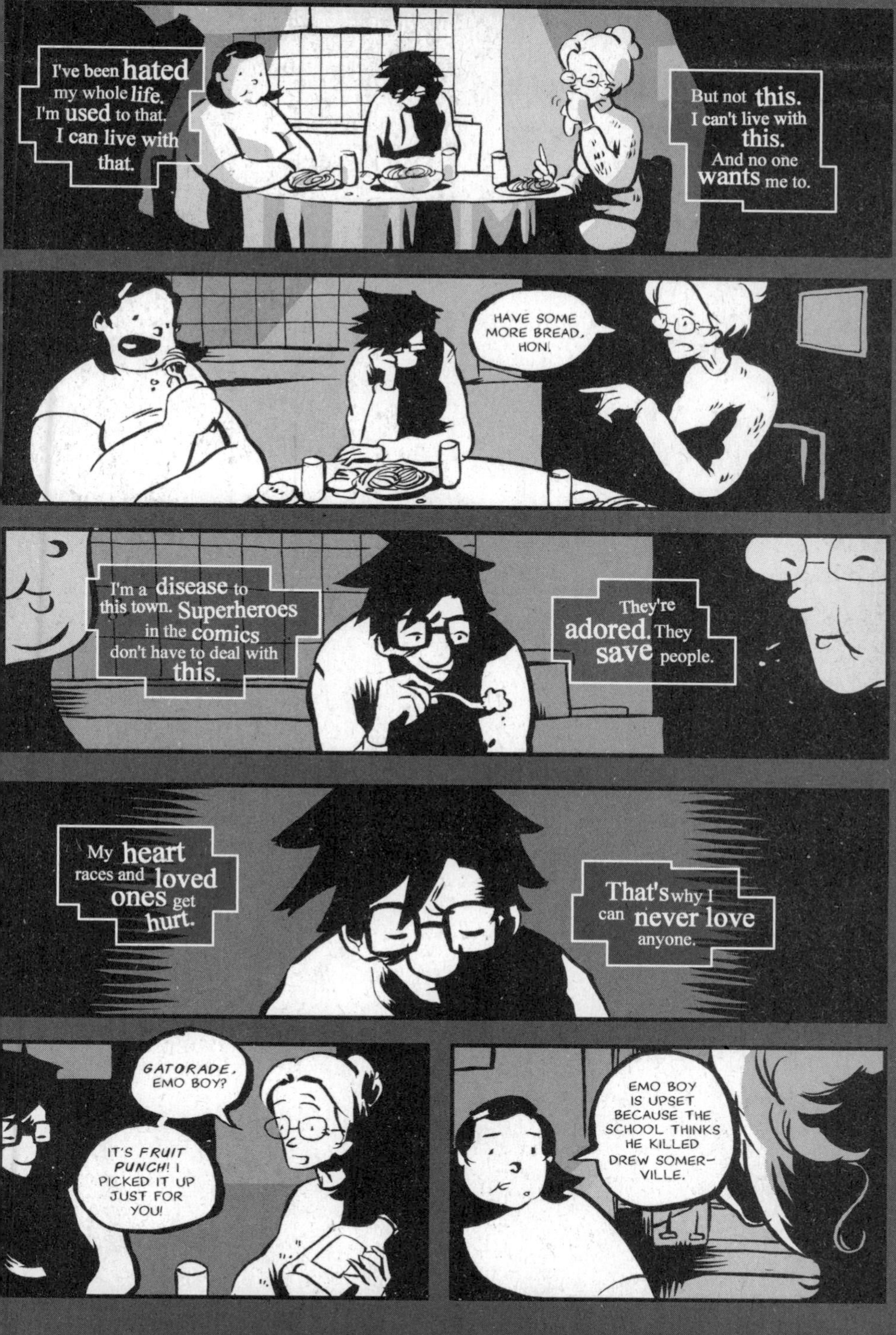

I've been hated my whole life. I'm used to that. I can live with that.
But not this. I can't live with this. And no one wants me to.
HAVE SOME MORE BREAD, HON.
I'm a disease to this town. Superheroes in the comics don't have to deal with this.
They're adored. They save people.
My heart races and loved ones get hurt.
That's why I can never love anyone.
GATORADE, EMO BOY?
IT'S FRUIT PUNCH! I PICKED IT UP JUST FOR YOU!
EMO BOY IS UPSET BECAUSE THE SCHOOL THINKS HE KILLED DREW SOMER-VILLE.

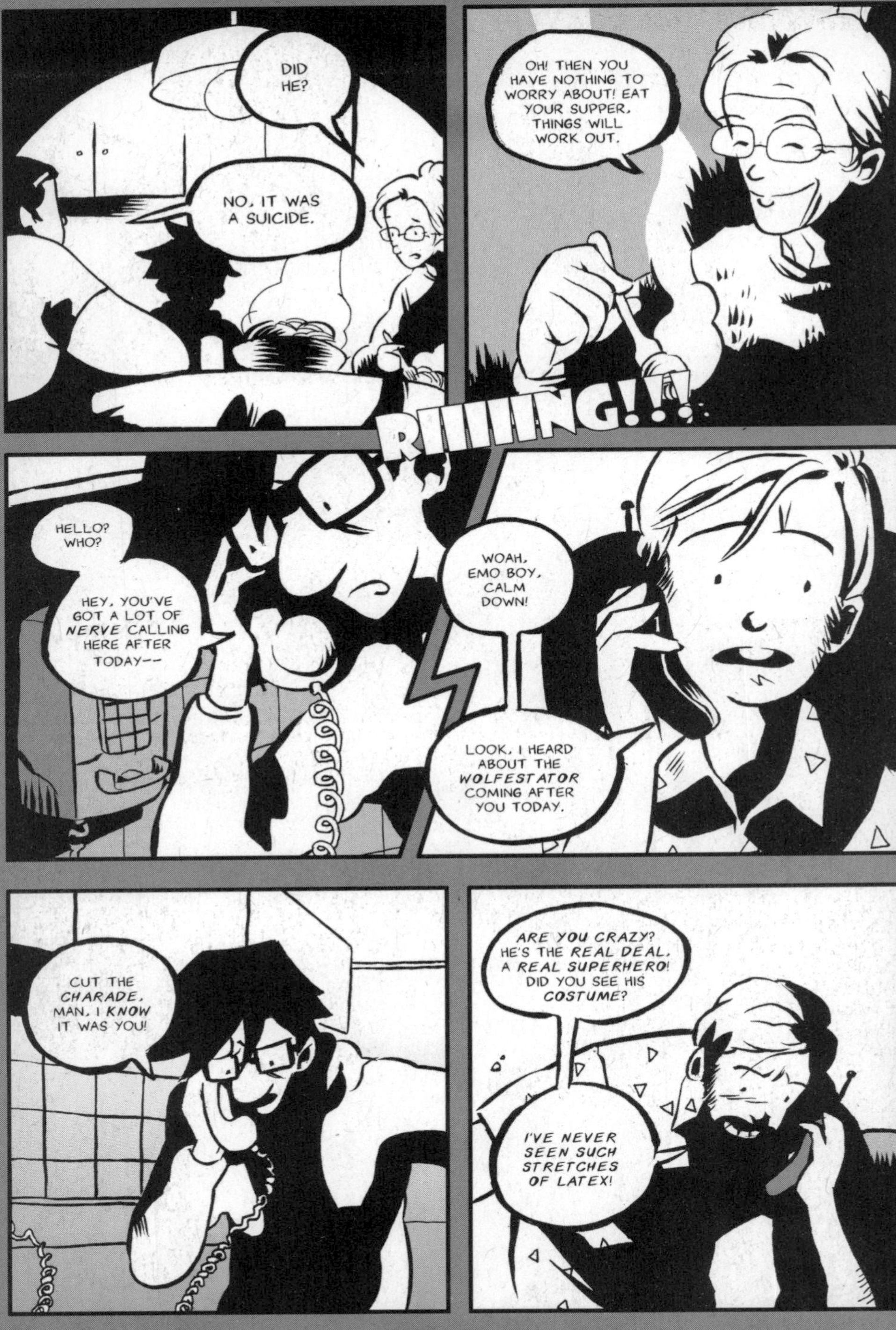
DID HE?
NO, IT WAS A SUICIDE.
OH! THEN YOU HAVE NOTHING TO WORRY ABOUT! EAT YOUR SUPPER, THINGS WILL WORK OUT.
RIIIIIING!!!
HELLO? WHO?
HEY, YOU'VE GOT A LOT OF NERVE CALLING HERE AFTER TODAY--
WOAH, EMO BOY, CALM DOWN!
LOOK, I HEARD ABOUT THE WOLFESTATOR COMING AFTER YOU TODAY.
CUT THE CHARADE, MAN, I KNOW IT WAS YOU!
ARE YOU CRAZY? HE'S THE REAL DEAL, A REAL SUPERHERO! DID YOU SEE HIS COSTUME?
I'VE NEVER SEEN SUCH STRETCHES OF LATEX!

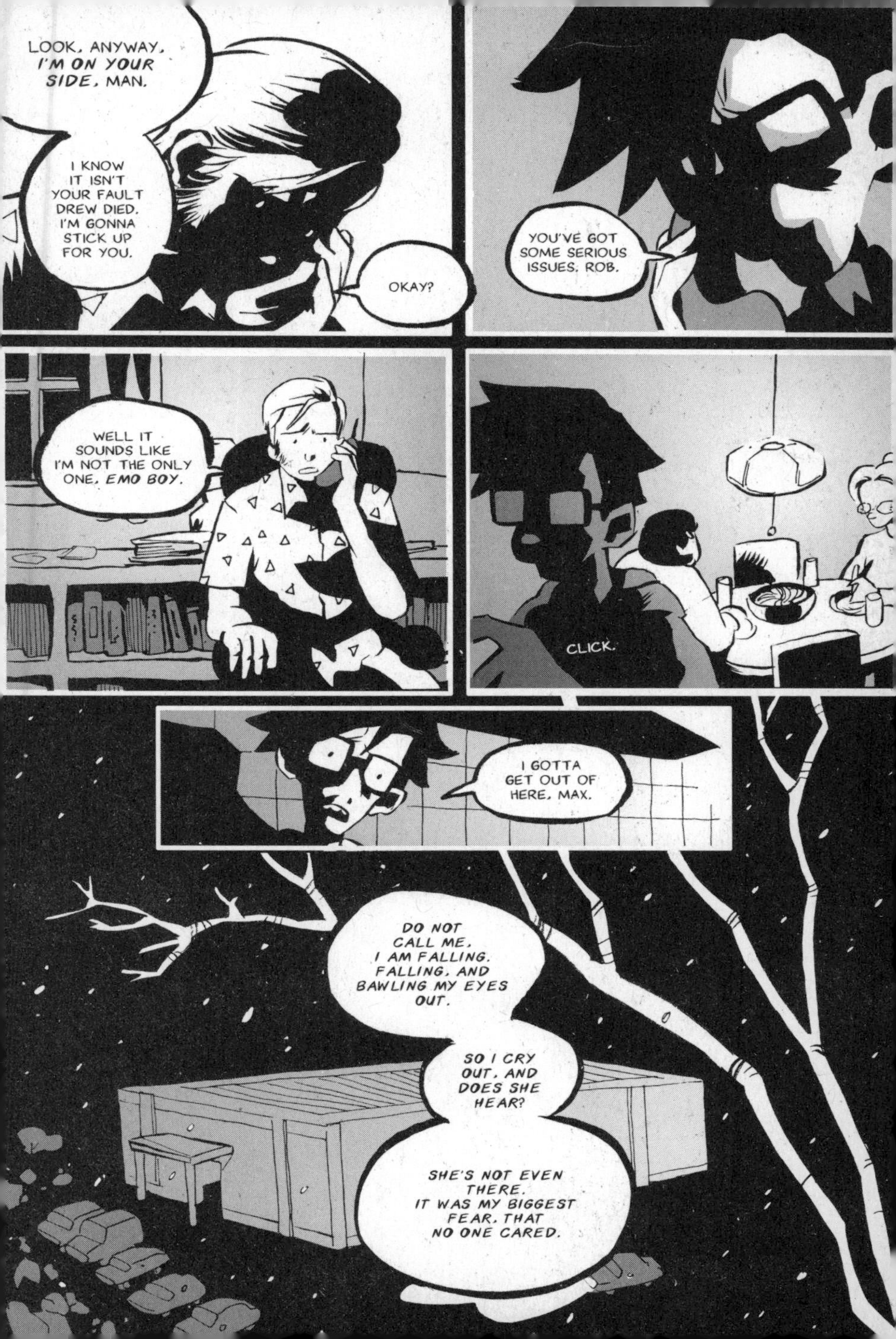
LOOK, ANYWAY, I'M ON YOUR SIDE, MAN.
I KNOW IT ISN'T YOUR FAULT DREW DIED. I'M GONNA STICK UP FOR YOU.
OKAY?
YOU'VE GOT SOME SERIOUS ISSUES, ROB.
WELL IT SOUNDS LIKE I'M NOT THE ONLY ONE, EMO BOY.
CLICK.
I GOTTA GET OUT OF HERE, MAX.
DO NOT CALL ME, I AM FALLING. FALLING, AND BAWLING MY EYES OUT.
SO I CRY OUT, AND DOES SHE HEAR?
SHE'S NOT EVEN THERE. IT WAS MY BIGGEST FEAR, THAT NO ONE CARED.

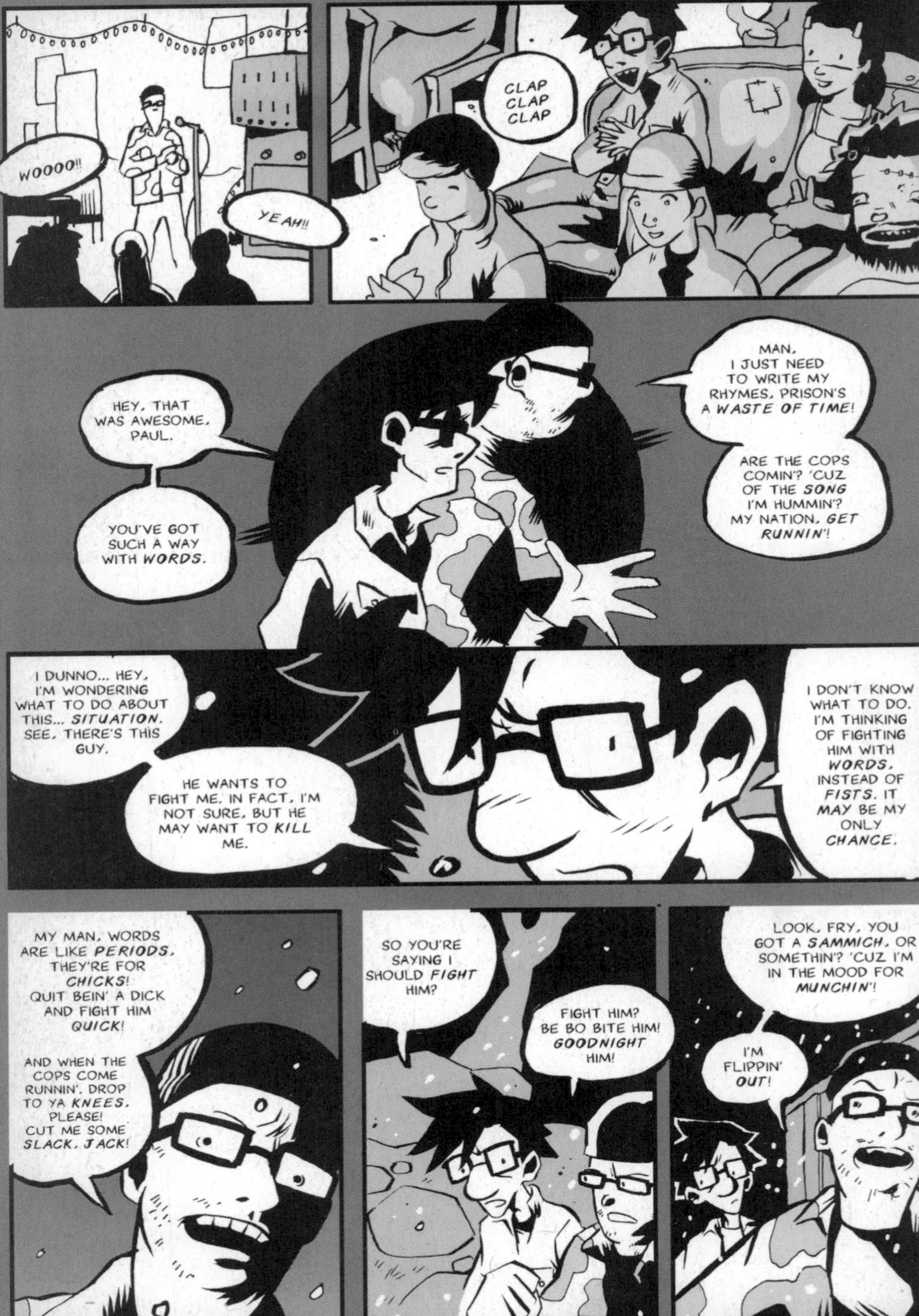
WOOOO!!
YEAH!!
CLAP CLAP CLAP
HEY, THAT WAS AWESOME, PAUL.
YOU'VE GOT SUCH A WAY WITH WORDS.
MAN, I JUST NEED TO WRITE MY RHYMES. PRISON'S A WASTE OF TIME!
ARE THE COPS COMIN'? 'CUZ OF THE SONG I'M HUMMIN'? MY NATION, GET RUNNIN'!
I DUNNO... HEY, I'M WONDERING WHAT TO DO ABOUT THIS... SITUATION. SEE, THERE'S THIS GUY.
HE WANTS TO FIGHT ME. IN FACT, I'M NOT SURE, BUT HE MAY WANT TO KILL ME.
I DON'T KNOW WHAT TO DO. I'M THINKING OF FIGHTING HIM WITH WORDS, INSTEAD OF FISTS. IT MAY BE MY ONLY CHANCE.
MY MAN, WORDS ARE LIKE PERIODS, THEY'RE FOR CHICKS! QUIT BEIN' A DICK AND FIGHT HIM QUICK!
AND WHEN THE COPS COME RUNNIN', DROP TO YA KNEES, PLEASE! CUT ME SOME SLACK, JACK!
SO YOU'RE SAYING I SHOULD FIGHT HIM?
FIGHT HIM? BE BO BITE HIM! GOODNIGHT HIM!
LOOK, FRY, YOU GOT A SAMMICH, OR SOMETHIN'? 'CUZ I'M IN THE MOOD FOR MUNCHIN'!
I'M FLIPPIN' OUT!

And I am under the **stars** and on **destiny's** doorstep.

I feel **emo.**

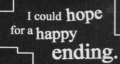

I find myself wishing this was a **tv show.** The music would cue, and swell; it would **drown** out my **thoughts.**

I could **hope** for a **happy ending.**

YOU *CAME.* GOOD BOY.

HOPE YOU'RE READY FOR A *FIGHT.*

I AM. I'M GOING TO FIGHT YOU, SULLY.

ONCE, WITH WORDS. AND IF THAT FAILS, THEN I'M GOING TO FIGHT YOU WITH MY FISTS.

WIN OR LOSE.

AND YOU'D JUST HAVE A CHANCE, TOO.

BUT DREW WAS MY TEAM MATE.

AND YOU KILLED HIM. YOU'RE A *KILLER.* AND I'M NOT ABOUT TO *DIE,* SO I BROUGHT SOME FRIENDS ALONG.

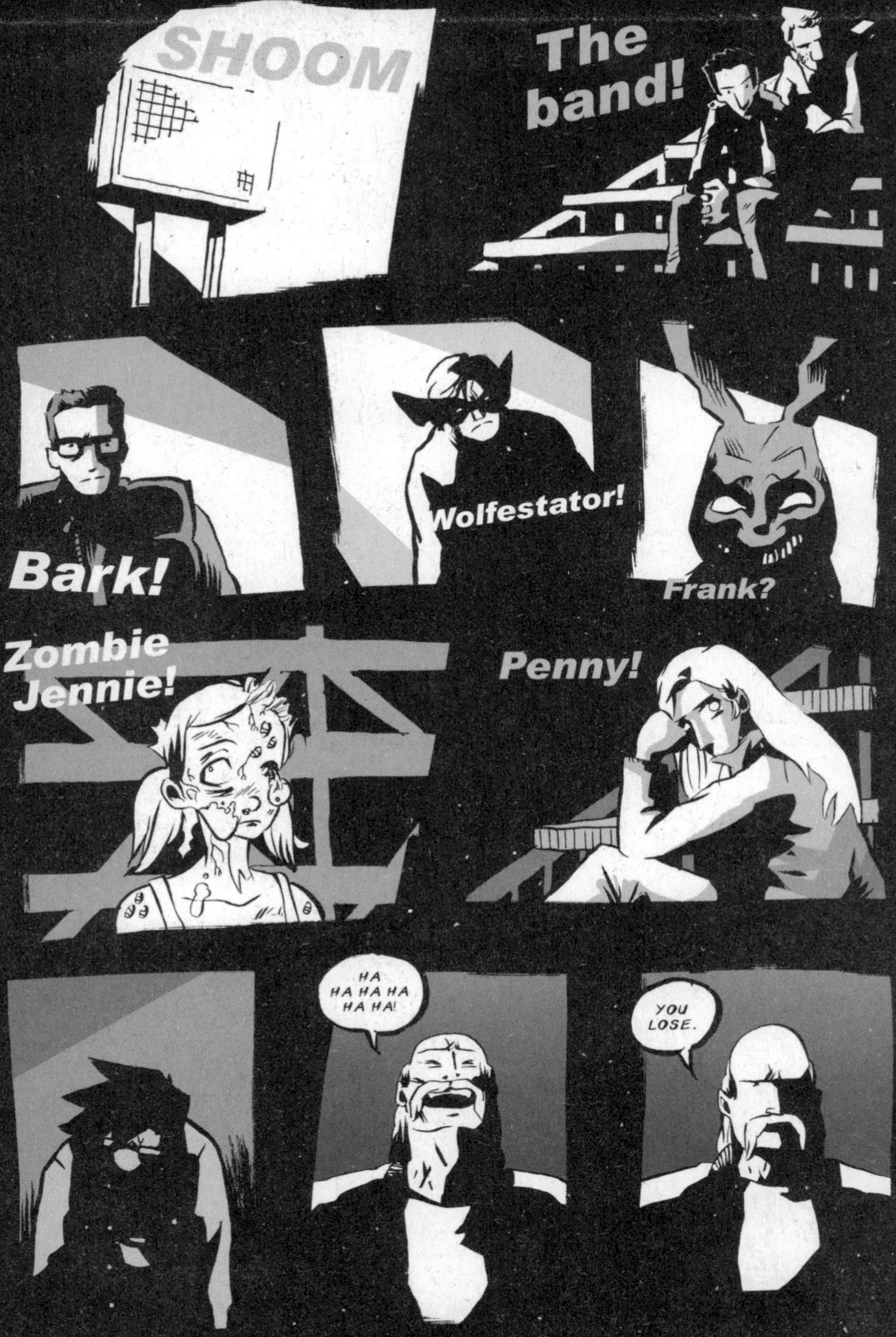
SHOOM
The band!
Bark!
Wolfestator!
Frank?
Zombie Jennie!
Penny!
HA HA HA HA HA HA!
YOU LOSE.

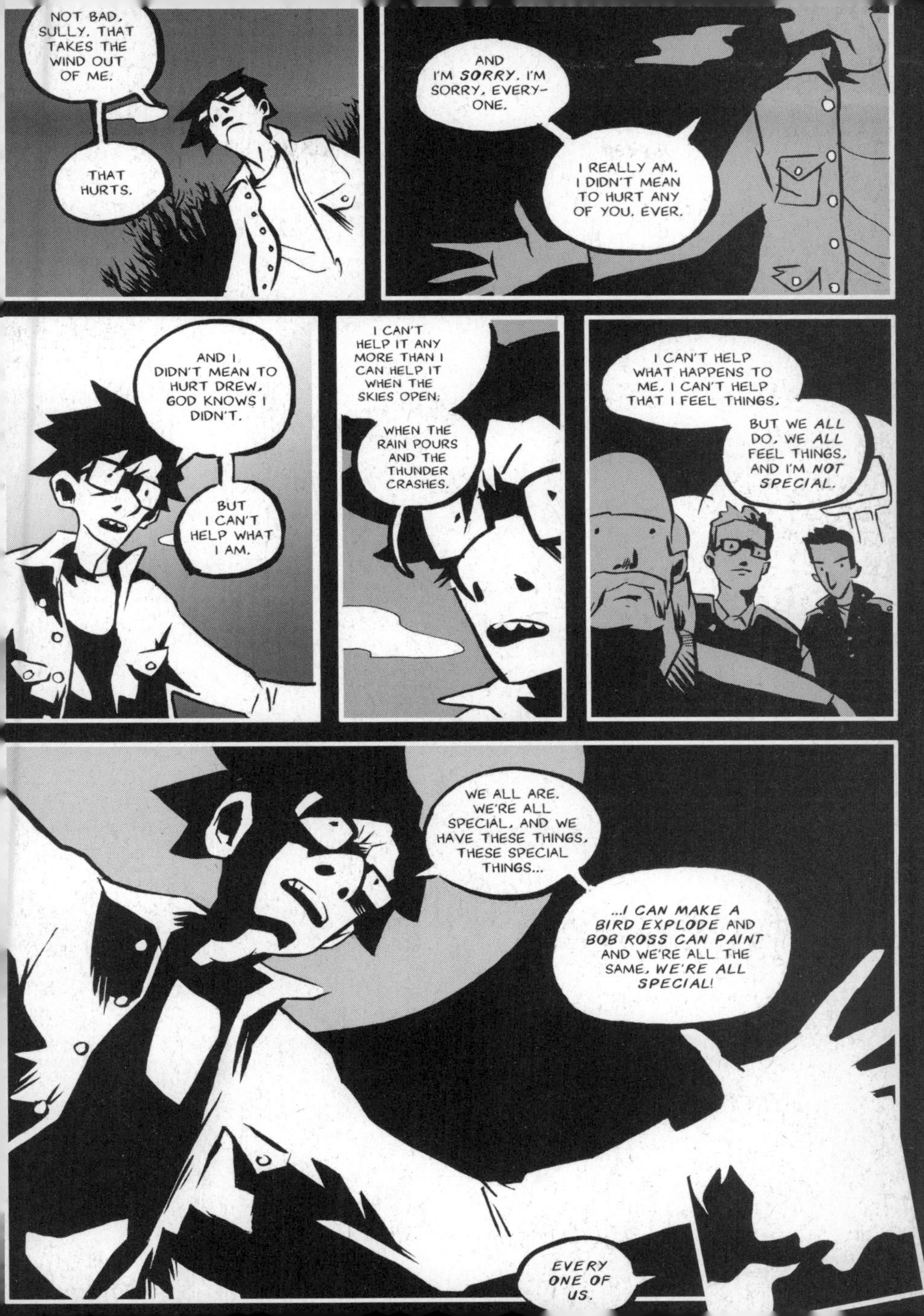
NOT BAD, SULLY. THAT TAKES THE WIND OUT OF ME.
THAT HURTS.
AND I'M SORRY. I'M SORRY, EVERY-ONE.
I REALLY AM. I DIDN'T MEAN TO HURT ANY OF YOU, EVER.
AND I DIDN'T MEAN TO HURT DREW, GOD KNOWS I DIDN'T.
BUT I CAN'T HELP WHAT I AM.
I CAN'T HELP IT ANY MORE THAN I CAN HELP IT WHEN THE SKIES OPEN;
WHEN THE RAIN POURS AND THE THUNDER CRASHES.
I CAN'T HELP WHAT HAPPENS TO ME, I CAN'T HELP THAT I FEEL THINGS,
BUT WE ALL DO, WE ALL FEEL THINGS, AND I'M NOT SPECIAL.
WE ALL ARE. WE'RE ALL SPECIAL, AND WE HAVE THESE THINGS, THESE SPECIAL THINGS...
...I CAN MAKE A BIRD EXPLODE AND BOB ROSS CAN PAINT AND WE'RE ALL THE SAME, WE'RE ALL SPECIAL!
EVERY ONE OF US.

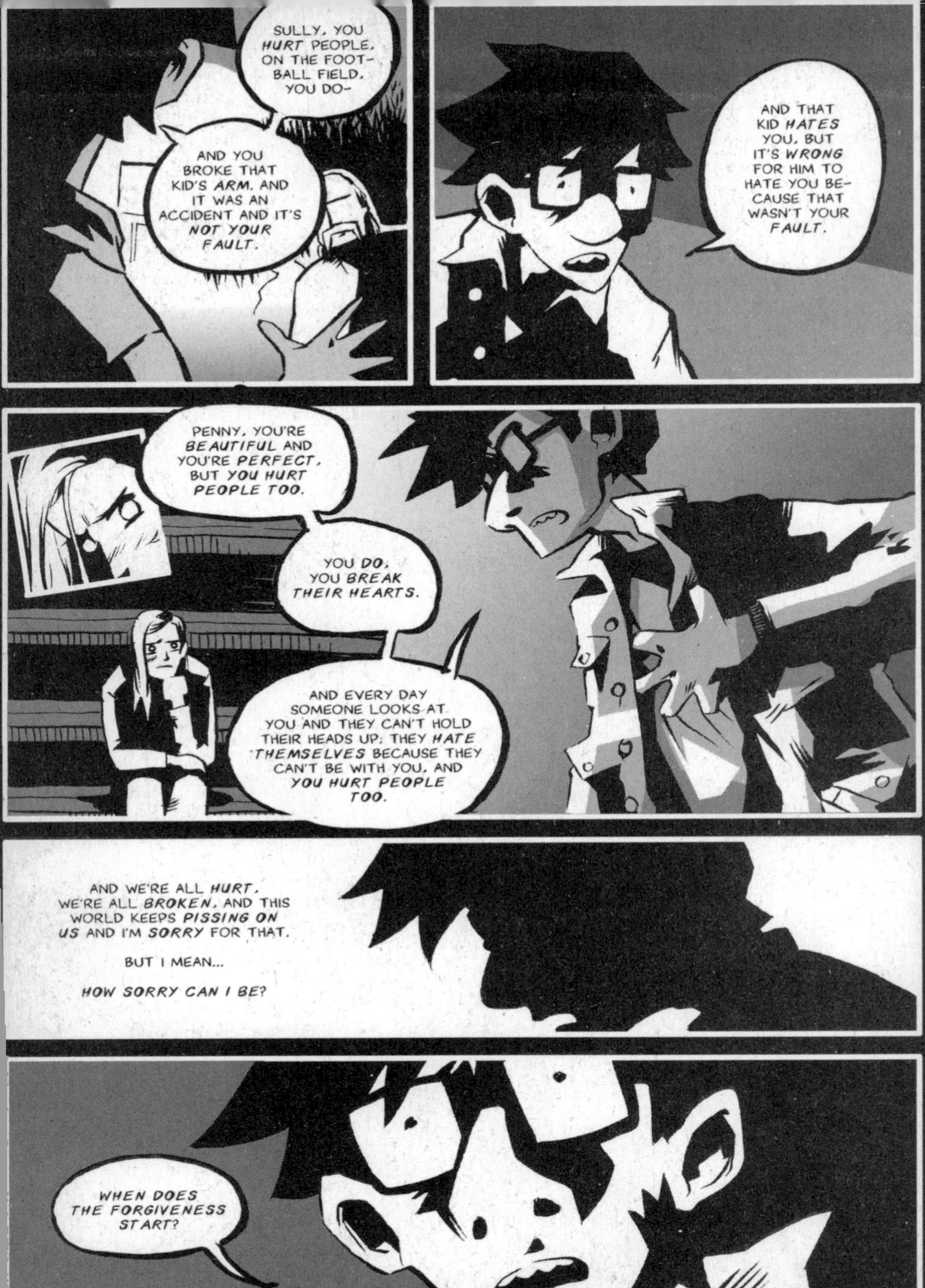

SULLY, YOU HURT PEOPLE. ON THE FOOTBALL FIELD, YOU DO-
AND YOU BROKE THAT KID'S ARM. AND IT WAS AN ACCIDENT AND IT'S NOT YOUR FAULT.
AND THAT KID HATES YOU, BUT IT'S WRONG FOR HIM TO HATE YOU BECAUSE THAT WASN'T YOUR FAULT.
PENNY, YOU'RE BEAUTIFUL AND YOU'RE PERFECT, BUT YOU HURT PEOPLE TOO.
YOU DO, YOU BREAK THEIR HEARTS.
AND EVERY DAY SOMEONE LOOKS AT YOU AND THEY CAN'T HOLD THEIR HEADS UP; THEY HATE THEMSELVES BECAUSE THEY CAN'T BE WITH YOU, AND YOU HURT PEOPLE TOO.
AND WE'RE ALL HURT, WE'RE ALL BROKEN, AND THIS WORLD KEEPS PISSING ON US AND I'M SORRY FOR THAT.
BUT I MEAN...
HOW SORRY CAN I BE?
WHEN DOES THE FORGIVENESS START?

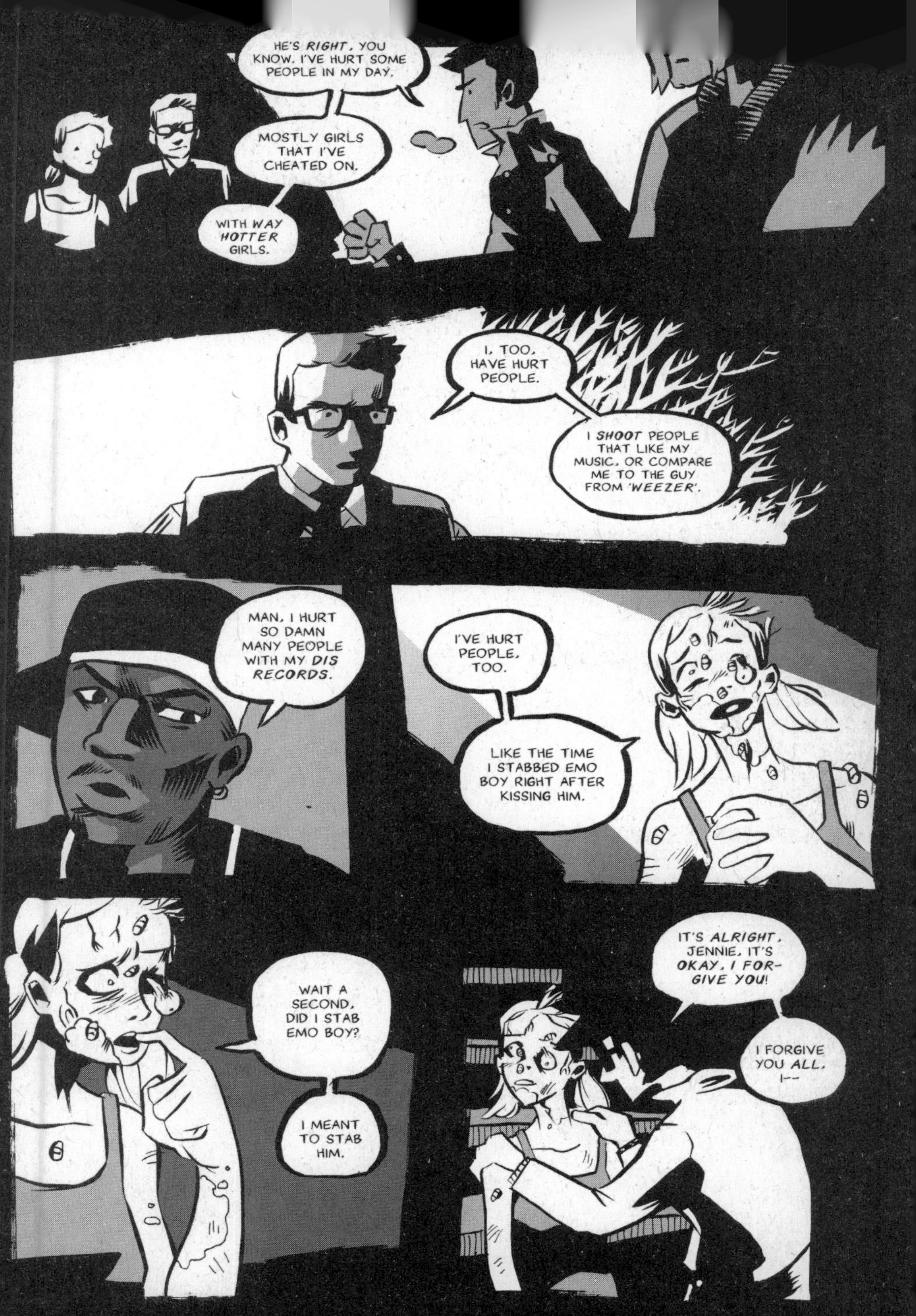
HE'S RIGHT, YOU KNOW. I'VE HURT SOME PEOPLE IN MY DAY.
MOSTLY GIRLS THAT I'VE CHEATED ON.
WITH WAY HOTTER GIRLS.
I, TOO, HAVE HURT PEOPLE.
I SHOOT PEOPLE THAT LIKE MY MUSIC, OR COMPARE ME TO THE GUY FROM 'WEEZER'.
MAN, I HURT SO DAMN MANY PEOPLE WITH MY DIS RECORDS.
I'VE HURT PEOPLE, TOO.
LIKE THE TIME I STABBED EMO BOY RIGHT AFTER KISSING HIM.
WAIT A SECOND, DID I STAB EMO BOY?
I MEANT TO STAB HIM.
IT'S ALRIGHT, JENNIE, IT'S OKAY, I FORGIVE YOU!
I FORGIVE YOU ALL. I--

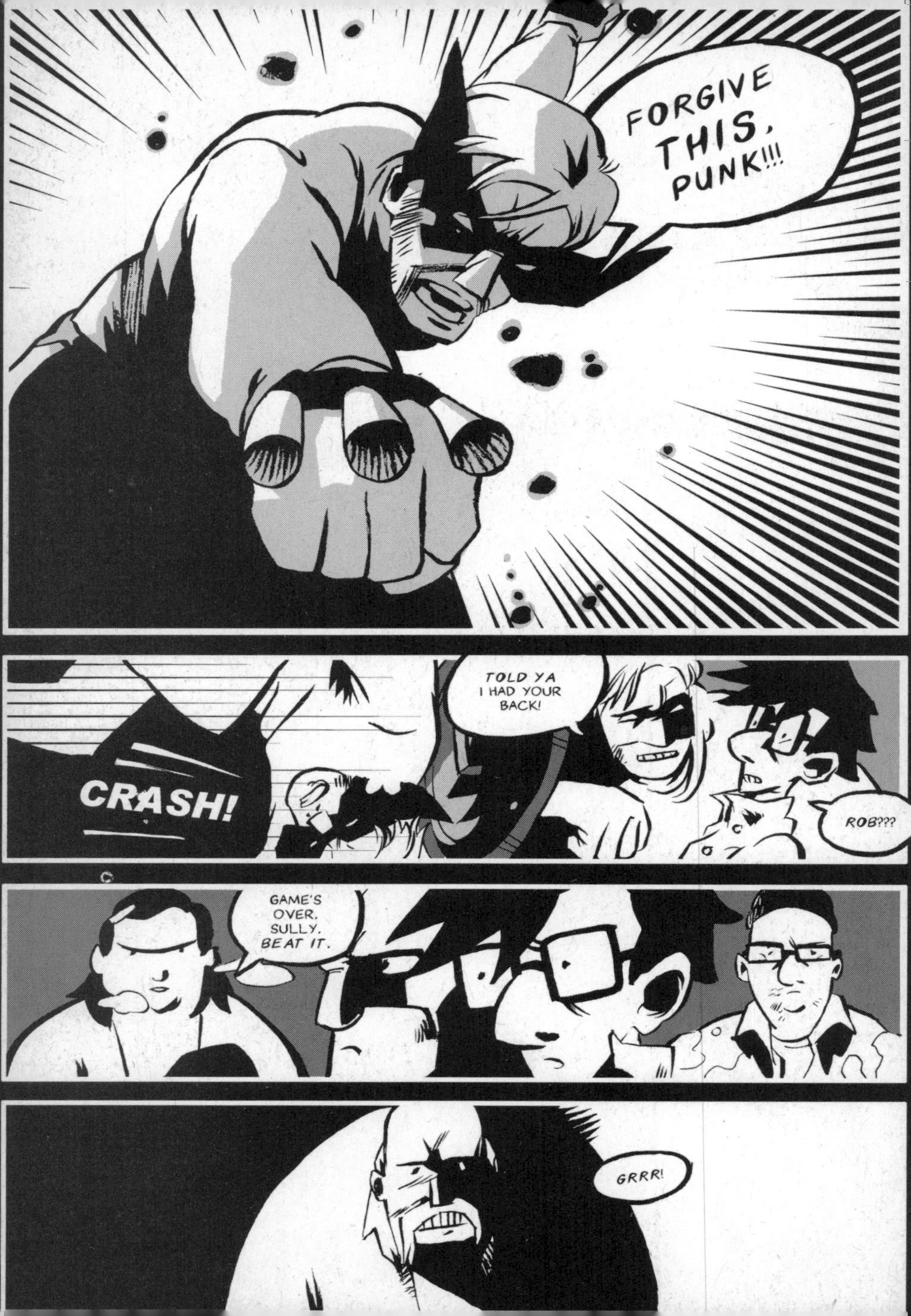
FORGIVE THIS, PUNK!!!
CRASH!
TOLD YA I HAD YOUR BACK!
ROB???
GAME'S OVER, SULLY. BEAT IT.
GRRR!

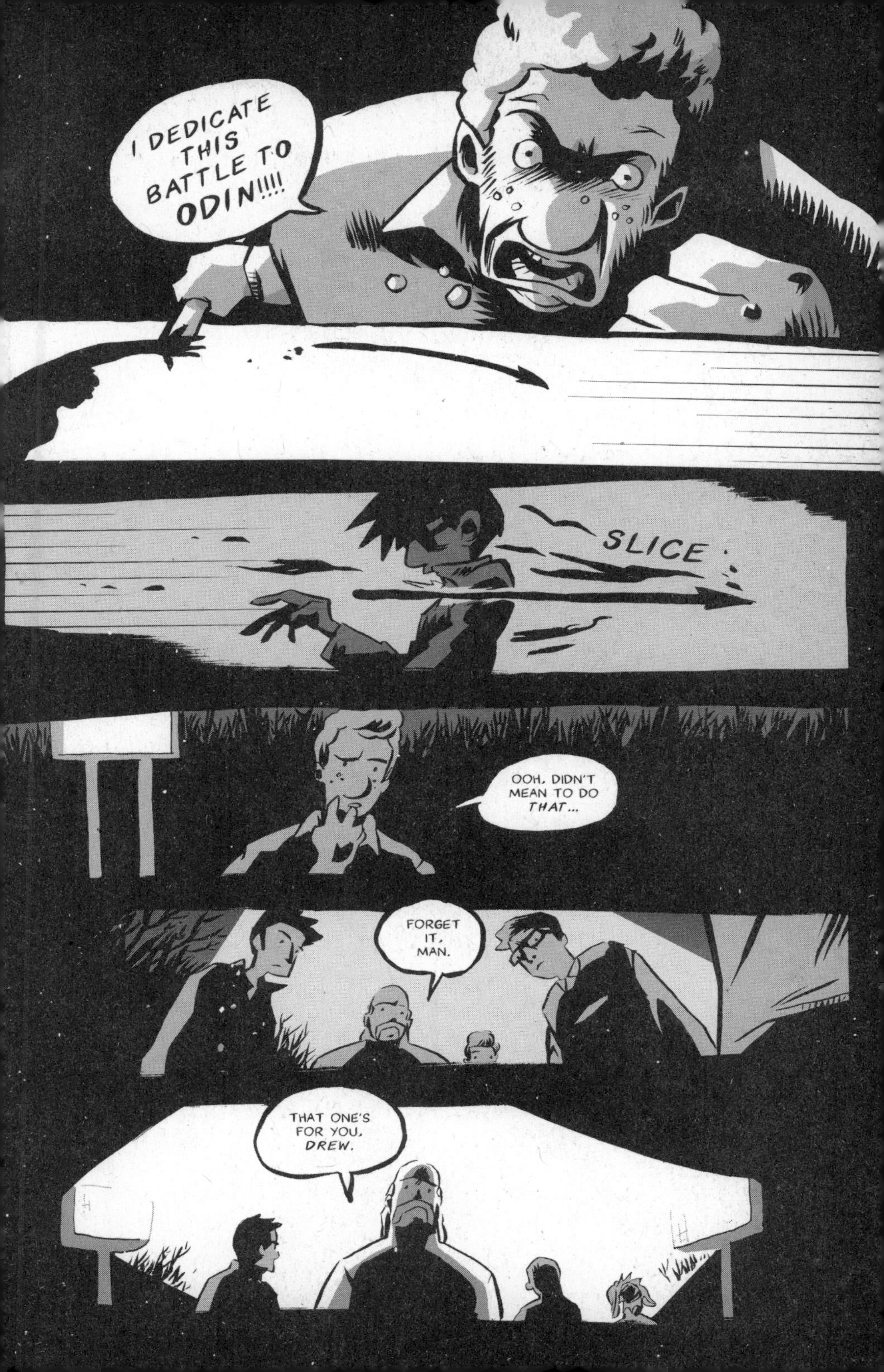
I DEDICATE THIS BATTLE TO ODIN!!!!
SLICE
OOH, DIDN'T MEAN TO DO THAT...
FORGET IT, MAN.
THAT ONE'S FOR YOU, DREW.

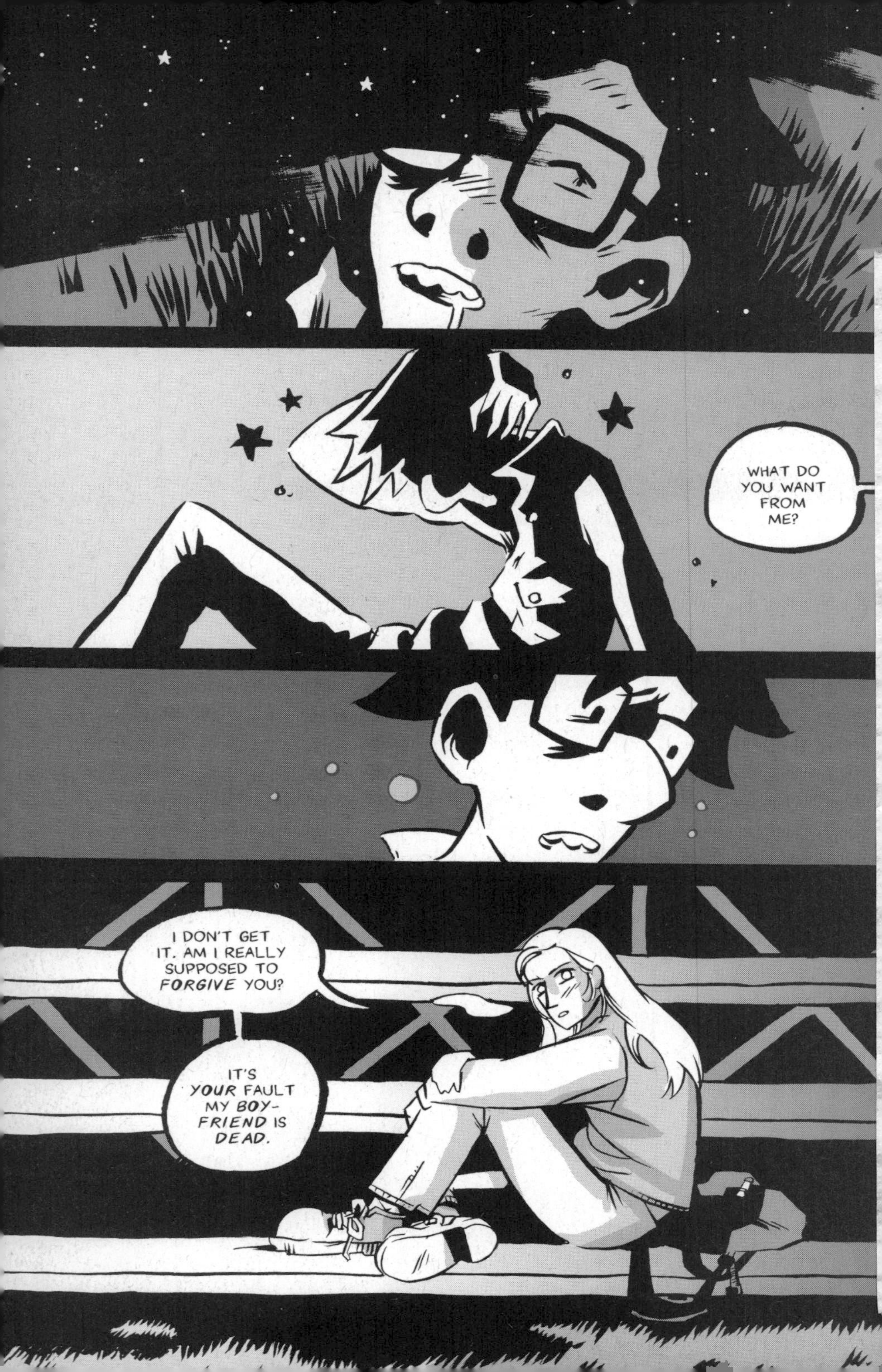

WHAT DO YOU WANT FROM ME?
I DON'T GET IT. AM I REALLY SUPPOSED TO FORGIVE YOU?
IT'S YOUR FAULT MY BOY-FRIEND IS DEAD.

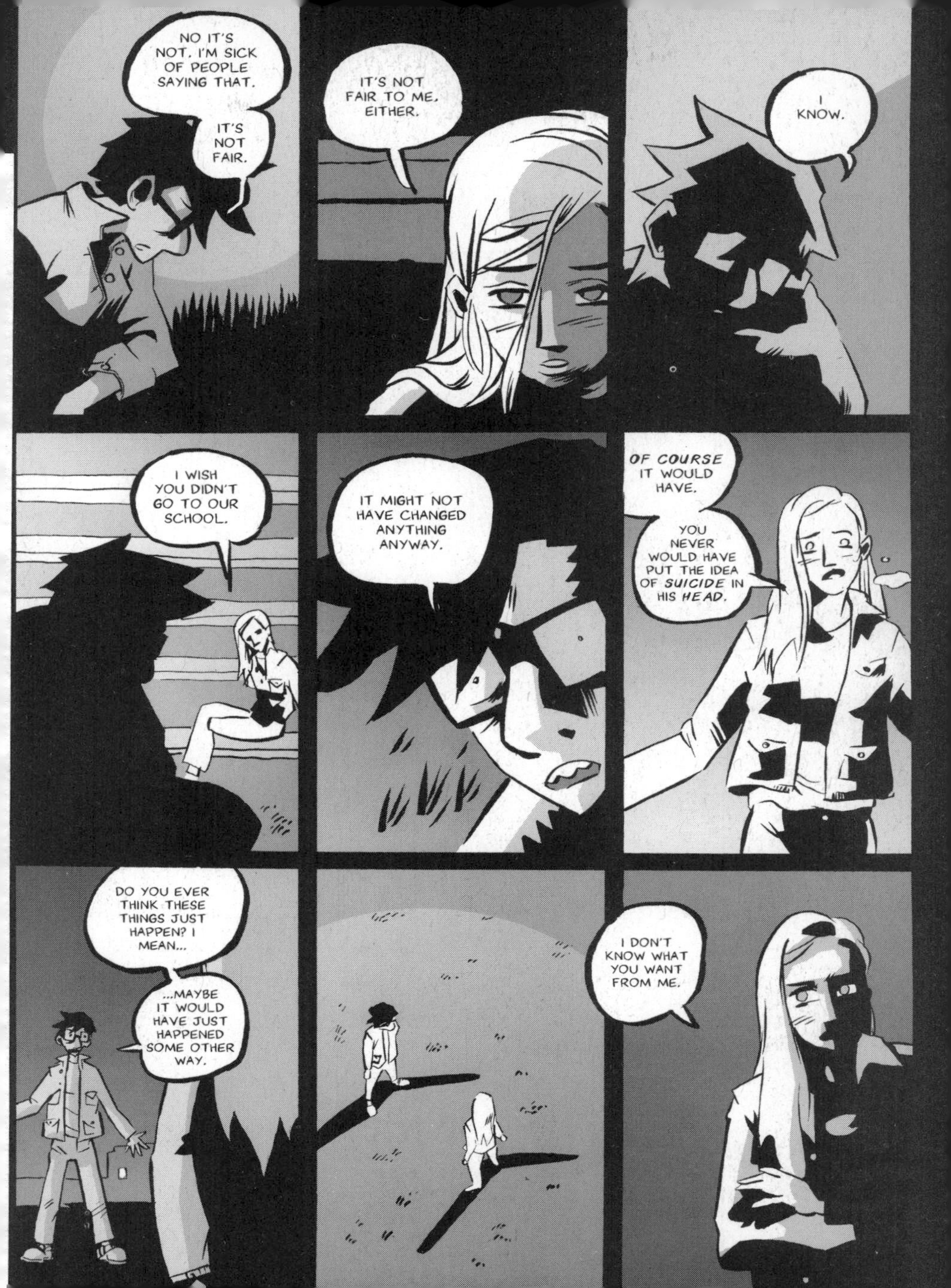
NO IT'S NOT. I'M SICK OF PEOPLE SAYING THAT.
IT'S NOT FAIR.
IT'S NOT FAIR TO ME, EITHER.
I KNOW.
I WISH YOU DIDN'T GO TO OUR SCHOOL.
IT MIGHT NOT HAVE CHANGED ANYTHING ANYWAY.
OF COURSE IT WOULD HAVE.
YOU NEVER WOULD HAVE PUT THE IDEA OF *SUICIDE* IN HIS *HEAD*.
DO YOU EVER THINK THESE THINGS JUST HAPPEN? I MEAN...
...MAYBE IT WOULD HAVE JUST HAPPENED SOME OTHER WAY.
I DON'T KNOW WHAT YOU WANT FROM ME.

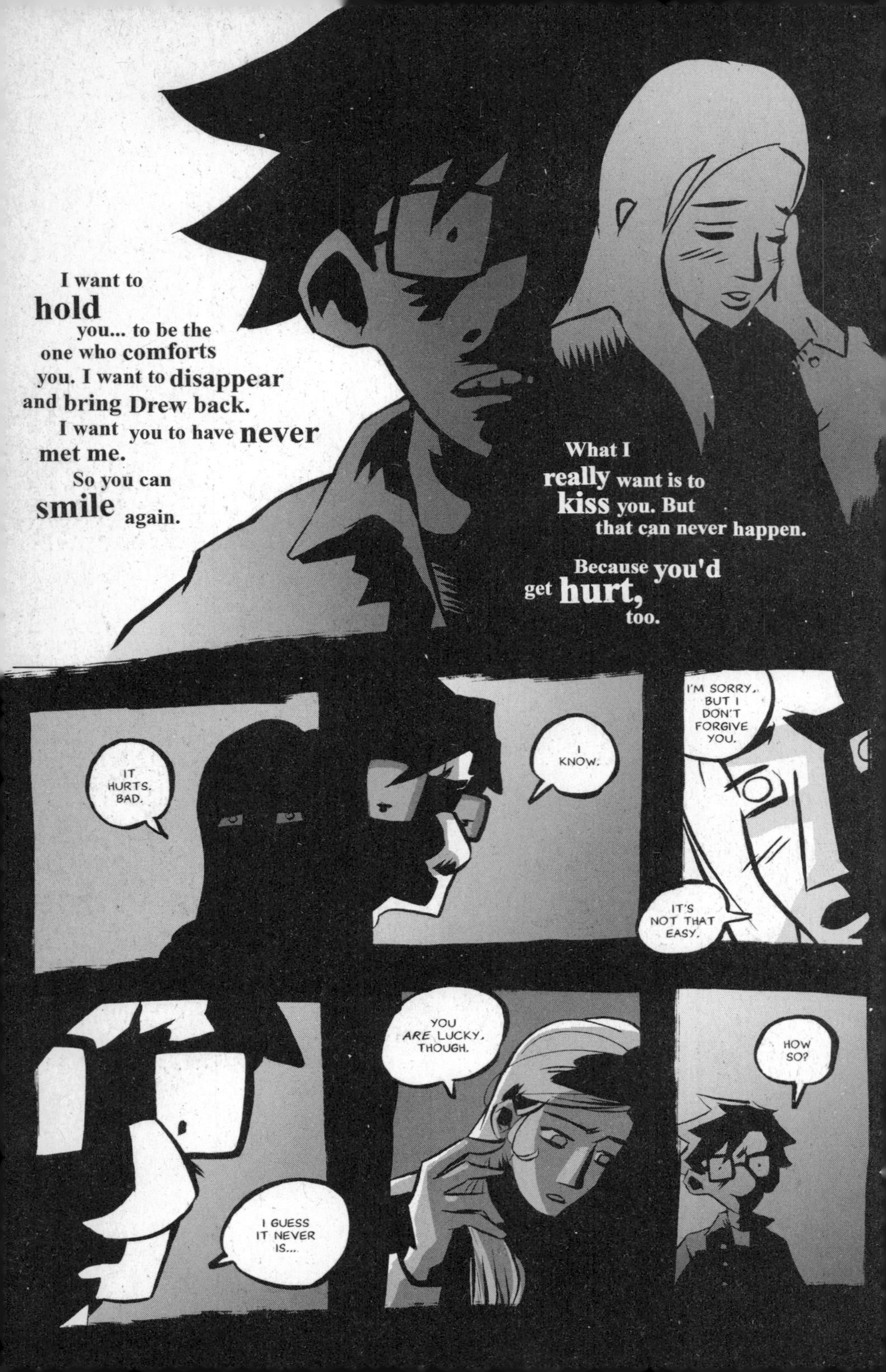

I want to hold you... to be the one who comforts you. I want to disappear and bring Drew back. I want you to have never met me. So you can smile again.
What I really want is to kiss you. But that can never happen.
Because you'd get hurt, too.
IT HURTS. BAD.
I KNOW.
I'M SORRY, BUT I DON'T FORGIVE YOU.
IT'S NOT THAT EASY.
I GUESS IT NEVER IS...
YOU ARE LUCKY, THOUGH.
HOW SO?

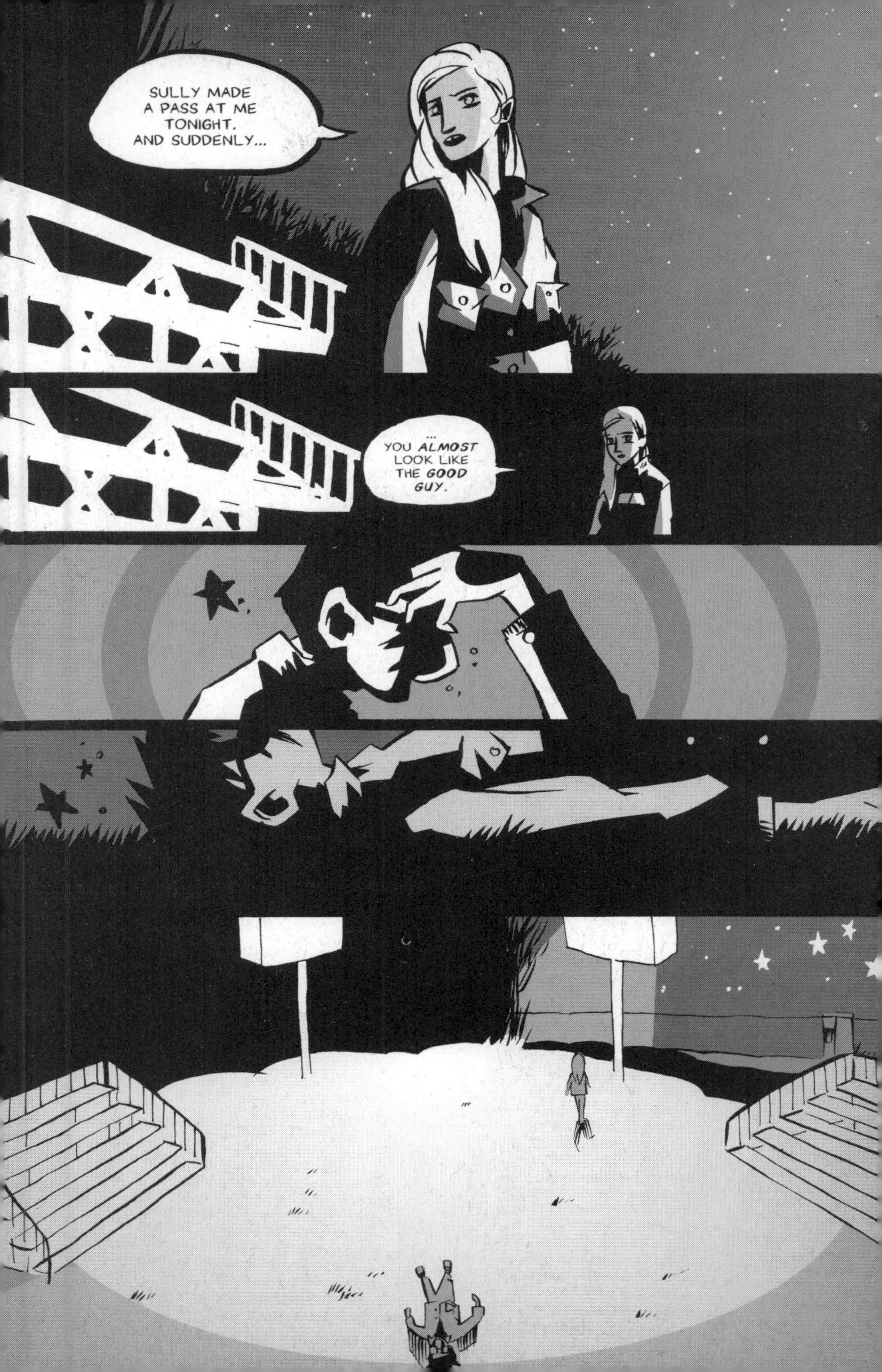
SULLY MADE A PASS AT ME TONIGHT, AND SUDDENLY...
... YOU *ALMOST* LOOK LIKE THE *GOOD GUY*.

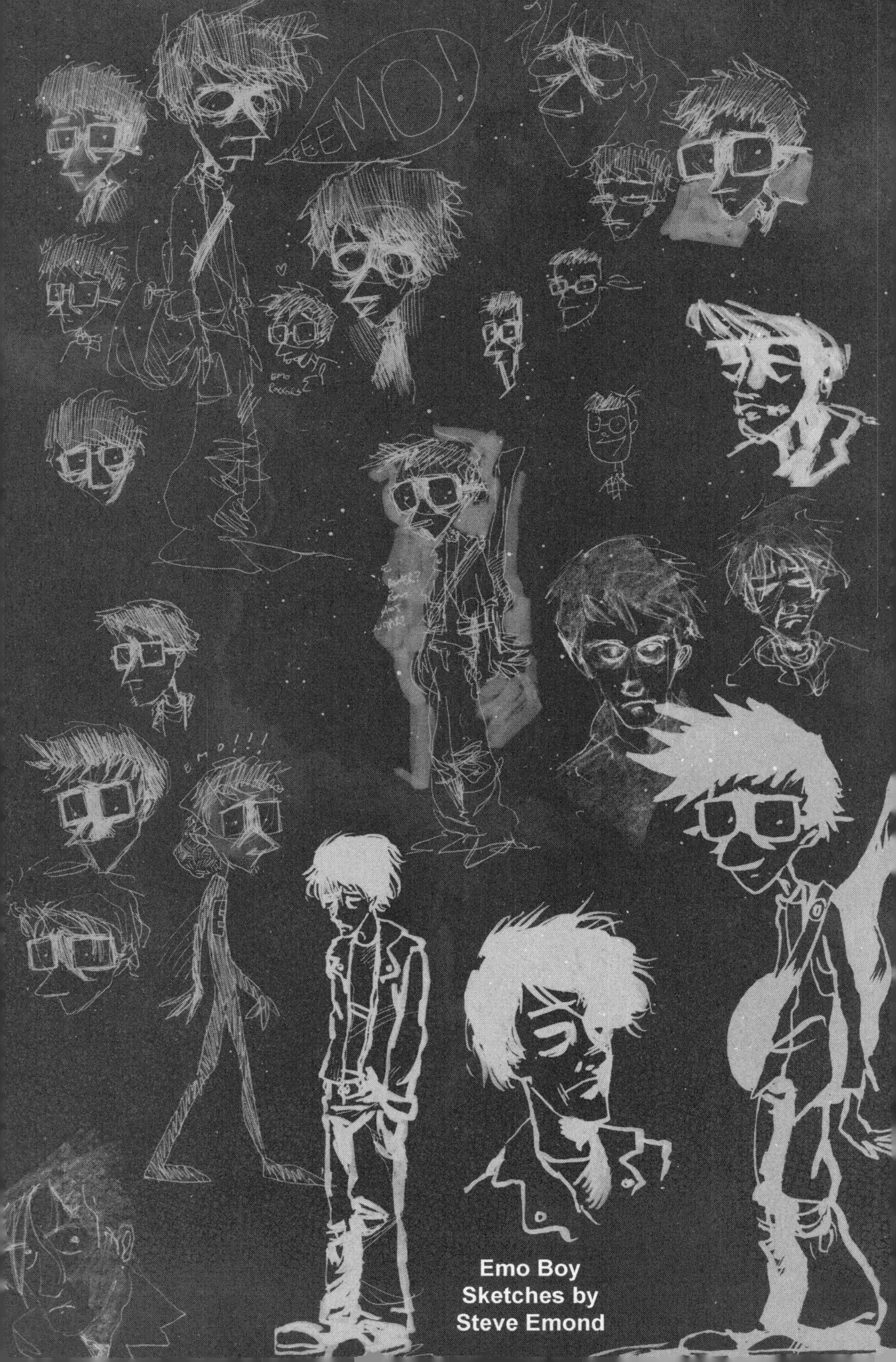
EMO!
EMO!!!

Emo Boy
Sketches by
Steve Emond

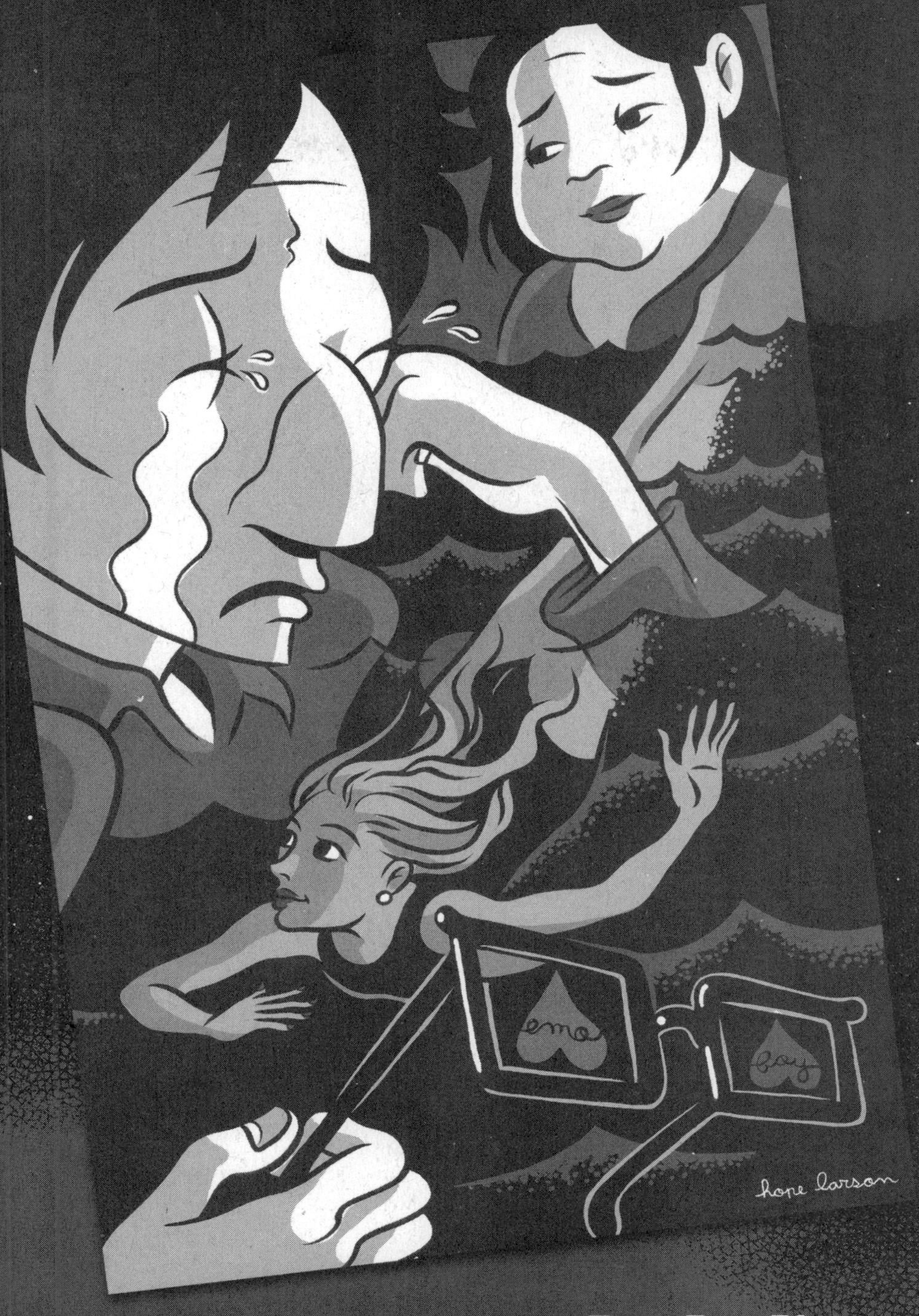
emo
boy
hope larson

Emo Boy Pinup
by Hope Larson

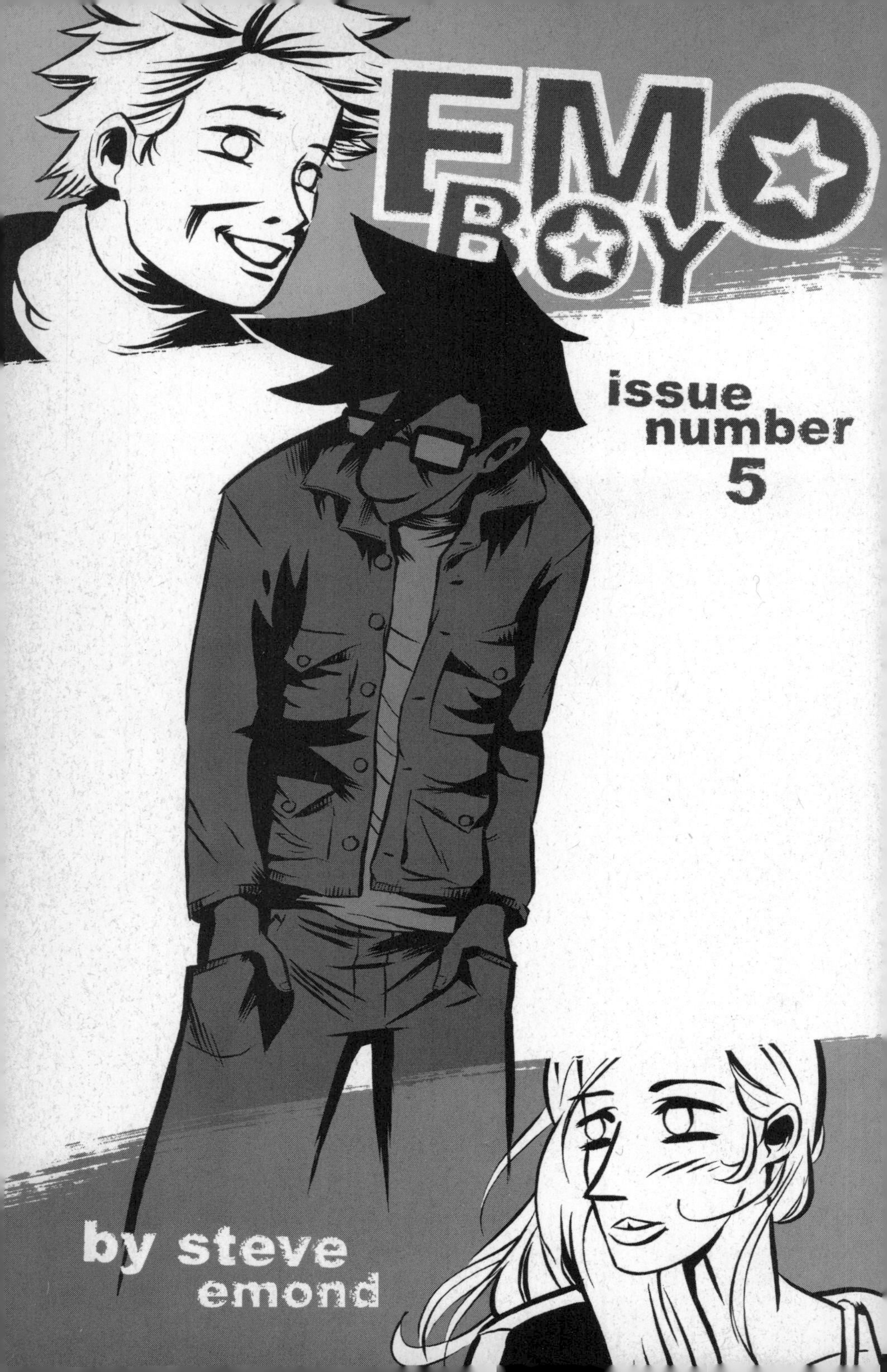
EMO BOY
issue number 5
by steve emond

I turn the volume up loud. I always do. I turn it louder and louder until it drains out my thoughts. Until it kills everyone around me and I am alone. Until it numbs me, until I feel nothing.

The beat sinks into my bones, and my arms become guitars, my heart a drum, my head an amplifier. I cease to exist beyond my role as a vessel for the music to live through.

I am everything and nothing. The music blares and the world goes silent.

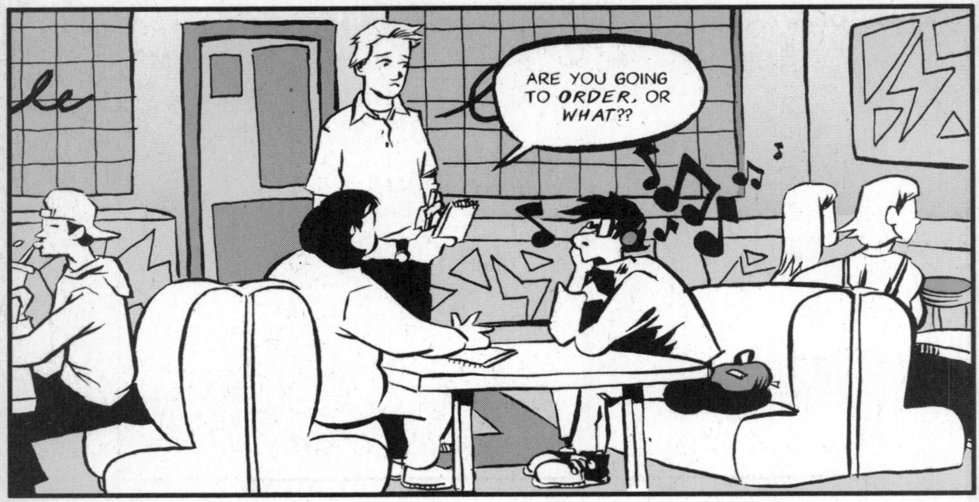
ARE YOU GOING TO ORDER, OR WHAT??

Emo Boy Issue 5:

"HOMO'S THE NEW HETERO"

Story and Art by Steve Emond

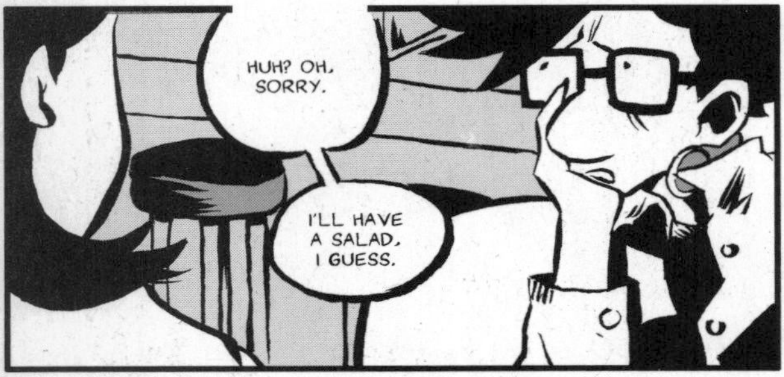
HUH? OH, SORRY.
I'LL HAVE A SALAD, I GUESS.

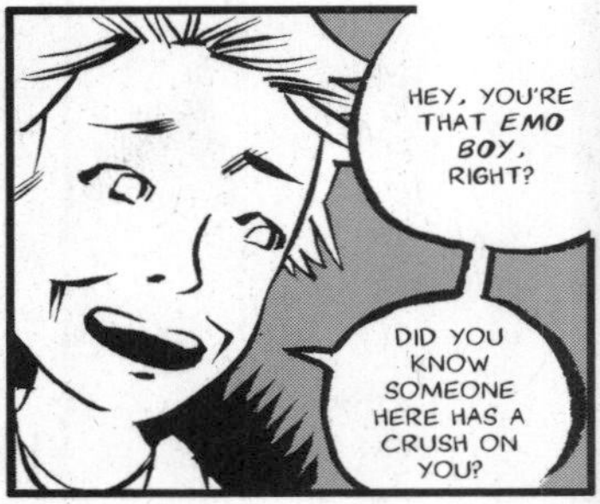
HEY, YOU'RE THAT EMO BOY, RIGHT?
DID YOU KNOW SOMEONE HERE HAS A CRUSH ON YOU?

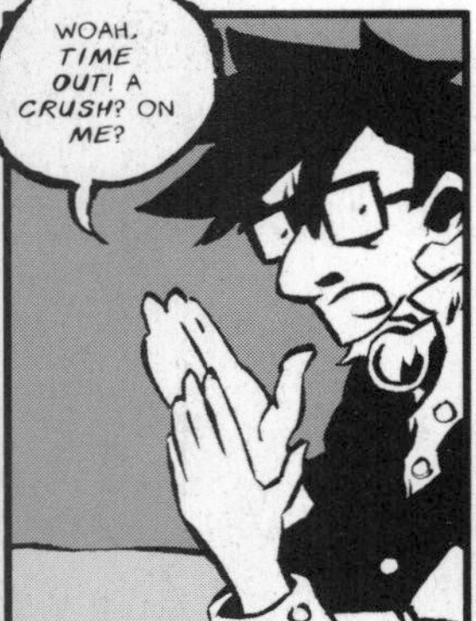
WOAH, TIME OUT! A CRUSH? ON ME?

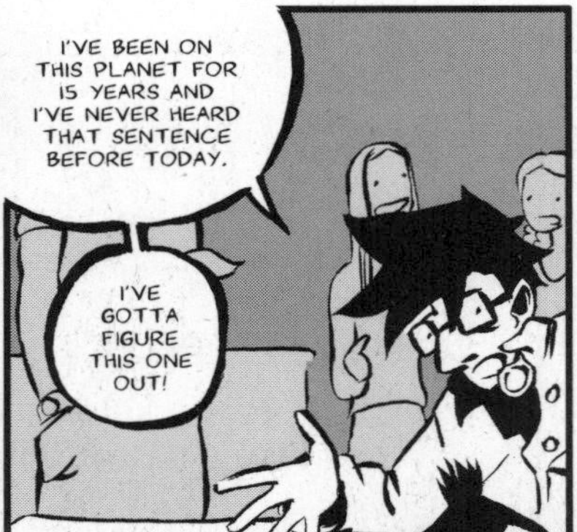
I'VE BEEN ON THIS PLANET FOR 15 YEARS AND I'VE NEVER HEARD THAT SENTENCE BEFORE TODAY.
I'VE GOTTA FIGURE THIS ONE OUT!

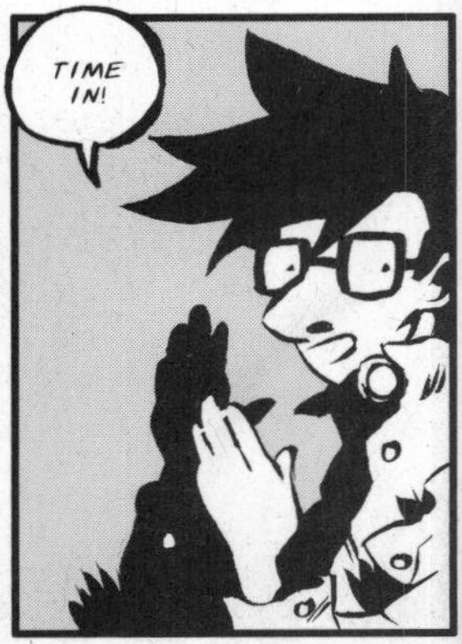
TIME IN!

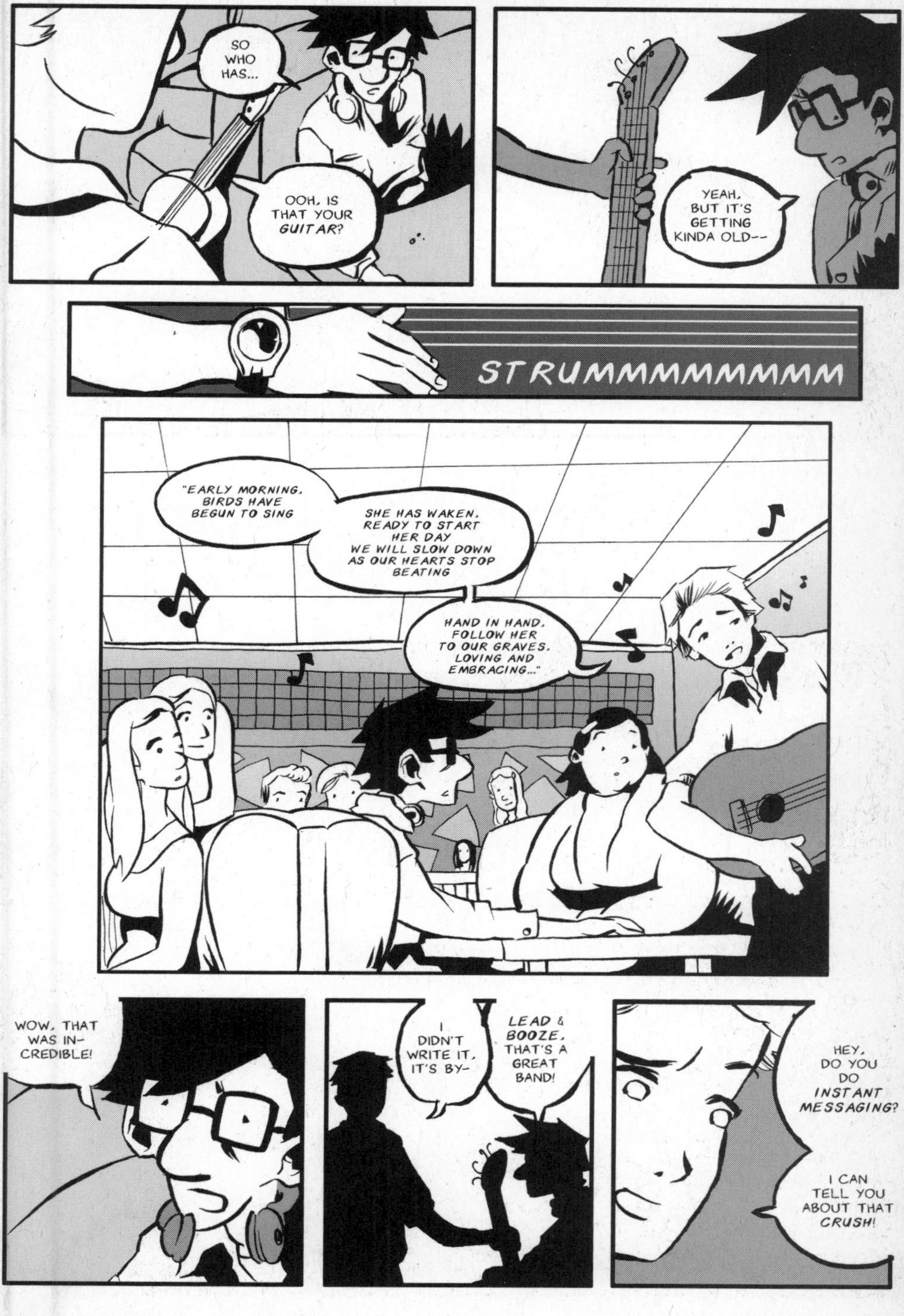

SO WHO HAS...
OOH, IS THAT YOUR GUITAR?
YEAH, BUT IT'S GETTING KINDA OLD--
STRUMMMMMMMM
"EARLY MORNING, BIRDS HAVE BEGUN TO SING
SHE HAS WAKEN, READY TO START HER DAY WE WILL SLOW DOWN AS OUR HEARTS STOP BEATING
HAND IN HAND, FOLLOW HER TO OUR GRAVES, LOVING AND EMBRACING..."
WOW, THAT WAS IN-CREDIBLE!
I DIDN'T WRITE IT, IT'S BY-
LEAD & BOOZE, THAT'S A GREAT BAND!
HEY, DO YOU DO INSTANT MESSAGING?
I CAN TELL YOU ABOUT THAT CRUSH!

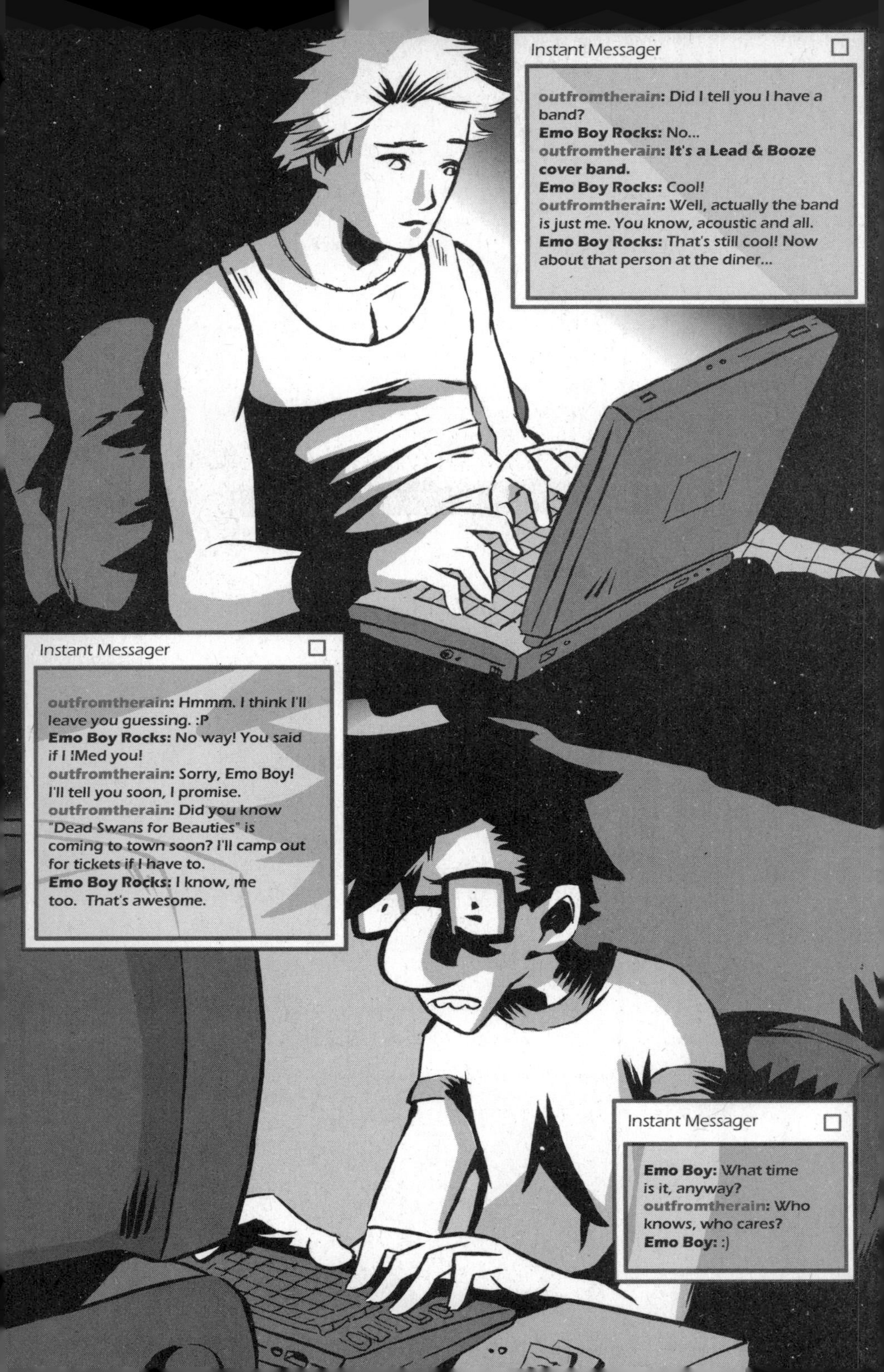

Instant Messager
outfromtherain: Did I tell you I have a band?
Emo Boy Rocks: No...
outfromtherain: It's a Lead & Booze cover band.
Emo Boy Rocks: Cool!
outfromtherain: Well, actually the band is just me. You know, acoustic and all.
Emo Boy Rocks: That's still cool! Now about that person at the diner...
Instant Messager
outfromtherain: Hmmm. I think I'll leave you guessing. :P
Emo Boy Rocks: No way! You said if I !Med you!
outfromtherain: Sorry, Emo Boy! I'll tell you soon, I promise.
outfromtherain: Did you know "Dead Swans for Beauties" is coming to town soon? I'll camp out for tickets if I have to.
Emo Boy Rocks: I know, me too. That's awesome.
Instant Messager
Emo Boy: What time is it, anyway?
outfromtherain: Who knows, who cares?
Emo Boy: :)

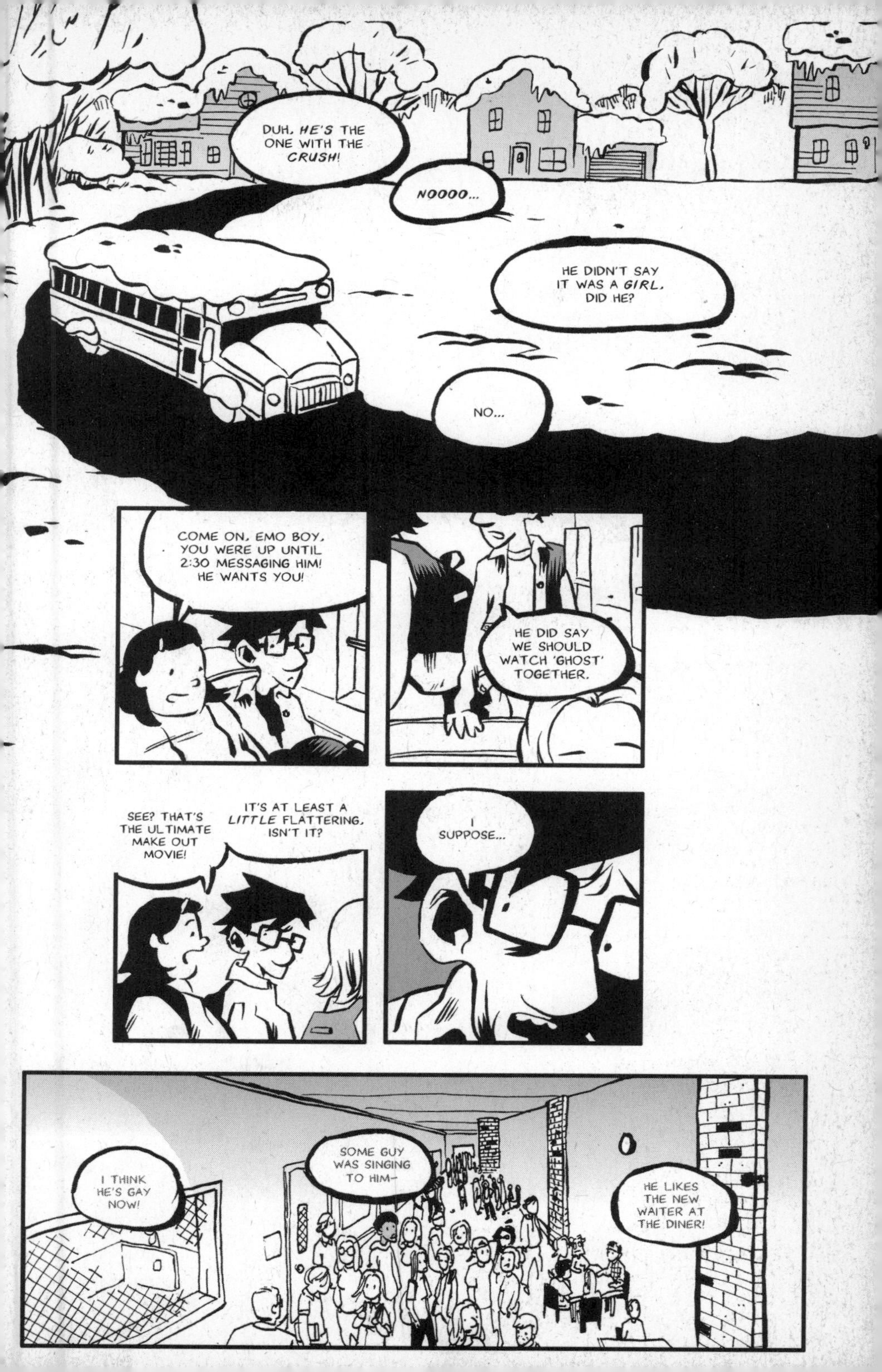
DUH, HE'S THE ONE WITH THE CRUSH!
NOOOO...
HE DIDN'T SAY IT WAS A GIRL, DID HE?
NO...
COME ON, EMO BOY, YOU WERE UP UNTIL 2:30 MESSAGING HIM! HE WANTS YOU!
HE DID SAY WE SHOULD WATCH 'GHOST' TOGETHER.
SEE? THAT'S THE ULTIMATE MAKE OUT MOVIE!
IT'S AT LEAST A LITTLE FLATTERING, ISN'T IT?
I SUPPOSE...
I THINK HE'S GAY NOW!
SOME GUY WAS SINGING TO HIM-
HE LIKES THE NEW WAITER AT THE DINER!

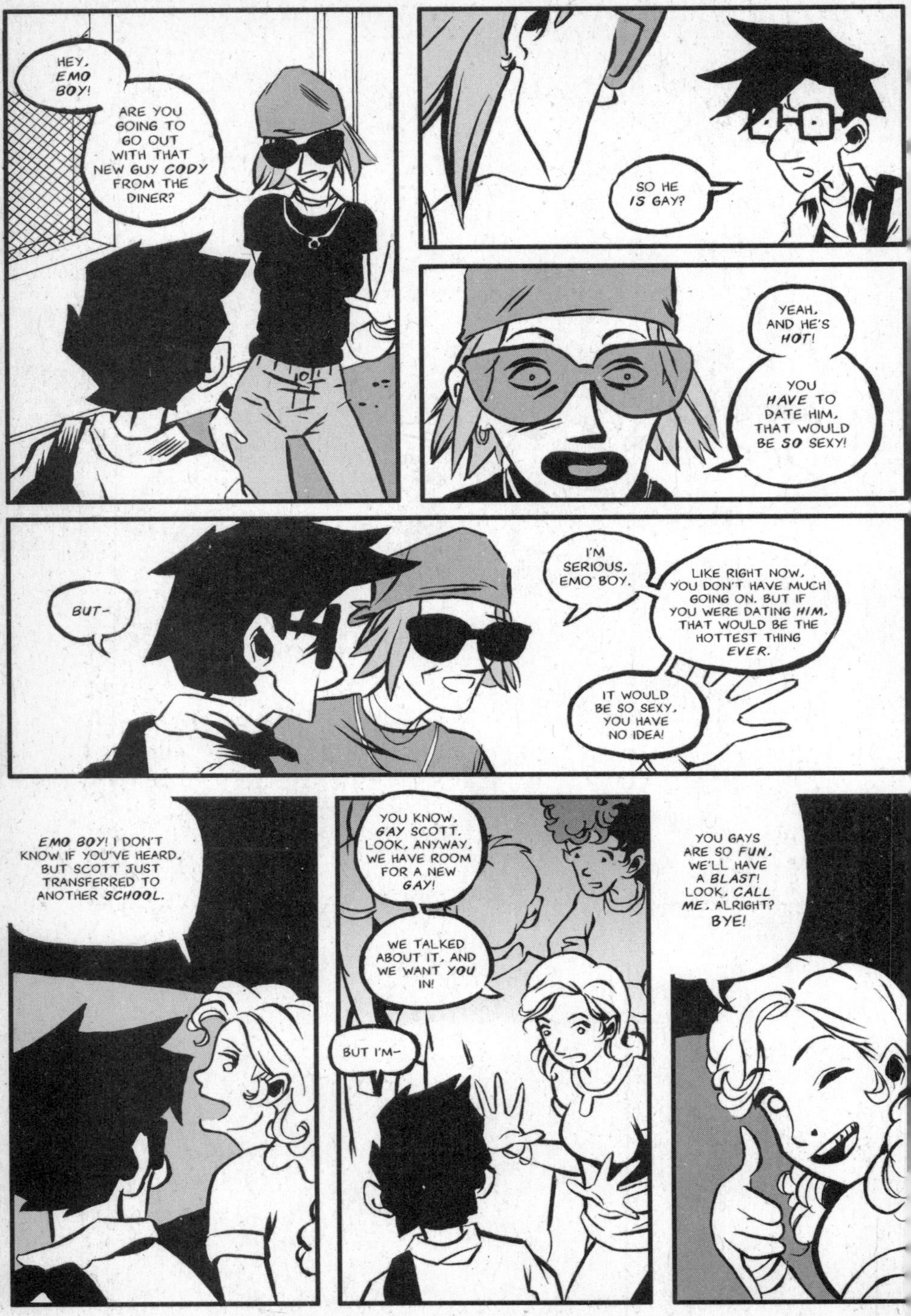
HEY, EMO BOY!
ARE YOU GOING TO GO OUT WITH THAT NEW GUY CODY FROM THE DINER?
SO HE IS GAY?
YEAH, AND HE'S HOT!
YOU HAVE TO DATE HIM, THAT WOULD BE SO SEXY!
BUT-
I'M SERIOUS, EMO BOY.
LIKE RIGHT NOW, YOU DON'T HAVE MUCH GOING ON. BUT IF YOU WERE DATING HIM, THAT WOULD BE THE HOTTEST THING EVER.
IT WOULD BE SO SEXY, YOU HAVE NO IDEA!
EMO BOY! I DON'T KNOW IF YOU'VE HEARD, BUT SCOTT JUST TRANSFERRED TO ANOTHER SCHOOL.
YOU KNOW, GAY SCOTT. LOOK, ANYWAY, WE HAVE ROOM FOR A NEW GAY!
WE TALKED ABOUT IT, AND WE WANT YOU IN!
BUT I'M-
YOU GAYS ARE SO FUN, WE'LL HAVE A BLAST! LOOK, CALL ME, ALRIGHT? BYE!

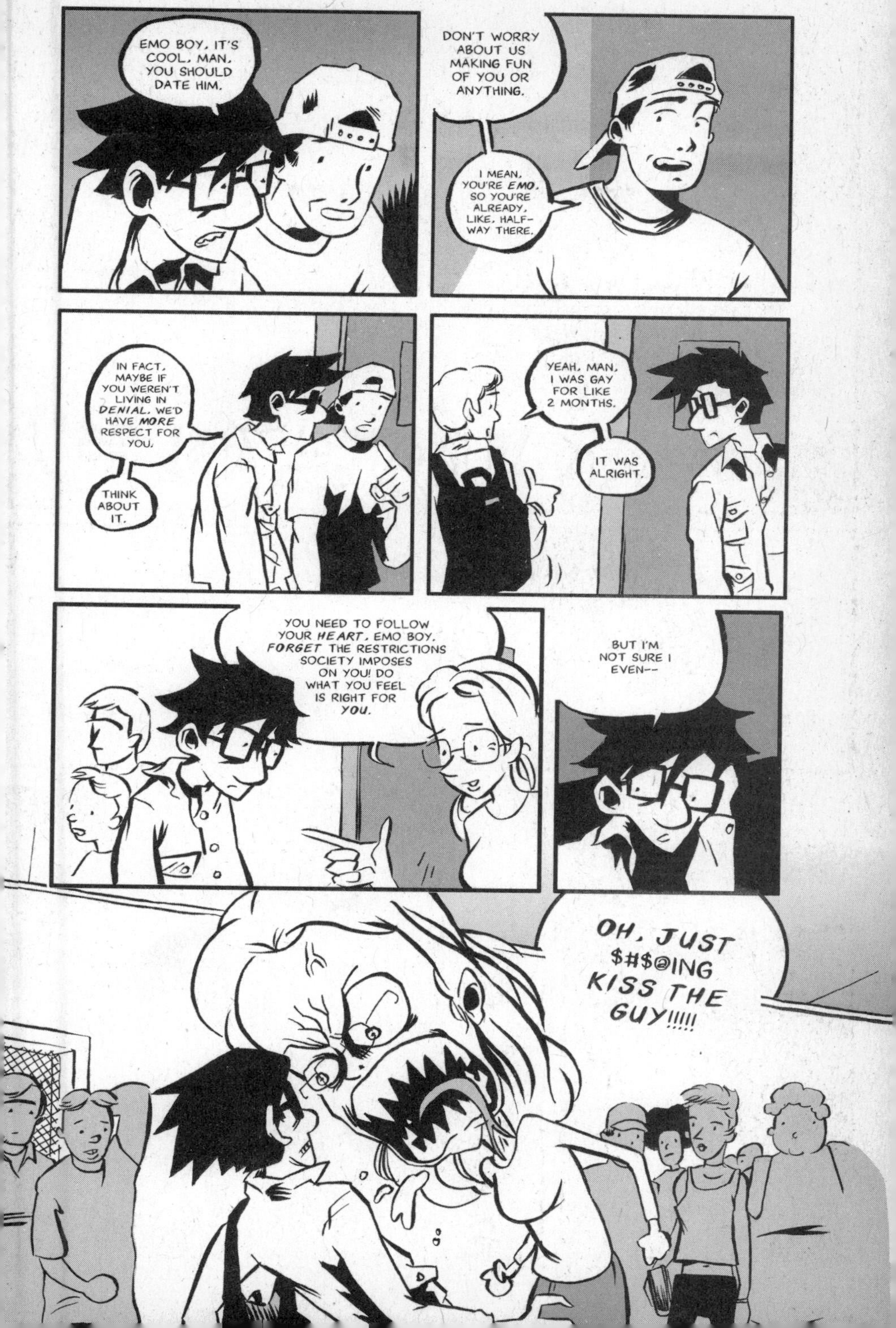
EMO BOY, IT'S COOL, MAN. YOU SHOULD DATE HIM.
DON'T WORRY ABOUT US MAKING FUN OF YOU OR ANYTHING.
I MEAN, YOU'RE EMO, SO YOU'RE ALREADY, LIKE, HALF-WAY THERE.
IN FACT, MAYBE IF YOU WEREN'T LIVING IN DENIAL, WE'D HAVE MORE RESPECT FOR YOU.
THINK ABOUT IT.
YEAH, MAN, I WAS GAY FOR LIKE 2 MONTHS.
IT WAS ALRIGHT.
YOU NEED TO FOLLOW YOUR HEART, EMO BOY. FORGET THE RESTRICTIONS SOCIETY IMPOSES ON YOU! DO WHAT YOU FEEL IS RIGHT FOR YOU.
BUT I'M NOT SURE I EVEN--
OH, JUST $#$@ING KISS THE GUY!!!!!

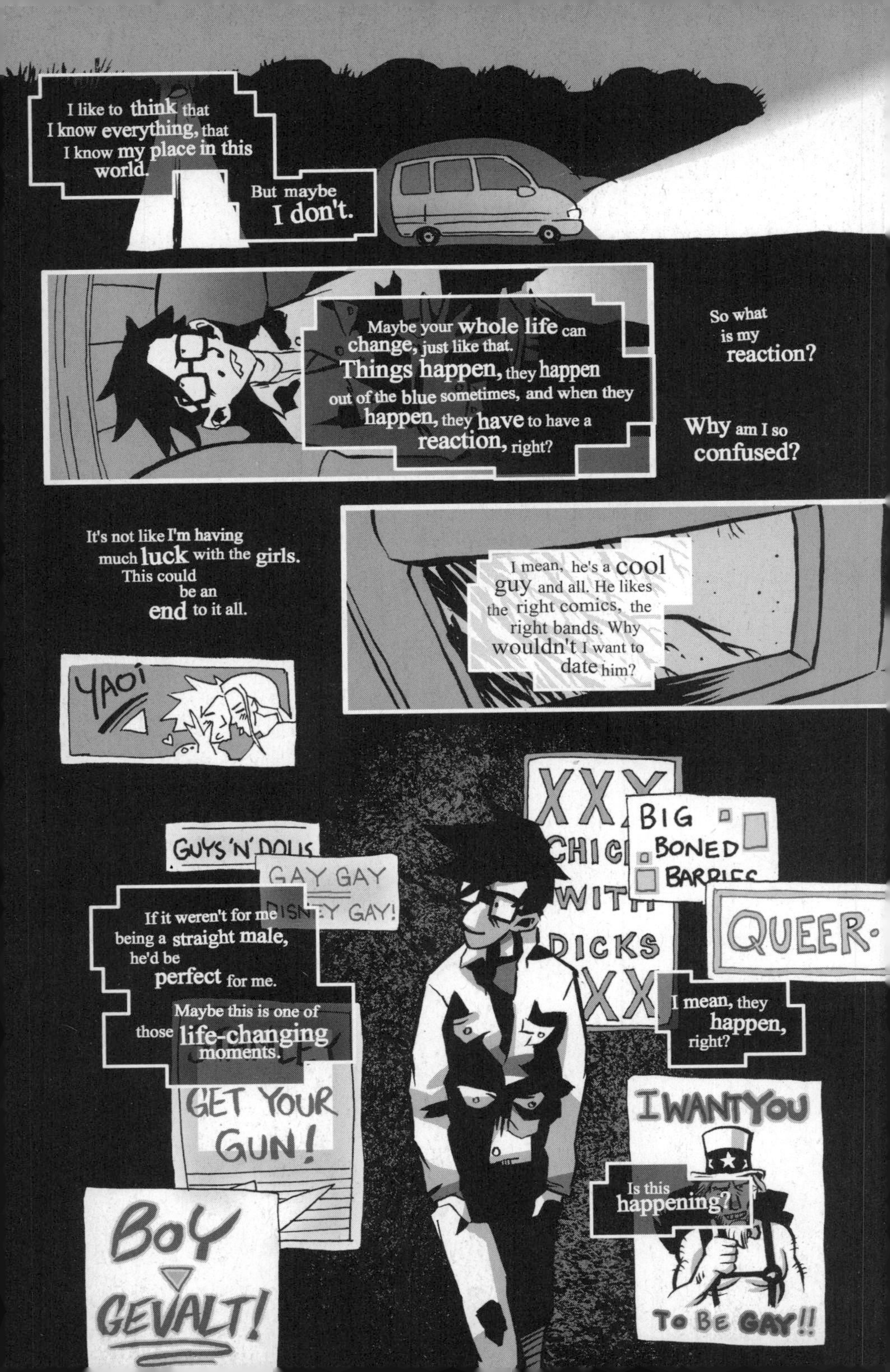

I like to think that I know everything, that I know my place in this world.
But maybe I don't.
Maybe your whole life can change, just like that. Things happen, they happen out of the blue sometimes, and when they happen, they have to have a reaction, right?
So what is my reaction?
Why am I so confused?
It's not like I'm having much luck with the girls. This could be an end to it all.
I mean, he's a cool guy and all. He likes the right comics, the right bands. Why wouldn't I want to date him?
YAOI
GUYS 'N' DOLLS
GAY GAY
DISNEY GAY!
If it weren't for me being a straight male, he'd be perfect for me.
Maybe this is one of those life-changing moments.
GET YOUR GUN!
BOY GEVALT!
BIG BONED BARBIES
QUEER
I mean, they happen, right?
I WANT YOU
Is this happening?
TO BE GAY!!

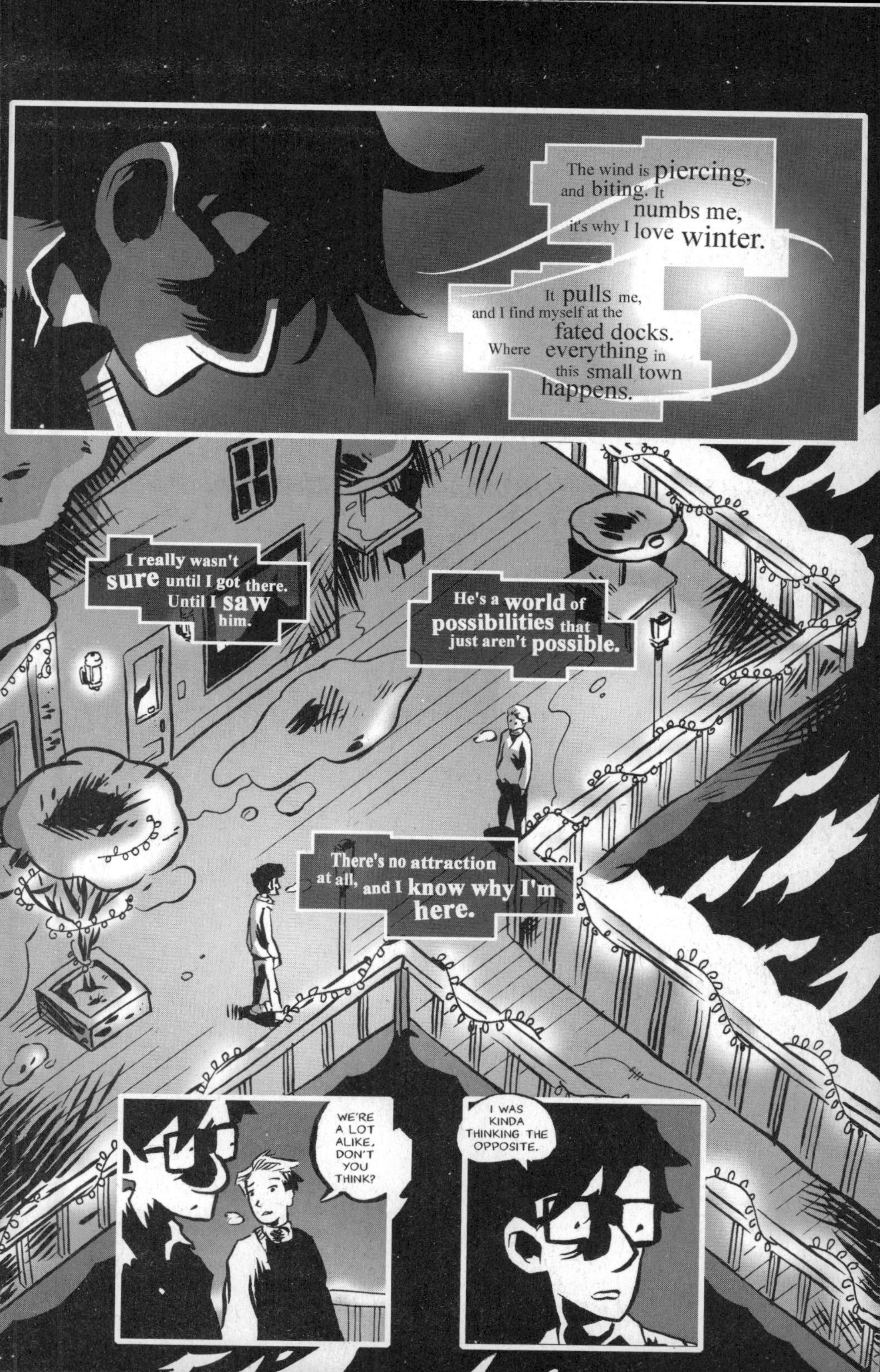

The wind is piercing, and biting. It numbs me, it's why I love winter.
It pulls me, and I find myself at the fated docks. Where everything in this small town happens.
I really wasn't sure until I got there. Until I saw him.
He's a world of possibilities that just aren't possible.
There's no attraction at all, and I know why I'm here.
WE'RE A LOT ALIKE, DON'T YOU THINK?
I WAS KINDA THINKING THE OPPOSITE.

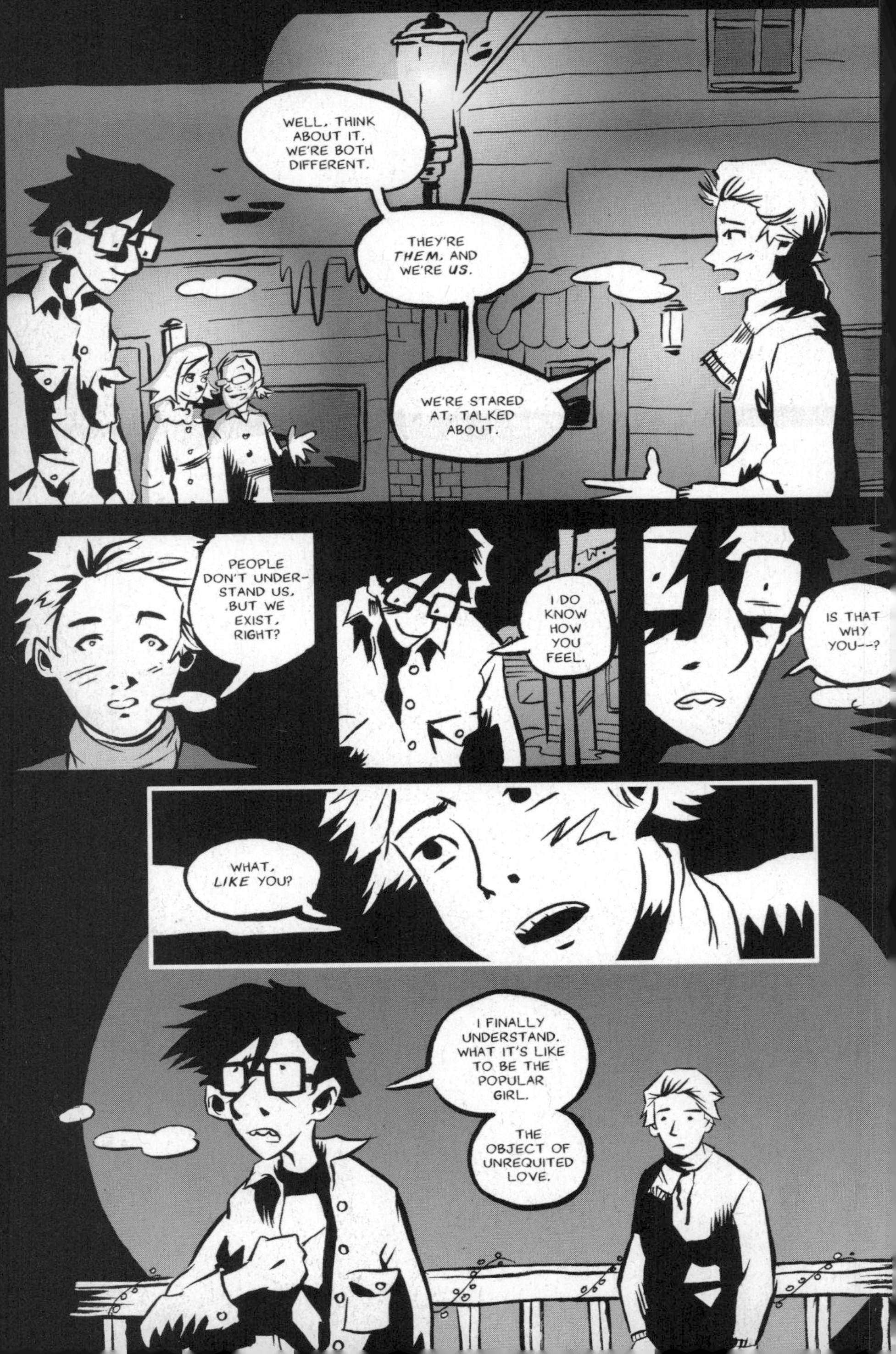
WELL, THINK ABOUT IT. WE'RE BOTH DIFFERENT.
THEY'RE *THEM*, AND WE'RE *US*.
WE'RE STARED AT; TALKED ABOUT.
PEOPLE DON'T UNDER-STAND US, BUT WE EXIST, RIGHT?
I DO KNOW HOW YOU FEEL.
IS THAT WHY YOU--?
WHAT, *LIKE* YOU?
I FINALLY UNDERSTAND. WHAT IT'S LIKE TO BE THE POPULAR GIRL.
THE OBJECT OF UNREQUITED LOVE.

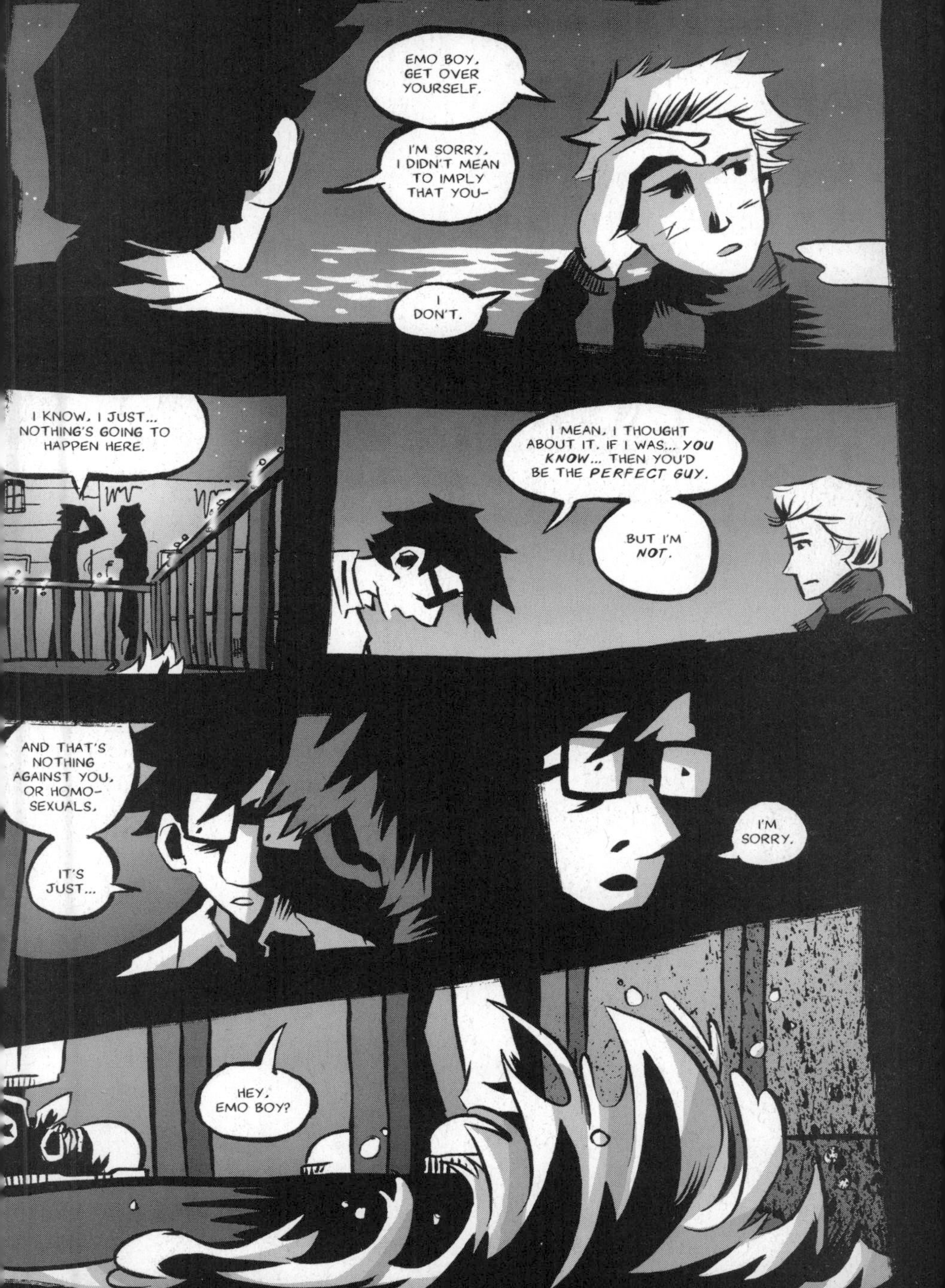
EMO BOY, GET OVER YOURSELF.
I'M SORRY, I DIDN'T MEAN TO IMPLY THAT YOU-
I DON'T.
I KNOW, I JUST... NOTHING'S GOING TO HAPPEN HERE.
I MEAN, I THOUGHT ABOUT IT. IF I WAS... *YOU KNOW*... THEN YOU'D BE THE *PERFECT GUY*.
BUT I'M *NOT*.
AND THAT'S NOTHING AGAINST YOU, OR HOMO-SEXUALS.
IT'S JUST...
I'M SORRY.
HEY, EMO BOY?

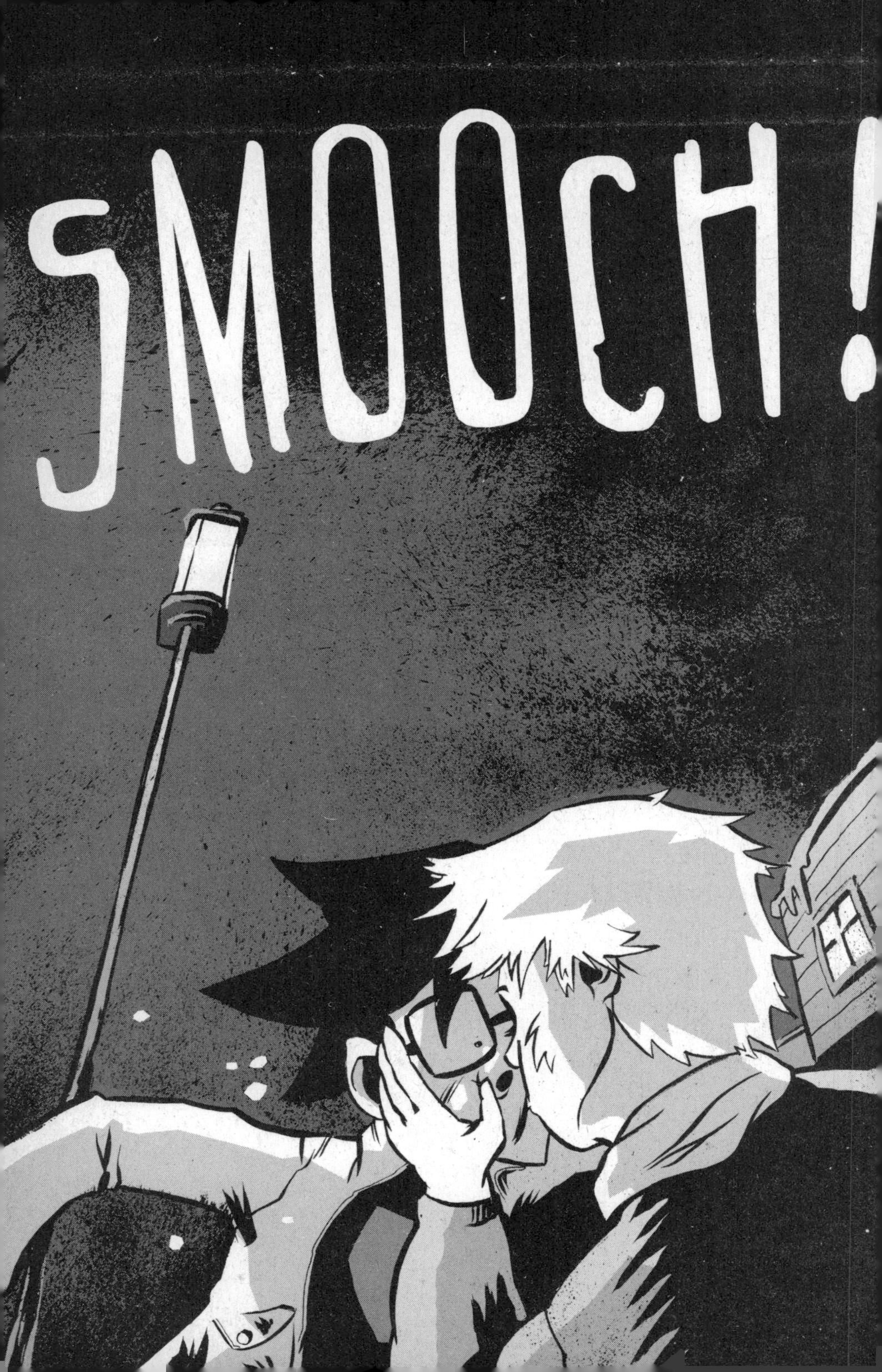
SMOOCH!

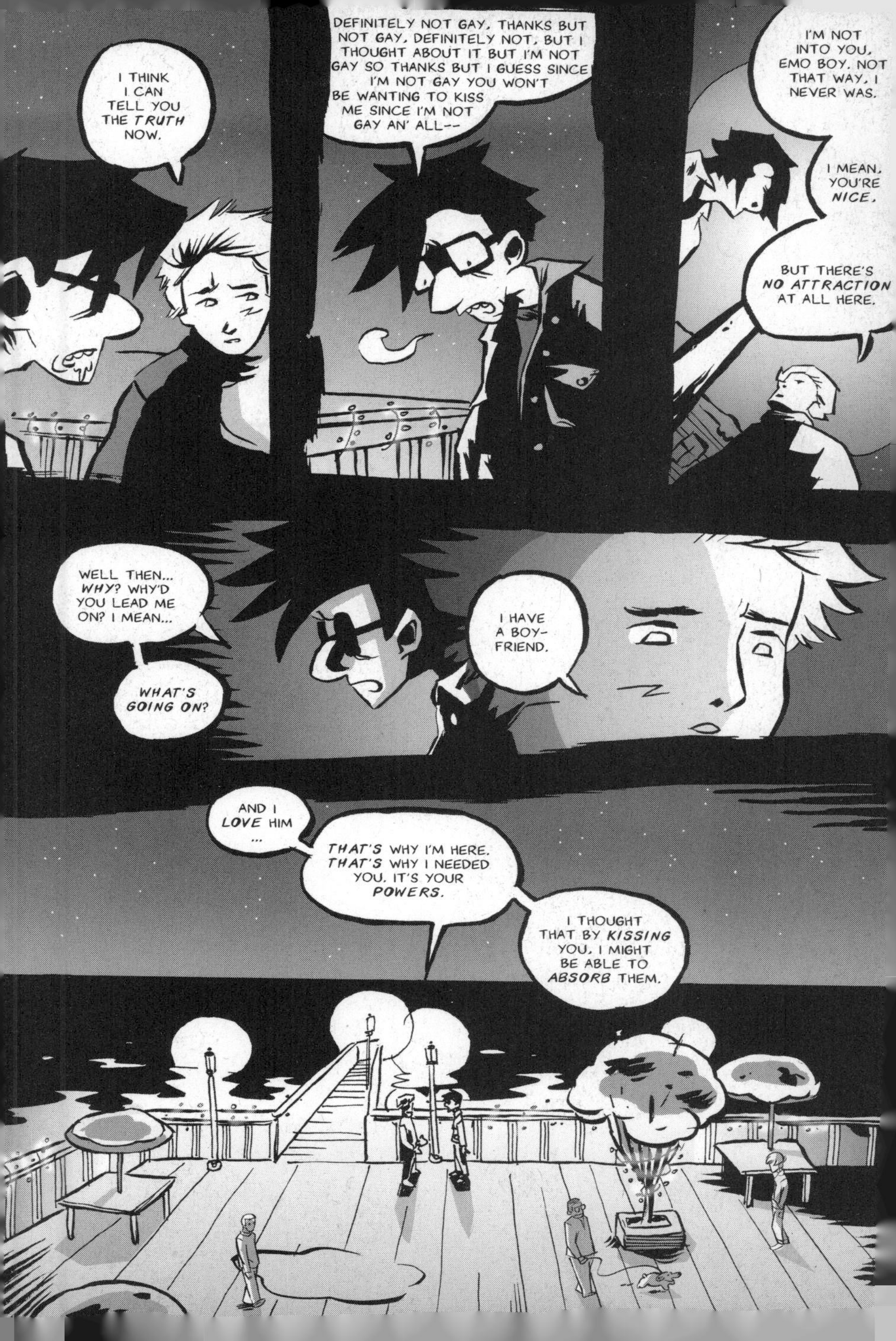
I THINK I CAN TELL YOU THE TRUTH NOW.
DEFINITELY NOT GAY. THANKS BUT NOT GAY. DEFINITELY NOT. BUT I THOUGHT ABOUT IT BUT I'M NOT GAY SO THANKS BUT I GUESS SINCE I'M NOT GAY YOU WON'T BE WANTING TO KISS ME SINCE I'M NOT GAY AN' ALL--
I'M NOT INTO YOU, EMO BOY. NOT THAT WAY. I NEVER WAS.
I MEAN, YOU'RE NICE.
BUT THERE'S NO ATTRACTION AT ALL HERE.
WELL THEN... WHY? WHY'D YOU LEAD ME ON? I MEAN...
WHAT'S GOING ON?
I HAVE A BOY-FRIEND.
AND I LOVE HIM ...
THAT'S WHY I'M HERE. THAT'S WHY I NEEDED YOU. IT'S YOUR POWERS.
I THOUGHT THAT BY KISSING YOU, I MIGHT BE ABLE TO ABSORB THEM.

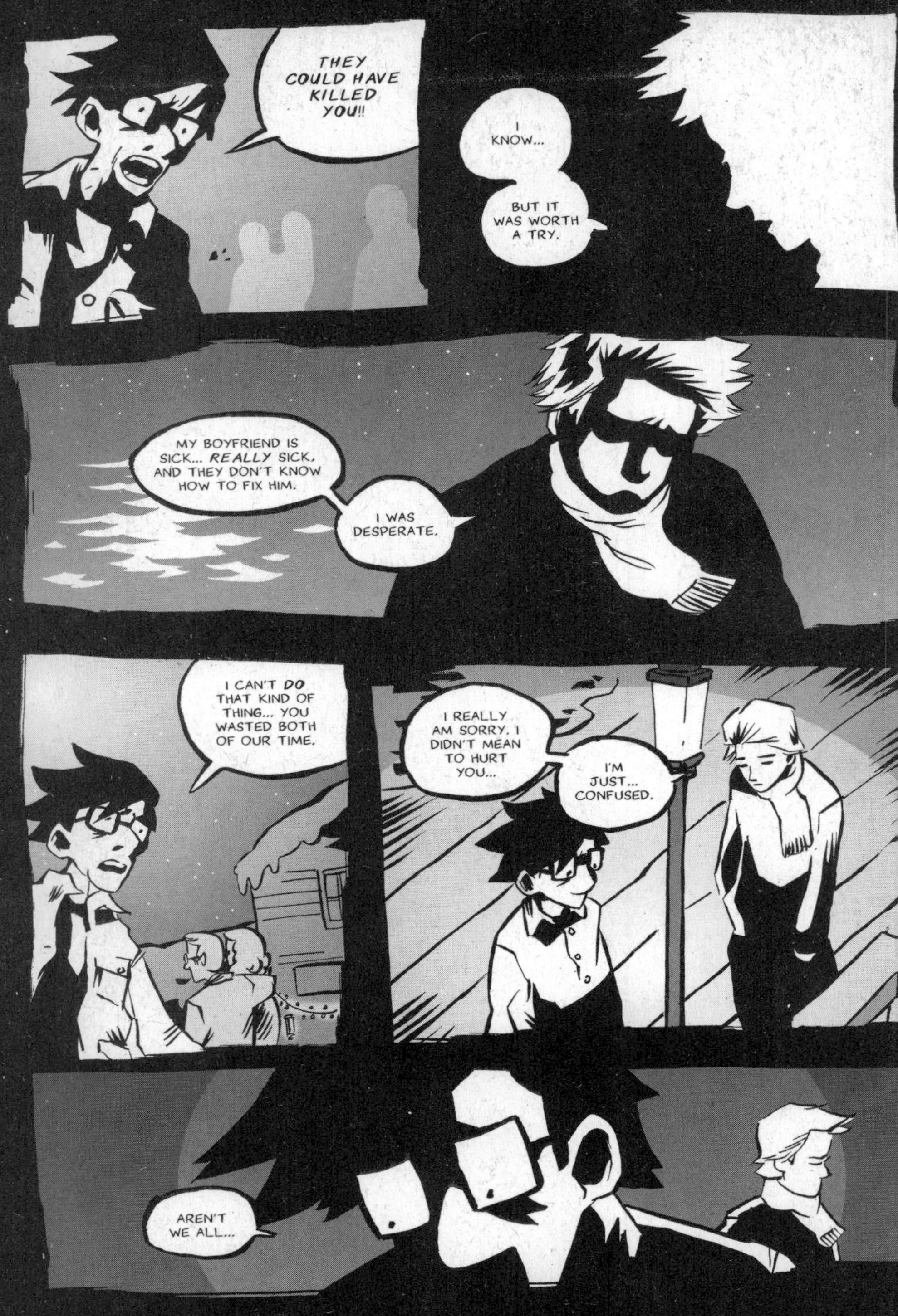
THEY COULD HAVE KILLED YOU!!
I KNOW...
BUT IT WAS WORTH A TRY.
MY BOYFRIEND IS SICK... REALLY SICK, AND THEY DON'T KNOW HOW TO FIX HIM.
I WAS DESPERATE.
I CAN'T DO THAT KIND OF THING... YOU WASTED BOTH OF OUR TIME.
I REALLY AM SORRY. I DIDN'T MEAN TO HURT YOU...
I'M JUST... CONFUSED.
AREN'T WE ALL...

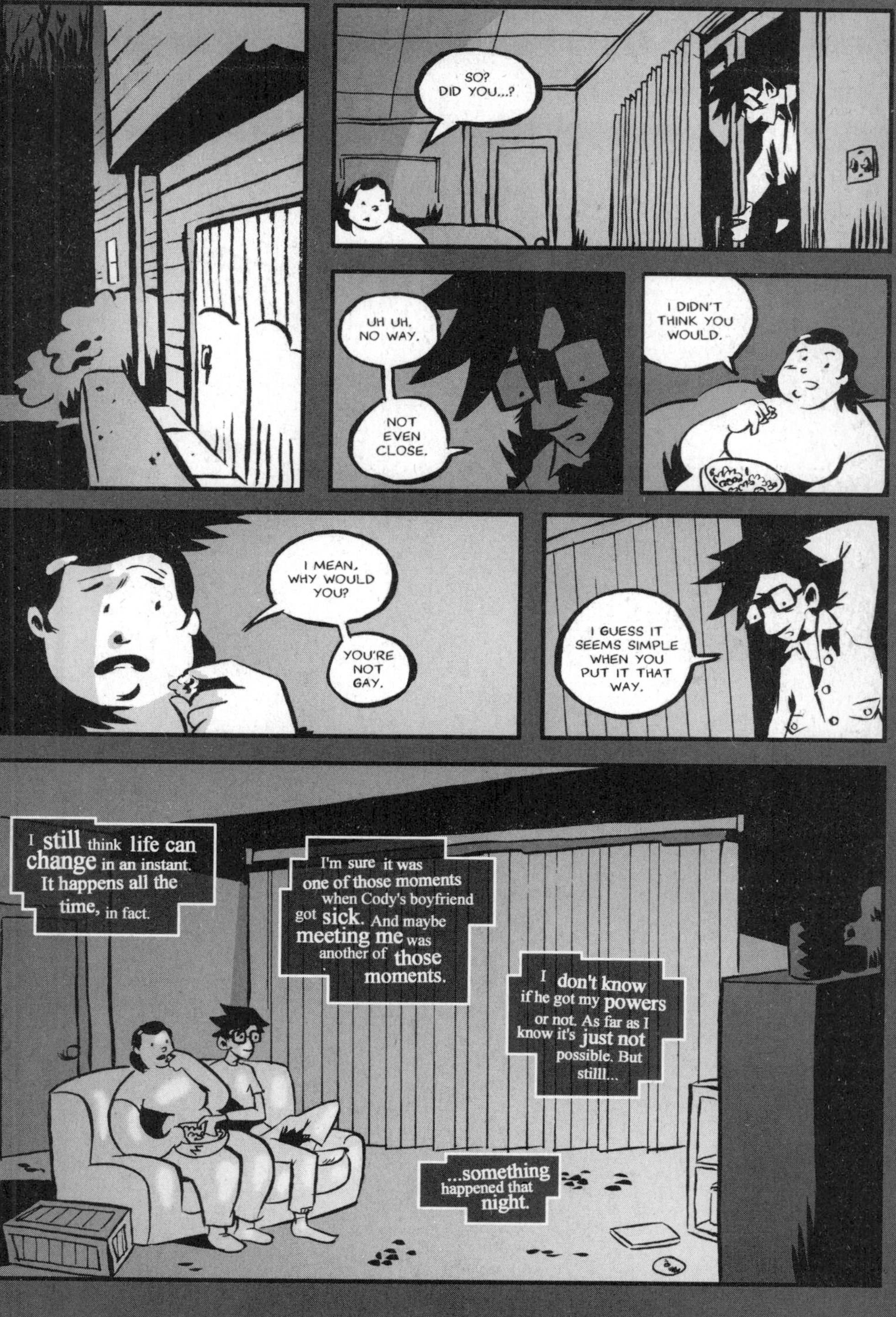
SO?
DID YOU...?
UH UH.
NO WAY.
NOT EVEN CLOSE.
I DIDN'T THINK YOU WOULD.
I MEAN, WHY WOULD YOU?
YOU'RE NOT GAY.
I GUESS IT SEEMS SIMPLE WHEN YOU PUT IT THAT WAY.
I still think life can change in an instant. It happens all the time, in fact.
I'm sure it was one of those moments when Cody's boyfriend got sick. And maybe meeting me was another of those moments.
I don't know if he got my powers or not. As far as I know it's just not possible. But stilll...
...something happened that night.

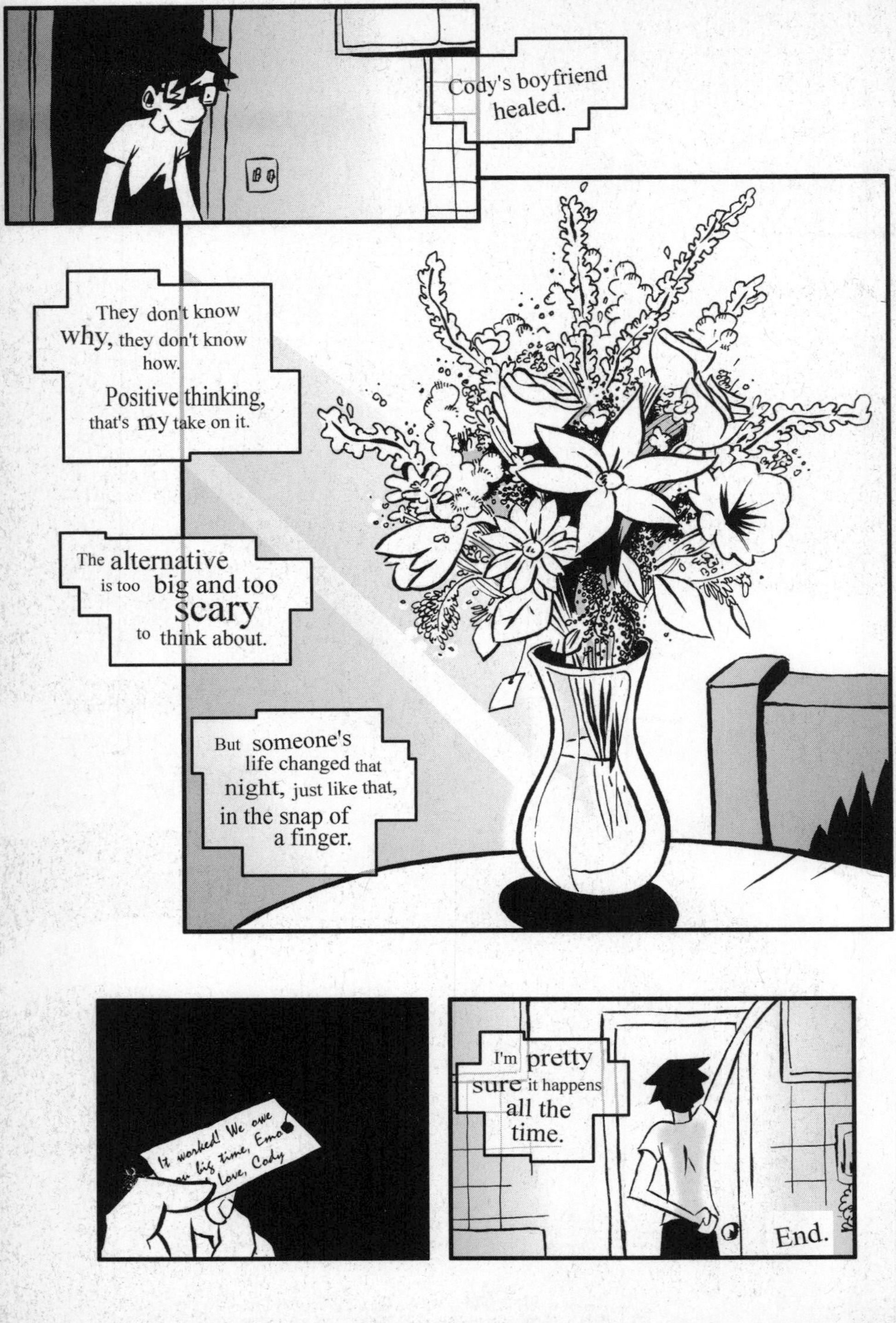
Cody's boyfriend healed.
They don't know why, they don't know how.
Positive thinking, that's my take on it.
The alternative is too big and too scary to think about.
But someone's life changed that night, just like that, in the snap of a finger.
It worked! We owe
big time, Emo
Love, Cody
I'm pretty sure it happens all the time.
End.

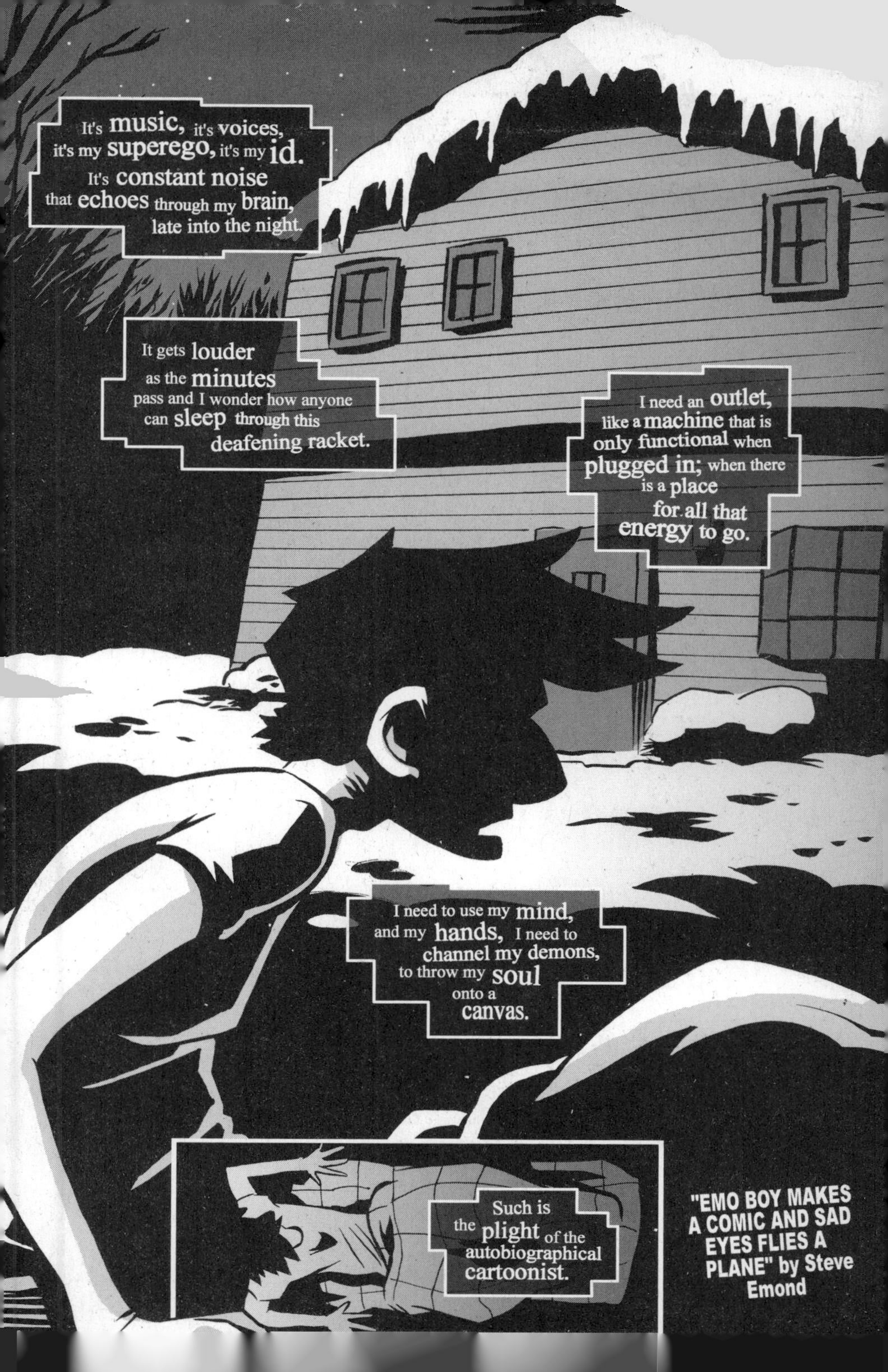
It's music, it's voices, it's my superego, it's my id. It's constant noise that echoes through my brain, late into the night.
It gets louder as the minutes pass and I wonder how anyone can sleep through this deafening racket.
I need an outlet, like a machine that is only functional when plugged in; when there is a place for all that energy to go.
I need to use my mind, and my hands, I need to channel my demons, to throw my soul onto a canvas.
Such is the plight of the autobiographical cartoonist.
"EMO BOY MAKES A COMIC AND SAD EYES FLIES A PLANE" by Steve Emond

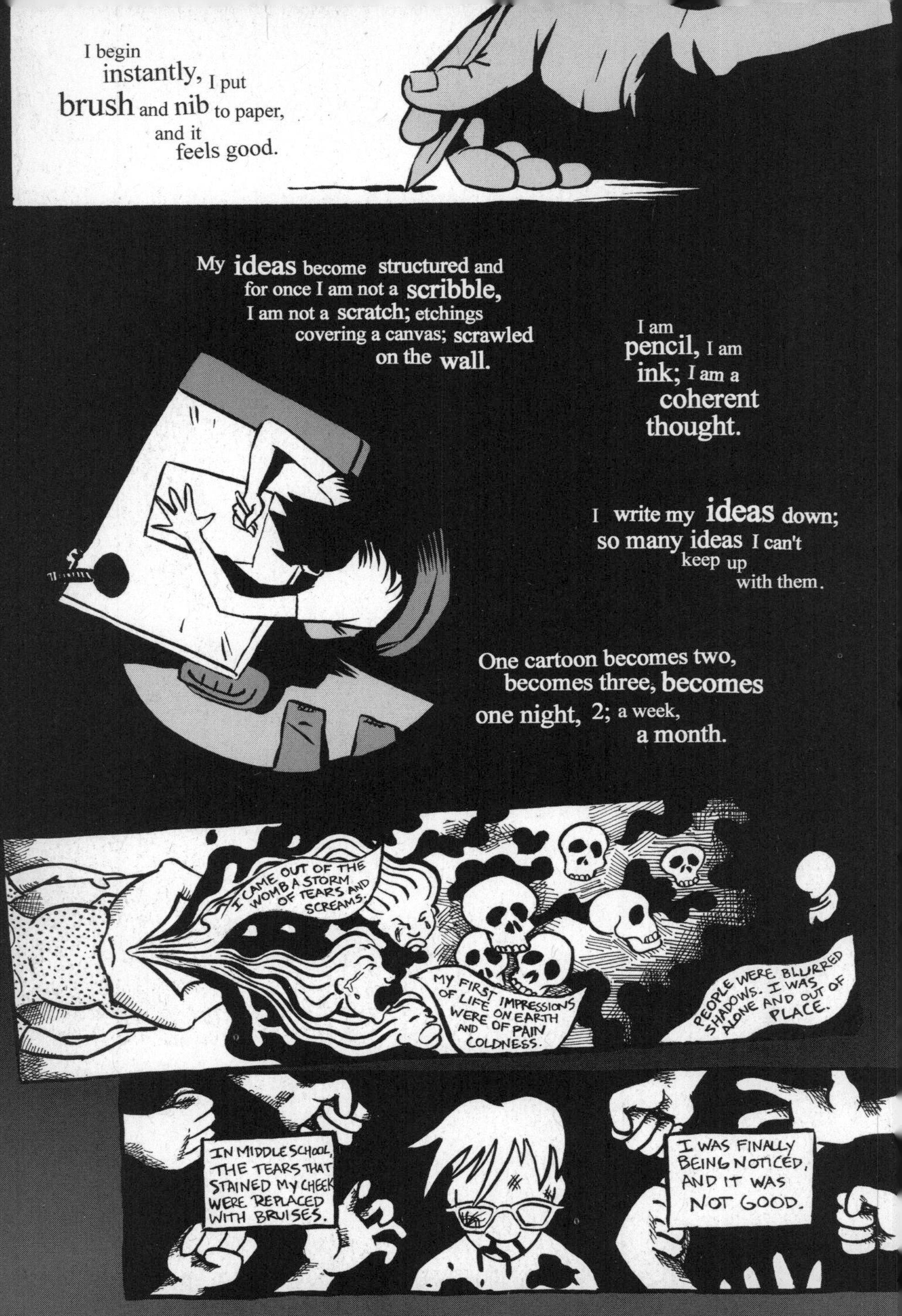
I begin instantly, I put brush and nib to paper, and it feels good.
My ideas become structured and for once I am not a scribble, I am not a scratch; etchings covering a canvas; scrawled on the wall.
I am pencil, I am ink; I am a coherent thought.
I write my ideas down; so many ideas I can't keep up with them.
One cartoon becomes two, becomes three, becomes one night, 2; a week, a month.
I CAME OUT OF THE WOMB A STORM OF TEARS AND SCREAMS.
MY FIRST IMPRESSIONS OF LIFE ON EARTH WERE OF PAIN AND COLDNESS.
PEOPLE WERE BLURRED SHADOWS. I WAS ALONE AND OUT OF PLACE.
IN MIDDLE SCHOOL, THE TEARS THAT STAINED MY CHEEK WERE REPLACED WITH BRUISES.
I WAS FINALLY BEING NOTICED, AND IT WAS NOT GOOD.

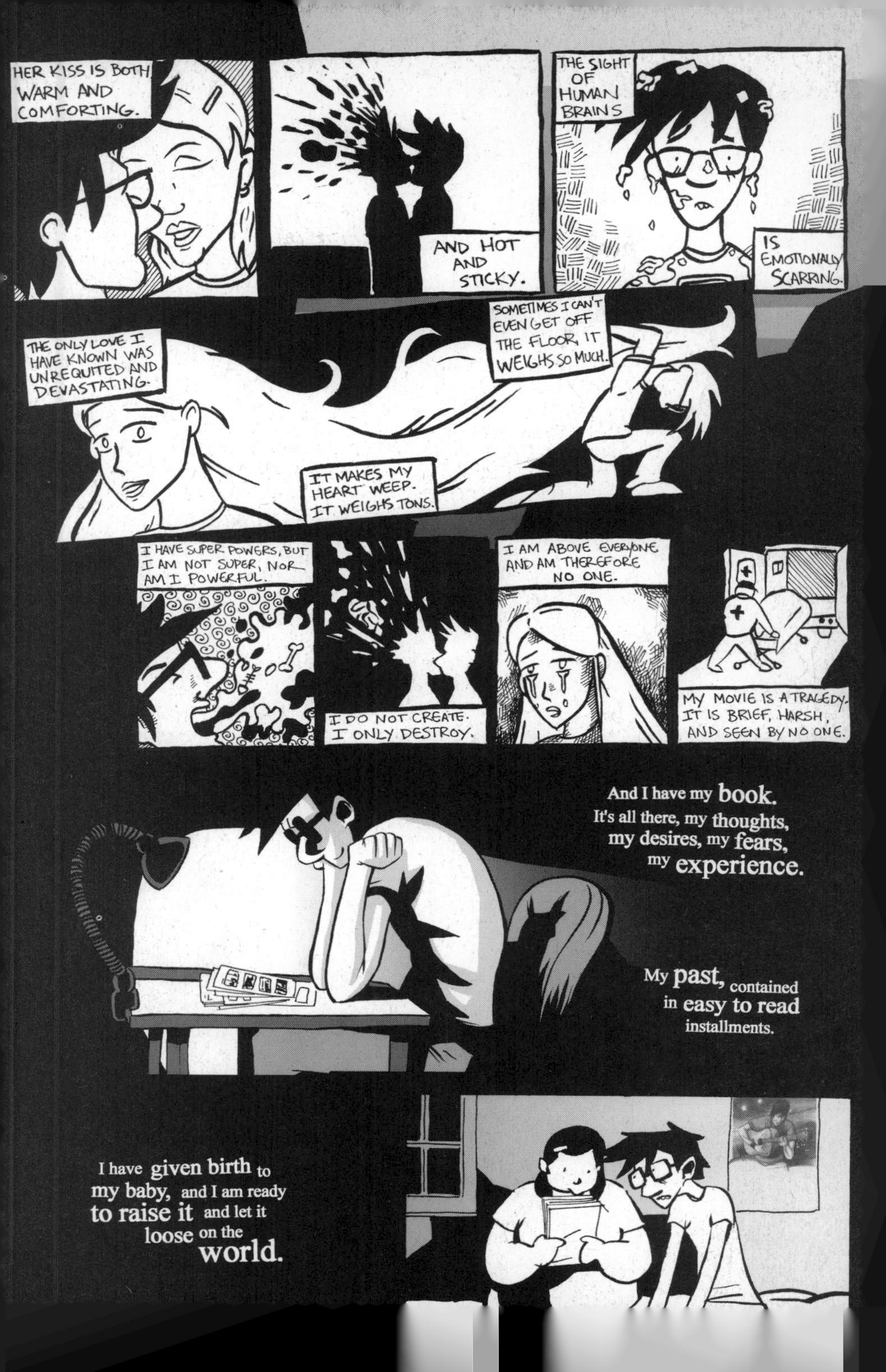

HER KISS IS BOTH WARM AND COMFORTING.
AND HOT AND STICKY.
THE SIGHT OF HUMAN BRAINS
IS EMOTIONALLY SCARRING.
THE ONLY LOVE I HAVE KNOWN WAS UNREQUITED AND DEVASTATING.
SOMETIMES I CAN'T EVEN GET OFF THE FLOOR, IT WEIGHS SO MUCH.
IT MAKES MY HEART WEEP. IT WEIGHS TONS.
I HAVE SUPER POWERS, BUT I AM NOT SUPER, NOR AM I POWERFUL.
I DO NOT CREATE. I ONLY DESTROY.
I AM ABOVE EVERYONE AND AM THEREFORE NO ONE.
MY MOVIE IS A TRAGEDY. IT IS BRIEF, HARSH, AND SEEN BY NO ONE.
And I have my book. It's all there, my thoughts, my desires, my fears, my experience.
My past, contained in easy to read installments.
I have given birth to my baby, and I am ready to raise it and let it loose on the world.

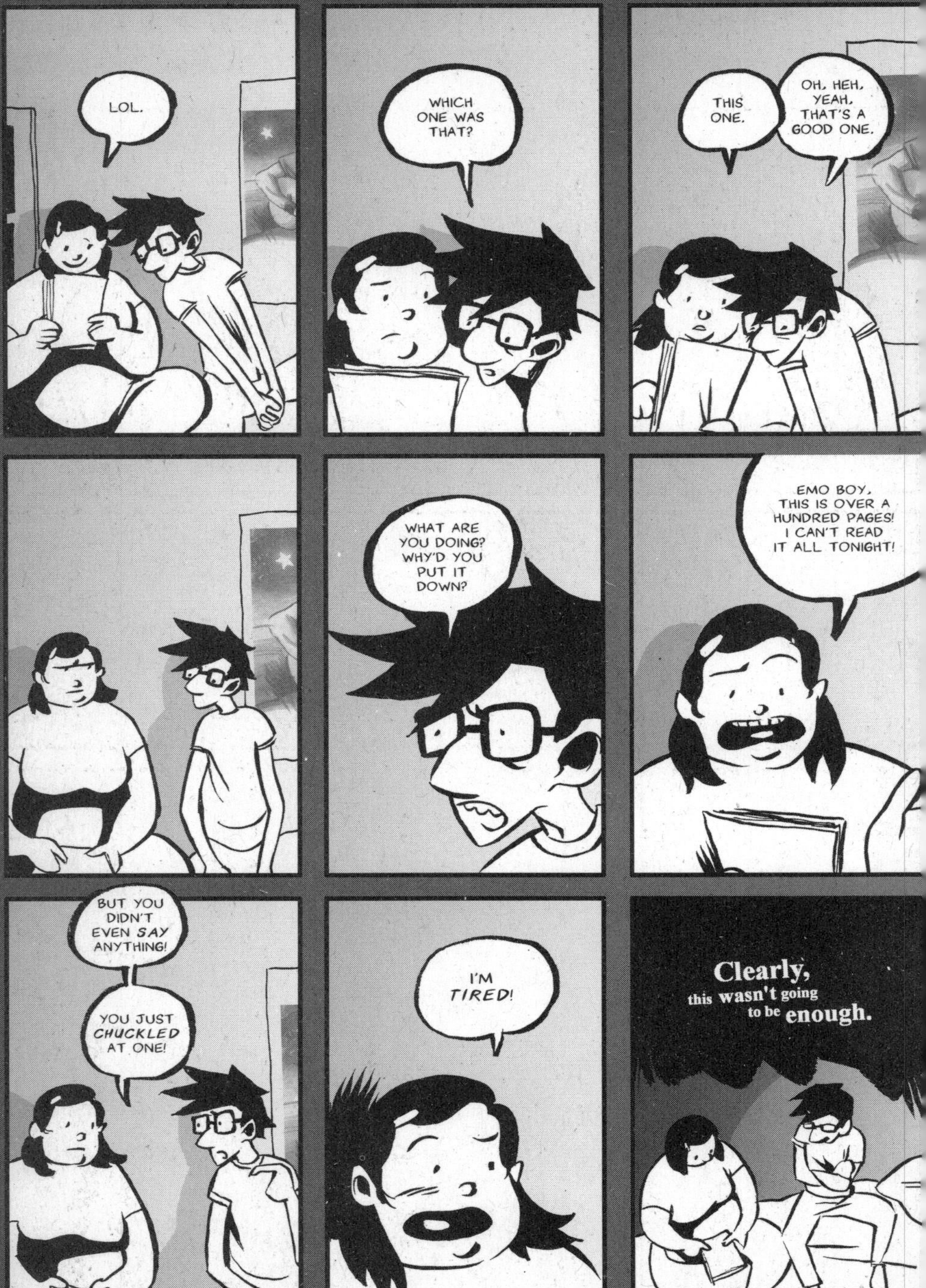
LOL.
WHICH ONE WAS THAT?
THIS ONE.
OH, HEH, YEAH, THAT'S A GOOD ONE.
WHAT ARE YOU DOING? WHY'D YOU PUT IT DOWN?
EMO BOY, THIS IS OVER A HUNDRED PAGES! I CAN'T READ IT ALL TONIGHT!
BUT YOU DIDN'T EVEN SAY ANYTHING!
YOU JUST CHUCKLED AT ONE!
I'M TIRED!
Clearly, this wasn't going to be enough.

I take it to the comic book convention circuit.

The next logical step is to find a publisher; someone to raise my baby with.

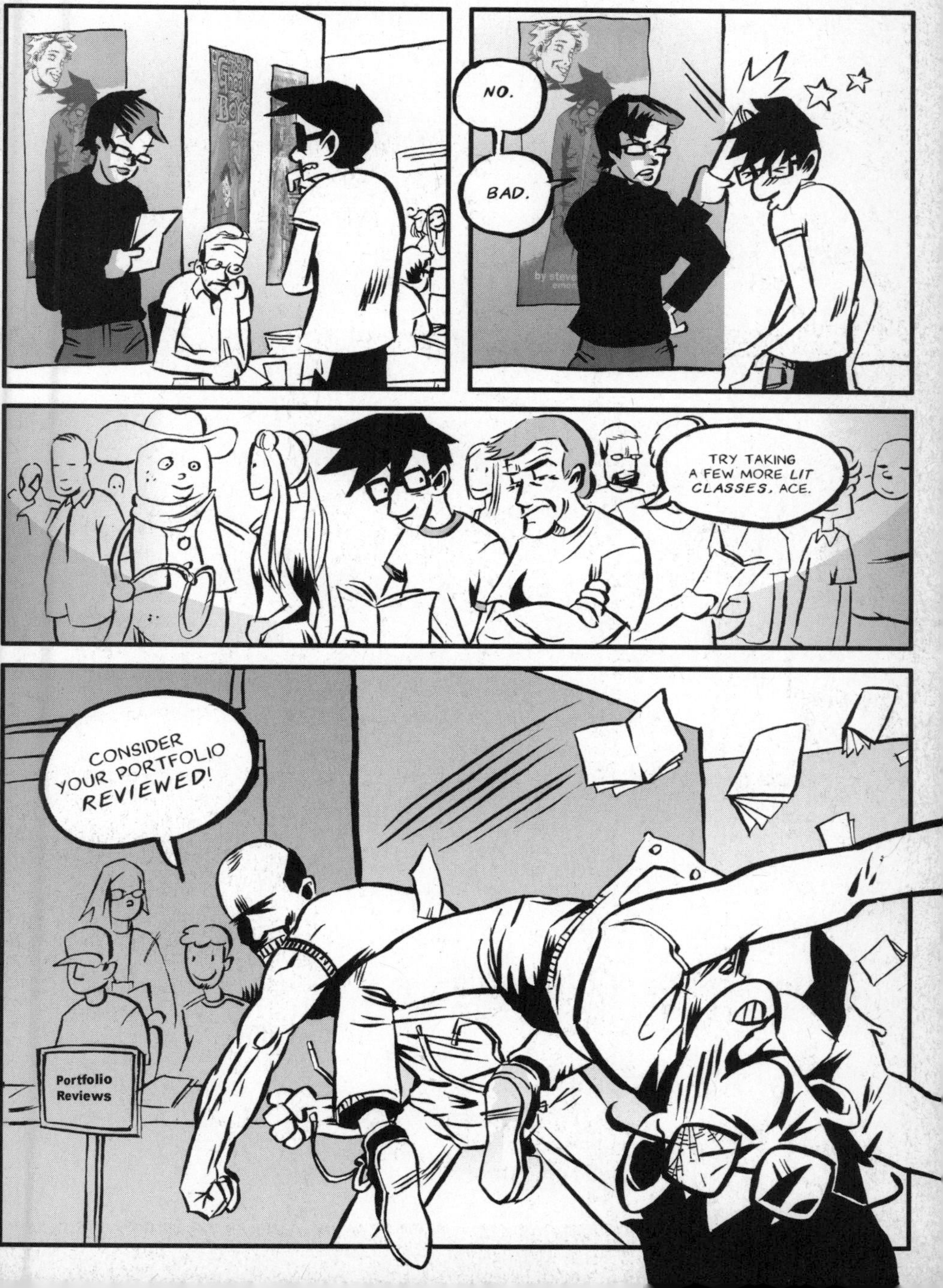
NO.
BAD.
TRY TAKING A FEW MORE LIT CLASSES, ACE.
CONSIDER YOUR PORTFOLIO REVIEWED!
Portfolio Reviews

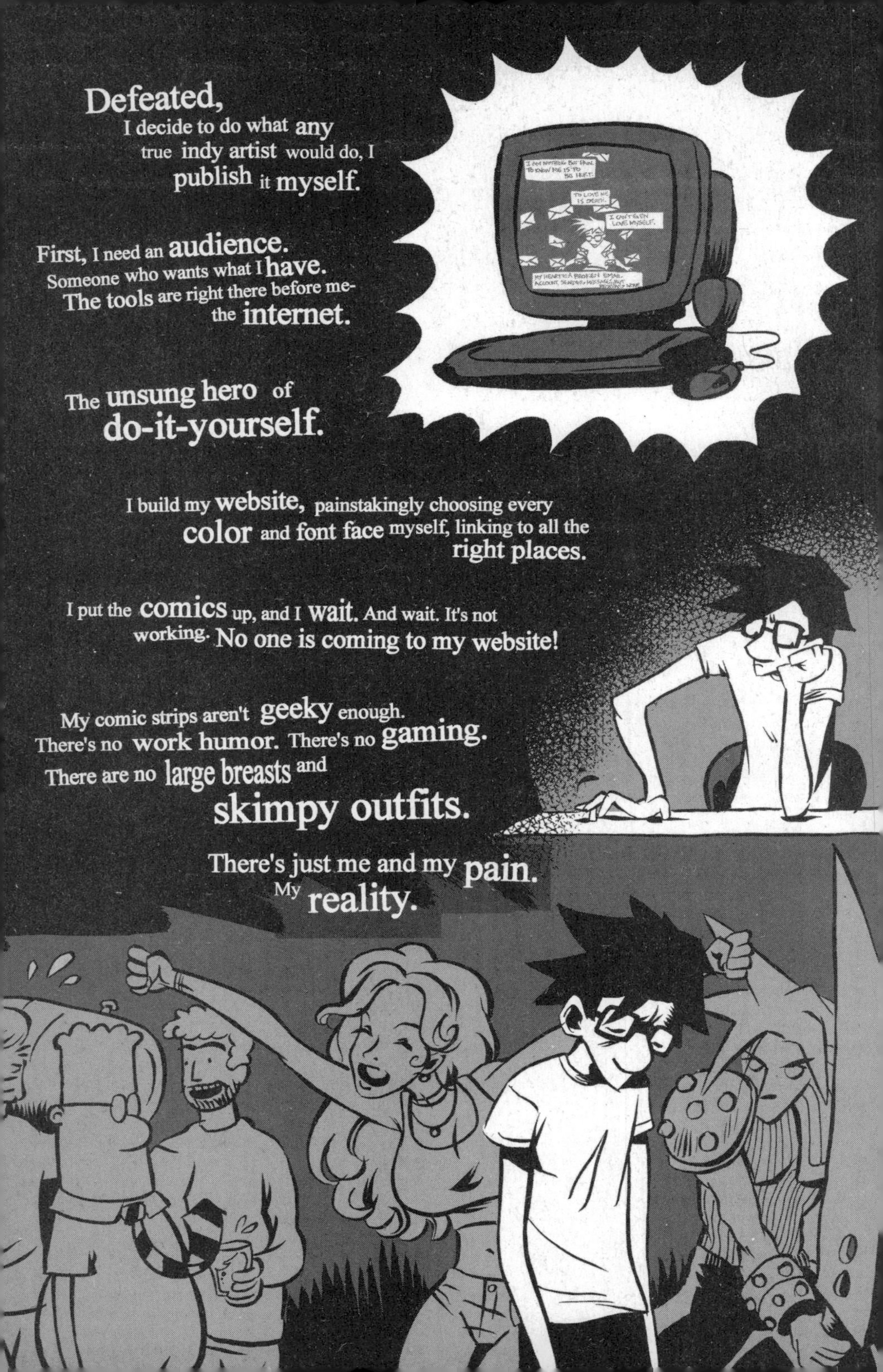
Defeated,
I decide to do what any true indy artist would do, I publish it myself.
First, I need an audience. Someone who wants what I have. The tools are right there before me- the internet.
The unsung hero of do-it-yourself.
I build my website, painstakingly choosing every color and font face myself, linking to all the right places.
I put the comics up, and I wait. And wait. It's not working. No one is coming to my website!
My comic strips aren't geeky enough. There's no work humor. There's no gaming. There are no large breasts and skimpy outfits.
There's just me and my pain. My reality.

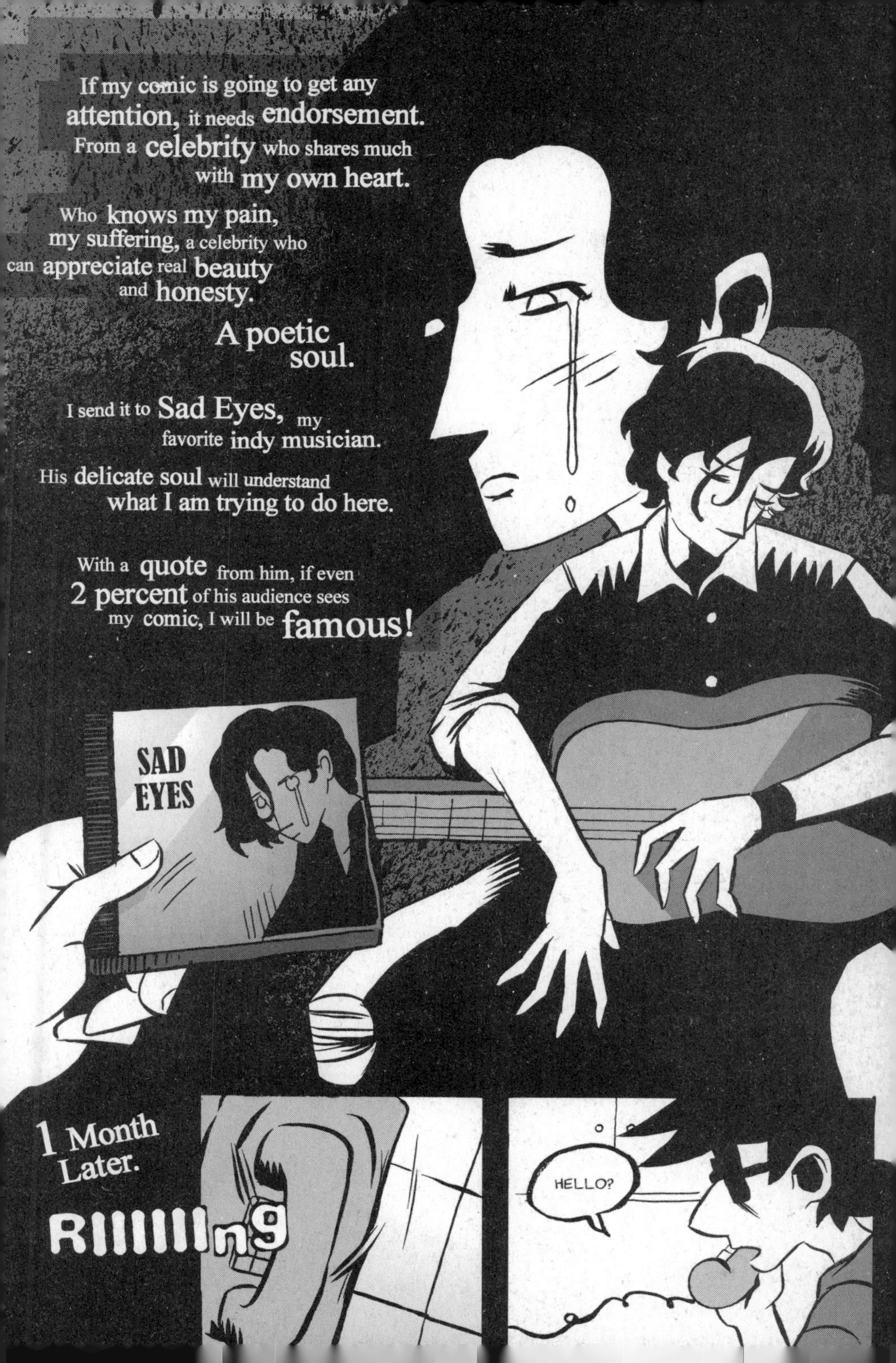
If my comic is going to get any attention, it needs endorsement. From a celebrity who shares much with my own heart.
Who knows my pain, my suffering, a celebrity who can appreciate real beauty and honesty.
A poetic soul.
I send it to Sad Eyes, my favorite indy musician.
His delicate soul will understand what I am trying to do here.
With a quote from him, if even 2 percent of his audience sees my comic, I will be famous!
SAD EYES
1 Month Later.
RIIIIIIng
HELLO?

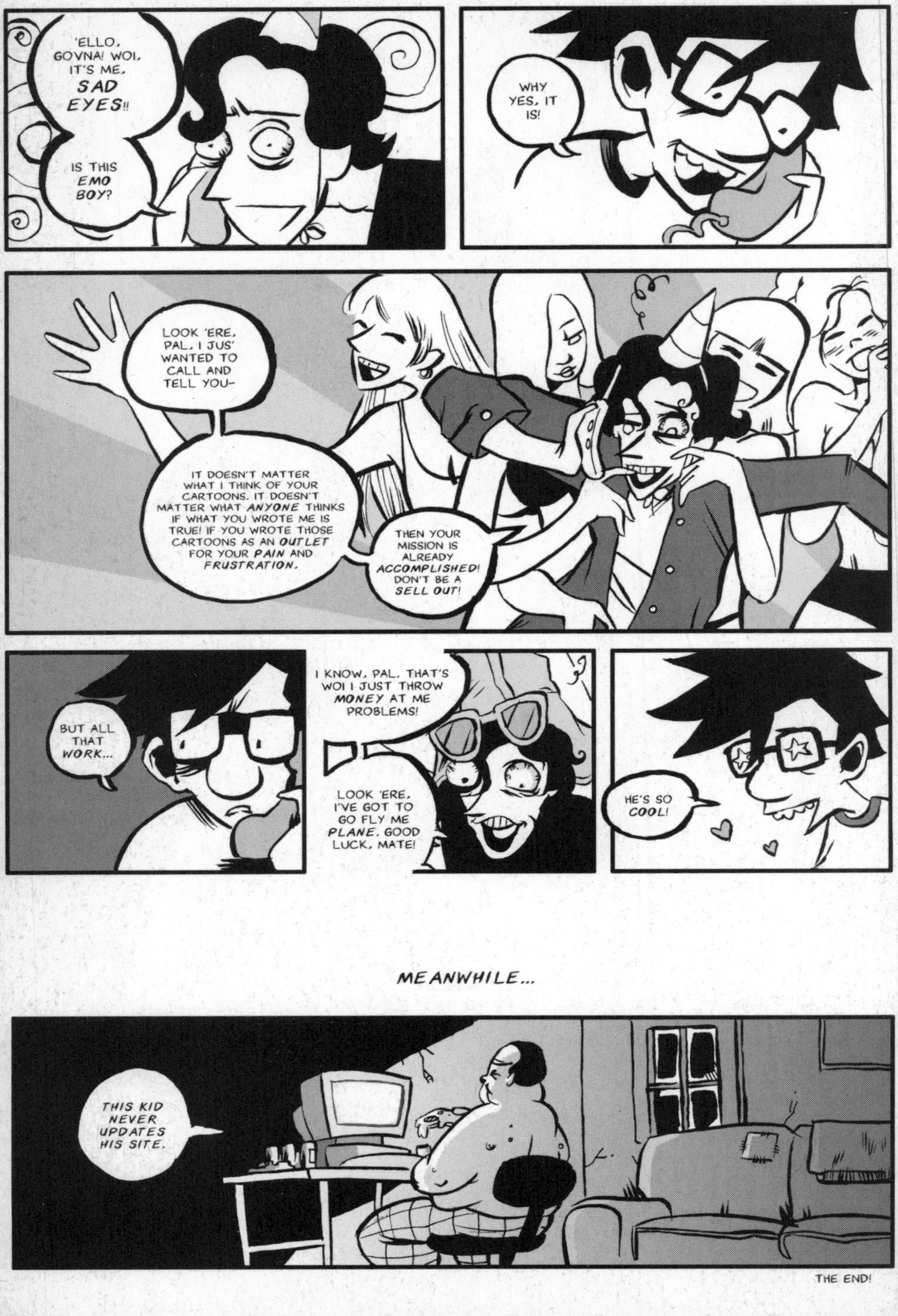
'ELLO, GOVNA! WOI, IT'S ME, SAD EYES!!
IS THIS EMO BOY?
WHY YES, IT IS!
LOOK 'ERE, PAL, I JUS' WANTED TO CALL AND TELL YOU-
IT DOESN'T MATTER WHAT I THINK OF YOUR CARTOONS. IT DOESN'T MATTER WHAT ANYONE THINKS IF WHAT YOU WROTE ME IS TRUE! IF YOU WROTE THOSE CARTOONS AS AN OUTLET FOR YOUR PAIN AND FRUSTRATION,
THEN YOUR MISSION IS ALREADY ACCOMPLISHED! DON'T BE A SELL OUT!
BUT ALL THAT WORK...
I KNOW, PAL. THAT'S WOI I JUST THROW MONEY AT ME PROBLEMS!
LOOK 'ERE, I'VE GOT TO GO FLY ME PLANE. GOOD LUCK, MATE!
HE'S SO COOL!
MEANWHILE...
THIS KID NEVER UPDATES HIS SITE.
THE END!

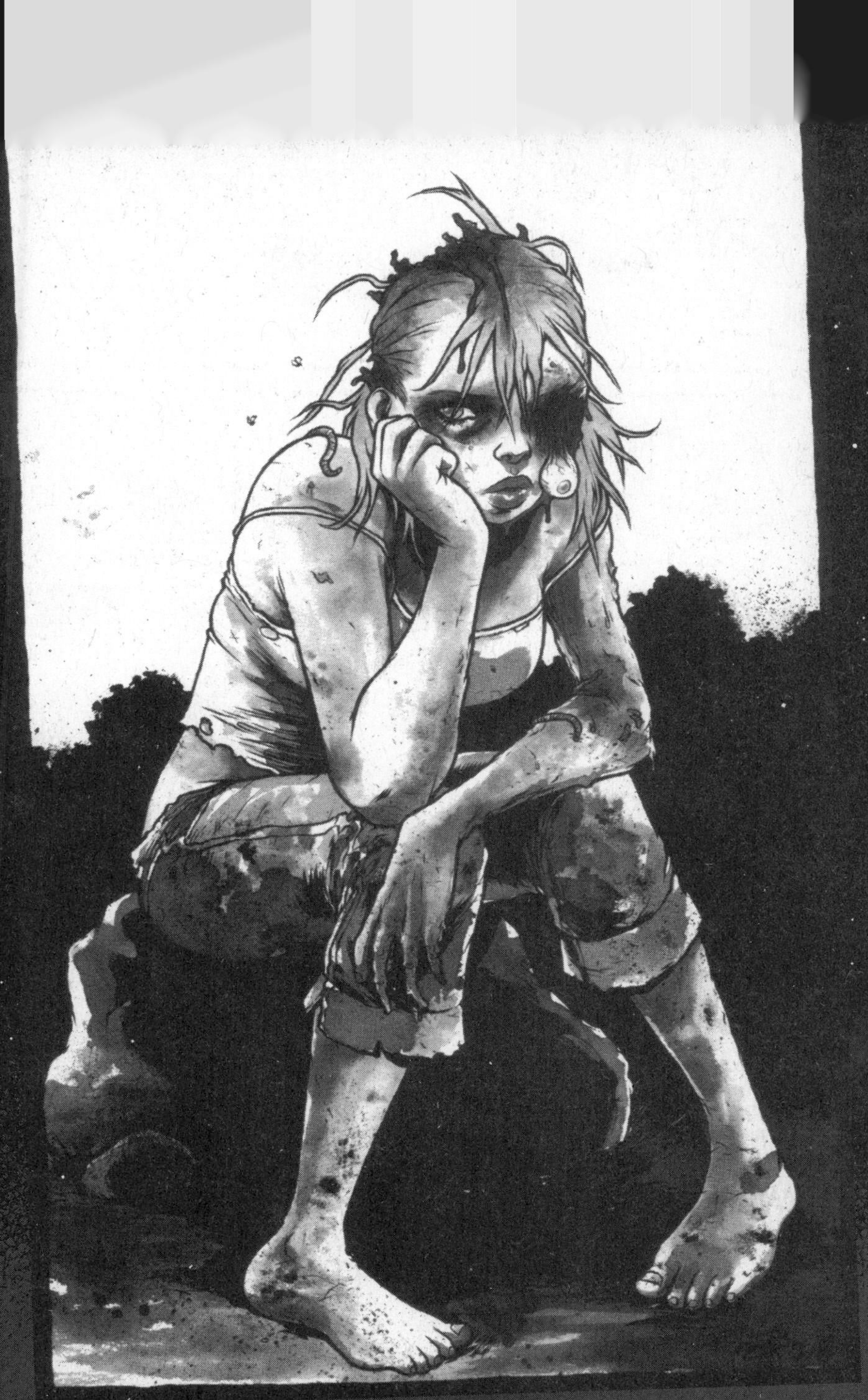

Emo Boy
Pinup by
Ross Campbell

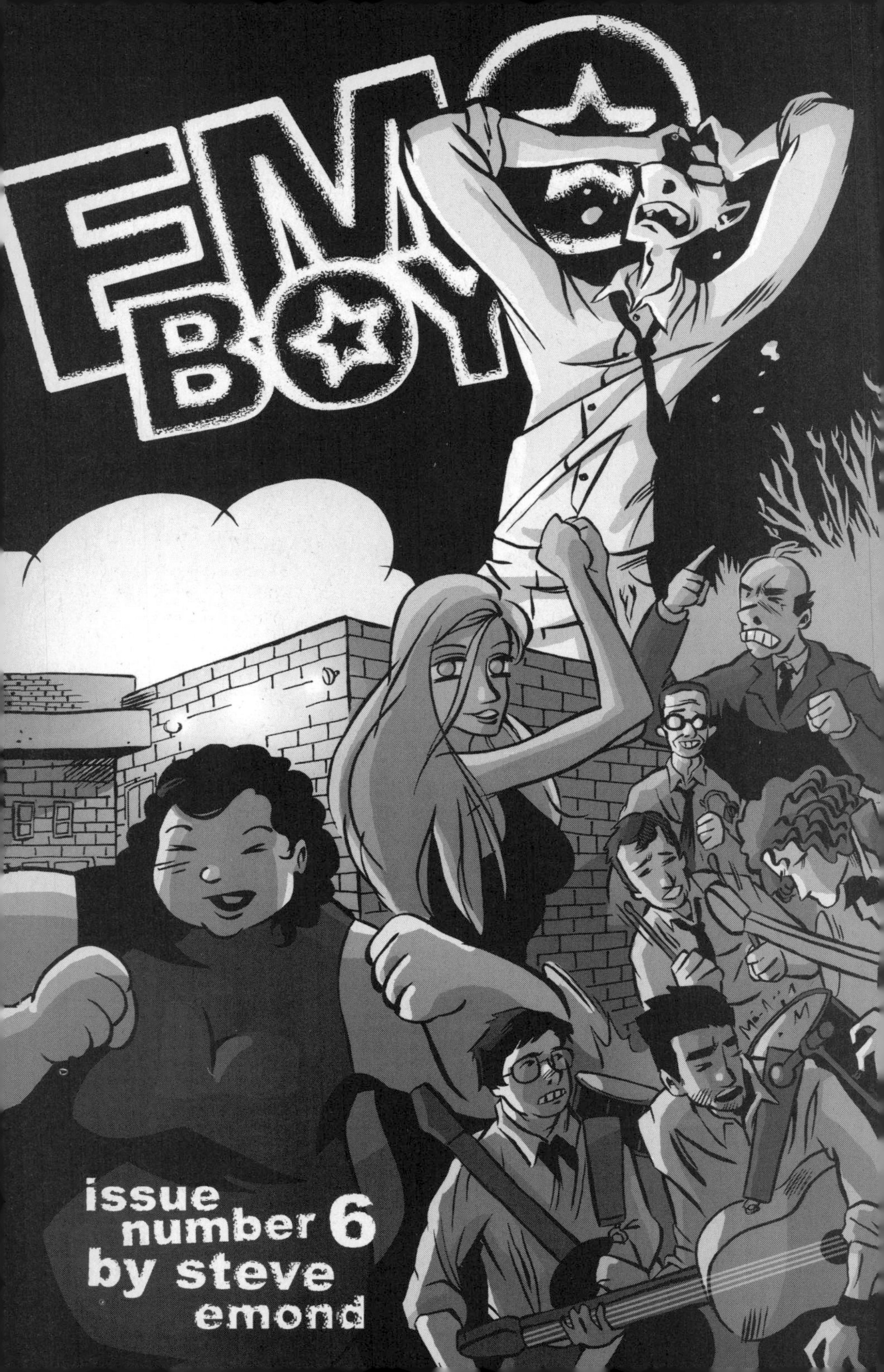
EM BOY
issue number 6
by steve emond

"JUST BECAUSE"
written and drawn
by STEVE EMOND

Emo Boy sits and stares in disbelief - an 'F-' graces the top of his paper. The paper details comic story at hand - both what the reader is now, and what they are about to read.
The halls are bus

"JUST BECAUSE" DANCE!!!

When: April 1
Who: You!
Where: Gym
Why? Just Because!
How: Huh?
What: Dancin', Fool!

BOO YAA!

s ffff..."
lliteratio
n't ca
stand is
a failure

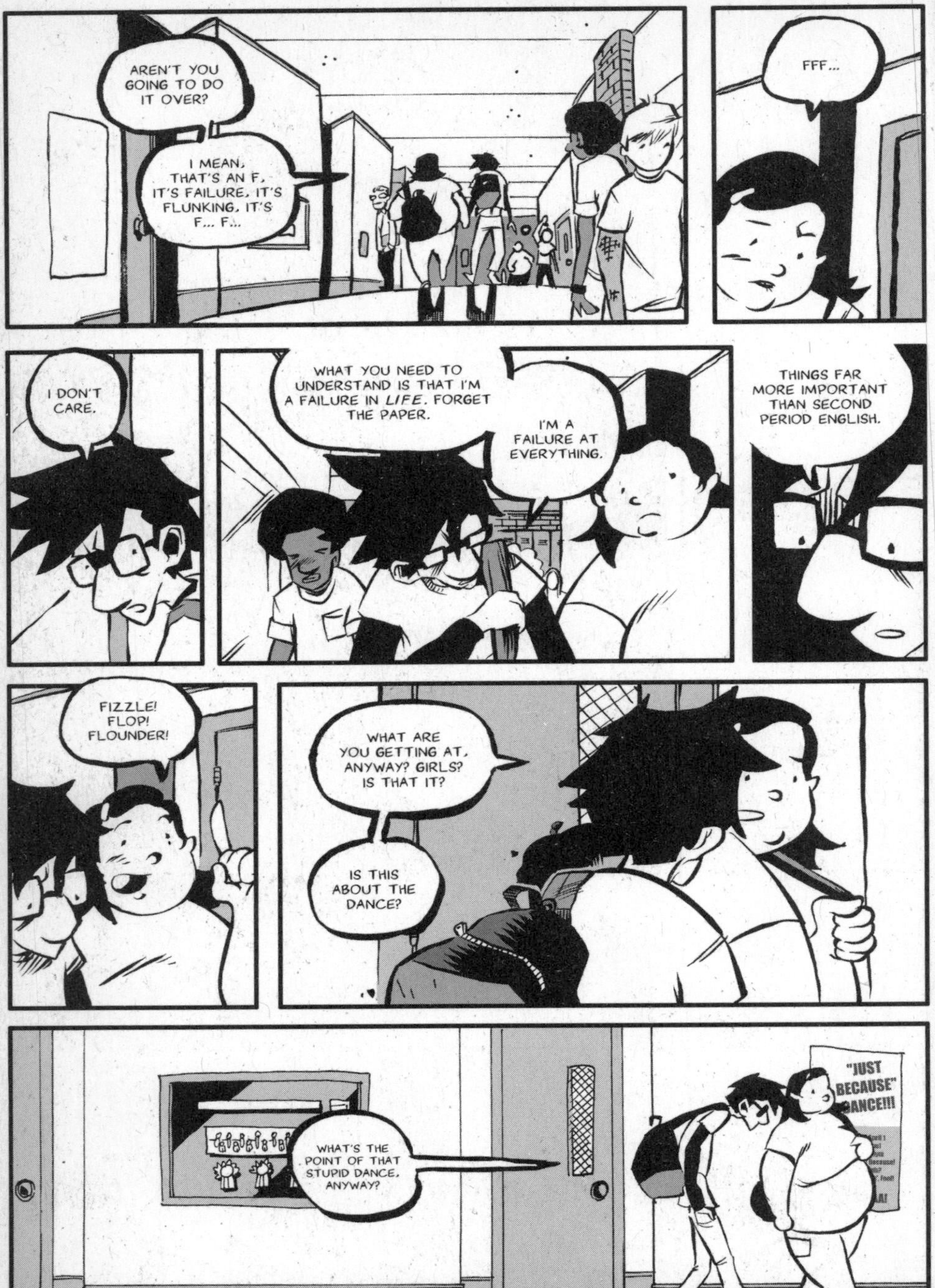
AREN'T YOU GOING TO DO IT OVER?
I MEAN, THAT'S AN F, IT'S FAILURE, IT'S FLUNKING, IT'S F... F...
FFF...
I DON'T CARE.
WHAT YOU NEED TO UNDERSTAND IS THAT I'M A FAILURE IN *LIFE*. FORGET THE PAPER.
I'M A FAILURE AT EVERYTHING.
THINGS FAR MORE IMPORTANT THAN SECOND PERIOD ENGLISH.
FIZZLE! FLOP! FLOUNDER!
WHAT ARE YOU GETTING AT, ANYWAY? GIRLS? IS THAT IT?
IS THIS ABOUT THE DANCE?
"JUST BECAUSE"
WHAT'S THE POINT OF THAT STUPID DANCE, ANYWAY?

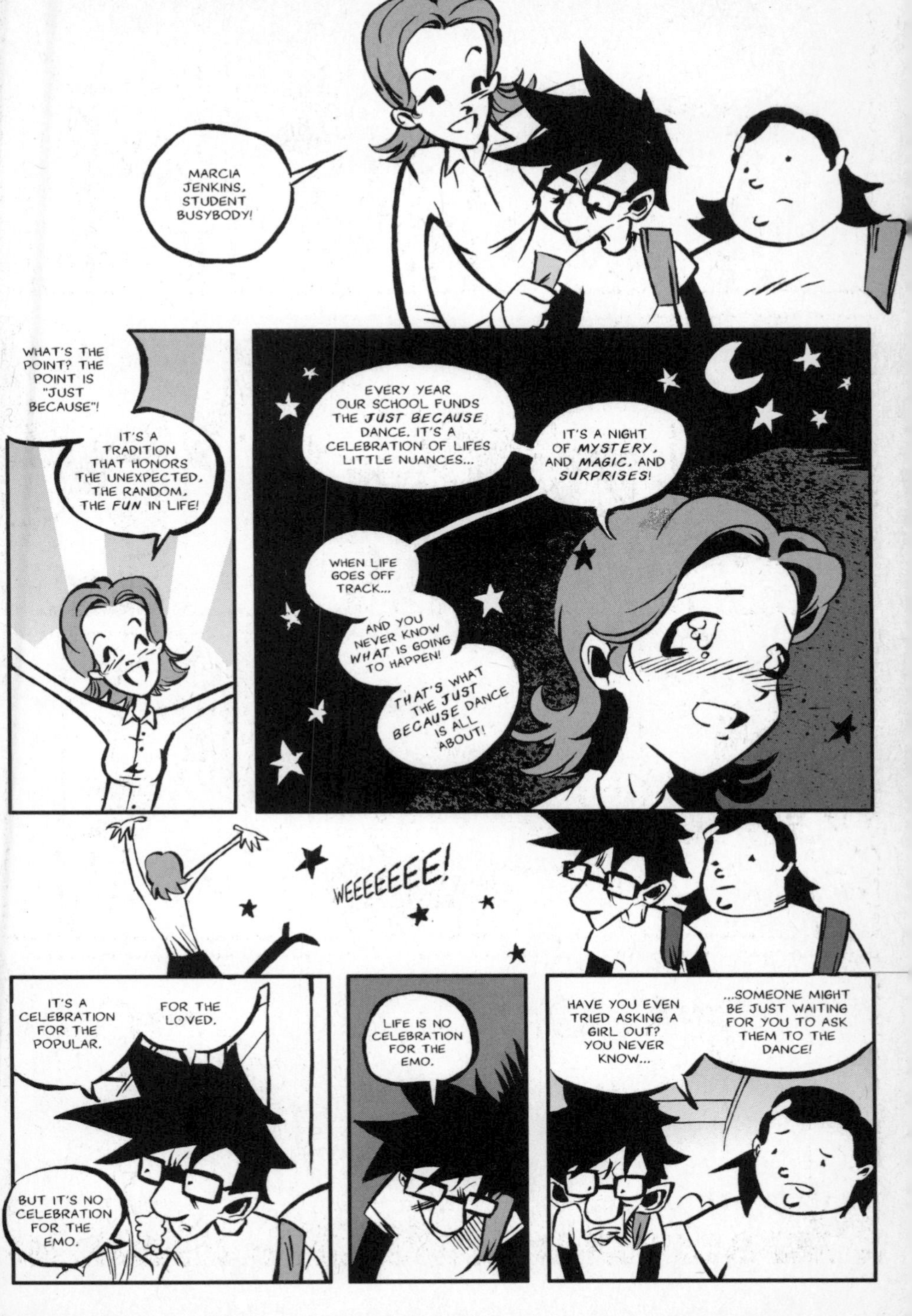
MARCIA JENKINS, STUDENT BUSYBODY!
WHAT'S THE POINT? THE POINT IS "JUST BECAUSE"!
IT'S A TRADITION THAT HONORS THE UNEXPECTED, THE RANDOM, THE FUN IN LIFE!
EVERY YEAR OUR SCHOOL FUNDS THE JUST BECAUSE DANCE. IT'S A CELEBRATION OF LIFES LITTLE NUANCES...
IT'S A NIGHT OF MYSTERY, AND MAGIC, AND SURPRISES!
WHEN LIFE GOES OFF TRACK...
AND YOU NEVER KNOW WHAT IS GOING TO HAPPEN!
THAT'S WHAT THE JUST BECAUSE DANCE IS ALL ABOUT!
WEEEEEEE!
IT'S A CELEBRATION FOR THE POPULAR.
FOR THE LOVED.
BUT IT'S NO CELEBRATION FOR THE EMO.
LIFE IS NO CELEBRATION FOR THE EMO.
HAVE YOU EVEN TRIED ASKING A GIRL OUT? YOU NEVER KNOW...
...SOMEONE MIGHT BE JUST WAITING FOR YOU TO ASK THEM TO THE DANCE!

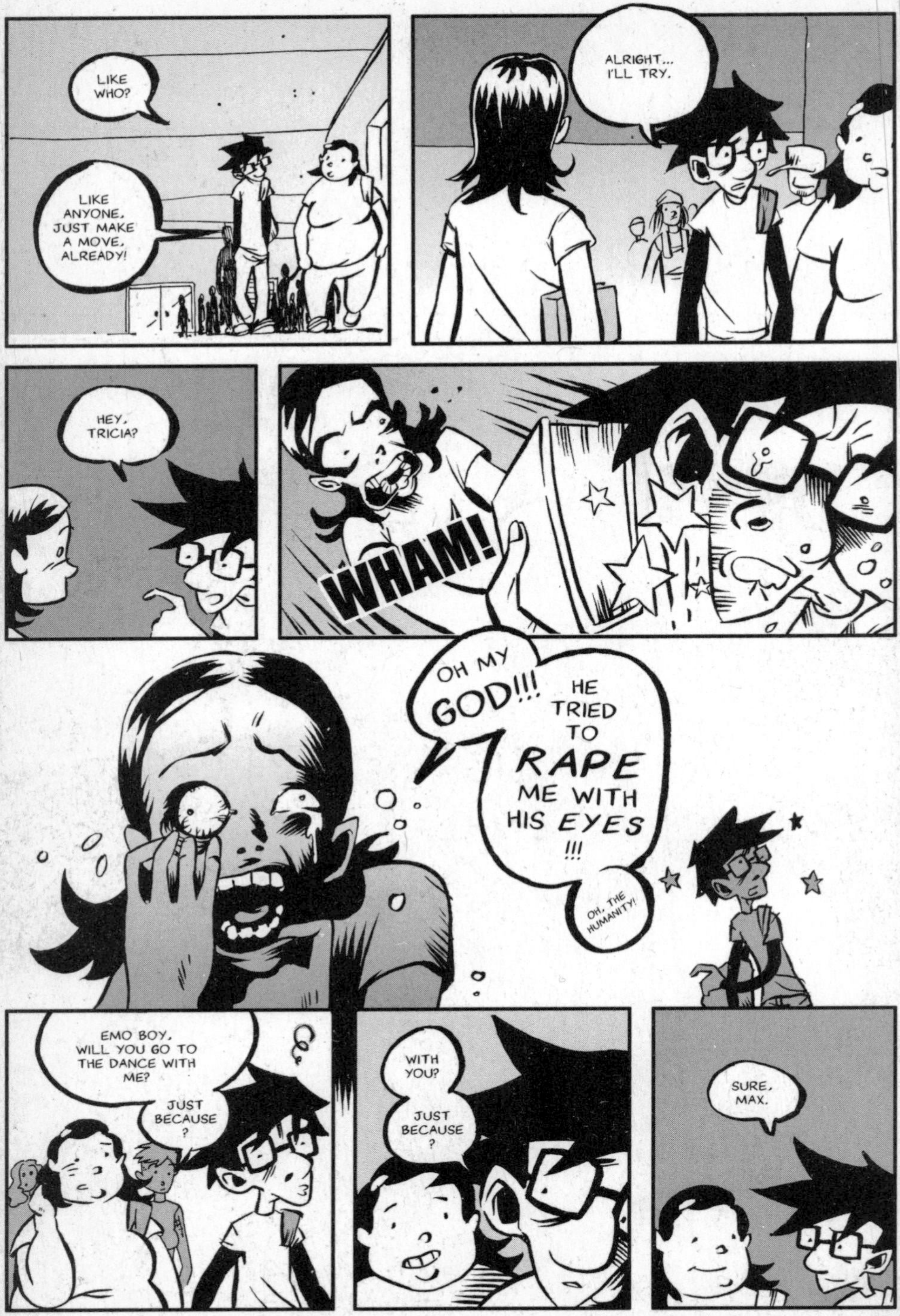
LIKE WHO?
LIKE ANYONE, JUST MAKE A MOVE, ALREADY!
ALRIGHT... I'LL TRY.
HEY, TRICIA?
WHAM!
OH MY GOD!!!
HE TRIED TO RAPE ME WITH HIS EYES !!!
OH, THE HUMANITY!
EMO BOY, WILL YOU GO TO THE DANCE WITH ME?
JUST BECAUSE ?
WITH YOU?
JUST BECAUSE ?
SURE, MAX.

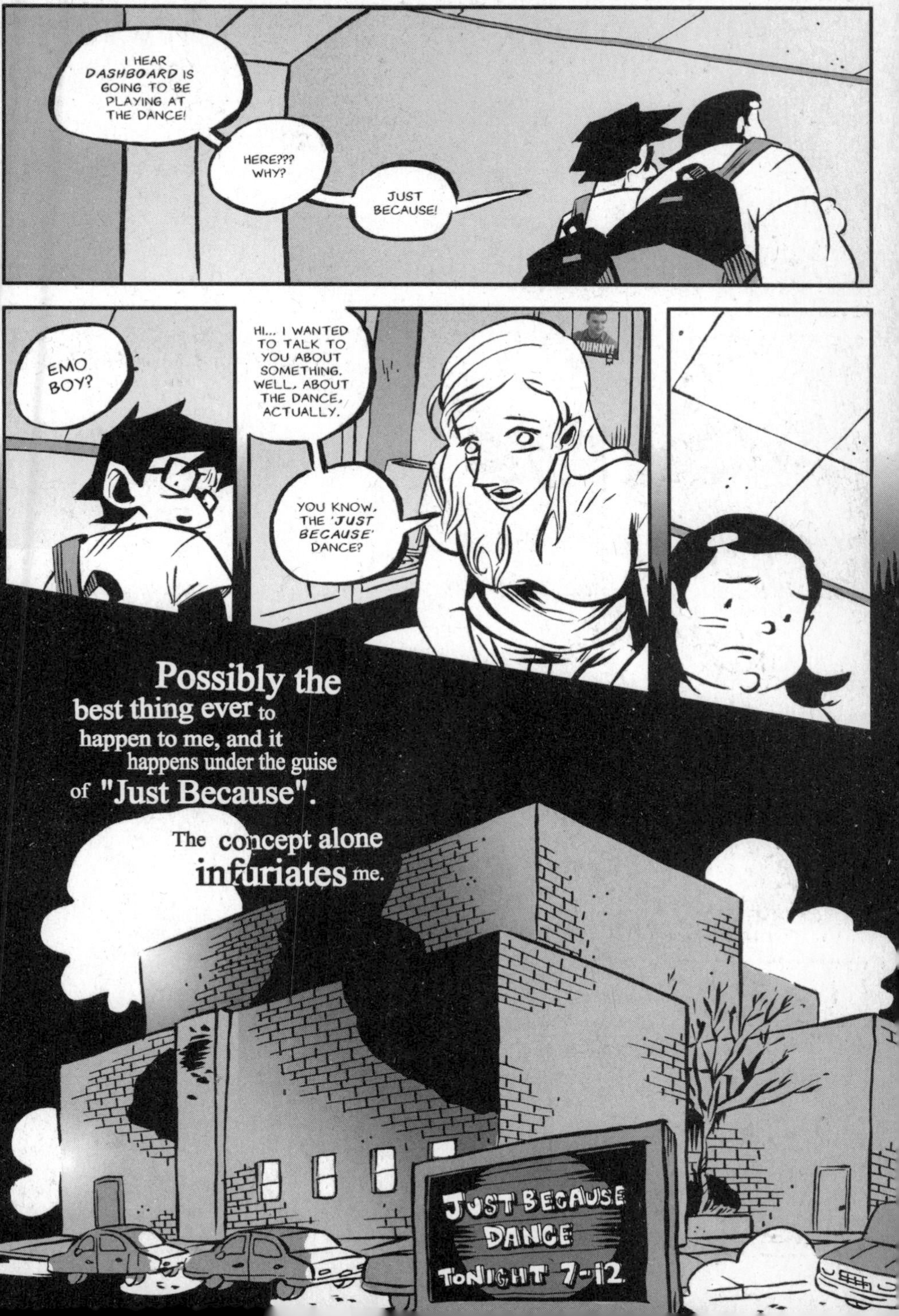
I HEAR DASHBOARD IS GOING TO BE PLAYING AT THE DANCE!
HERE??? WHY?
JUST BECAUSE!
EMO BOY?
HI... I WANTED TO TALK TO YOU ABOUT SOMETHING. WELL, ABOUT THE DANCE, ACTUALLY.
YOU KNOW, THE 'JUST BECAUSE' DANCE?
JOHNNY!
Possibly the best thing ever to happen to me, and it happens under the guise of "Just Because".
The concept alone infuriates me.
JUST BECAUSE DANCE TONIGHT 7-12

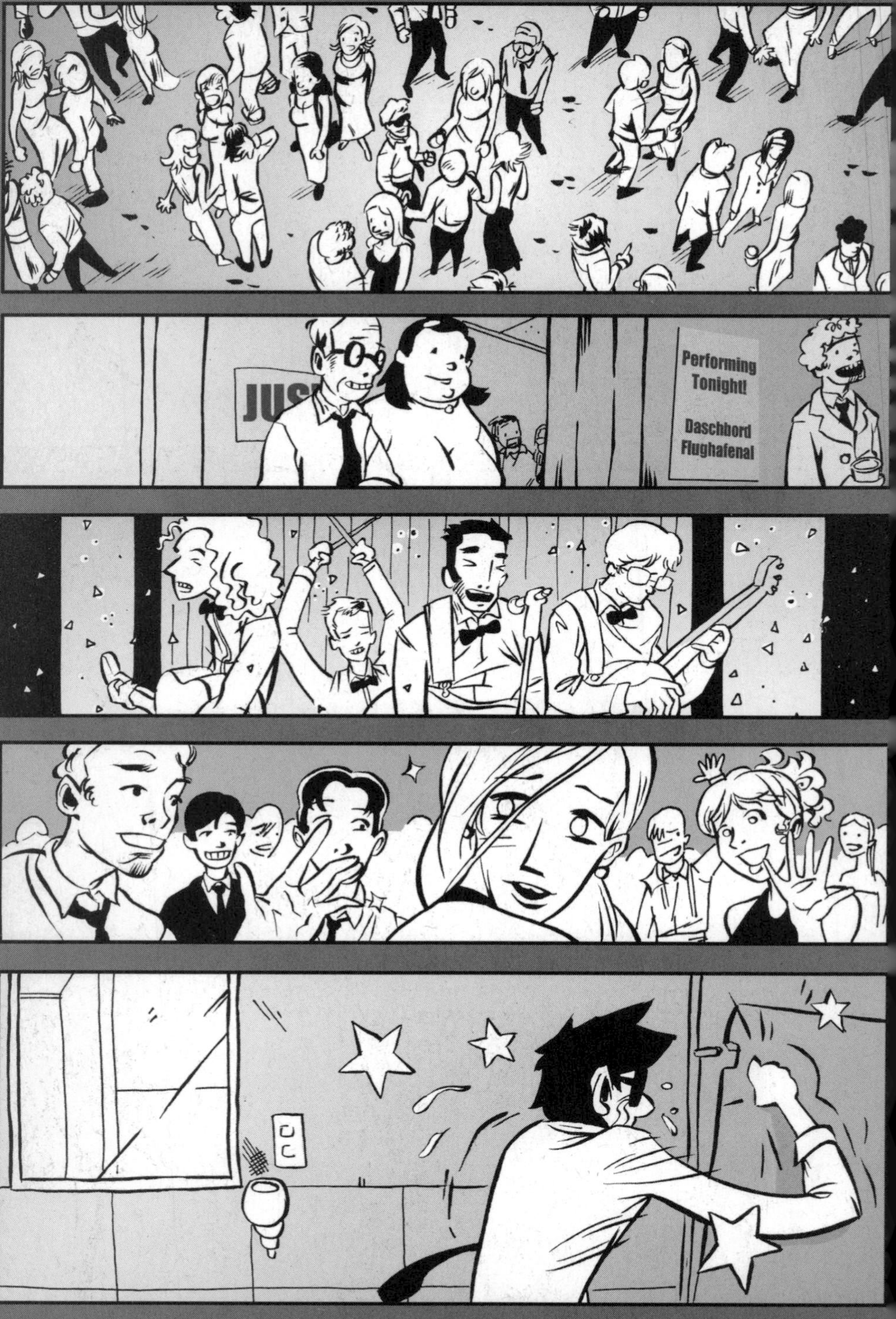

JUS
Performing Tonight!
Daschbord Flughafenal

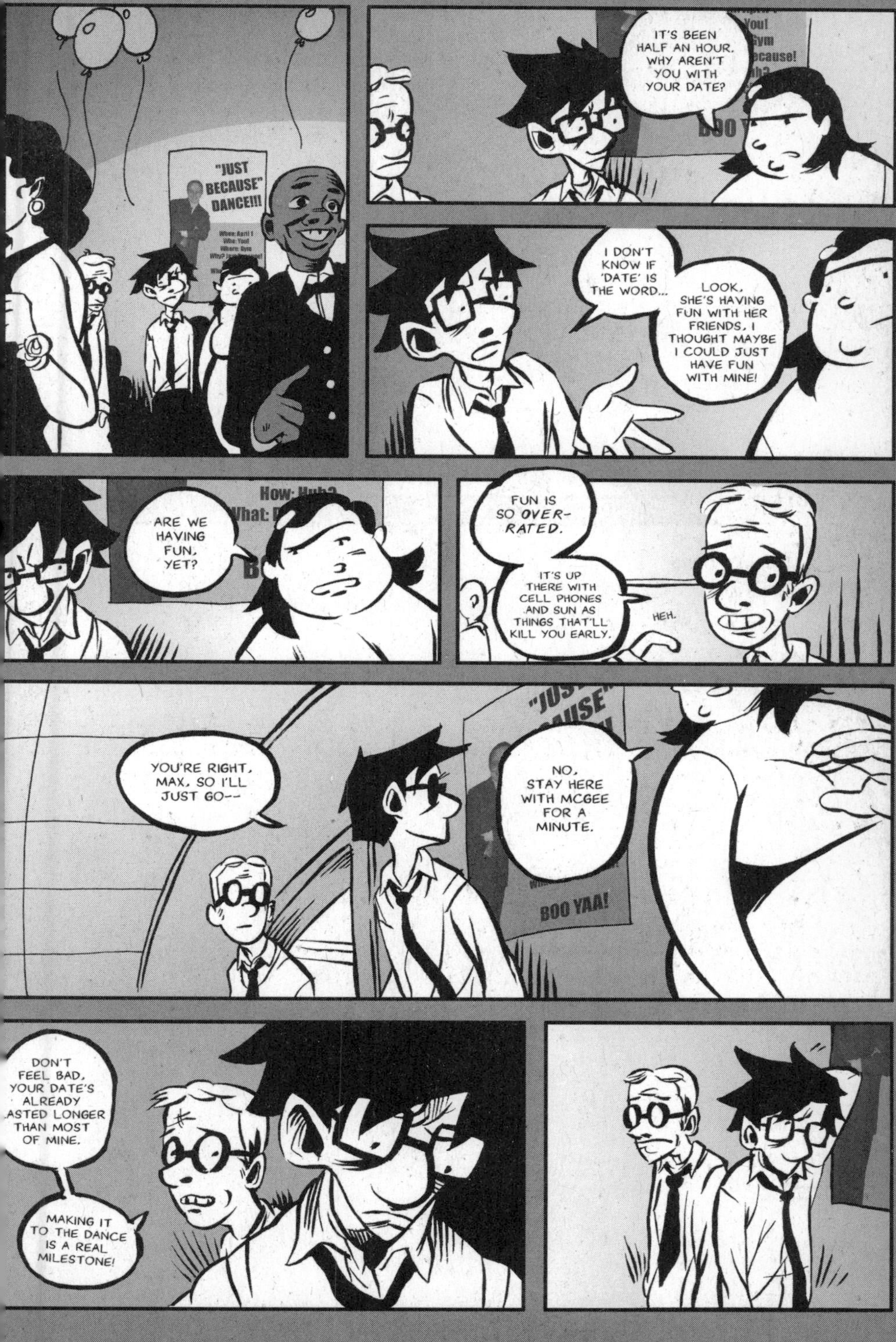
"JUST BECAUSE" DANCE!!!
IT'S BEEN HALF AN HOUR. WHY AREN'T YOU WITH YOUR DATE?
I DON'T KNOW IF 'DATE' IS THE WORD...
LOOK, SHE'S HAVING FUN WITH HER FRIENDS, I THOUGHT MAYBE I COULD JUST HAVE FUN WITH MINE!
ARE WE HAVING FUN, YET?
FUN IS SO *OVER-RATED.*
IT'S UP THERE WITH CELL PHONES AND SUN AS THINGS THAT'LL KILL YOU EARLY.
HEH.
YOU'RE RIGHT, MAX, SO I'LL JUST GO--
NO, STAY HERE WITH MCGEE FOR A MINUTE.
BOO YAA!
DON'T FEEL BAD, YOUR DATE'S ALREADY LASTED LONGER THAN MOST OF MINE.
MAKING IT TO THE DANCE IS A REAL MILESTONE!

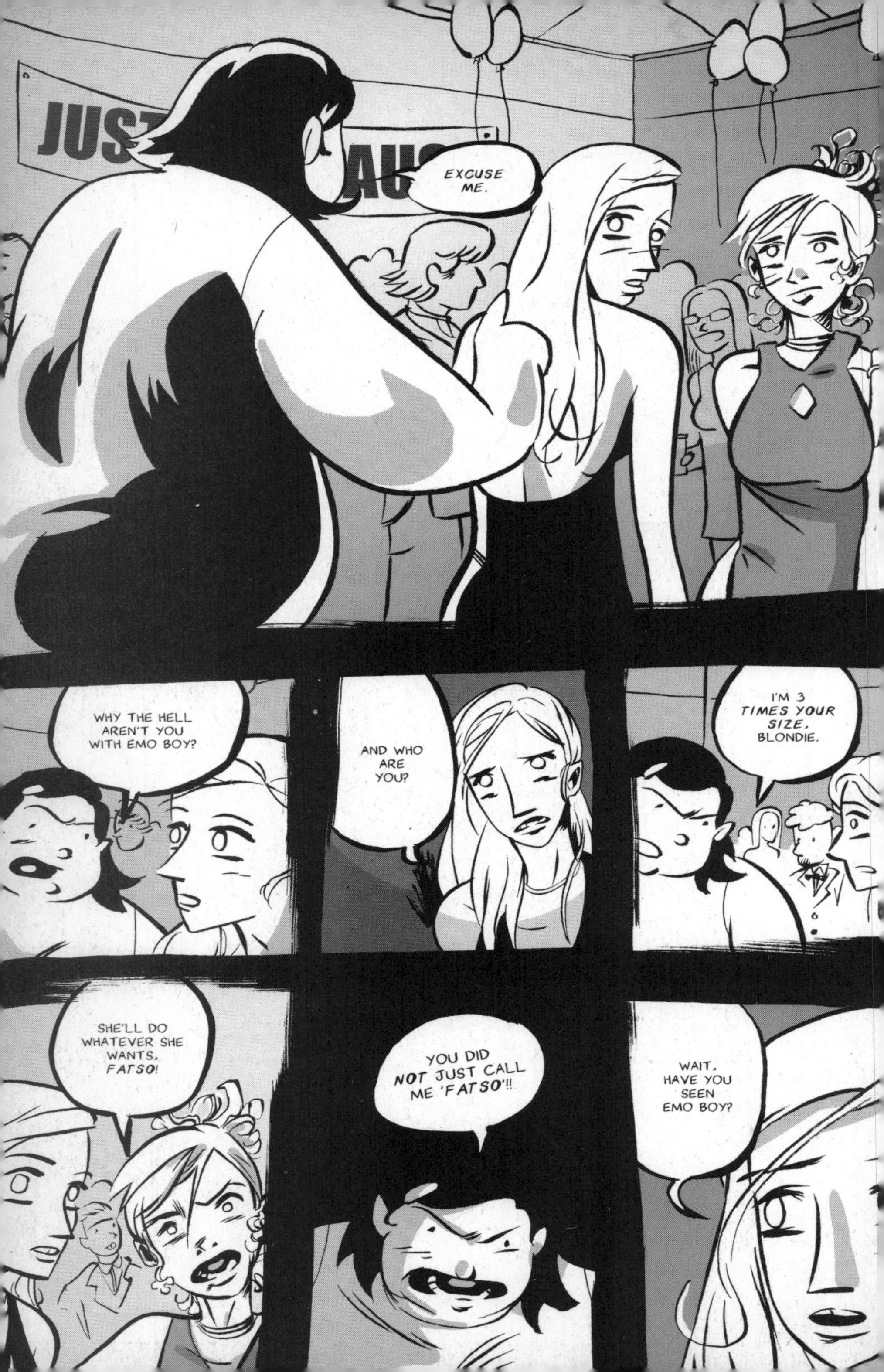
JUST
AUS
EXCUSE ME.
WHY THE HELL AREN'T YOU WITH EMO BOY?
AND WHO ARE YOU?
I'M 3 *TIMES YOUR SIZE*, BLONDIE.
SHE'LL DO WHATEVER SHE WANTS, *FATSO*!
YOU DID *NOT* JUST CALL ME '*FATSO*'!!
WAIT, HAVE YOU SEEN EMO BOY?

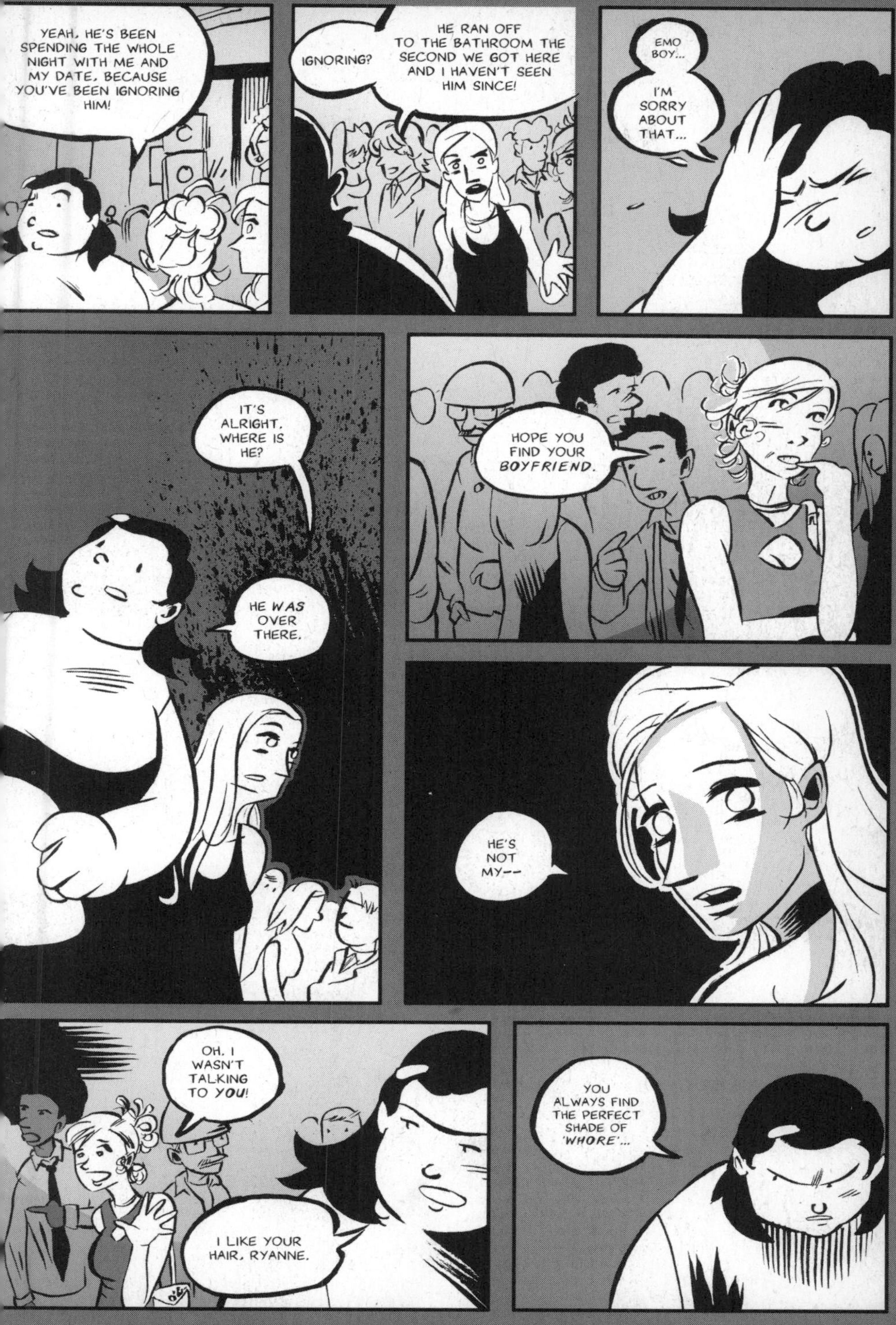
YEAH, HE'S BEEN SPENDING THE WHOLE NIGHT WITH ME AND MY DATE, BECAUSE YOU'VE BEEN IGNORING HIM!
IGNORING?
HE RAN OFF TO THE BATHROOM THE SECOND WE GOT HERE AND I HAVEN'T SEEN HIM SINCE!
EMO BOY...
I'M SORRY ABOUT THAT...
IT'S ALRIGHT. WHERE IS HE?
HE *WAS* OVER THERE.
HOPE YOU FIND YOUR ***BOYFRIEND***.
HE'S NOT MY--
OH. I WASN'T TALKING TO ***YOU***!
I LIKE YOUR HAIR, RYANNE.
YOU ALWAYS FIND THE PERFECT SHADE OF '***WHORE***'...

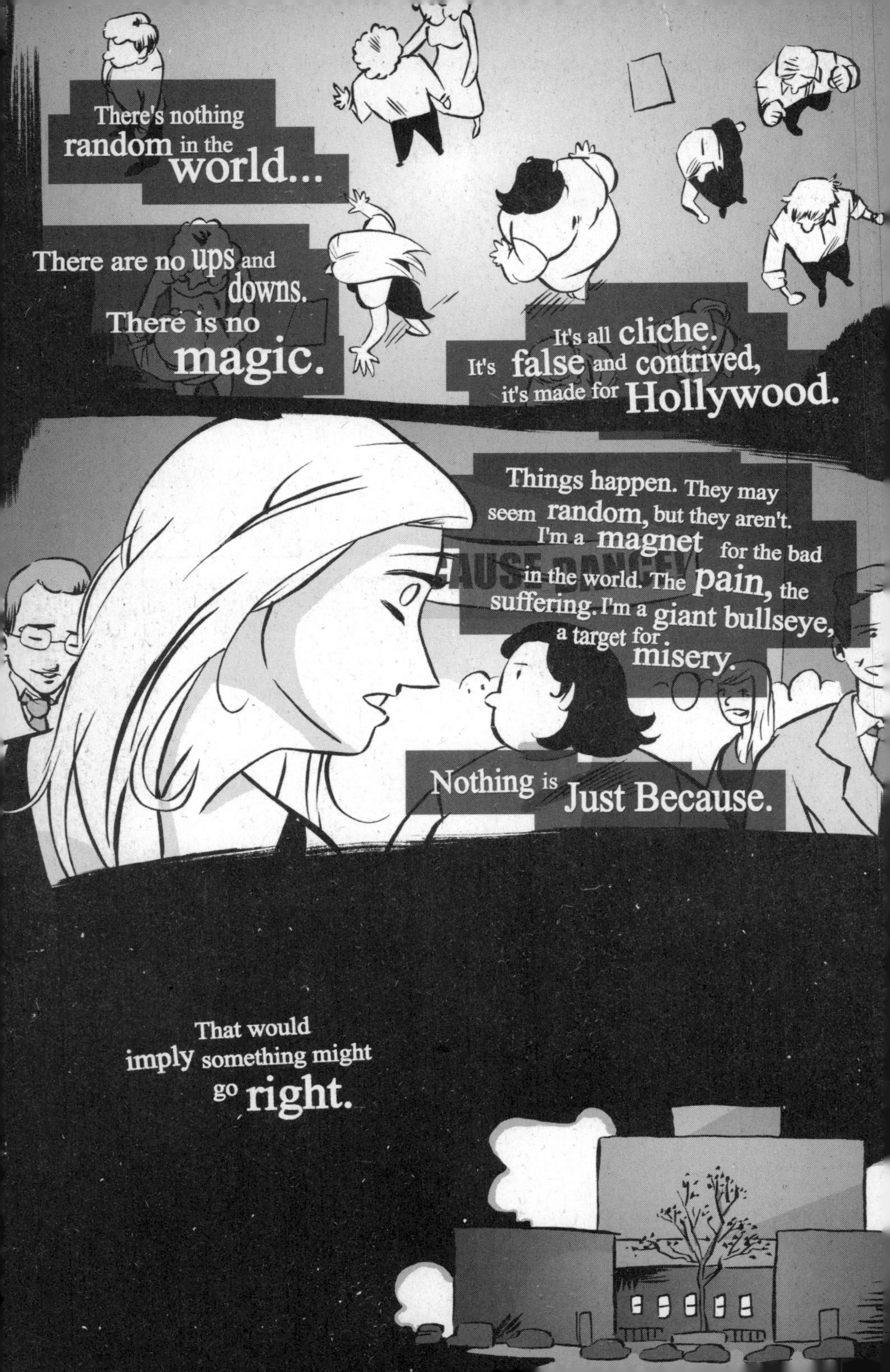
There's nothing random in the world...
There are no ups and downs. There is no magic.
It's all cliche. It's false and contrived, it's made for Hollywood.
Things happen. They may seem random, but they aren't. I'm a magnet for the bad in the world. The pain, the suffering. I'm a giant bullseye, a target for misery.
Nothing is Just Because.
That would imply something might go right.

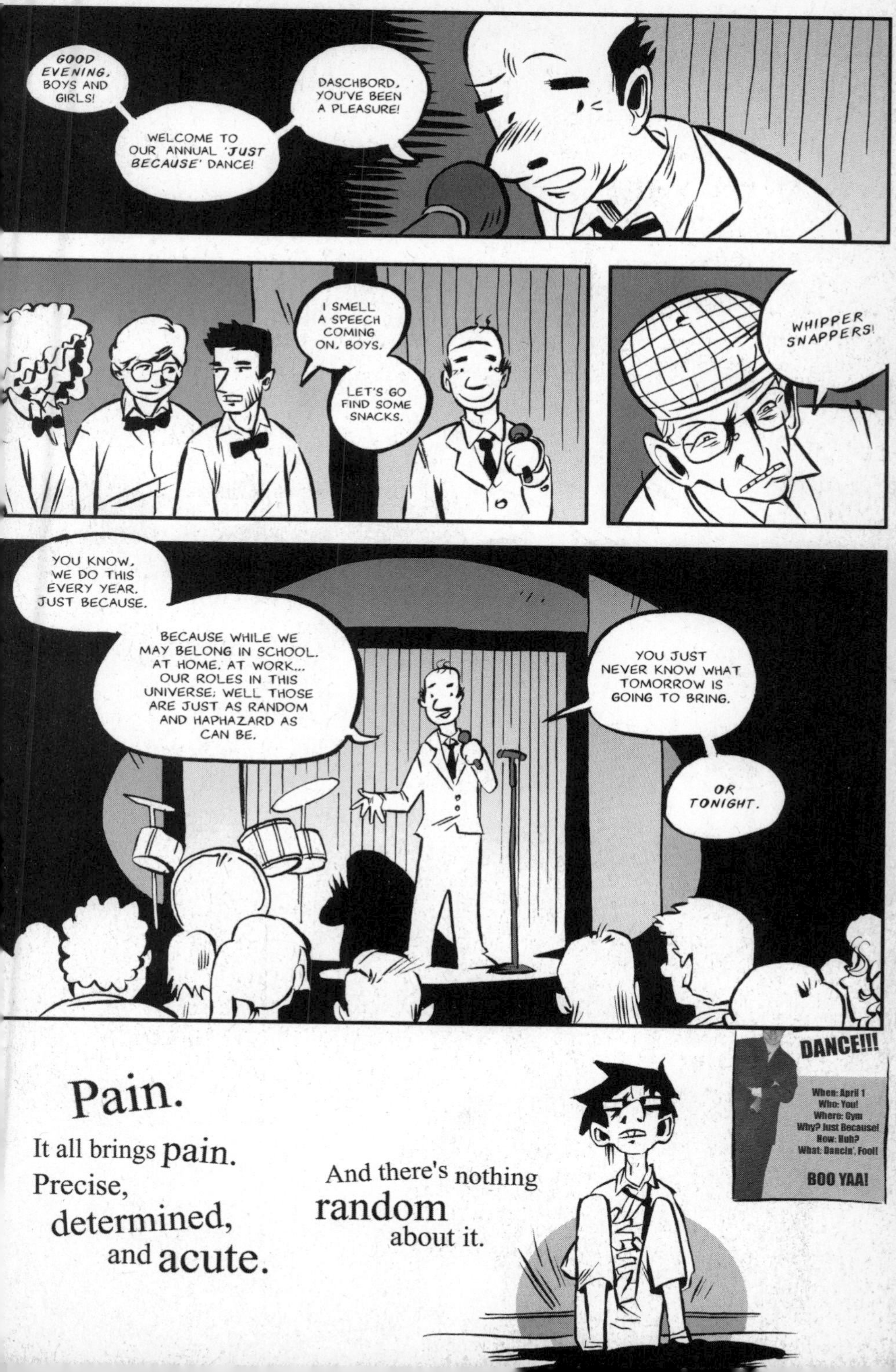
GOOD EVENING, BOYS AND GIRLS!
WELCOME TO OUR ANNUAL 'JUST BECAUSE' DANCE!
DASCHBORD, YOU'VE BEEN A PLEASURE!
I SMELL A SPEECH COMING ON, BOYS.
LET'S GO FIND SOME SNACKS.
WHIPPER SNAPPERS!
YOU KNOW, WE DO THIS EVERY YEAR. JUST BECAUSE.
BECAUSE WHILE WE MAY BELONG IN SCHOOL, AT HOME, AT WORK... OUR ROLES IN THIS UNIVERSE; WELL THOSE ARE JUST AS RANDOM AND HAPHAZARD AS CAN BE.
YOU JUST NEVER KNOW WHAT TOMORROW IS GOING TO BRING.
OR TONIGHT.
Pain.
It all brings pain.
Precise, determined, and acute.
And there's nothing random about it.
DANCE!!!
When: April 1
Who: You!
Where: Gym
Why? Just Because!
How: Huh?
What: Dancin', Fool!
BOO YAA!

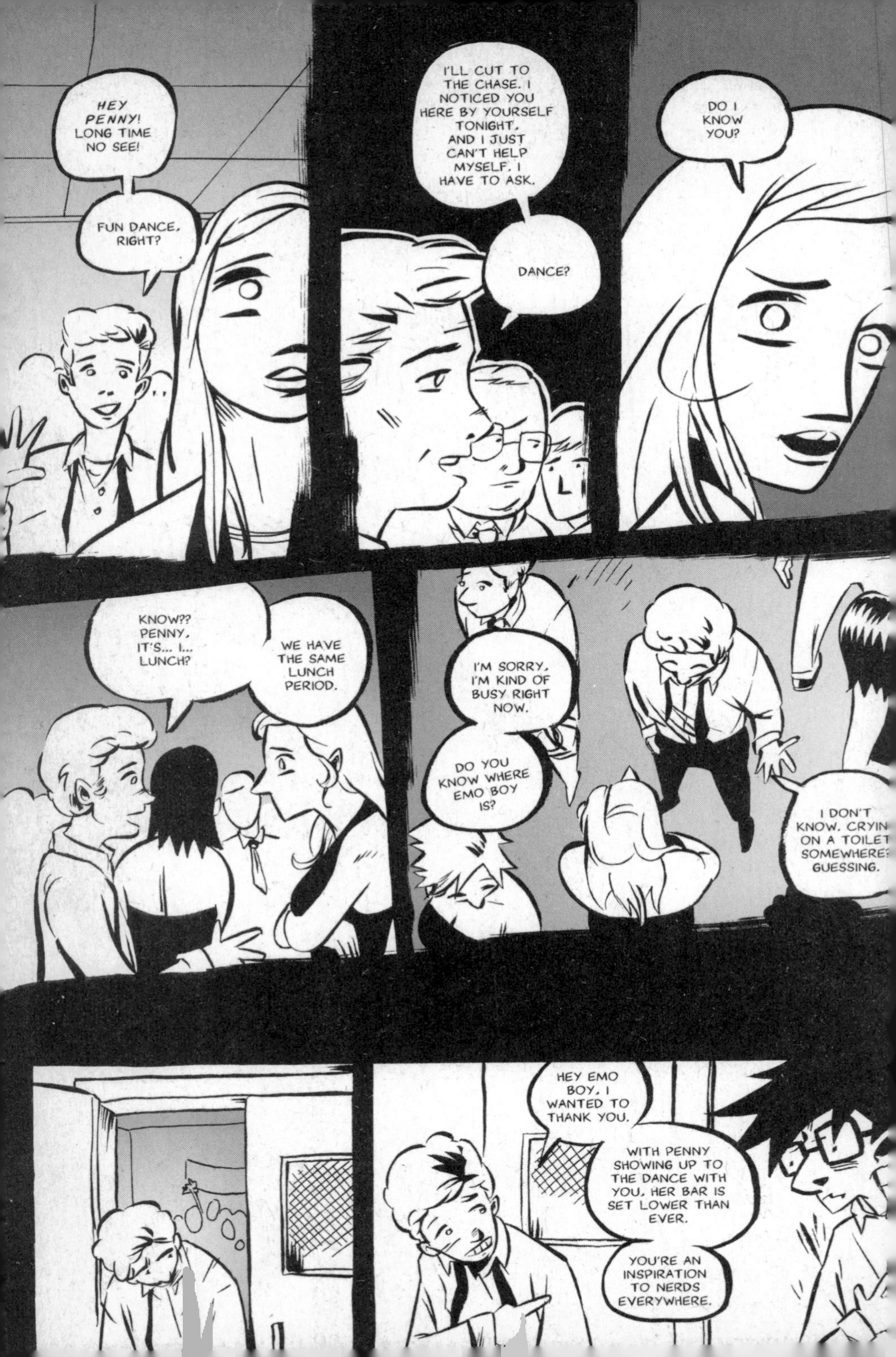
HEY PENNY! LONG TIME NO SEE!
FUN DANCE, RIGHT?
...
I'LL CUT TO THE CHASE. I NOTICED YOU HERE BY YOURSELF TONIGHT, AND I JUST CAN'T HELP MYSELF. I HAVE TO ASK.
DANCE?
DO I KNOW YOU?
KNOW?? PENNY, IT'S... I... LUNCH?
WE HAVE THE SAME LUNCH PERIOD.
I'M SORRY, I'M KIND OF BUSY RIGHT NOW.
DO YOU KNOW WHERE EMO BOY IS?
I DON'T KNOW. CRYIN ON A TOILET SOMEWHERE? GUESSING.
HEY EMO BOY, I WANTED TO THANK YOU.
WITH PENNY SHOWING UP TO THE DANCE WITH YOU, HER BAR IS SET LOWER THAN EVER.
YOU'RE AN INSPIRATION TO NERDS EVERYWHERE.

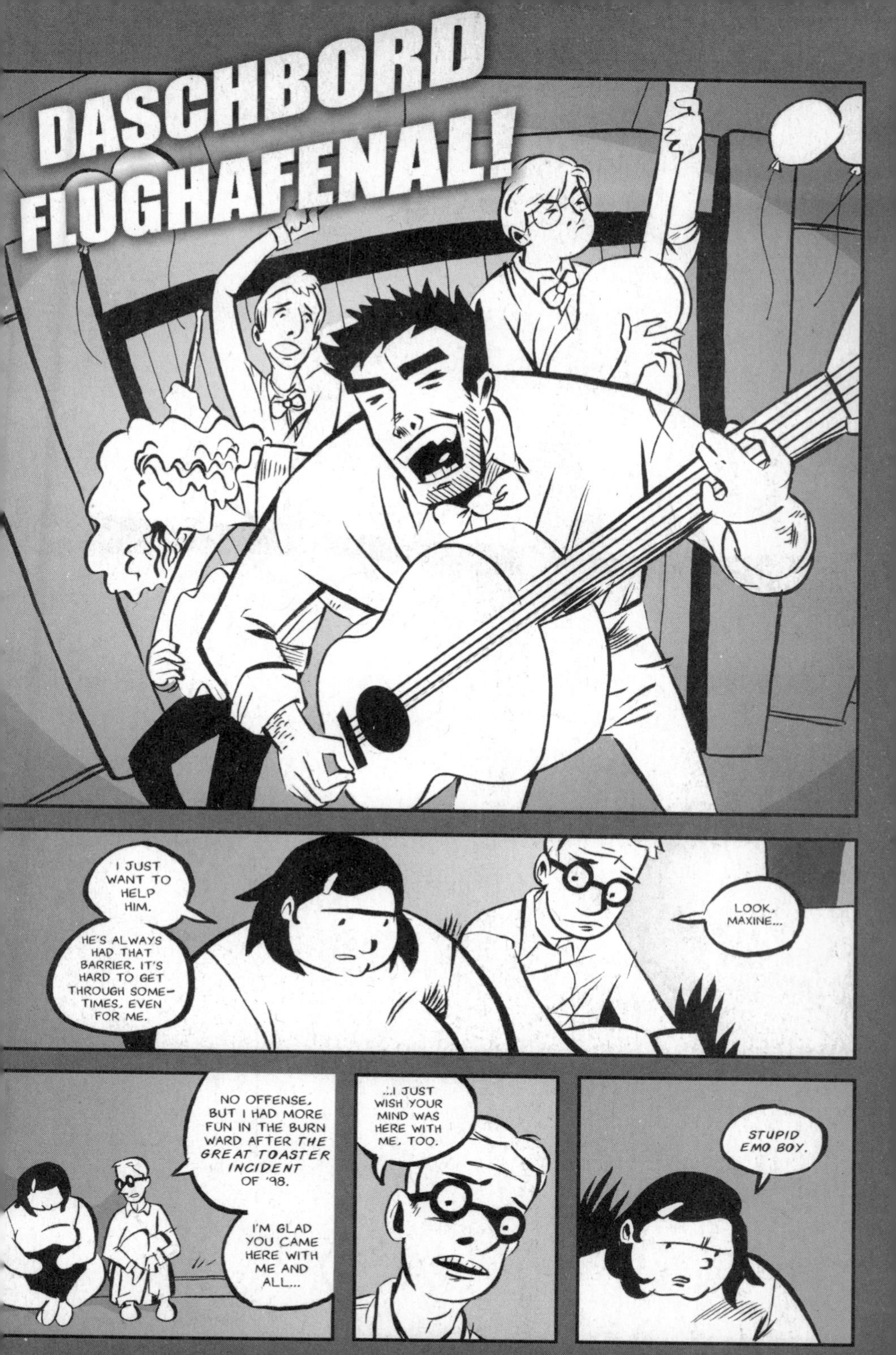
DASCHBORD FLUGHAFENAL!
I JUST WANT TO HELP HIM.
HE'S ALWAYS HAD THAT BARRIER. IT'S HARD TO GET THROUGH SOME-TIMES. EVEN FOR ME.
LOOK, MAXINE...
NO OFFENSE, BUT I HAD MORE FUN IN THE BURN WARD AFTER *THE GREAT TOASTER INCIDENT* OF '98.
I'M GLAD YOU CAME HERE WITH ME AND ALL...
...I JUST WISH YOUR MIND WAS HERE WITH ME, TOO.
STUPID EMO BOY.

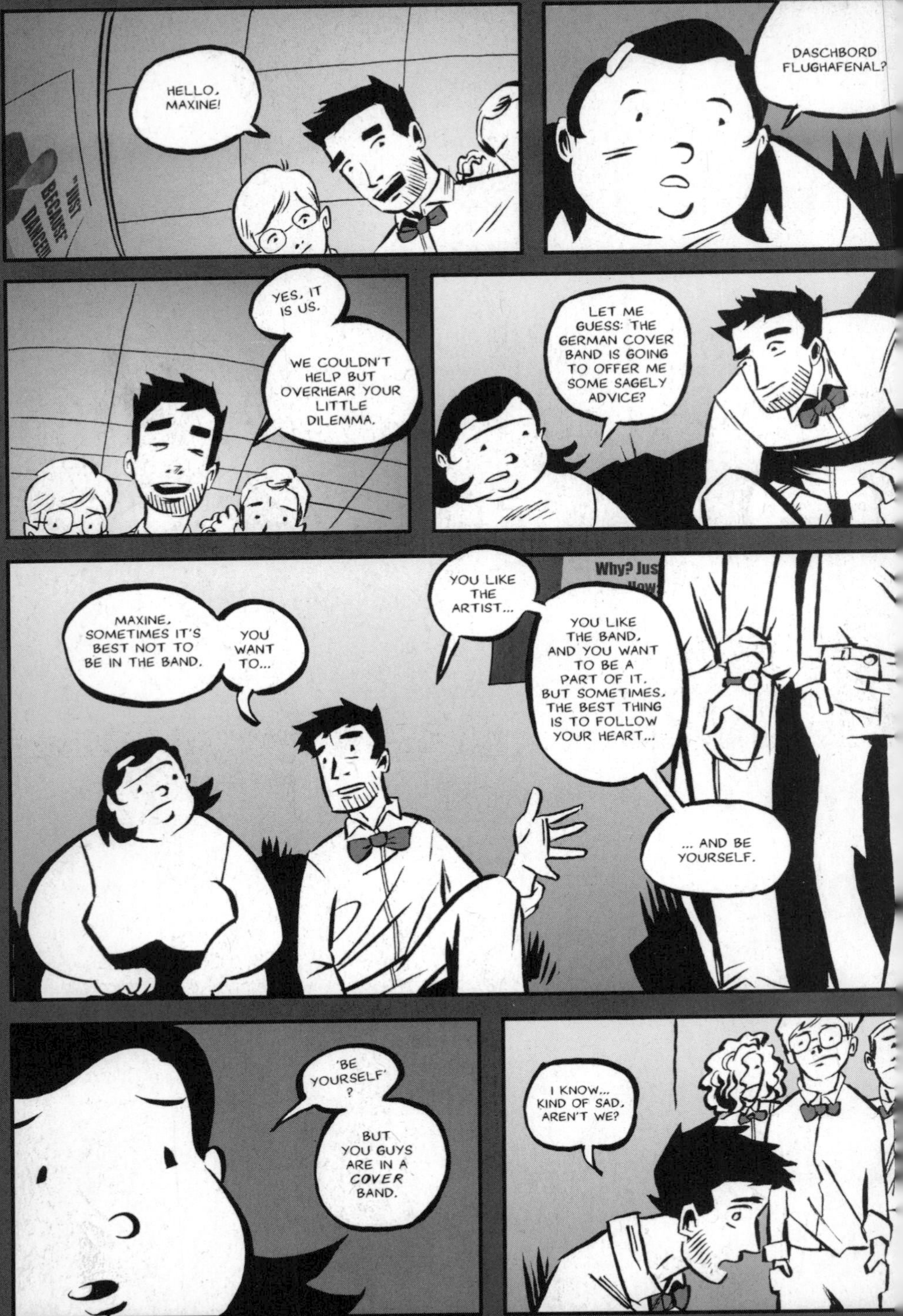
HELLO, MAXINE!
DASCHBORD FLUGHAFENAL?
YES, IT IS US.
WE COULDN'T HELP BUT OVERHEAR YOUR LITTLE DILEMMA.
LET ME GUESS: THE GERMAN COVER BAND IS GOING TO OFFER ME SOME SAGELY ADVICE?
MAXINE, SOMETIMES IT'S BEST NOT TO BE IN THE BAND.
YOU WANT TO...
YOU LIKE THE ARTIST...
YOU LIKE THE BAND, AND YOU WANT TO BE A PART OF IT. BUT SOMETIMES, THE BEST THING IS TO FOLLOW YOUR HEART...
... AND BE YOURSELF.
'BE YOURSELF'?
BUT YOU GUYS ARE IN A COVER BAND.
I KNOW... KIND OF SAD, AREN'T WE?

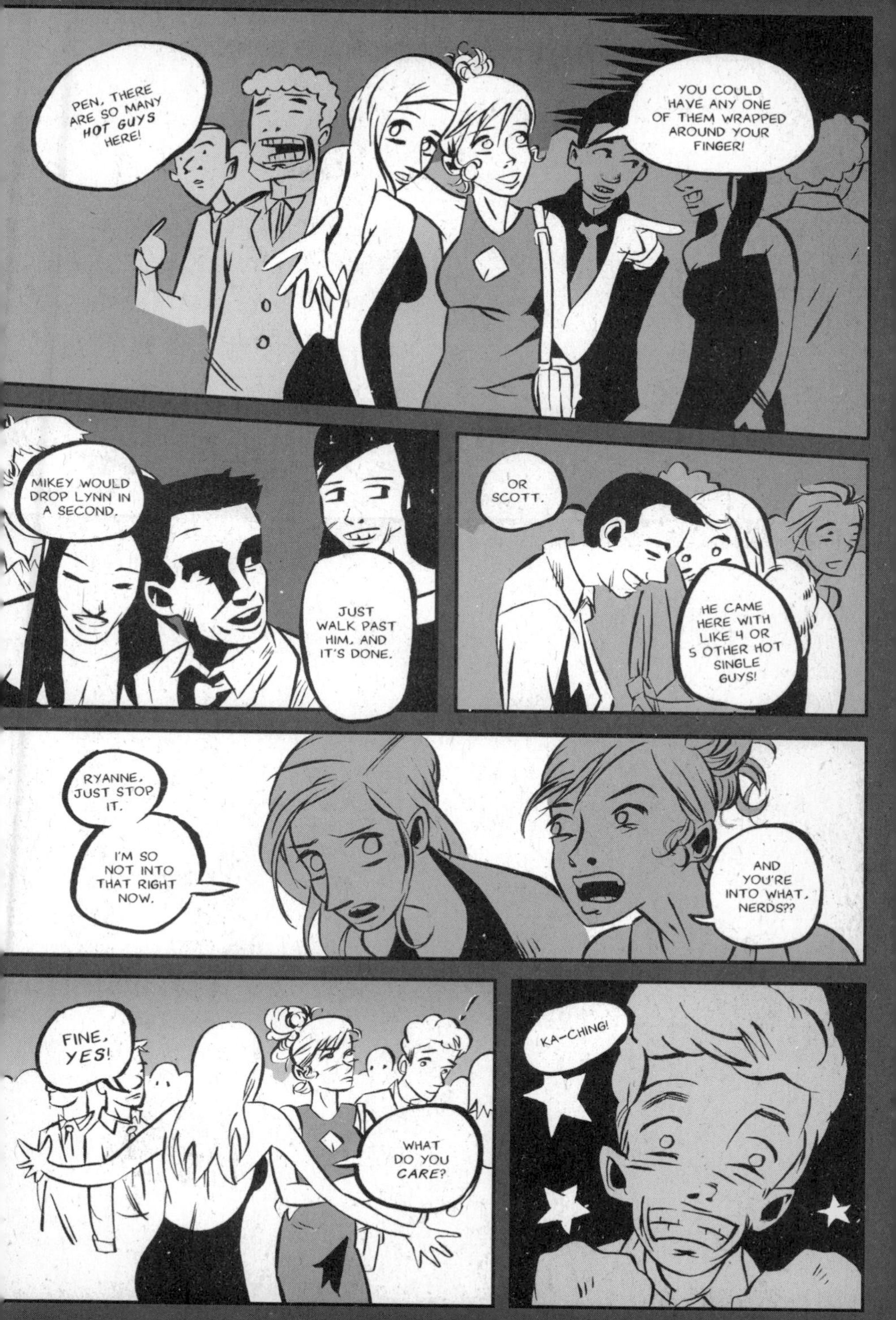
PEN, THERE ARE SO MANY HOT GUYS HERE!
YOU COULD HAVE ANY ONE OF THEM WRAPPED AROUND YOUR FINGER!
MIKEY WOULD DROP LYNN IN A SECOND.
JUST WALK PAST HIM, AND IT'S DONE.
OR SCOTT.
HE CAME HERE WITH LIKE 4 OR 5 OTHER HOT SINGLE GUYS!
RYANNE, JUST STOP IT.
I'M SO NOT INTO THAT RIGHT NOW.
AND YOU'RE INTO WHAT, NERDS??
FINE, YES!
WHAT DO YOU CARE?
KA-CHING!

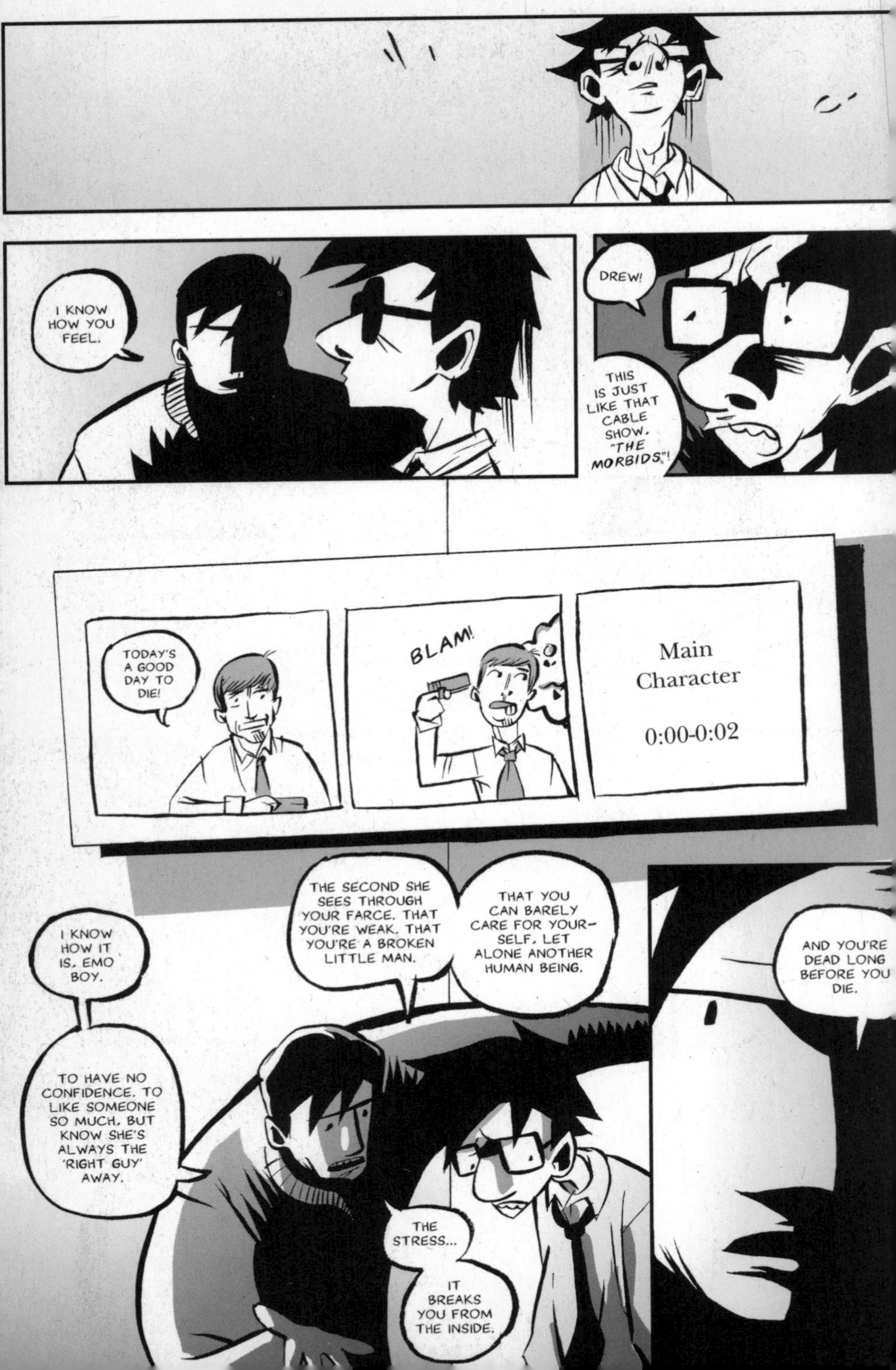
I KNOW HOW YOU FEEL.
DREW!
THIS IS JUST LIKE THAT CABLE SHOW, "THE MORBIDS"!
TODAY'S A GOOD DAY TO DIE!
BLAM!
Main Character
0:00-0:02
I KNOW HOW IT IS, EMO BOY.
TO HAVE NO CONFIDENCE. TO LIKE SOMEONE SO MUCH, BUT KNOW SHE'S ALWAYS THE 'RIGHT GUY' AWAY.
THE SECOND SHE SEES THROUGH YOUR FARCE. THAT YOU'RE WEAK. THAT YOU'RE A BROKEN LITTLE MAN.
THAT YOU CAN BARELY CARE FOR YOURSELF, LET ALONE ANOTHER HUMAN BEING.
THE STRESS...
IT BREAKS YOU FROM THE INSIDE.
AND YOU'RE DEAD LONG BEFORE YOU DIE.

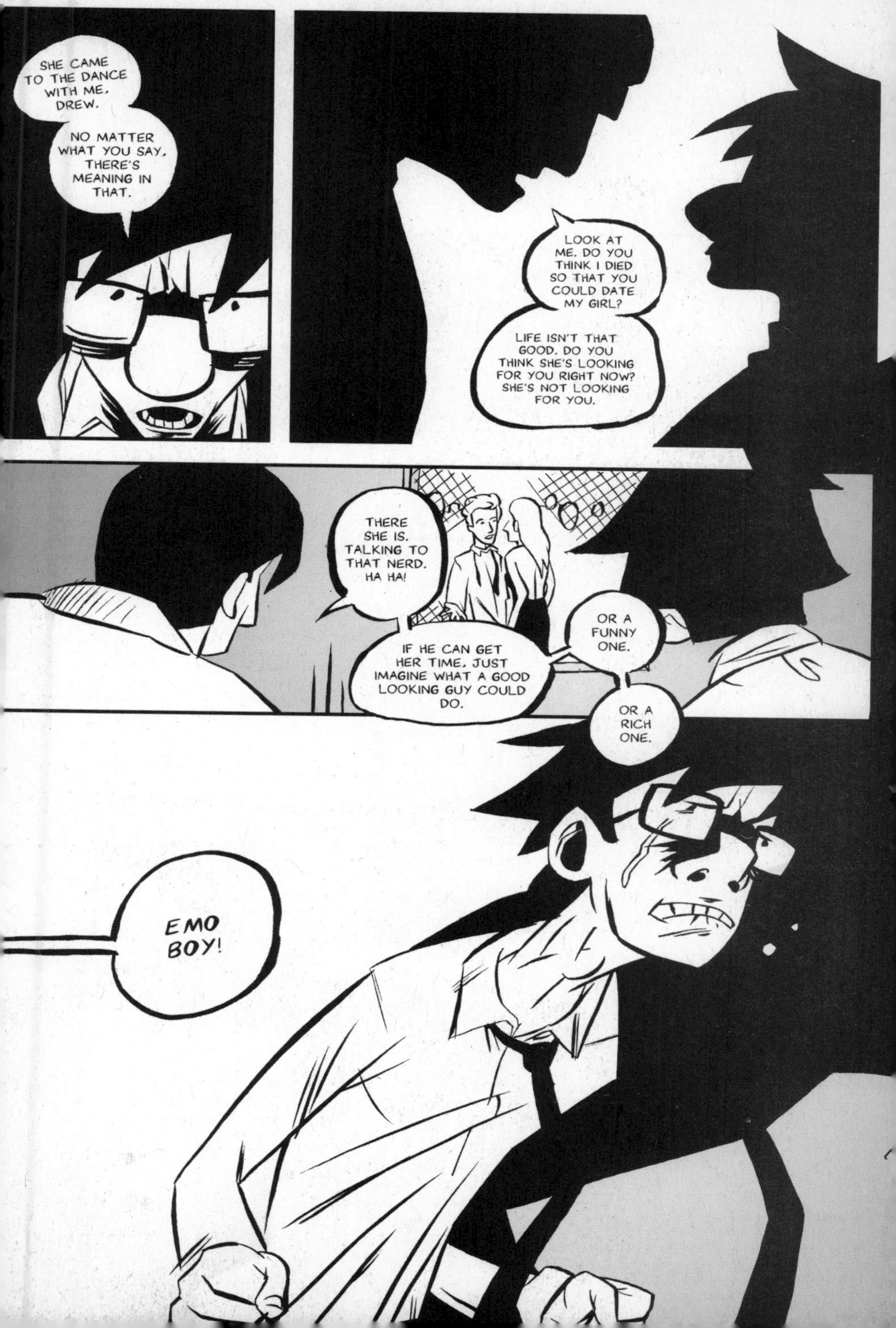
SHE CAME TO THE DANCE WITH ME, DREW.
NO MATTER WHAT YOU SAY, THERE'S MEANING IN THAT.
LOOK AT ME. DO YOU THINK I DIED SO THAT YOU COULD DATE MY GIRL?
LIFE ISN'T THAT GOOD. DO YOU THINK SHE'S LOOKING FOR YOU RIGHT NOW? SHE'S NOT LOOKING FOR YOU.
THERE SHE IS. TALKING TO THAT NERD. HA HA!
IF HE CAN GET HER TIME, JUST IMAGINE WHAT A GOOD LOOKING GUY COULD DO.
OR A FUNNY ONE.
OR A RICH ONE.
EMO BOY!

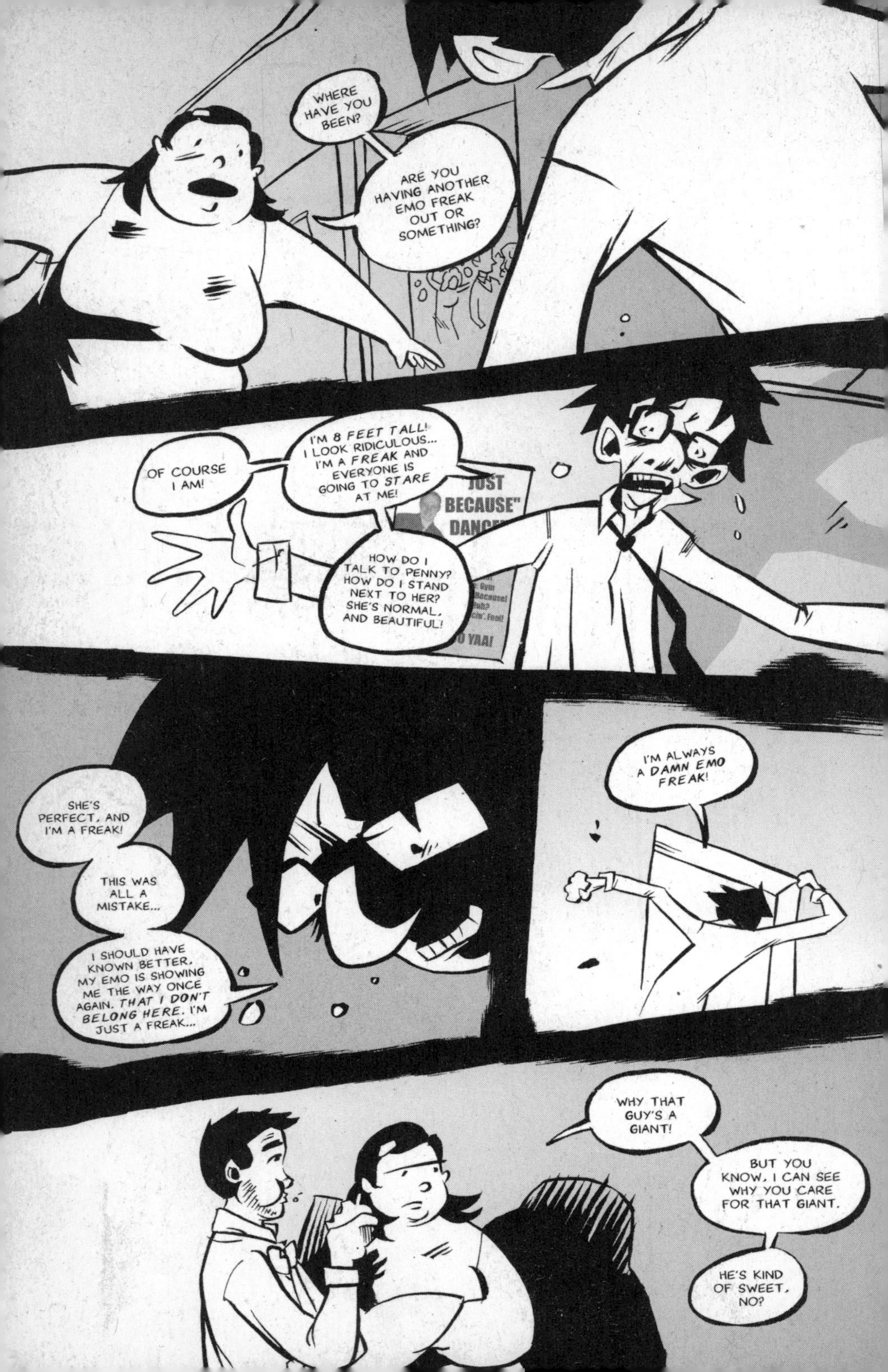
WHERE HAVE YOU BEEN?
ARE YOU HAVING ANOTHER EMO FREAK OUT OR SOMETHING?
OF COURSE I AM!
I'M 8 FEET TALL! I LOOK RIDICULOUS... I'M A FREAK AND EVERYONE IS GOING TO STARE AT ME!
"JUST BECAUSE"
HOW DO I TALK TO PENNY? HOW DO I STAND NEXT TO HER? SHE'S NORMAL, AND BEAUTIFUL!
SHE'S PERFECT, AND I'M A FREAK!
THIS WAS ALL A MISTAKE...
I SHOULD HAVE KNOWN BETTER, MY EMO IS SHOWING ME THE WAY ONCE AGAIN. THAT I DON'T BELONG HERE. I'M JUST A FREAK...
I'M ALWAYS A DAMN EMO FREAK!
WHY THAT GUY'S A GIANT!
BUT YOU KNOW, I CAN SEE WHY YOU CARE FOR THAT GIANT.
HE'S KIND OF SWEET, NO?

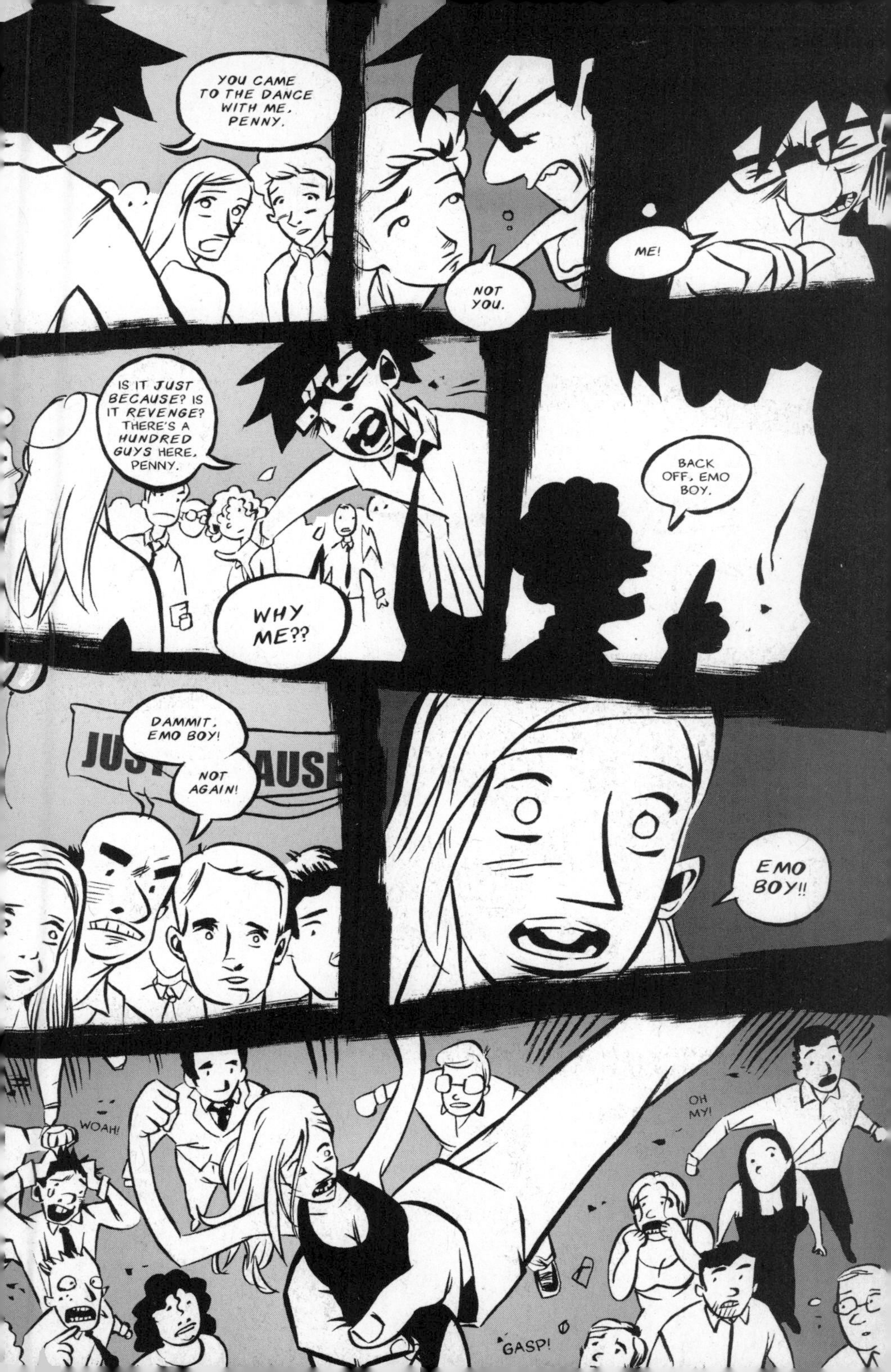
YOU CAME TO THE DANCE WITH ME, PENNY.
NOT YOU.
ME!
IS IT JUST BECAUSE? IS IT REVENGE? THERE'S A HUNDRED GUYS HERE, PENNY.
WHY ME??
BACK OFF, EMO BOY.
JUST AUSE
DAMMIT, EMO BOY!
NOT AGAIN!
EMO BOY!!
WOAH!
OH MY!
GASP!

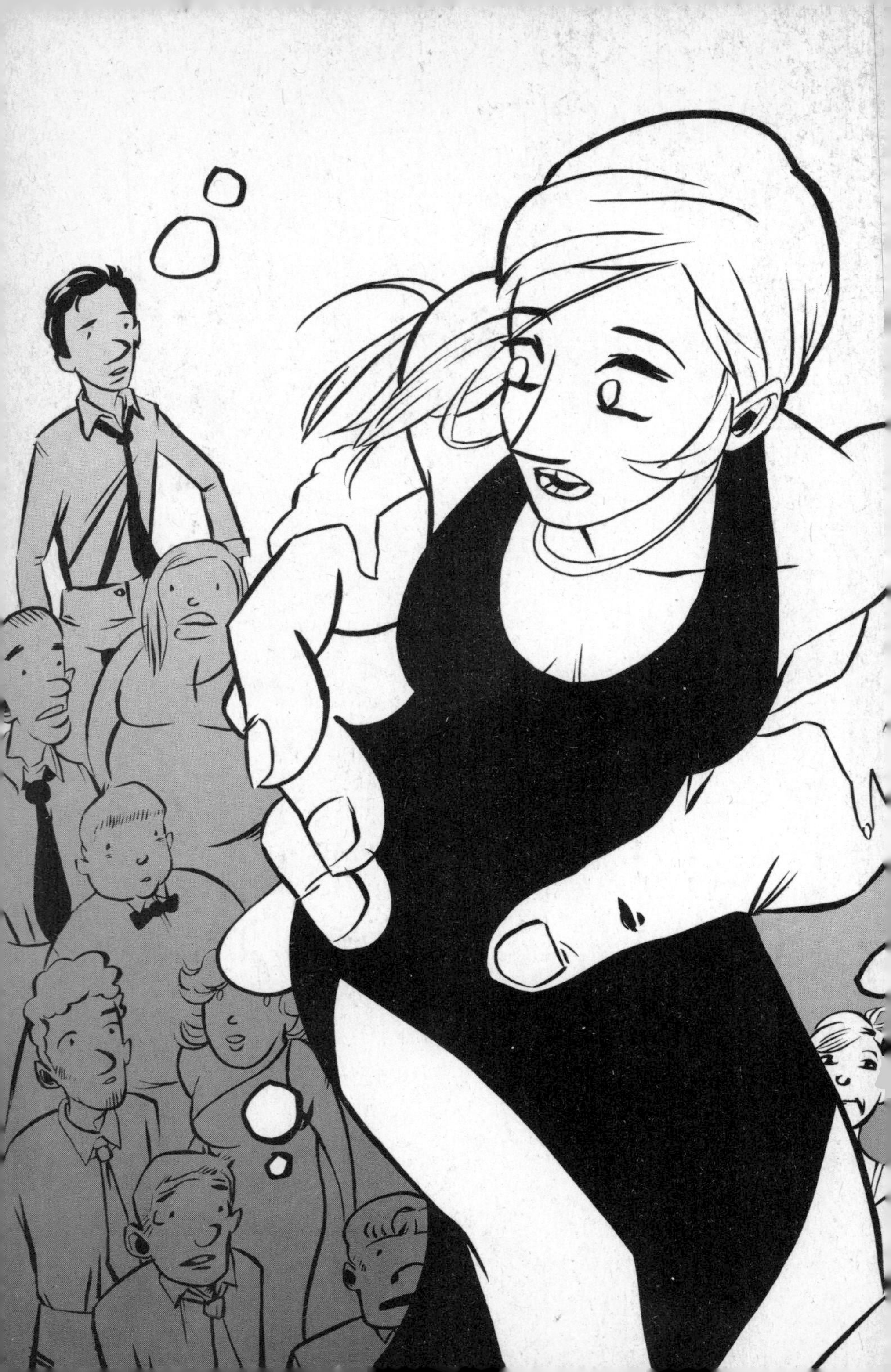

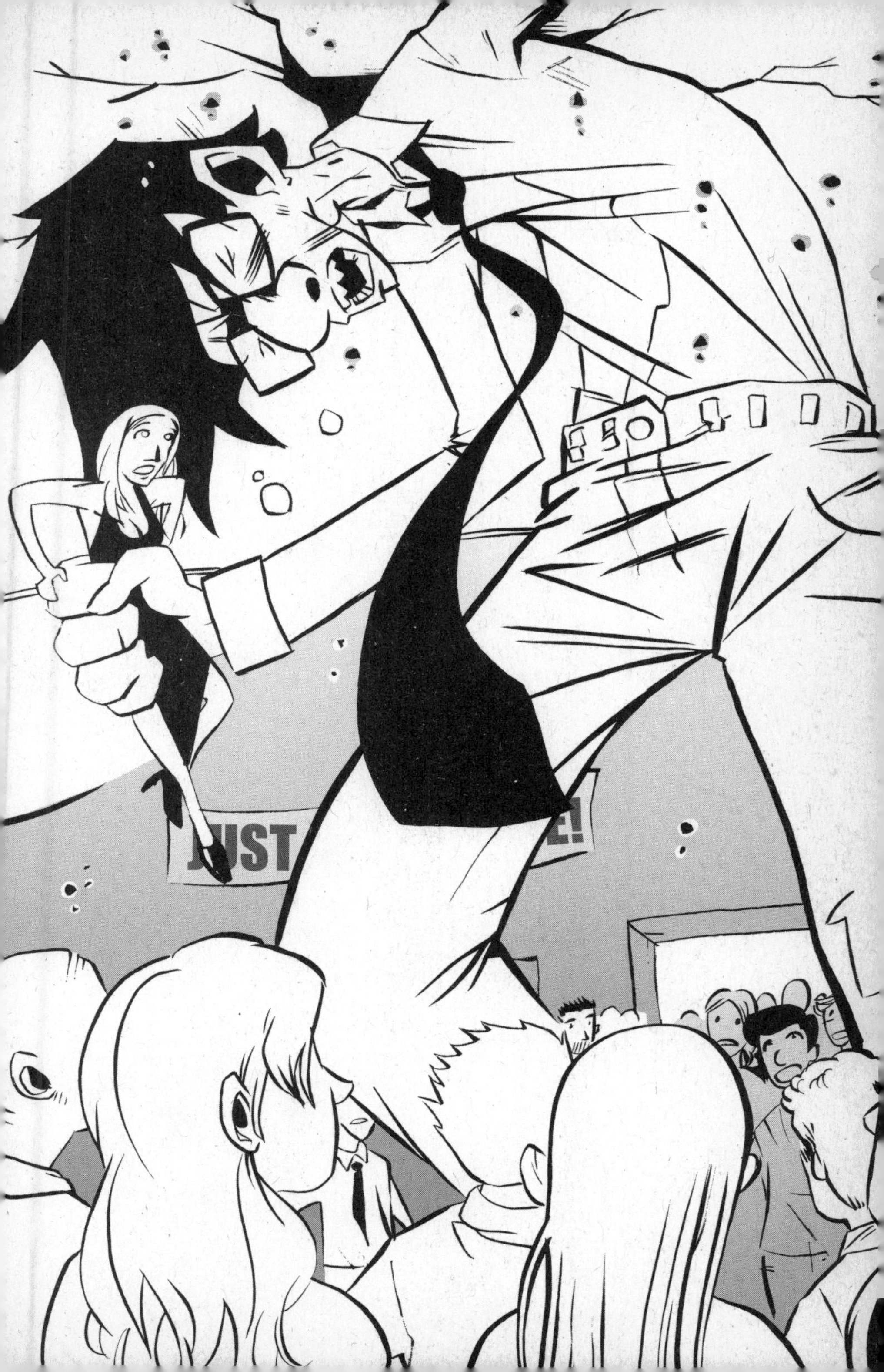
JUST
E!

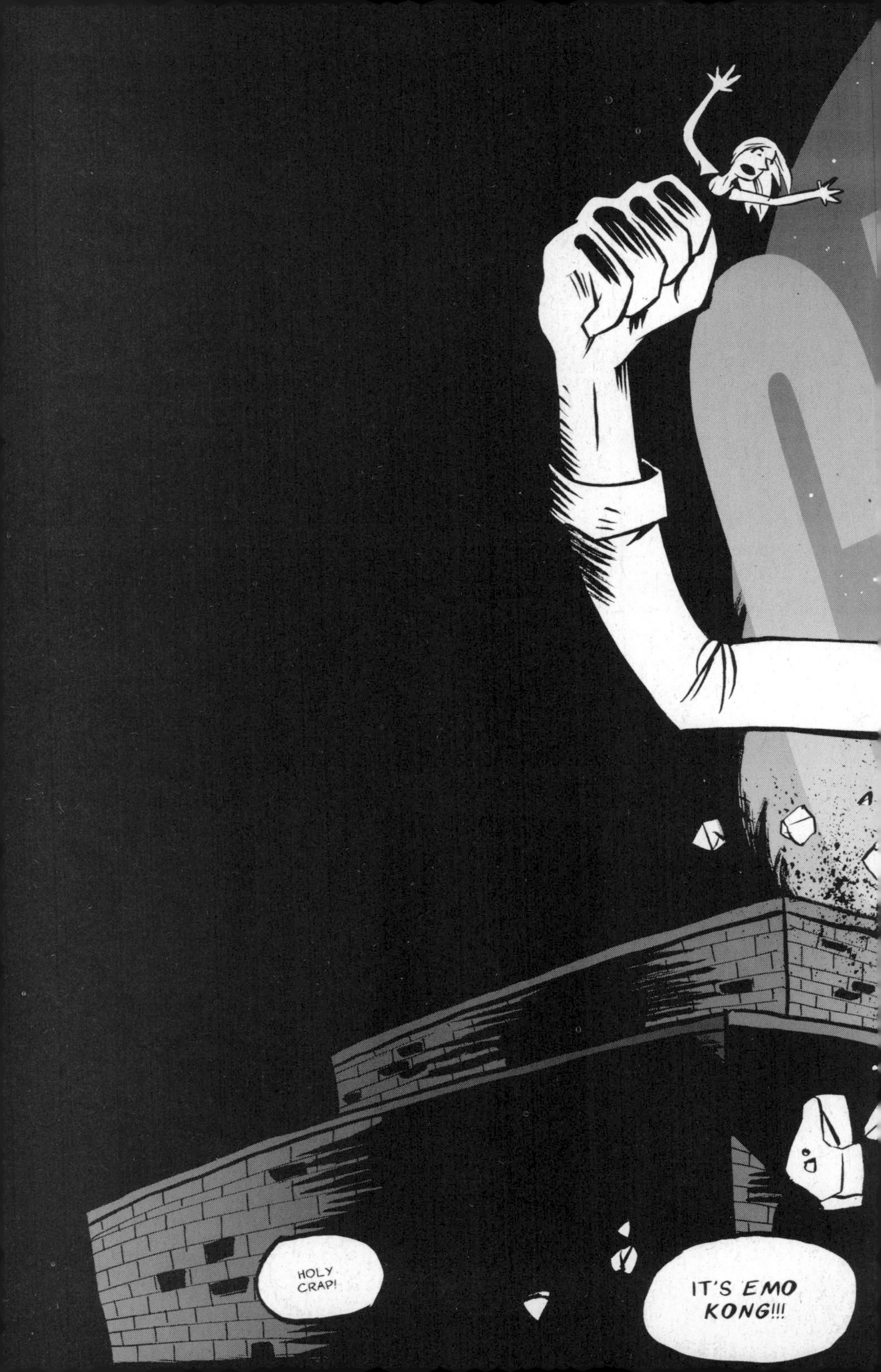
HOLY CRAP!
IT'S EMO KONG!!!

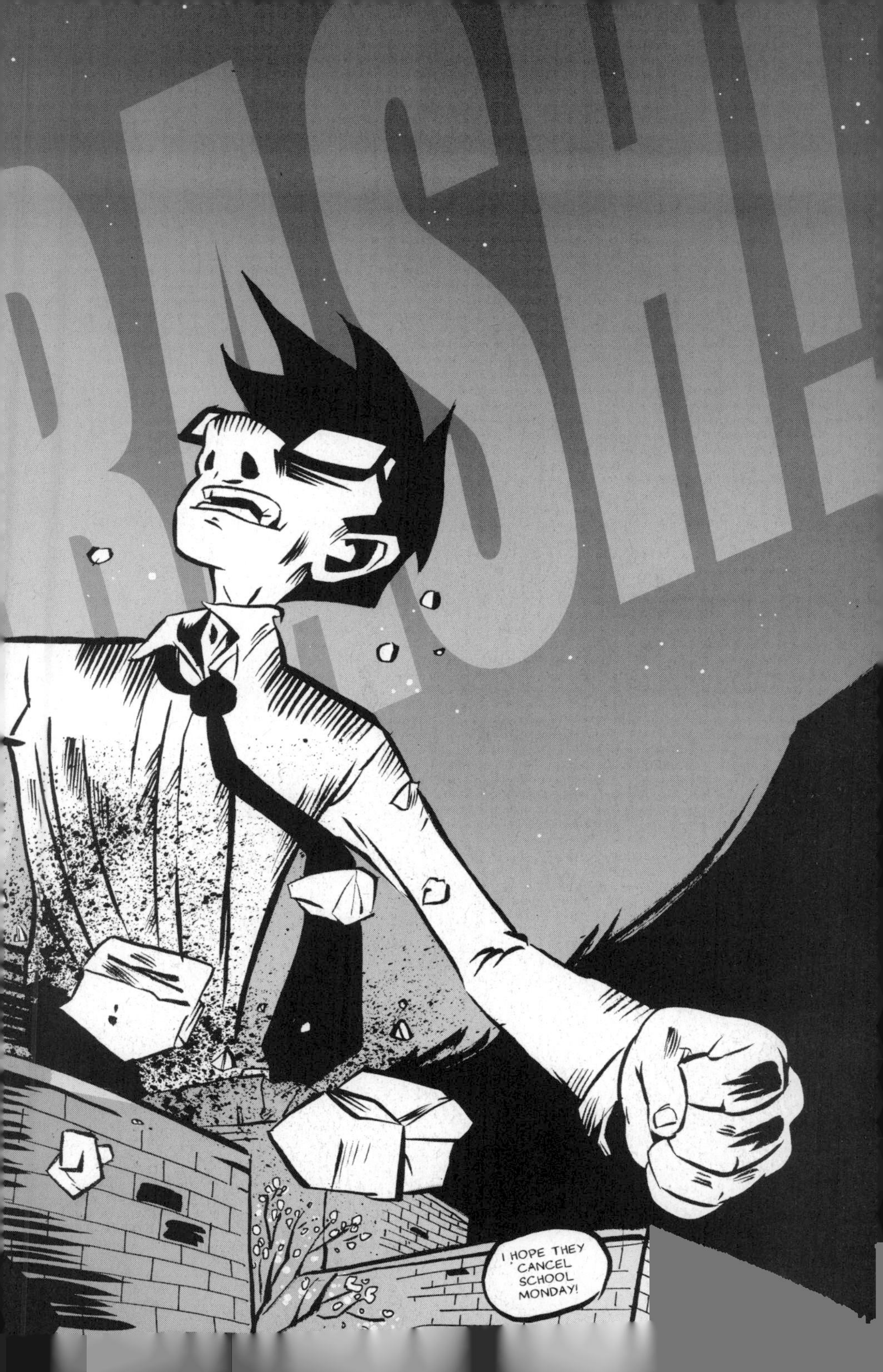
I HOPE THEY CANCEL SCHOOL MONDAY!

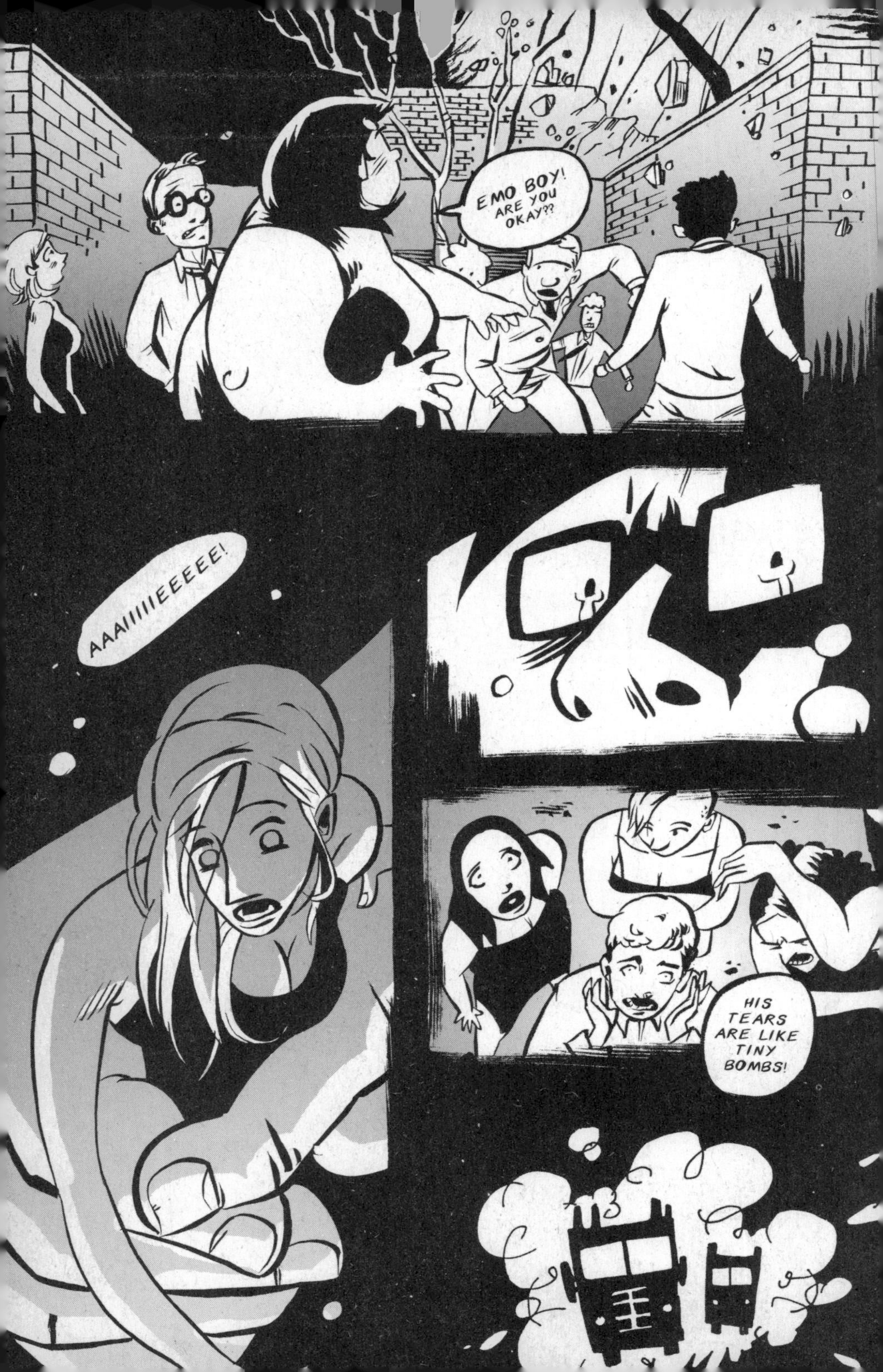
EMO BOY! ARE YOU OKAY??
AAAIIIIIIEEEEE!
HIS TEARS ARE LIKE TINY BOMBS!

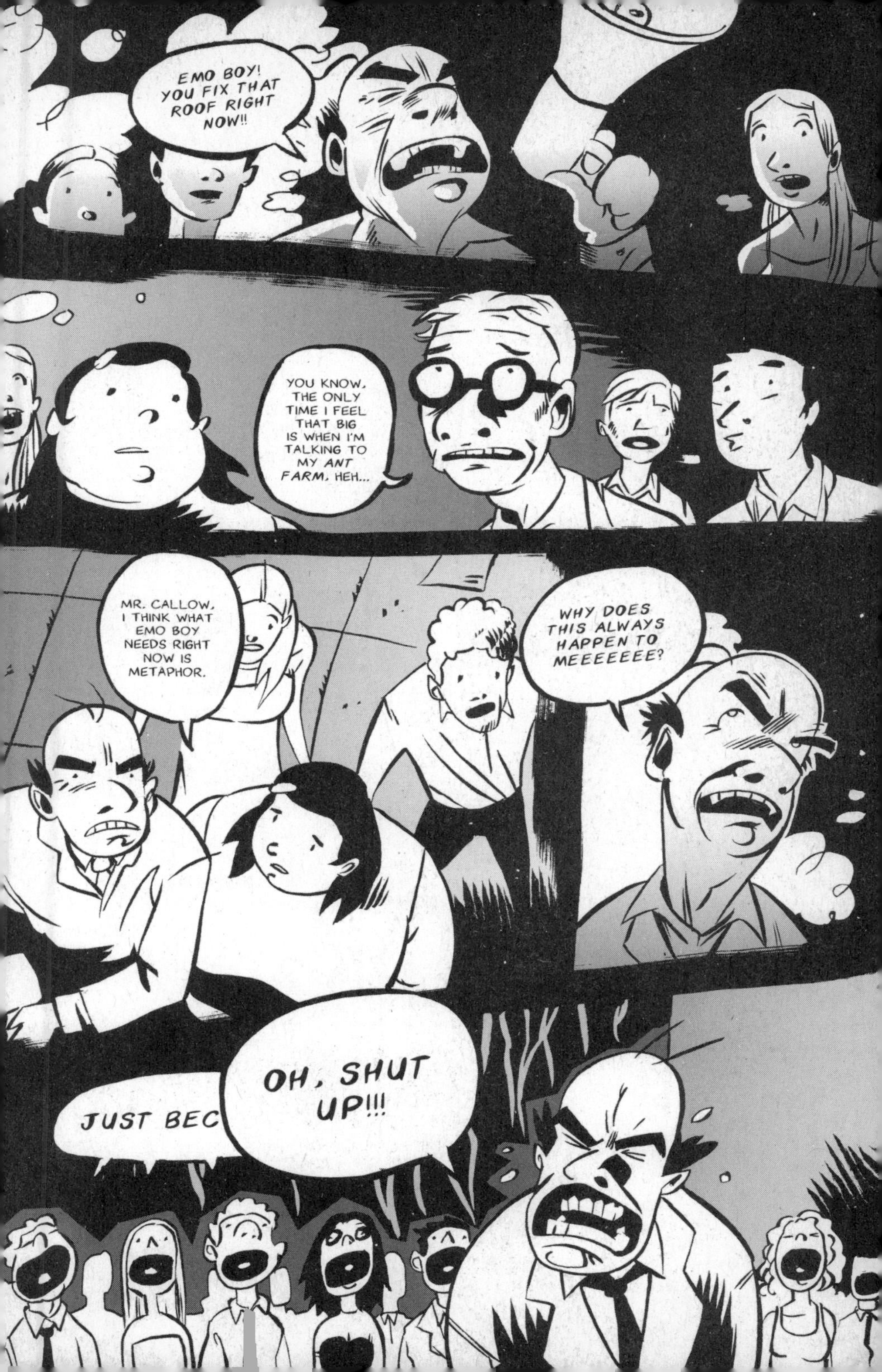
EMO BOY! YOU FIX THAT ROOF RIGHT NOW!!
YOU KNOW, THE ONLY TIME I FEEL THAT BIG IS WHEN I'M TALKING TO MY *ANT* FARM, HEH...
MR. CALLOW, I THINK WHAT EMO BOY NEEDS RIGHT NOW IS METAPHOR.
WHY DOES THIS ALWAYS HAPPEN TO MEEEEEEE?
JUST BEC
OH, SHUT UP!!!

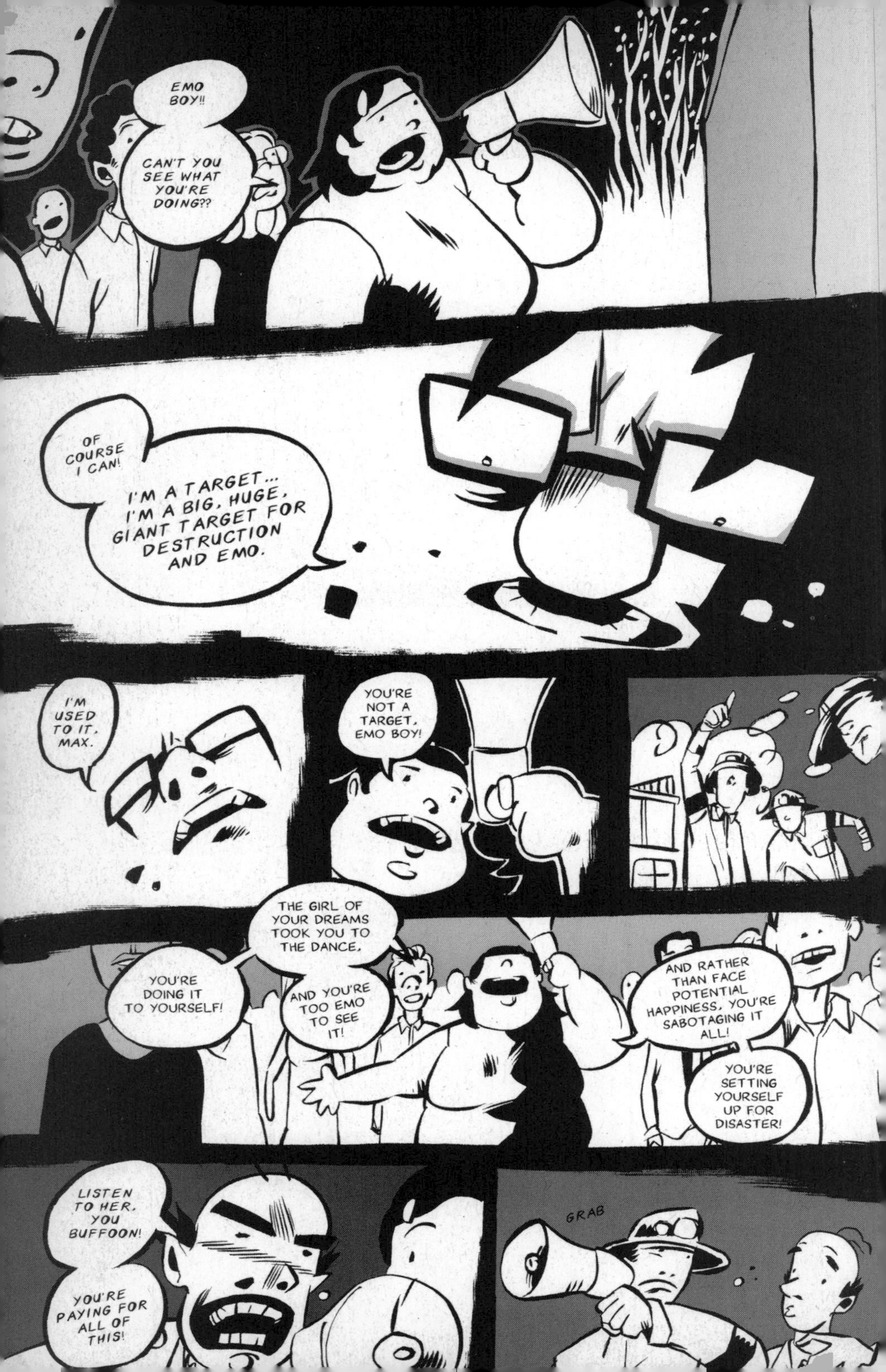
EMO BOY!!
CAN'T YOU SEE WHAT YOU'RE DOING??
OF COURSE I CAN!
I'M A TARGET... I'M A BIG, HUGE, GIANT TARGET FOR DESTRUCTION AND EMO.
I'M USED TO IT, MAX.
YOU'RE NOT A TARGET, EMO BOY!
YOU'RE DOING IT TO YOURSELF!
THE GIRL OF YOUR DREAMS TOOK YOU TO THE DANCE,
AND YOU'RE TOO EMO TO SEE IT!
AND RATHER THAN FACE POTENTIAL HAPPINESS, YOU'RE SABOTAGING IT ALL!
YOU'RE SETTING YOURSELF UP FOR DISASTER!
LISTEN TO HER, YOU BUFFOON!
YOU'RE PAYING FOR ALL OF THIS!
GRAB

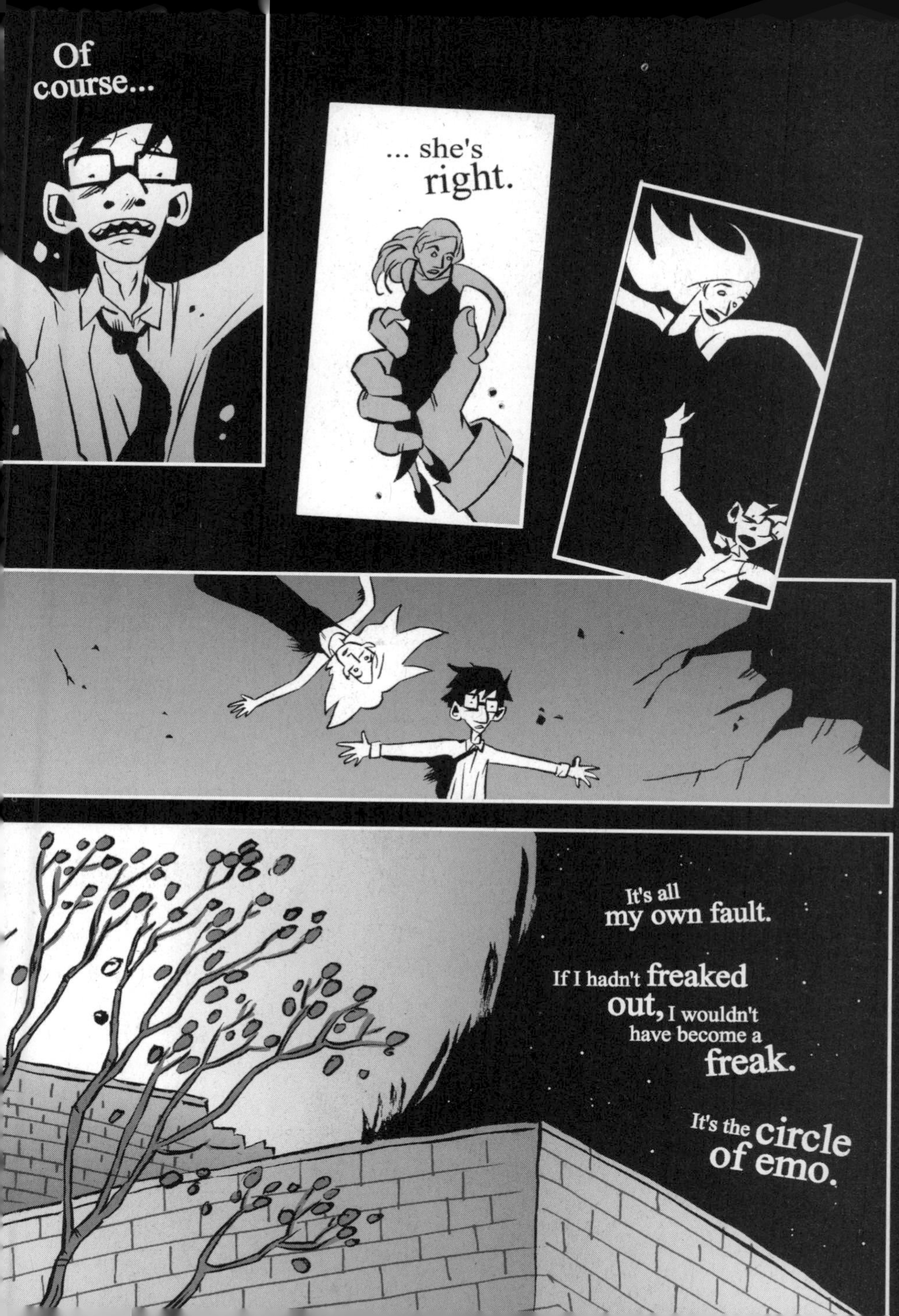
Of course...
... she's right.
It's all my own fault.
If I hadn't freaked out, I wouldn't have become a freak.
It's the circle of emo.

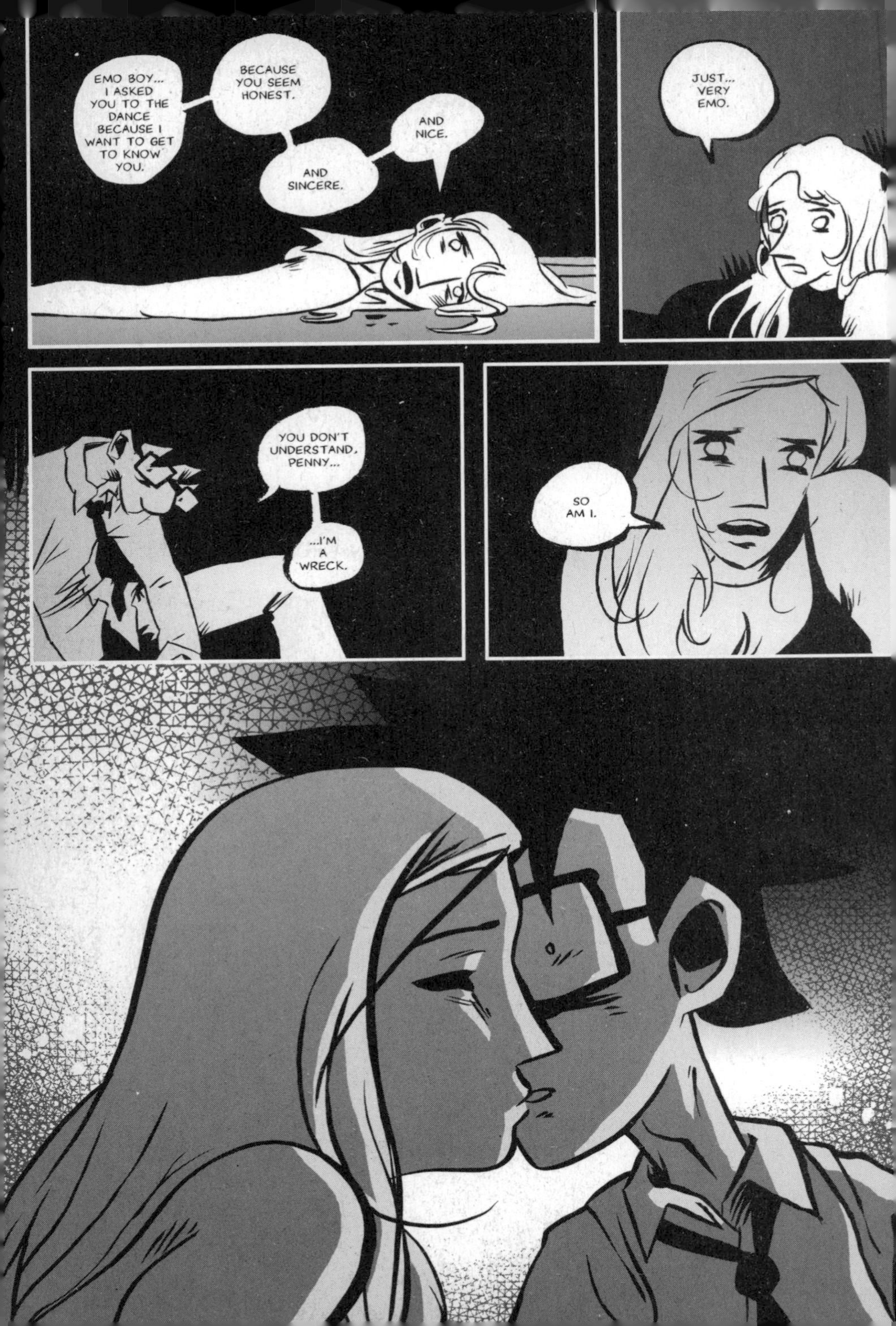
EMO BOY... I ASKED YOU TO THE DANCE BECAUSE I WANT TO GET TO KNOW YOU.
BECAUSE YOU SEEM HONEST.
AND SINCERE.
AND NICE.
JUST... VERY EMO.
YOU DON'T UNDERSTAND, PENNY...
...I'M A WRECK.
SO AM I.

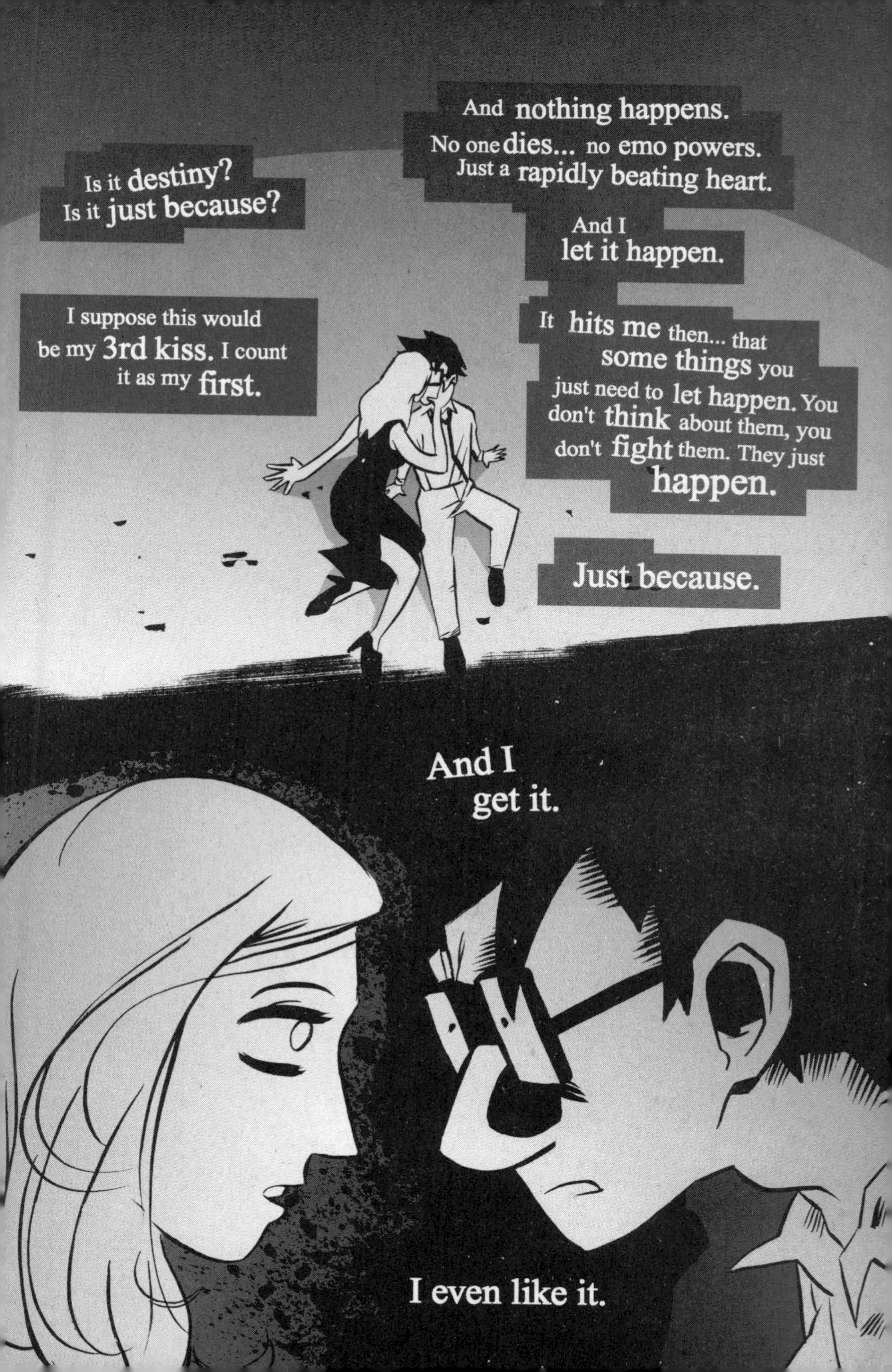
Is it destiny?
Is it just because?
And nothing happens.
No one dies... no emo powers.
Just a rapidly beating heart.
And I
let it happen.
I suppose this would be my 3rd kiss. I count it as my first.
It hits me then... that some things you just need to let happen. You don't think about them, you don't fight them. They just happen.
Just because.
And I
get it.
I even like it.

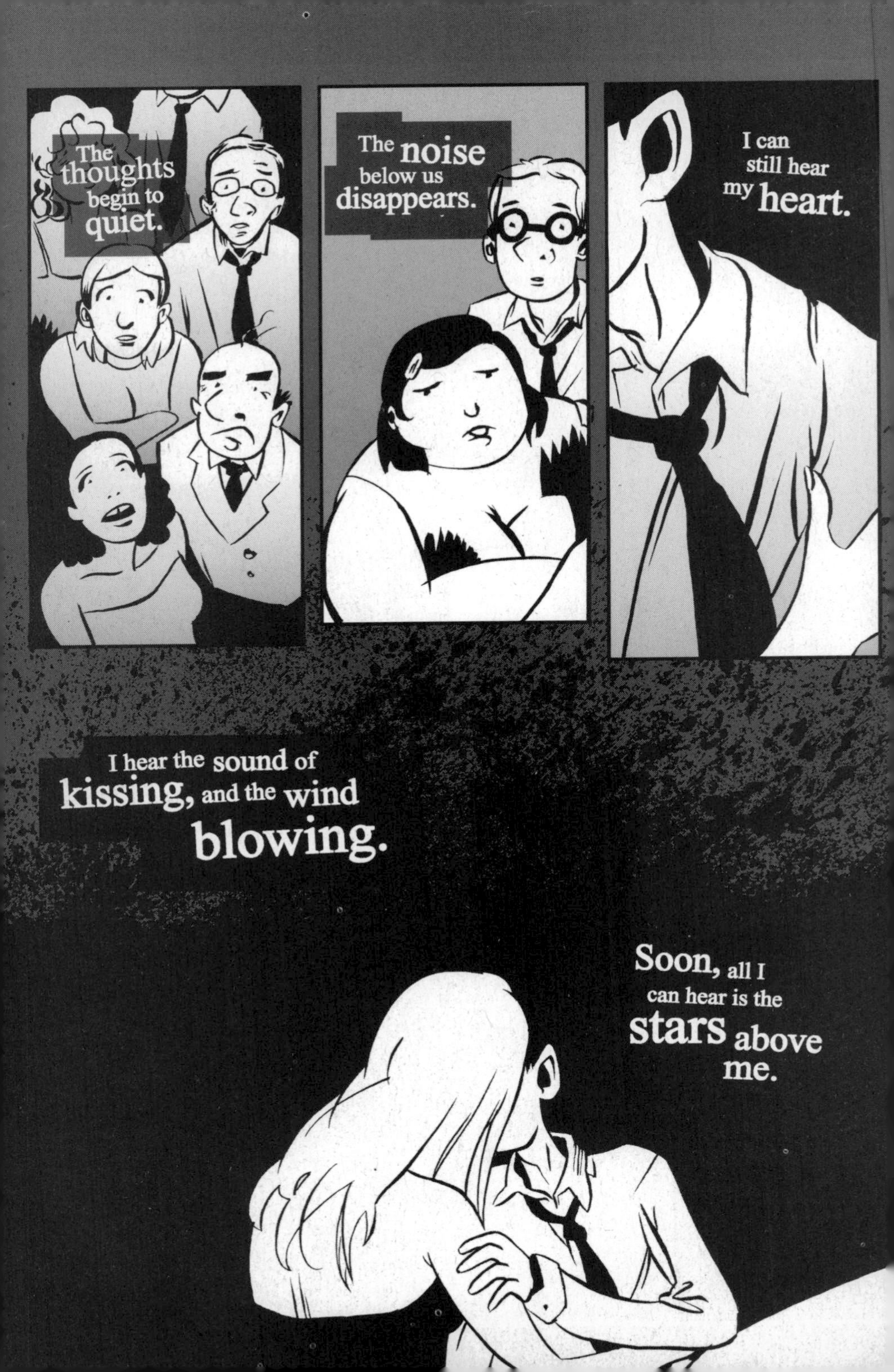
The thoughts begin to quiet.
The noise below us disappears.
I can still hear my heart.
I hear the sound of kissing, and the wind blowing.
Soon, all I can hear is the stars above me.

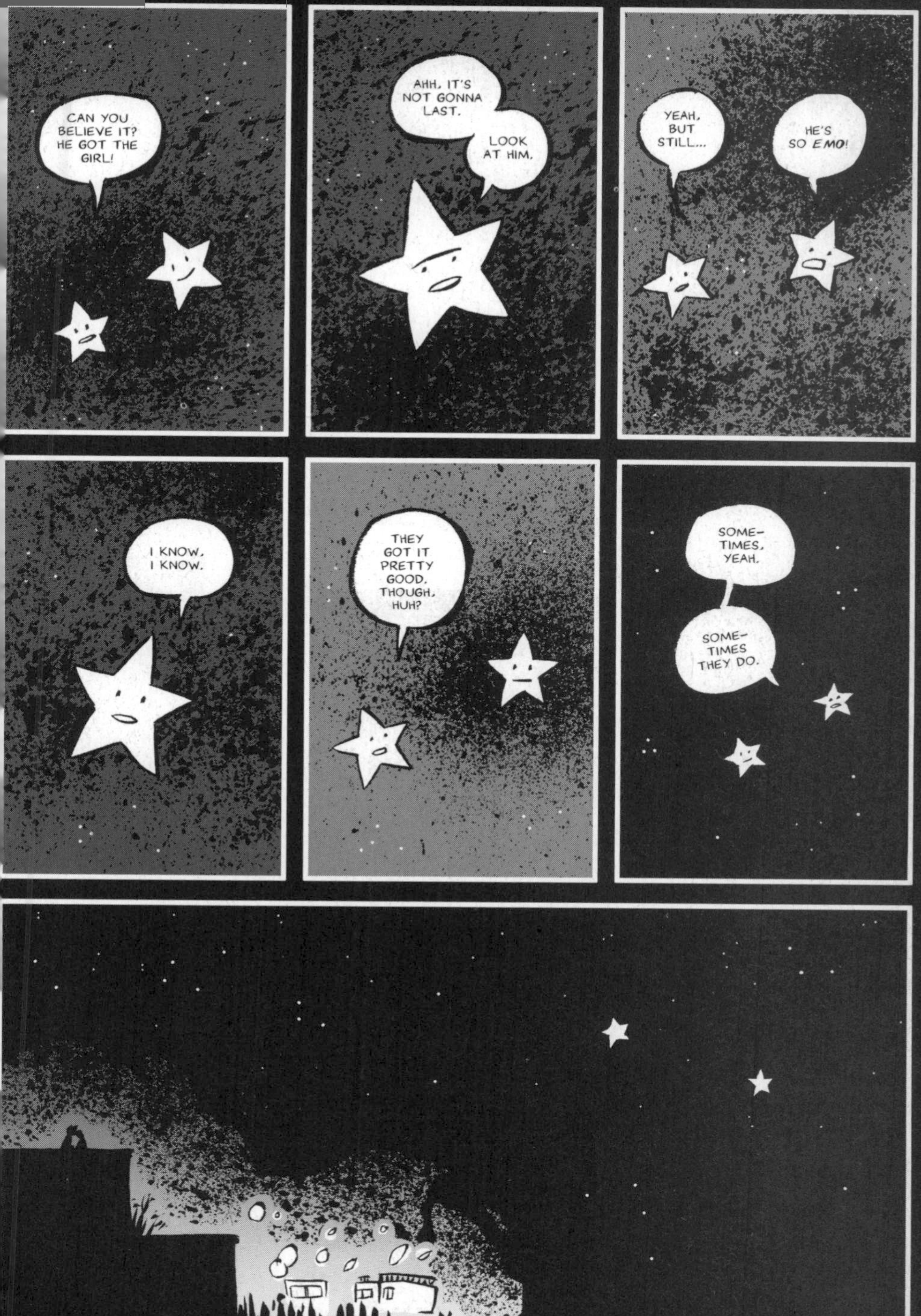
CAN YOU BELIEVE IT? HE GOT THE GIRL!
AHH, IT'S NOT GONNA LAST.
LOOK AT HIM.
YEAH, BUT STILL...
HE'S SO EMO!
I KNOW, I KNOW.
THEY GOT IT PRETTY GOOD, THOUGH, HUH?
SOME-TIMES, YEAH.
SOME-TIMES THEY DO.

"CATCHING UP WITH EMO BOY"

story and art by steve emond.

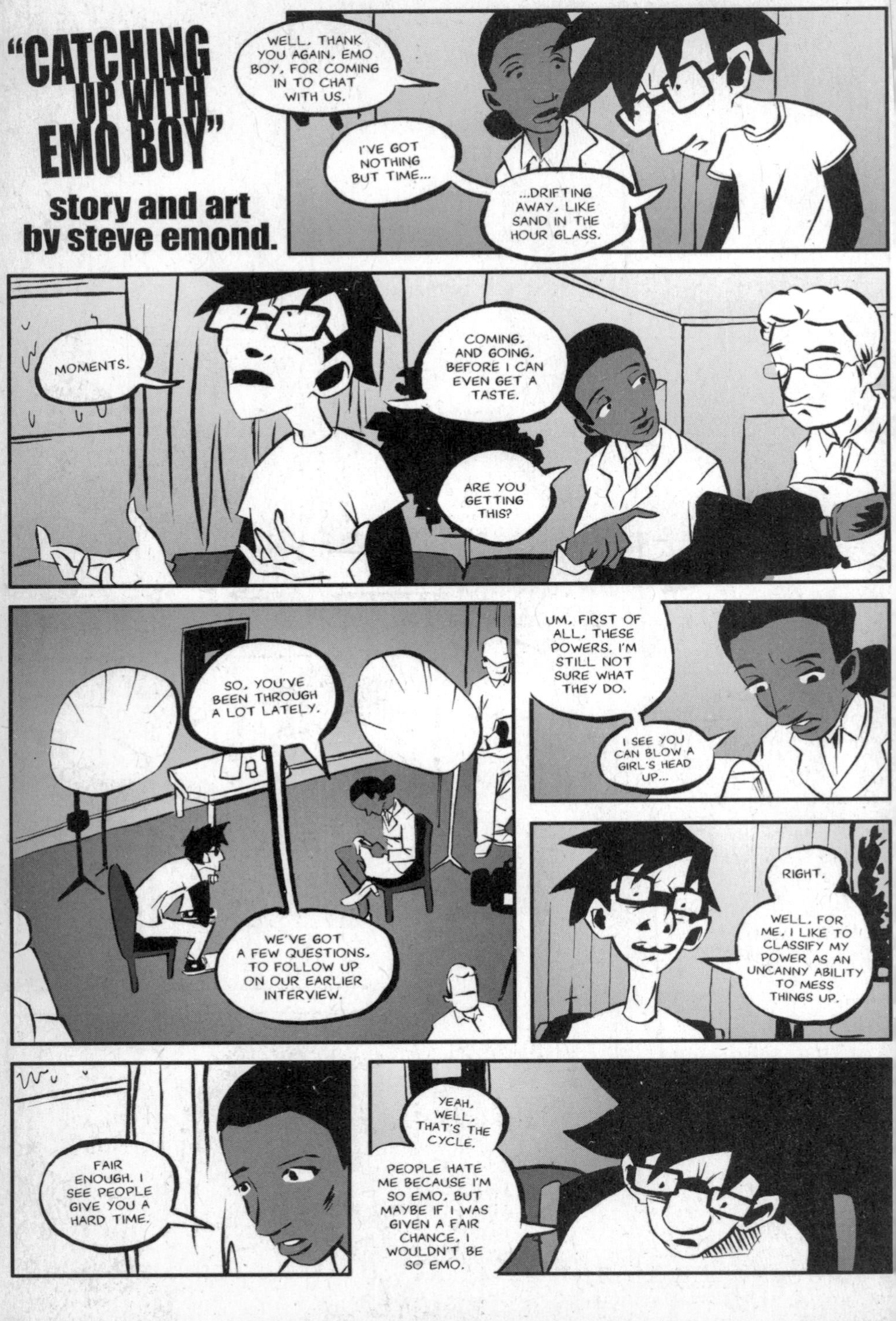
WELL, THANK YOU AGAIN, EMO BOY, FOR COMING IN TO CHAT WITH US.
I'VE GOT NOTHING BUT TIME...
...DRIFTING AWAY, LIKE SAND IN THE HOUR GLASS.
MOMENTS.
COMING, AND GOING, BEFORE I CAN EVEN GET A TASTE.
ARE YOU GETTING THIS?
SO, YOU'VE BEEN THROUGH A LOT LATELY.
WE'VE GOT A FEW QUESTIONS, TO FOLLOW UP ON OUR EARLIER INTERVIEW.
UM, FIRST OF ALL, THESE POWERS, I'M STILL NOT SURE WHAT THEY DO.
I SEE YOU CAN BLOW A GIRL'S HEAD UP...
RIGHT.
WELL, FOR ME, I LIKE TO CLASSIFY MY POWER AS AN UNCANNY ABILITY TO MESS THINGS UP.
FAIR ENOUGH. I SEE PEOPLE GIVE YOU A HARD TIME.
YEAH, WELL, THAT'S THE CYCLE.
PEOPLE HATE ME BECAUSE I'M SO EMO, BUT MAYBE IF I WAS GIVEN A FAIR CHANCE, I WOULDN'T BE SO EMO.

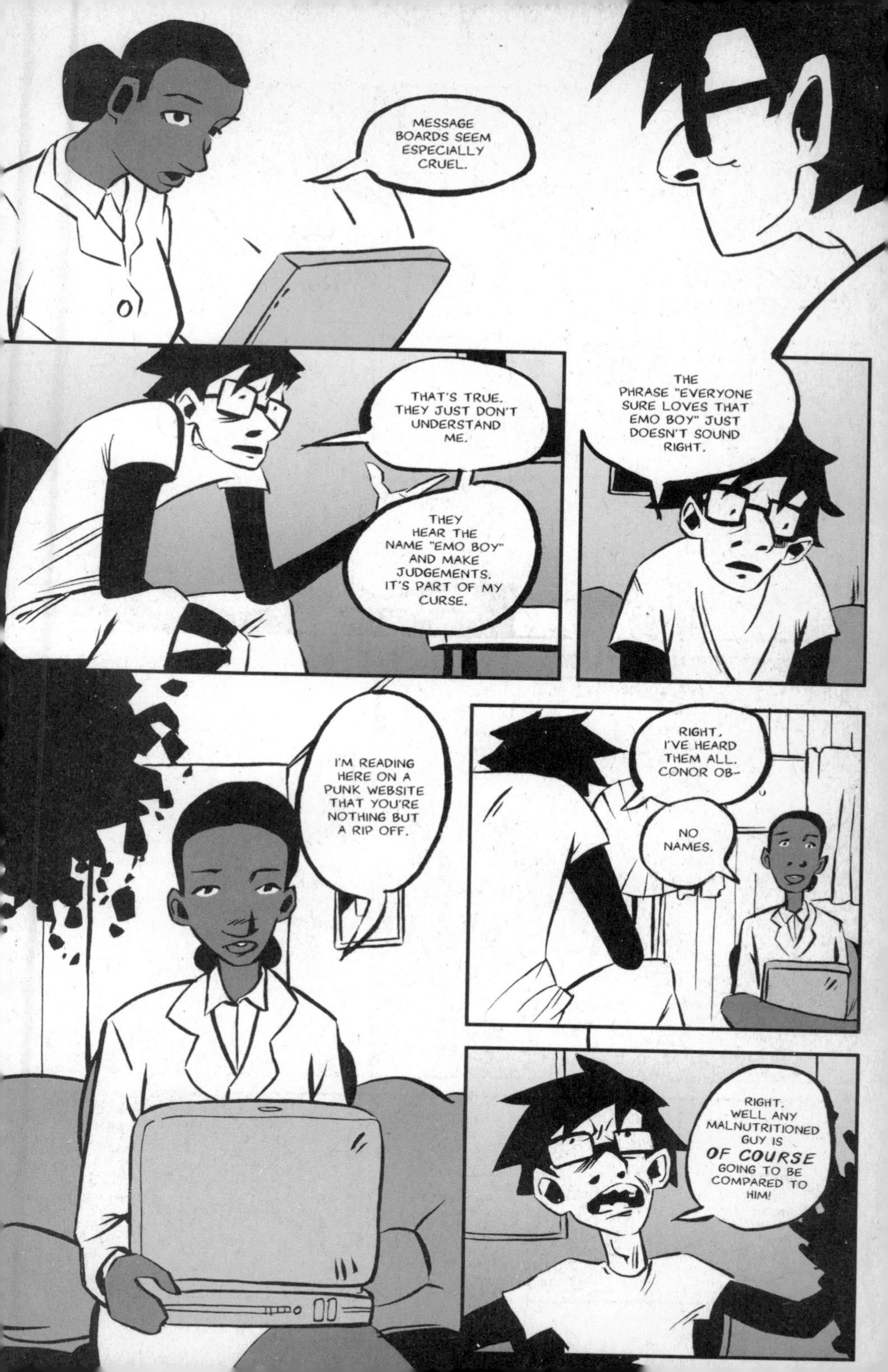
MESSAGE BOARDS SEEM ESPECIALLY CRUEL.
THAT'S TRUE. THEY JUST DON'T UNDERSTAND ME.
THEY HEAR THE NAME "EMO BOY" AND MAKE JUDGEMENTS. IT'S PART OF MY CURSE.
THE PHRASE "EVERYONE SURE LOVES THAT EMO BOY" JUST DOESN'T SOUND RIGHT.
I'M READING HERE ON A PUNK WEBSITE THAT YOU'RE NOTHING BUT A RIP OFF.
RIGHT, I'VE HEARD THEM ALL. CONOR OB-
NO NAMES.
RIGHT. WELL ANY MALNUTRITIONED GUY IS OF COURSE GOING TO BE COMPARED TO HIM!

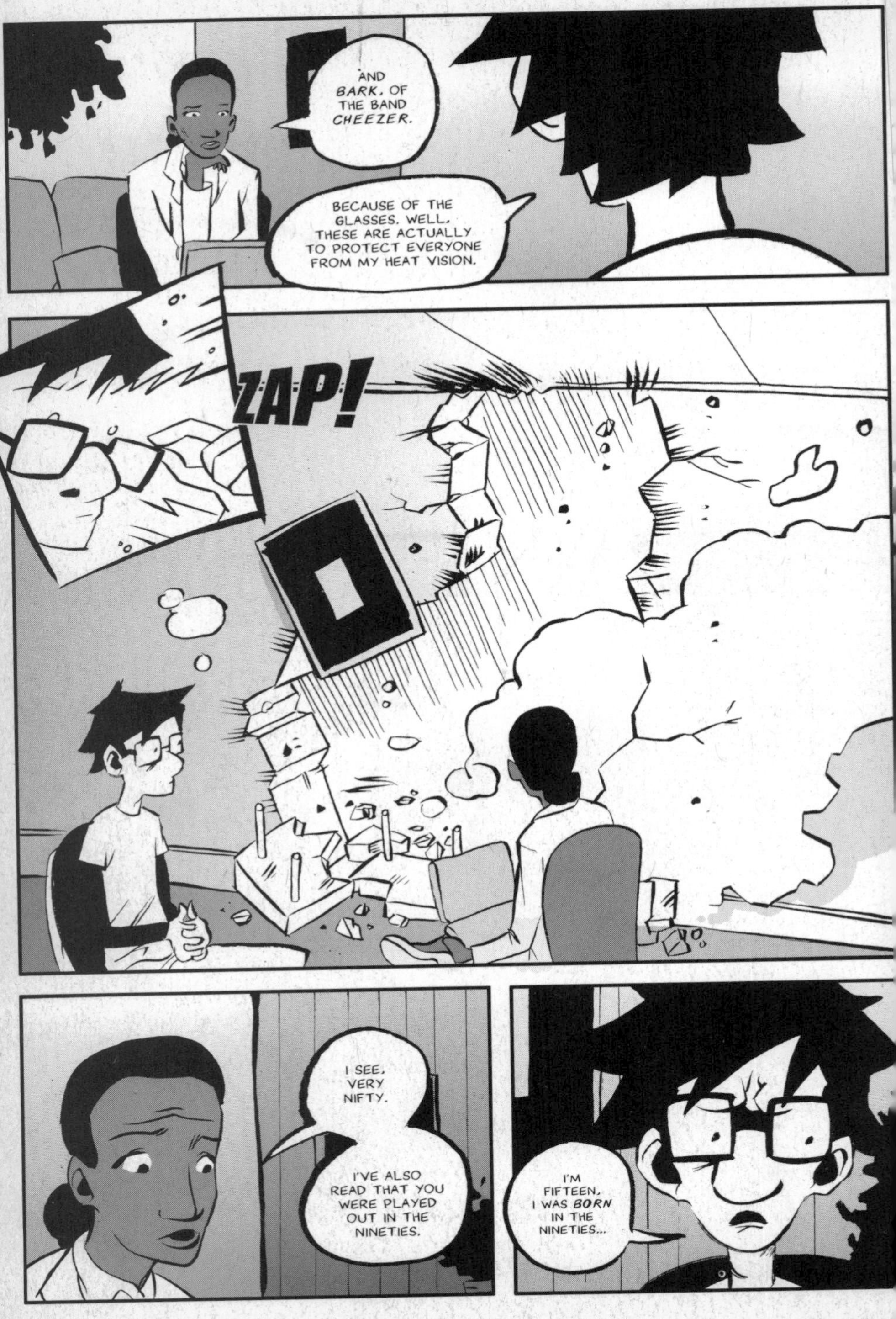

AND BARK, OF THE BAND CHEEZER.
BECAUSE OF THE GLASSES. WELL, THESE ARE ACTUALLY TO PROTECT EVERYONE FROM MY HEAT VISION.
ZAP!
I SEE, VERY NIFTY.
I'VE ALSO READ THAT YOU WERE PLAYED OUT IN THE NINETIES.
I'M FIFTEEN, I WAS BORN IN THE NINETIES...

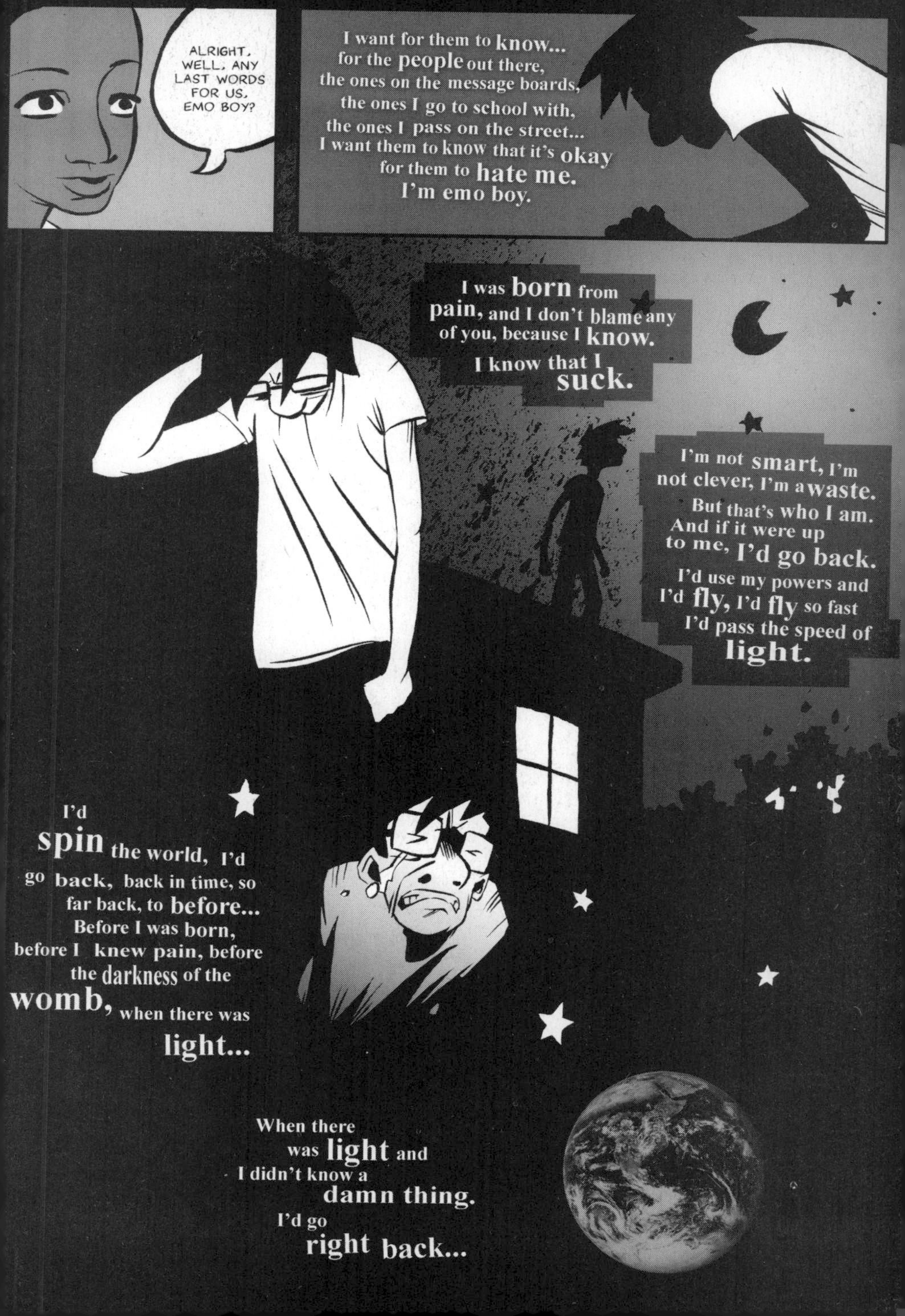
ALRIGHT, WELL, ANY LAST WORDS FOR US, EMO BOY?
I want for them to know... for the people out there, the ones on the message boards, the ones I go to school with, the ones I pass on the street... I want them to know that it's okay for them to hate me. I'm emo boy.
I was born from pain, and I don't blame any of you, because I know. I know that I suck.
I'm not smart, I'm not clever, I'm a waste. But that's who I am. And if it were up to me, I'd go back. I'd use my powers and I'd fly, I'd fly so fast I'd pass the speed of light.
I'd spin the world, I'd go back, back in time, so far back, to before... Before I was born, before I knew pain, before the darkness of the womb, when there was light...
When there was light and I didn't know a damn thing. I'd go right back...

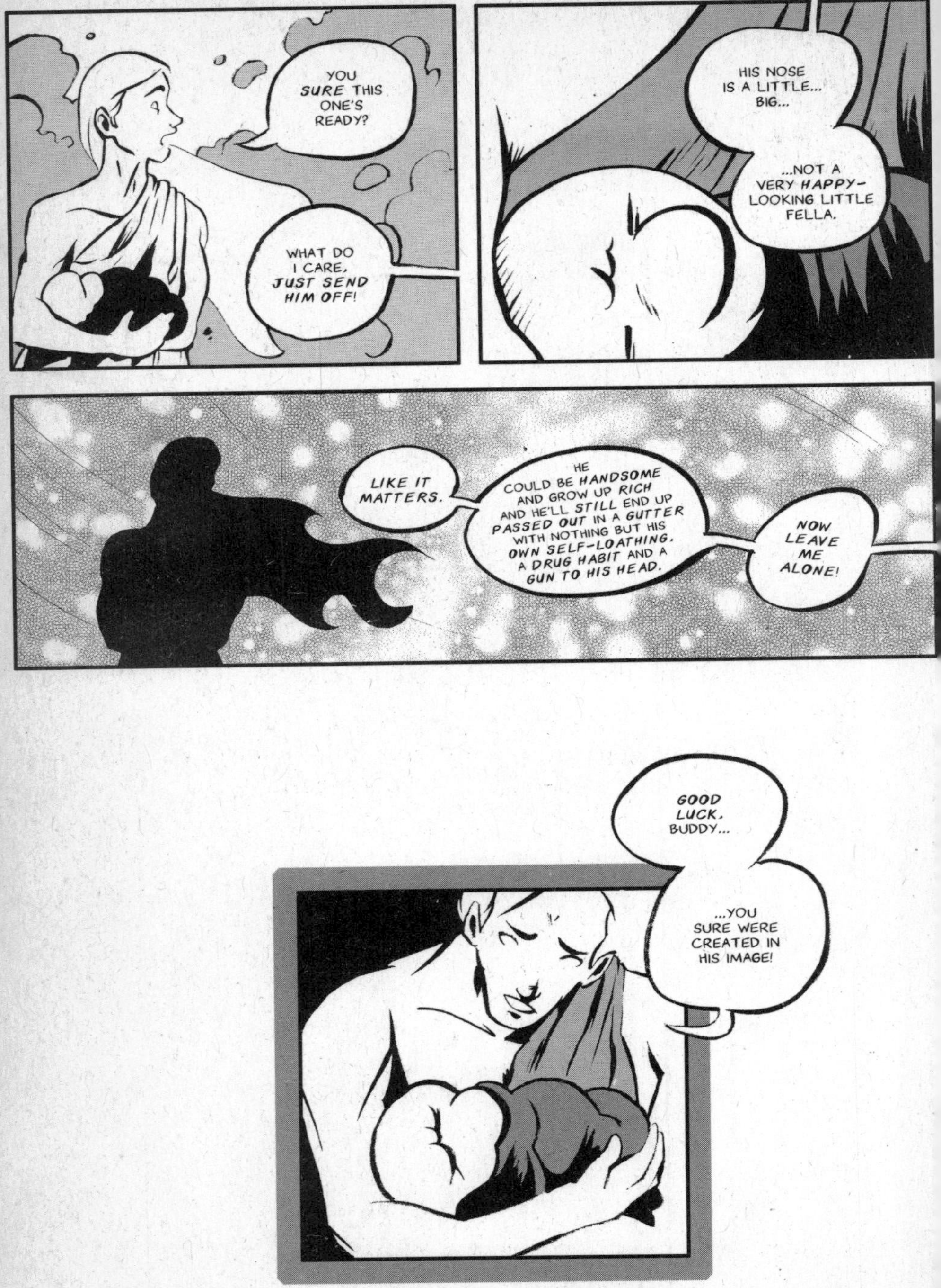
YOU SURE THIS ONE'S READY?
WHAT DO I CARE, JUST SEND HIM OFF!
HIS NOSE IS A LITTLE... BIG...
...NOT A VERY HAPPY-LOOKING LITTLE FELLA.
LIKE IT MATTERS.
HE COULD BE HANDSOME AND GROW UP RICH AND HE'LL STILL END UP PASSED OUT IN A GUTTER WITH NOTHING BUT HIS OWN SELF-LOATHING, A DRUG HABIT AND A GUN TO HIS HEAD.
NOW LEAVE ME ALONE!
GOOD LUCK, BUDDY...
...YOU SURE WERE CREATED IN HIS IMAGE!

The story continues! Check out Emo Boy issues 7 and up, available at your local comic bo store or online at http://store.slavelabor.com, or wait for the Emo Boy: Volume 2 Collection